Lust for Life

Irving Stone was born in San Francisco in 1903 and received his B.A. from the University of California, Berkley in 1923 and his Master's degree from the University of Southern California in 1924. He wrote plays and supported himself by writing detective stories until the publication of *Lust for Life*, his first novel, in 1934. Stone called his work "bio-history" and based his novels on meticulous and extensive reserach into the lives of the historical characters at the heart of his novels. He maried his editor, Jean Factor, in 1934. He founded the Academy of American Poets in 1962. He died in Los Angeles in 1989.

D1500241

Lust For Life

Irving Stone

JUN 2 3 2008

arrow books

Reprinted by Arrow Books in 2001

7 9 10 8

Copyright © Irving Stone 1935

The right of Irving Stone to be identified as the author of this work
has been asserted by him in accordance with the Copyright, Designs
and Patents Act, 1988

First published in the United Kingdom in 1935 by Bodley Head Limited
This edition first published by Mandarin Paperbacks in 1997
(and reprinted 17 times)

Arrow Books
The Random House Group Limited
20 Vauxhall Bridge Road, London SW1V 2SA

www.rbooks.co.uk

Addresses for companies within The Random House Group Limited
can be found at:
www.randomhouse.co.uk/offices.htm

The Random House Group Limited Reg. No. 954009

A CIP catalogue record for this book
is available from the British Library

ISBN 9780099416425

The Random House Group Limited makes every effort to ensure
that the papers used in its books are made from trees that
have been legally sourced from well-managed and credibly
certified forests. Our paper procurement policy can be found at:
www.randomhouse.co.uk/paper.htm

Printed and bound in the United Kingdom by
Cox & Wyman Ltd, Reading, Berkshire

To the memory of my mother

PAULINE STONE

CONTENTS

LUST FOR LIFE

LONDON

1

"Monsieur Van Gogh! It's time to wake up!"

Vincent had been waiting for Ursula's voice even while he slept.

"I was awake, Mademoiselle Ursula," he called back.

"No you weren't," the girl laughed, "but you are now." He heard her go down the stairs and into the kitchen.

Vincent put his hands under him, gave a shove, and sprang out of bed. His shoulders and chest were massive, his arms thick and powerful. He slipped into his clothes, poured some cold water out of the ewer, and stropped his razor.

Vincent enjoyed the daily ritual of the shave; down the broad cheek from the right sideburn to the corner of the voluptuous mouth; the right half of the upper lip from the nostril out, then the left half; then down the chin, a huge, rounded slab of warm granite.

He stuck his face into the wreath of Brabantine grass and oak leaves on the chiffonier. His brother Theo had gathered it from the heath near Zundert and sent it to London for him. The smell of Holland in his nose started the day off right.

"Monsieur Van Gogh," called Ursula, knocking on the door again, "the postman just left this letter for you."

He recognized his mother's handwriting as he tore open the envelope. "Dear Vincent," he read, "I am going to put a word to bed on paper for you."

His face felt cold and damp so he stuck the letter into his trouser pocket, intending to read it during one of his many leisure moments at Goupils. He combed back his long, thick, yellow-red hair, put on a stiff white shirt, low collar and a large knotted four-in-hand black tie and descended to breakfast and Ursula's smile.

Ursula Loyer and her mother, the widow of a Provençal curate, kept a kindergarten for boys in a little house in the back garden. Ursula was nineteen, a smiling, wide-eyed creature with a delicate, oval face, pastel colouring and a small, slender figure. Vincent loved to watch the sheen of laughter which, like the glow from a highly coloured parasol, was spread over her piquant face.

Ursula served with quick, dainty movements, chatting vivaciously while he ate. He was twenty-one and in love for the first time. Life opened out before him. He thought he would be a fortunate man if he could eat breakfast opposite Ursula for the rest of his days.

Ursula brought in a rasher of bacon, an egg, and a cup of strong, black tea. She fluttered into a chair across the table from him, patted the brown curls at the back of her head, and smiled at him while she passed the salt, pepper, butter and toast in quick succession.

"Your mignonette is coming up a bit," she said, wetting her lips with her tongue. "Will you have a look at it before you go to the gallery?"

"Yes," he replied. "Will you, that is, would you . . . show me?"

"What a droll person he is! He plants the mignonette himself and then doesn't know where to find it." She had a habit of speaking about people as though they were not in the room.

Vincent gulped. His manner, like his body, was heavy and he did not seem able to find the right words for Ursula. They went into the yard. It was a cool April morning, but the apple trees had already blossomed. A little garden separated the Loyer House from the kindergarten. Just a few days before, Vincent had sown poppies and sweet peas. The mignonette was pushing through the earth. Vincent and Ursula squatted on either side of it, their heads almost touching. Ursula had a strong, natural perfume of the hair.

"Mademoiselle Ursula," he said.

"Yes?" She withdrew her head, but smiled at him questioningly.

"I . . . I . . . that is . . ."

"Dear me, what can you be stuttering about?" she asked, and jumped up. He followed her to the door of the kindergarten. "My *poupons* will be here soon," she said. "Won't you be late at the gallery?"

"I have time. I walk to the Strand in forty-five minutes."

She could think of nothing to say, so she reached behind her with both arms to catch up a tiny wisp of hair that was escaping. The curves of her body were surprisingly ample for so slender a figure.

12

"Whatever have you done with that Brabant picture you promised me for the kindergarten?" she asked.

"I sent a reproduction of one of Caesar de Cock's sketches to Paris. He is going to inscribe it for you."

"Oh, delightful!" She clapped her hands, swung a short way about on her hips, then turned back again. "Sometimes, Monsieur, just sometimes, you can be most charming."

She smiled at him with her eyes and mouth, and tried to go. He caught her by the arm. "I thought of a name for you after I went to bed," he said. "I called you *l'ange aux poupons.*"

Ursula threw back her head and laughed heartily. *'L'ange aux poupons!'* she cried. "I must go tell it to Mother!"

She broke loose from his grip, laughed at him over a raised shoulder, ran through the garden and into the house.

2

Vincent put on his top hat, took his gloves, and stepped out into the road of Clapham. The houses were scattered at this distance from the heart of London. In every garden the lilacs and hawthorn and laburnums were in bloom.

It was eight-fifteen; he did not have to be at Goupils until nine. He was a vigorous walker, and as the houses thickened he passed an increasing number of business men on their way to work. He felt extremely friendly to them all; they too knew what a splendid thing it was to be in love.

He walked along the Thames Embankment, crossed Westminster Bridge, passed by Westminster Abbey and the Houses of Parliament, and turned into number 17 Southampton Street, Strand, the London quarters of Goupil and Company, Art Dealers and Publishers of Engravings.

As he walked through the main salon, with its thick carpets and rich draperies, he saw a canvas representing a kind of fish or dragon six yards long, with a little man hovering over it. It was called *The Archangel Michael Killing Satan.*

"There is a package for you on the lithograph table," one of the clerks told him as he passed.

The second room of the shop, after one passed the picture salon in which were exhibited the paintings of Millais, Boughton, and Turner, was devoted to etchings and lithographs. It was in the third room, which looked more like a place of business than either of the others, that most of the

13

sales were carried on. Vincent laughed as he thought of the woman who had made the last purchase the evening before.

"I can't fancy this picture, Harry, can you?" she asked her husband. "The dog looks a rare bit like the one that bit me in Brighton last summer."

"Look here, old fellow," said Harry, "must we have a dog? They mostly put the missus in a stew."

Vincent was conscious of the fact that he was selling very poor stuff indeed. Most of the people who came in knew absolutely nothing about what they were buying. They paid high prices for a cheap commodity, but what business was it of his? All he had to do was make the print room successful.

He opened the package from Goupils in Paris. It had been sent by Caesar de Cock and was inscribed, "To Vincent, and Ursula Loyer: *Les amis de mes amis sont mes amis.*"

"I'll ask Ursula tonight when I give her this," he murmured to himself. "I'll be twenty-two in a few days and I'm earning five pounds a month. No need to wait any longer."

The time in the quiet back room of Goupils passed very quickly. He sold on an average of fifty photographs a day for the Musée Goupil and Company, and although he would have preferred to deal in oil canvases and etchings, he was pleased to be taking in so much money for the house. He liked his fellow clerks and they liked him; they spent many pleasant hours together talking of things European.

As a young chap he had been slightly morose and had avoided companionship. People had thought him queer, a bit eccentric. But Ursula had changed his nature completely. She had made him want to be agreeable and popular; she had brought him out of himself and helped him to see the goodness in the ordinary pattern of daily life.

At six o'clock the store closed. Mr. Obach stopped Vincent on his way out. "I had a letter from your Uncle Vincent Van Gogh about you," he said. "He wanted to know how you were coming on. I was happy to tell him that you are one of the best clerks in the store."

"It was very good of you to say that, sir."

"Not at all. After your summer vacation I want you to leave the back room and come forward into the etchings and lithographs."

"That means a great deal to me at this moment, sir, because I ... I'm going to be married!"

"Really? This is news. When is it to take place?"

14

"This summer, I suppose." He hadn't thought of the date before.

"Well, my boy, that's splendid. You just had an increase the first of the year, but when you come back from your wedding trip I dare say we can manage another."

3

"I'll get the picture for you, Mademoiselle Ursula," said Vincent after dinner, pushing back his chair.

Ursula was wearing a modishly embroidered dress of verdigris faye. "Did the artist write something nice for me?" she asked.

"Yes. If you'll get a lamp I'll hang it in the kindergarten for you."

She pursed her lips to a highly kissable *moue* and looked at him sideways. "I must help Mother. Shall we make it in a half hour?"

Vincent rested his elbows on the chiffonier in his room and gazed into the mirror. He had rarely thought about his appearance; in Holland such things had not seemed important. He had noticed that in comparison to the English his face and head were ponderous. His eyes were buried in deep crevices of horizontal rock; his nose was high ridged, broad and straight as a shinbone; his dome-like forehead was as high as the distance from his thick eyebrows to the sensuous mouth; his jaws were wide and powerful, his neck a bit squat and thick, and his massive chin a living monument to Dutch character.

He turned away from the mirror and sat idly on the edge of the bed. He had been brought up in an austere home. He had never loved a girl before; he had never even looked at one or engaged in the casual banter between the sexes. In his love for Ursula there was nothing of passion or desire. He was young; he was an idealist; he was in love for the first time.

He glanced at his watch. Only five minutes had passed. The twenty-five minutes that stretched ahead seemed interminable. He drew a note from his brother Theo out of his mother's letter and reread it. Theo was four years younger than Vincent and was now taking Vincent's place in Goupils in The Hague. Theo and Vincent, like their father Theodorus and Uncle Vincent, had been favourite brothers all through their youth.

15

Vincent picked up a book, rested some paper on it, and wrote Theo a note. From the top drawer of the chiffonier he drew out a few rough sketches that he had made along the Thames Embankment and put them into an envelope for Theo along with a photograph of *Young Girl with a Sword*, by Jacquet.

"My word," he exclaimed aloud, "I've forgotten all about Ursula!" He looked at his watch; he was already a quarter of an hour late. He snatched up a comb, tried to straighten out the tangle of wavy red hair, took Caesar de Cock's picture from the table, and flung open the door.

"I thought you had forgotten me," Ursula said as he came into the parlour. She was pasting together some paper toys for her *poupons*. "Did you bring my picture? May I see it?"

"I would like to put it up before you look. Did you fix a lamp?"

"Mother has it."

When he returned from the kitchen she gave him a scarf of blue marine to wrap about her shoulders. He thrilled to the silken touch of it. In the garden there was the smell of apple blossoms. The path was dark and Ursula put the ends of her fingers lightly on the sleeve of his rough, black coat. She stumbled once, gripped his arm more tightly and laughed in high glee at her own clumsiness. He did not understand why she thought it funny to trip, but he liked to watch her body carry the laughter down the dark path. He held open the door of the kindergarten for her and as she passed, her delicately moulded face almost brushing his, she looked deep into his eyes and seemed to answer his question before he asked it.

He set the lamp down on the table. "Where would you like me to hang the picture?" he asked.

"Over my desk, don't you think?"

There were perhaps fifteen low chairs and tables in the room of what had formerly been a summer house. At one end was a little platform supporting Ursula's desk. He and Ursula stood side by side, groping for the right position for the picture. Vincent was nervous; he dropped the pins as fast as he tried to stick them into the wall. She laughed at him in a quiet, intimate tone.

"Here, clumsy, let me do it."

She lifted both arms above her head and worked with deft movements of every muscle of her body. She was quick in her gestures, and graceful. Vincent wanted to take her in his arms,

16

there in the dim light of the lamp, and settle with one sure embrace this whole tortuous business. But Ursula, though she touched him frequently in the dark, never seemed to get into position for it. He held the lamp up high while she read the inscription. She was pleased, clapped her hands, rocked back on her heels. She moved so much he could never catch up with her.

"That makes him my friend too, doesn't it?" she asked. "I've always wanted to know an artist."

Vincent tried to say something tender, something that would pave the way for his declaration. Ursula turned her face to him in the half shadow. The gleam from the lamp put tiny spots of light in her eyes. The oval of her face was framed in the darkness and something he could not name moved within him when he saw her red, moist lips stand out from the smooth paleness of her skin.

There was a meaningful pause. He could feel her reaching out to him, waiting for him to utter the unnecessary words of love. He wetted his lips several times. Ursula turned her head, looked into his eyes over a slightly raised shoulder, and ran out the door.

Terror stricken that his opportunity would pass, he pursued her. She stopped for a moment under the apple tree.

"Ursula, please."

She turned and looked at him, shivering a bit. There were cold stars out. The night was black. He had left the lamp behind him. The only light came from the dim glow of the kitchen window. The perfume of Ursula's hair was in his nostrils. She pulled the silk scarf tightly about her shoulders and crossed her arms on her chest.

"You're cold," he said.

"Yes. We had better go in."

"No! Please, I . . . ." He planted himself in her path.

She lowered her chin into the warmth of the scarf and looked up at him with wide, wondering eyes. "Why Monsieur Van Gogh, I'm afraid I don't understand."

"I only wanted to talk to you. You see . . . I . . . that is . . ."

"Please, not now. I'm shivering."

"I thought you should know. I was promoted today . . . I'm going forward into the lithograph room . . . it will be my second increase in a year . . ."

Ursula stepped back, unwrapped the scarf, and stood resolutely in the night, quite warm without any protection.

17

"Precisely what are you trying to tell me, Monsieur Van Gogh?"

He felt the coolness in her voice and cursed himself for being so awkward. The emotion in him suddenly shut down; he felt calm and possessed. He tried a number of voices in his mind and chose the one he liked best.

"I am trying to tell you, Ursula, something you know already. That I love you with all my heart and can only be happy if you will be my wife."

He observed how startled she looked at his sudden command of himself. He wondered if he ought to take her in his arms.

"Your wife!" Her voice rose a few tones. "Why Monsieur Van Gogh, that's impossible!"

He looked at her from under mountain crags, and she saw his eyes clearly in the darkness. "Now I'm afraid it's I who do not . . ."

"How extraordinary that you shouldn't know. I've been engaged for over a year."

He did not know how long he stood there, or what he thought or felt. "Who is the man?" he asked dully.

"Oh, you've never met my fiancé? He had your room before you came. I thought you knew."

"How would I have?"

She stood on tiptoes and peered in the direction of the kitchen. "Well, I . . . I . . . thought someone might have told you."

"Why did you keep this from me all year, when you knew I was falling in love with you?" There was no hesitation or fumbling in his voice now.

"Was it my fault that you fell in love with me? I only wanted to be friends with you."

"Has he been to visit you since I've been in the house?"

"No. He's in Wales. He's coming to spend his summer holiday with me."

"You haven't seen him for over a year? Then you've forgotten him! I'm the one you love now!"

He threw sense and discretion to the winds, grabbed her to him and kissed her rudely on the unwilling mouth. He tasted the moistness of her lips, the sweetness of her mouth, the perfume of her hair; all the intensity of his love rose up within him.

"Ursula, you don't love him. I won't let you. You're going

18

to be my wife. I couldn't bear to lose you. I'll never stop until you forget him and marry me!"

"Marry you!" she cried. "Do I have to marry every man that falls in love with me? Now let go of me, do you hear, or I shall call for help."

She wrenched herself free and ran breathlessly down the dark path. When she gained the steps she turned and spoke in a low carrying whisper that struck him like a shout.

"*Red-headed fool!*"

4

The next morning no one called him. He climbed lethargically out of bed. He shaved around his face in a circular swash, leaving several patches of beard. Ursula did not appear at breakfast. He walked downtown to Goupils. As he passed the same men that he had seen the morning before he noticed that they had altered. They looked like such lonely souls, hurrying away to their futile labours.

He did not see the laburnums in bloom nor the chestnut trees that lined the road. The sun was shining even more brightly than the morning before. He did not know it.

During the day he sold twenty *épreuves d'artiste* in colour of the *Venus Anadyomene* after Ingres. There was a big profit in these pictures for Goupils, but Vincent had lost his sense of delight in making money for the gallery. He had very little patience with the people who came in to buy. They not only could not tell the difference between good and bad art, but seemed to have a positive talent for choosing the artificial, the obvious, and the cheap.

His fellow clerks had never thought him a jolly chap, but he had done his best to make himself pleasant and agreeable. "What do you suppose is bothering the member of our illustrious Van Gogh family?" one of the clerks asked another.

"I dare say he got out of the wrong side of bed this morning."

"A jolly lot he has to worry about. His uncle, Vincent Van Gogh, is half owner of all the Goupil Galleries in Paris, Berlin, Brussels, The Hague, and Amsterdam. The old man is sick and has no children; everyone says he's leaving his half of the business to this chap."

19

"Some people have all the luck."

"That's only half the story. His uncle, Hendrik Van Gogh, owns big art shops in Brussels and Amsterdam, and still another uncle, Cornelius Van Gogh, is the head of the biggest firm in Holland. Why, the Van Goghs are the greatest family of picture dealers in Europe. One day our red-headed friend in the next room will practically control Continental art!"

When Vincent walked into the dining room of the Loyers' that night he found Ursula and her mother talking together in undertones. They stopped as soon as he came in, and left a sentence hanging in mid-air.

Ursula ran into the kitchen. "Good evening," said Madame Loyer with a curious glint in her eye.

Vincent ate his dinner alone at the large table. Ursula's blow had stunned but not defeated him. He simply was not going to take "no" for an answer. He would crowd the other man out of Ursula's mind.

It was almost a week before he could catch her standing still long enough to speak to her. He had eaten and slept very little during that week; his stolidity had given way to nervousness. His sales at the gallery had dropped off considerably. The greenness had gone from his eyes and left them a pain-shot blue. He had more difficulty than ever in finding words when he wanted to speak.

He followed her into the garden after the big Sunday dinner. "Mademoiselle Ursula," he said, "I'm sorry if I frightened you the other night."

She glanced up at him out of large, cool eyes, as though surprised that he should have followed her.

"Oh, it doesn't matter. It was of no importance. Let's forget it, shall we?"

"I'd like very much to forget that I was rude to you. But the things I said were true."

He took a step toward her. She moved away.

"Why speak of it again?" Ursula asked. "The whole episode has quite gone out of my mind." She turned her back on him and walked down the path. He hurried after her.

"I must speak of it again. Ursula, you don't understand how much I love you! You don't know how unhappy I've been this past week. Why do you keep running away from me?"

"Shall we go in? I think Mother is expecting callers."

"It can't be true that you love this other man. I would have seen it in your eyes if you had."

20

"I'm afraid I've not got any more time to spare. When did you say you were going home for your holiday?"

He gulped. "In July."

"How fortunate. My fiancé is coming to spend his July holiday with me, and we'll need his old room."

"I'll never give you up to him, Ursula."

"You'll simply have to stop this sort of thing. If you don't, Mother says you can find new lodgings."

He spent the next two months trying to dissuade her. All his early characteristics returned; if he could not be with Ursula he wanted to be by himself so that no one could interfere with his thinking about her. He was unfriendly to the people at the store. The world that had been awakened by Ursula's love went fast asleep again and he became the sombre, morose lad his parents had known in Zundert.

July came, and with it his holiday. He did not wish to leave London for two weeks. He had the feeling that Ursula could not love anyone else as long as he was in the house.

He went down into the parlour. Ursula and her mother were sitting there. They exchanged one of their significant looks.

"I'm taking only one grip with me, Madame Loyer," he said. "I shall leave everything in my room just as it is. Here is the money for the two weeks that I shall be away."

"I think you had better take all your things with you, Monsieur Van Gogh," said Madame.

"But why?"

"Your room is rented from Monday morning. We think it better if you live elsewhere."

"We?"

He turned and looked at Ursula from under the deep ridge of brow. That look made no statement. It only asked a question.

"Yes, we," replied her mother. "My daughter's fiancé has written that he wants you out of the house. I'm afraid, Monsieur Van Gogh, that it would have been better if you had never come here at all."

5

Theodorus Van Gogh met his son at the Breda station with a carriage. He had on his heavy, black ministerial coat, the wide lapelled vest, starched white shirt, and huge black bow tie covering all but a narrow strip of the high collar. With a quick glance Vincent took in his father's two facial characteristics: the right lid drooped down lower than the left, covering a considerable portion of the eye; the left side of his mouth was a thin, taut line, the right side full and sensuous. His eyes were passive; their expression simply said, "This is me."

The people of Zundert often remarked that the dominie Theodorus went about doing good with a high silk hat on.

He never understood to the day of his death why he was not more successful. He felt that he should have been called to an important pulpit in Amsterdam or The Hague years before. He was called the handsome dominie by his parishioners, was well educated, of a loving nature, had fine spiritual qualities, and was indefatigable in the service of God. Yet for twenty-five years he had been buried and forgotten in the little village of Zundert. He was the only one of the six Van Gogh brothers who had not achieved national importance.

The parsonage at Zundert, where Vincent had been born, was a wooden frame building across the road from the market place and *stadhuis*. There was a garden back of the kitchen with acacias and a number of little paths running through the carefully tended flowers. The church was a tiny wooden building hidden in the trees just behind the garden. There were two small Gothic windows of plain glass on either side, perhaps a dozen hard benches on the wooden floor, and a number of warming pans attached permanently to the planks. At the rear there was a stairway leading up to an old hand organ. It was a severe and simple place of worship, dominated by the spirit of Calvin and his reformation.

Vincent's mother, Anna Cornelia, was watching from the front window and had the door open before the carriage came to a full stop. Even while taking him with loving tenderness to her ample bosom, she perceived that something was wrong with her boy.

"Myn lieve zoon," she murmured. "My Vincent."–

Her eyes, now blue, now green, were always wide open, gently inquiring, seeing through a person without judging too harshly. A faint line from the side of each nostril down to the corners of the mouth deepened with the passage of the years, and the deeper these lines became, the stronger impression they gave of a face slightly lifted in smile.

Anna Cornelia Carbentus was from The Hague, where her father carried the title of "Bookbinder to the King." William

Carbentus's business flourished and when he was chosen to bind the first Constitution of Holland he became known throughout the country. His daughters, one of whom married Uncle Vincent Van Gogh, and a third the well known Reverend Stricker of Amsterdam, were *bien élevées*.

Anna Cornelia was a good woman. She saw no evil in the world and knew of none. She knew only of weakness, temptation, hardship, and pain. Theodorus Van Gogh was also a good man, but he understood evil very thoroughly and condemned every last vestige of it.

The dining room was the centre of the Van Gogh house, and the big table, after the supper dishes had been cleared off, the centre of family life. Here everyone gathered about the friendly oil lamp to pass the evening. Anna Cornelia was worried about Vincent; he was thin, and had become jumpy in his mannerisms.

"Is anything wrong, Vincent?" she asked after supper that night. "You don't look well to me."

Vincent glanced about the table where Anna, Elizabeth, and Willemien, three strange young girls who happened to be his sisters, were sitting.

"No," he said, "nothing is wrong."

"Do you find London agreeable?" asked Theodorus. "If you don't like it I'll speak to your Uncle Vincent. I think he would transfer you to one of the Paris shops."

Vincent became very agitated. "No, no, you mustn't do that!" he exclaimed. "I don't want to leave London, I . . ." He quieted himself. "When Uncle Vincent wants to transfer me, I'm sure he'll think of it for himself."

"Just as you wish," said Theodorus.

"It's that girl," said Anna Cornelia to herself. "Now I understand what was wrong with his letters."

There were pine woods and clumps of oaks on the heath near Zundert. Vincent spent his days walking alone in the fields, gazing down into the numerous ponds with which the heath was dotted. The only diversion he enjoyed was drawing; he made a number of sketches of the garden, the Saturday afternoon market seen from the window of the parsonage, the front door of the house. It kept his mind off Ursula for moments at a time.

Theodorus had always been disappointed that his oldest son had not chosen to follow in his footsteps. They went to visit a sick peasant and when they drove back that evening across the heath the two men got out of the carriage and walked awhile. The sun was setting red behind the pine trees, the evening sky was reflected in the pools, and the heath and yellow sand were full of harmony.

"My father was a parson, Vincent, and I had always hoped you would continue the line."

"What makes you think I want to change?"

"I was only saying, in case you wanted to ... You could live with Uncle Jan in Amsterdam while you attend the University. And the Reverend Stricker has offered to direct your education."

"Are you advising me to leave Goupils?"

"Oh no, certainly not. But if you are unhappy there ... sometimes people change...."

"I know. But I have no intention of leaving Goupils."

His mother and father drove him to Breda the day he was to leave for London. "Are we to write to the same address, Vincent?" Anna Cornelia asked.

"No. I'm moving."

"I'm glad you're leaving the Loyers," said his father. "I never liked that family. They had too many secrets."

Vincent stiffened. His mother laid a warm hand over his and said gently, so that Theodorus might not hear, "Don't be unhappy, my dear. You will be better off with a nice Dutch girl, later, later, when you are more established. She would not be good for you, that Ursula girl. She is not your kind."

He wondered how his mother knew.

6

Back in London he took furnished rooms in Kensington New Road. His landlady was a little old woman who retired every evening at eight. There was never the faintest sound in the house. Each night he had a fierce battle on his hands; he yearned to run directly to the Loyers'. He would lock the door on himself and swear resolutely that he was going to sleep. In a quarter of an hour he would find himself mysteriously on the street, hurrying to Ursula's.

When he got within a block of her house he felt himself enter her aura. It was torture to have this feel of her and yet have her so inaccessible; it was a thousand times worse torture to stay in Ivy Cottage and not get within that penumbra of haunting personality.

Pain did curious things to him. It made him sensitive to the pain of others. It made him intolerant of everything that was cheap and blatantly successful in the world about him. He was no longer of any value at the gallery. When customers asked him what he thought about a particular print he told them in no uncertain terms how horrible it was, and they did not buy. The only pictures in which he could find reality and emotional depth were the ones in which the artists had expressed pain.

In October a stout matron with a high lace collar, a high bosom, a sable coat, and a round velvet hat with a blue plume, came in and asked to be shown some pictures for her new town house. She fell to Vincent.

"I want the very best things you have in stock," she said. "You needn't concern yourself over the expense. Here are the dimensions; in the drawing room there are two uninterrupted walls of fifty feet, one wall broken by two windows with a space between . . ."

He spent the better part of the afternoon trying to sell her some etchings after Rembrandt, an excellent reproduction of a Venetian water scene after Turner, some lithographs after Thys Maris, and museum photographs after Corot and Daubigny. The woman had a sure instinct for picking out the very worst expression of the painter's art to be found in any group that Vincent showed her. She had an equal talent for being able to reject at first sight, and quite peremptorily, everything he knew to be authentic. As the hours passed, the woman, with her pudgy features and condescending puerilities, became for him a perfect symbol of middle-class fatuity and the commercial life.

"There," she exclaimed with a self-satisfied air, "I think I've chosen rather well."

"If you had closed your eyes and picked," said Vincent, "you couldn't have done any worse."

The woman rose to her feet heavily and swept the wide velvet skirt to one side. Vincent could see the turgid flow of blood creep from her propped-up bosom to her neck under the lace collar.

"Why!" she exclaimed, "why, you're nothing but a . . . a . . . country boor!"

She stormed out, the tall feather in her velvet hat waving back and forth.

Mr. Obach was outraged. "My dear Vincent," he exclaimed,

"whatever is the matter with you? You've muffed the biggest sale of the week, and insulted that woman!"

"Mr. Obach, would you answer me one question?"

"Well, what is it? I have a few questions to ask, myself."

Vincent shoved aside the woman's prints and put both hands on the edge of the table. "Then tell me how a man can justify himself for spending his one and only life selling very bad pictures to very stupid people?"

Obach made no attempt to answer. "If this sort of thing keeps up," he said, "I'll have to write to your uncle and have him transfer you to another branch. I can't have you ruining my business."

Vincent moved aside Obach's strong breath with a gesture of his hand. "How can we take such large profits for selling trash, Mr. Obach? And why is it that the only people who can afford to come in here are those who can't bear to look at anything authentic? Is it because their money has made them callous? And why is it that the poor people who can really appreciate good art haven't even a farthing to buy a print for their walls?"

Obach looked at him queerly. "What is this, socialism?"

When he reached home he picked up the volume of Renan lying on his table and turned to a page he had marked. "To act well in this world," he read, "one must die within oneself. Man is not on this earth only to be happy, he is not there to be simply honest, he is there to realize great things for humanity, to attain nobility and to surpass the vulgarity in which the existence of almost all individuals drags on."

About a week before Christmas the Loyers put up a dainty Christmas tree in their front window. Two nights later as he walked by he saw the house well lighted and neighbours going in the front door. He heard the sound of laughing voices inside. The Loyers were giving their Christmas party. Vincent ran home, shaved hurriedly, put on a fresh shirt and tie, and walked back as fast as he could to Clapham. He had to wait several minutes at the bottom of the stairs to catch his breath.

This was Christmas; the spirit of kindliness and forgiveness was in the air. He walked up the stairs. He pounded on the knocker. He heard a familiar footstep come through the hall, a familiar voice call back something to the people in the parlour. The door was opened. The light from the lamp fell on his face. He looked at Ursula. She was wearing a sleeveless green

26

polonaise with large bows and lace cascades. He had never seen her so beautiful.

"Ursula," he said.

An expression passed over her face that repeated clearly all the things she had said to him in the garden. Looking at her, he remembered them.

"Go away," she said.

She slammed the door in his face.

The following morning he sailed for Holland.

Christmas was the busiest season for the Goupil Galleries. Mr. Obach wrote to Uncle Vincent, explaining that his nephew had taken a holiday without so much as a "with your leave." Uncle Vincent decided to put his nephew into the main gallery in Rue Chaptal in Paris.

Vincent calmly announced that he was through with the art business. Uncle Vincent was stunned and deeply hurt. He declared that in the future he would wash his hands of Vincent. After the holidays he stopped washing them long enough to secure his namesake a position as clerk in the bookshop of Blussé and Braam at Dordrecht. It was the very last thing the two Vincent Van Goghs ever had to do with each other.

He remained at Dordrecht almost four months. He was neither happy nor unhappy, successful nor unsuccessful. He simply was not there. One Saturday night he took the last train from Dordrecht to Oudenbosch and walked home to Zundert. It was beautiful on the heath with all the cool, pungent smells of night. Though it was dark he could distinguish the pine woods and moors extending far and wide. It reminded him of the print by Bodmer that hung in his father's study. The sky was overcast but the night stars were shining through the clouds. It was very early when he arrived at the churchyard at Zundert ; in the distance he could hear the larks singing in the black fields of yong corn.

His parents understood that he was going through a difficult time. Over the summer the family moved to Etten, a little market town just a few kilometres away, where Theodorus had been named dominie. Etten had a large, elm-lined public square and a steam train connecting it with the important city of Breda. For Theodorus it was a slight step up.

When early fall came it was necessary once again to make a decision. Ursula was not yet married.

"You are not fitted for all these shops, Vincent," said his

27

father. "Your heart has been leading you straight to the service of God."

"I know, Father."

"Then why not go to Amsterdam and study?"

"I would like to, but . . ."

"There is still hesitation in your heart?"

"Yes. I can't explain now. Give me a little more time."

Uncle Jan passed through Etten. "There is a room waiting for you in my house in Amsterdam, Vincent," he said.

"The Reverend Stricker has written that he can secure you good tutors," added his mother.

When he received the gift of pain from Ursula he had inherited the disinherited of the earth. He knew that the best training he could get was at the University at Amsterdam. The Van Gogh and Stricker families would take him in, encourage him, help him with money, books, and sympathy. But he could not make the clean break. Ursula was still in England, unmarried. In Holland he had lost the touch of her. He sent for some English newspapers, answered a number of advertisements, and finally secured a position as teacher at Ramsgate, a seaport town four and a half hours by train from London.

7

Mr. Stokes's schoolhouse stood on a square in the middle of which was a large lawn shut off by iron railings. There were twenty-four boys from ten to fourteen years of age at the school. Vincent had to teach French, German, and Dutch, keep an eye on the boys after hours, and help them with their weekly ablutions on Saturday night. He was given his board and lodging, but no pay.

Ramsgate was a melancholy spot but it suited his mood. Unconsciously he had come to cherish his pain as a dear companion; through it he kept Ursula constantly by his side. If he could not be with the girl he loved, it did not matter where he was. All he asked was that no one come between him and the heavy satiety with which Ursula crammed his brain and body.

"Can't you pay me just a small sum, Mr. Stokes?" asked Vincent. "Enough to buy tobacco and clothes?"

"No, I will certainly not do that," replied Stokes. "I can get teachers enough for just board and lodging."

Early the first Saturday morning Vincent started from

Ramsgate to London. It was a long walk, and the weather stayed hot until evening. Finally he reached Canterbury. He rested in the shade of the old trees surrounding the medieval cathedral. After a bit he walked still farther until he arrived at a few large beech and elm trees near a little pond. He slept there until four in the morning; the birds began to sing at dawn and awakened him. By afternoon he reached Chatham where he saw in the distance, between partly flooded low meadows, the Thames full of ships. Towards evening Vincent struck the familiar suburbs of London, and in spite of his fatigue, cut out briskly for the Loyers' house.

The thing for which he had come back to England, the contact with Ursula, reached out and gripped him the instant he came within sight of her home. In England she was still his because he could feel her.

He could not quiet the loud beating of his heart. He leaned against a tree, dully aching with an ache that existed outside the realm of words of articulate thought. At length the lamp in Ursula's parlour was extinguished, then the lamp in her bedroom. The house went dark. Vincent tore himself away and stumbled wearily down the road of Clapham. When he got out of sight of the house he knew that he had lost her again.

When he pictured his marriage to Ursula he no longer thought of her as the wife of a successful art dealer. He saw her as the faithful, uncomplaining wife of an evangelist, working by his side in the slums, to serve the poor.

Nearly every weekend he tried tramping to London, but he found it difficult to get back in time for the Monday morning classes. Sometimes he would walk all Friday and Saturday night just to see Ursula come out of her house on the way to church on Sunday morning. He had no money for food or lodgings, and as winter came on he suffered from the cold. When he got back to Ramsgate in the dawn of a Monday morning he would be shivering, exhausted and famished. It took him all week to recover.

After a few months he found a better position at Mr. Jones's Methodist school in Isleworth. Mr. Jones was a minister with a large parish. He employed Vincent as a teacher but soon turned him into a country curate.

Once again Vincent had to change all the pictures in his mind. Ursula was no longer to be the wife of an evangelist, working in the slums, but rather the wife of a country clergyman, helping her husband in the parish just as his mother helped his father. He saw Ursula looking on with approval, happy that he had left the narrow commercial life of Goupils and was now working for humanity.

He did not permit himself to realize that Ursula's wedding day was coming closer and closer. The other man had never existed as a reality in his mind. He always thought of Ursula's refusal as arising from some peculiar shortcoming on his part, a shortcoming which he must somehow remedy. What better way was there than serving God?

Mr. Jones's impoverished students came from London. The master gave Vincent the addresses of the parents and sent him there on foot to collect tuition. Vincent found them in the heart of Whitechapel. There were vile odours in the streets, large families herded into cold, barren rooms, hunger and illness staring out of every pair of eyes. A number of the fathers traded in diseased meat which the government prohibited from sale in the regular markets. Vincent came upon the families shivering in their rags and eating their supper of slops, dry crusts and putrid meat. He listened to their tales of destitution and misery until nightfall.

He had welcomed the trip to London because it would give him the chance to pass Ursula's house on the way home. The slums of Whitechapel drove her out of his mind and he forgot to take the road through Clapham. He returned to Isleworth without so much as a brass farthing for Mr. Jones.

One Thursday evening during the services the minister leaned over to his curate and feigned fatigue. "I'm feeling frightfully done in this evening, Vincent, You've been writing sermons straight along, haven't you? Then let's hear one of them. I want to see what kind of minister you're going to make."

Vincent mounted to the pulpit, trembling. His face went red and he did not know what to do with his hands. His voice was hoarse and halting. He had to stumble through his memory for the well-rounded phrases he had set down so neatly on paper. But he felt his spirit burst through the broken words and clumsy gestures.

"Nicely done, Vincent," said Mr. Jones. "I shall send you to Richmond next week."

It was a clear autumn day and a beautiful walk from Isleworth to Richmond along the Thames. The blue sky and great chestnut trees with their load of yellow leaves were mirrored in the water. The people of Richmond wrote Mr. Jones that they liked the young Dutch preacher, so the good man decided to give Vincent his chance. Mr. Jones's church at Turnham Green was an important one, the congregation large and critical. If Vincent could preach a good sermon there, he would be qualified to preach from any pulpit.

Vincent chose as his text, Psalms 119:19, "I am a stranger on the earth: hide not Thy commandments from me." He spoke with simple fervour. His youth, his fire, his heavy-handed power, his massive head, and penetrating eyes all had a tremendous effect on the congregation.

Many of them came up to thank him for his message. He shook their hands and smiled at them in a misty daze. As soon as everyone had gone, he slipped out the back door of the church and took the road to London.

A storm came up. He had forgotten his hat and overcoat. The Thames was yellowish, especially near the shore. At the horizon there was a dash of light, and above it immense grey clouds from which the rain poured down in slanting streaks. He was drenched to the skin, but he tramped on at an exhilarated speed.

At last he was successful! He had found himself. He had a triumph to lay at Ursula's feet, to share with her.

The rain pelted the dust on the little white path and swayed the hawthorn bushes. In the distance was a town that looked like a Durer engraving, a town with its turrets, mills, slate roofs and houses built in the Gothic style.

He battled his way into London, the water streaming down his face and sopping into his boots. It was late afternoon before he reached the Loyer house. A grey, murky dusk had fallen. From some distance he heard the sound of music, of violins, and wondered what was going on. Every room in the house had its lamp burning. A number of carriages stood out in the sheets of rain. Vincent saw people dancing in the parlour. An old cabby was sitting on his box under a huge umbrella, huddled away from the rain.

"What's going on here?" he asked.

"Weddin', I fancy."

Vincent leaned against the carriage, rivulets from his red hair streaming down his face. After a time the front door opened. Ursula and a tall, slim man were framed in the doorway. The crowd from the parlour surged out on the porch, laughing, shouting, throwing rice.

Vincent slunk around to the dark side of the carriage. Ursula and her husband got in. The cabby flicked his whip over the horses. They started slowly. Vincent took a few steps forward and pressed his face against the streaming windows. Ursula was locked tight in the man's arms, her mouth full on his. The carriage drew away.

Something thin snapped within Vincent, snapped neat and clean. The spell was broken. He had not known it could be so easy.

He trudged back to Isleworth in the slashing rain, collected his belongings, and left England for ever.

BOOK ONE

THE BORINAGE

1

Vice-Admiral Johannes Van Gogh, highest ranking officer in the Dutch Navy, stood on the *stoep* of his roomy, rent-free residence at the rear of the Navy Yard. In honour of his nephew's coming he had donned his dress uniform; a gold epaulet perched on each shoulder. Above the ponderous Van Gogh chin jutted a strong, straight-ridged nose that met the convex cliff of the forehead.

"I'm glad to have you here, Vincent," he said. "The house is very quiet, now that my children have married out of it."

They mounted a flight of broad, angular stairs and Uncle Jan threw open a door. Vincent entered the room and set down his bag. A large window overlooked the Yard. Uncle Jan sat on the edge of the bed and tried to look as informal as his gold braid would permit.

"I was pleased to hear that you had decided to study for the ministry," he said. "One member of the Van Gogh family has always done God's work."

Vincent reached for his pipe and loaded the bowl carefully with tobacco; it was a gesture he often made when he needed an extra moment to think. "I wanted to be an evangelist, you know, and get right to work."

"You wouldn't want to be an evangelist, Vincent. They're uneducated people, and Lord knows what sort of garbled theology they preach. No, my boy, the Van Gogh dominies have always been University graduates. But no doubt you would like to unpack now. Dinner is at eight."

The broad back of the vice-admiral had no sooner gone out of the door than a gentle melancholy descended upon Vincent. He looked about him. The bed was wide and comfortable, the bureau spacious, the low, smooth study table inviting. But he felt ill at ease, as he did in the presence of strangers. He snatched up his cap and walked rapidly across the *Dam*. There he found a Jewish book-seller who offered beautiful prints in an open bin. After a good deal of searching, Vincent selected thirteen pieces, stuck them under his arm and walked home along the waterfront, breathing in the strong odour of tar.

As he was pinning up his prints lightly, so as not to injure the fabric of the walls, there was a knock on the door. The Reverend Stricker entered. Stricker was also Vincent's uncle, but he was not a Van Gogh; his wife and Vincent's mother were sisters. He was a well-known clergyman in Amsterdam and by general admission a clever one. His black suit was of good material, smartly cut.

When the greetings were over the dominie said, "I have secured Mendes da Costa, one of our finest scholars of the classical languages, to tutor you in Latin and Greek. His home is in the Jewish quarter; you are to go there Monday after-noon at three for your first lesson. But what I came for was to ask your company at tomorrow's Sunday dinner. Your Aunt Wilhelmina and Cousin Kay are anxious to see you."

"I would like that very much. At what time shall I come?"

"We dine at noon, after my late morning service."

"Please present my compliments to your family," said Vincent, as the Reverend Stricker picked up his black hat and folio.

"Until tomorrow," said his uncle, and was gone.

2

The Keizersgracht, on which the Stricker family lived, was one of the most aristocratic streets in Amsterdam. It was the fourth horseshoe boulevard and canal which starts from the south side of the harbour, runs around the centrum and back to the harbour again on the north. It was clean and clear, far too important a canal to be covered with *kroos*, the mysterious green moss which for hundreds of years has laid a thick surface on the canals in the poorer districts.

The houses that line the street are pure Flemish; narrow, well built, tightly fitted together, a long line of prim Puritan soldiers standing at attention.

The following day, after listening to Uncle Stricker preach, Vincent set out for the dominie's house. A bright sun had waved away the ash-grey clouds that float eternally across the Dutch skies, and for a few moments the air was luminous. Vincent was early. He walked at a meditative gait and watched the canal boats being pushed upstream against the current.

They were largely sand boats, oblong except for the tapering ends; a water-worn black in colour, with great hollow spaces in the centre for the cargo. Long clothes-lines extended from prow to stern, on which hung the family wash. The father of the family thrust his pole into the mud, propped it against his shoulder, and struggled down the catwalk at twisted, tortuous angles while the boat slipped out from under him. The wife, a heavy, buxom, red-faced woman, sat immutably at the stern and worked the clumsy wooden tiller. The children played with the dog, and every few minutes ran down into the cabin hole that was their home.

The Reverend Stricker's home was of typical Flemish architecture; narrow, three-storied, with an oblong tower at the top containing the attic window, and decorated with flowing arabesques. A beam stuck out from the attic window with a long iron hook at the end of it.

Aunt Wilhelmina welcomed Vincent and led him into the dining room. A portrait of Calvin by Ary Scheffer hung on the wall, and a silver service gleamed on a sideboard. The walls were done in dark wood panelling.

Before Vincent could get used to the customary darkness of the room, a tall, lithe girl came out of the shadows and greeted him warmly.

"Of course you wouldn't know me," she said in a rich voice, "but I'm your Cousin Kay."

Vincent took her outstretched hand and felt the soft, warm flesh of a young woman for the first time in many months.

"We've never met," the girl went on in that intimate tone, "and I think it rather curious, since I'm twenty-six, and you must be ... ?"

Vincent gazed at her in silence. Several moments passed

before he realized that an answer was necessary. In order to make up for his stupidity, he blurted out in a loud, harsh voice, "Twenty-four. Younger than you."

"Yes. Well, I suppose it's not so curious after all. You have never visited Amsterdam and I have never been in the Brabant. But I'm afraid I'm being a poor hostess. Won't you sit down?"

He sat on the edge of a stiff chair. With one of the swift, strange metamorphoses that changed him from an awkward, country boor to a polished gentleman, he said, "Mother often wished you would come to visit us. I think the Brabant would have pleased you. The countryside is very *simpatico*."

"I know. Aunt Anna wrote and invited me several times. I must visit there very soon."

"Yes," replied Vincent, "you must."

It was only a remote portion of his mind that heard and answered the girl. The rest of him was soaking up her beauty with the passionate thirst of a man who has drunk too long at a celibate well. Kay had the hardy features of the Dutch women, but they had been filed down, chiselled away to delicate proportions. Her hair was neither the corn blonde nor the raw red of her country-women, but a curious intermingling in which the fire of one had caught up the light of the other in a glowing, subtle warmth. She had guarded her skin against the sun and wind; the whiteness of her chin crept into the flush of her cheek with all the artistry of a little Dutch master. Her eyes were a deep blue, dancing to the joy of life; her full-lipped mouth was slightly open, as though for its acceptance.

She noticed Vincent's silence and said, "What are you thinking about, Cousin? You seem preoccupied."

"I was thinking that Rembrandt would have liked to paint you."

Kay laughed low and with a ripe lusciousness in her throat. "Rembrandt only liked to paint ugly old women, didn't he?" she asked.

"No," replied Vincent. "He painted beautiful old women, women who were poor or in some way unhappy, but who through sorrow had gained a soul."

For the first time Kay really looked at Vincent. She had glanced at him only casually when he came in and noticed his mop of rust-red hair and rather heavy face. Now she saw the full mouth, the deep set, burning eyes, the high, symmetrical

35

forehead of the Van Goghs, and the uncrushable chin, stuck slightly out toward her.

"Forgive me for being stupid," she murmured, almost in a whisper. "I understand what you mean about Rembrandt. He gets at the real essence of beauty, doesn't he, when he paints those gnarled old people who have suffering and defeat carved into their faces."

"What have you children been talking about so earnestly?" asked the Reverend Stricker from the doorway.

"We have been getting acquainted," Kay answered. "Why didn't you tell me I had such a nice cousin?"

Another man came into the room, a slender chap with an easy smile and charming manner. Kay rose and kissed him eagerly. "Cousin Vincent," she said, "this is my husband, Mijnheer Vos."

She returned in a few moments with a tow-headed boy of two, a vivacious child with a wistful face and the light blue eyes of his mother. Kay reached down and lifted the boy. Vos put his arms about the two of them.

"Will you sit on this side of the table with me, Vincent?" asked Aunt Wilhelmina.

Opposite Vincent, with Vos on one side and Jan propped up on the other, sat Kay. She had forgotten about Vincent now that her husband was home. The colour deepened in her cheek. Once, as her husband said something pointed in a low, guarded tone, she leaned over with a quick alertness and kissed him.

The vibrant waves of their love reached out and engulfed Vincent. For the first time since that fateful Sunday the old pain for Ursula arose from some mysterious source within him and flooded the outermost ramparts of his body and brain. The little family before him, with its clinging unity and joyous affection, brought him to a realization that he had been hungry, desperately hungry for love all these weary months, and that it was a hunger not easily destroyed.

3

Vincent arose just before sunrise each morning to read his Bible. When the sun came up about five o'clock he went to the window which overlooked the Navy Yard and watched the gangs of workmen come through the gate, a long uneven line of black figures. Little steamers sailed to and fro in the Zuider

Zee and in the distance, near the village across the Y, he saw the swiftly moving, brown sails.

When the sun had fully risen and sponged the mist from the pile of lumber, Vincent turned from his window, breakfasted on a piece of dry bread and a glass of beer, and then sat down for a seven hour siege with his Latin and Greek.

After four or five hours of concentration his head became heavy; often it burned and his thoughts were confused. He did not see how he was going to persevere in simple, regular study after all those emotional years. He pounded rules into his head until the sun was already sliding down the other side of the heavens and it was time for him to go to Mendes da Costa for his lesson. On the way there he would walk along the Buitenkant, around the Oudezyds Chapel and the Old and South Church, through crooked streets with forges and coopers and lithograph shops.

Mendes reminded Vincent of the *Imitation of Jesus Christ* by Ruyperez; he was the classical type of Jew with profound, cavernous eyes, a thin, hollowed out, spiritual face, and the soft, pointed beard of the early rabbis. It was very close and sultry in mid-afternoon in the Jewish quarter; Vincent, gorged with seven hours of Greek and Latin, and more hours of Dutch History and Grammar, would talk to Mendes about lithographs. One day he brought his teacher the study of *A Baptism* by Maris.

Mendes held *A Baptism* in his bony, tapering fingers, letting the sharp stream of dusted sunlight from the high window fall upon it.

"It is good," he said in his throaty, Jewish voice. "It catches something of the spirit of universal religion."

Vincent's fatigue left him instantly. He launched into an enthusiastic description of Maris's art. Mendes shook his head imperceptibly. The Reverend Stricker was paying him a high price to instruct Vincent in Latin and Greek.

"Vincent," he said quietly, "Maris is very fine, but the time grows short and we had better get on with our studies, yes?"

Vincent understood. On the way home, after a two hour lesson, he would pause before the interiors of houses where the wood-choppers, carpenters, and ships' victuallers were at work. The doors stood open before a big wine cellar, and men with lights were running to and fro in the dark vault.

Uncle Jan went to Helvoort for a week; knowing that he was alone in the big house behind the Navy Yard, Kay and

Vos walked over late one afternoon to fetch Vincent for dinner.

"You must come to us every night until Uncle Jan gets back," Kay told him. "And Mother asks if you won't take Sunday dinner with us each week, after services?"

When dinner was over the family played cards, but since Vincent did not know how to play, he settled in a quiet corner and read August Gruson's "Histoire des Croisades." From where he was sitting he could watch Kay and the changes of her quick, provocative smile. She left the table and came to his side.

"What are you reading, Cousin Vincent?" she asked.

He told her and then said, "It's a fine little book, I should almost say written with the sentiment of Thys Maris."

Kay smiled. He was always making these funny literary allusions. "Why Thys Maris?" she demanded.

"Read this and see if it doesn't remind you of a Maris canvas, where the writer describes an old castle on a rock, with the autumn woods in twilight, and in the foreground the black fields, and a peasant who is ploughing with a white horse."

While Kay was reading, Vincent drew up a chair for her. When she looked at him a thoughtful expression darkened her blue eyes.

"Yes," she said, "it is just like a Maris. The writer and painter use their own medium to express the same thought."

Vincent took the book and ran his finger across the page eagerly. "This line might have been lifted straight from Michelet or Carlyle."

"You know, Cousin Vincent, for a man who has spent so little time in classrooms, you are surprisingly well educated. Do you still read a good many books?"

"No, I should like to, but I may not. Though in fact I need not long for it so much, for all things are found in the word of Christ—more perfect and more beautiful than in any other book."

"Oh, Vincent," exclaimed Kay, jumping to her feet, "that was so unlike you!"

Vincent stared at her in amazement.

"I think you are ever so much nicer when you're seeing Thys Maris in the 'Histoires des Croisades'—though Father says you ought to concentrate and not think of such things —than when you talk like a stuffy, provincial clergyman."

Vos strolled over and said, "We've dealt you a hand, Kay."

Kay looked for a moment into the live, burning coals under Vincent's overhanging brows, then took her husband's arm and joined the other card players.

4

Mendes da Costa knew that Vincent liked to talk to him about the more general things of life, so several times a week he invented excuses to accompany him back to town when their lesson was done.

One day he took Vincent through an interesting part of the city, the outskirts that extend from the Leidsche Poort, near the Vondel Park, to the Dutch railway station. It was full of sawmills, workmen's cottages with little gardens, and was very populous. The quarter was cut through with many small canals.

"It must be a splendid thing to be a clergyman in a quarter like this," said Vincent.

"Yes," replied Mendes, as he filled his pipe and passed the cone-shaped bag of tobacco to Vincent, "these people need God and religion more than our friends uptown."

They were crossing a tiny wooden bridge that might almost have been Japanese. Vincent stopped and said, "What do you mean, Mijnheer?"

"These workers," said Mendes with a gentle sweep of his arm, "have a hard life of it. When illness comes they have no money for a doctor. The food for tomorrow comes from today's labour, and hard labour it is, too. Their houses, as you see, are small and poor; they are never more than a stone's throw away from privation and want. They've made a bad bargain with life; they need the thought of God to comfort them."

Vincent lighted his pipe and dropped the match into the little canal below him. "And the people uptown?" he asked.

"They have good clothes to wear, secure positions, money put away against adversity. When they think of God, He is a prosperous old gentleman, rather well pleased with himself for the lovely way things are going on earth."

"In short," said Vincent, "they're a little stuffy."

"Dear me!" exclaimed Mendes. "I never said that."

"No, I did."

That night he spread his Greek books out before him, and then stared at the opposite wall for a long time. He

39

remembered the slums of London, the sordid poverty and suffering; he remembered his desire to become an evangelist and help those people. His mental image flashed to Uncle Stricker's church. The congregation was prosperous, well-educated, sensitive to and capable of acquiring the better things of life. Uncle Stricker's sermons were beautiful and comforting, but who in the congregation needed comfort?

Six months had passed since he first came to Amsterdam. He was at last beginning to understand that hard work is but a poor substitute for natural ability. He pushed aside his language books and opened his algebra. At midnight Uncle Jan came in.

"I saw the light under your door, Vincent," said the vice-admiral, "and the watchman told me he saw you walking in the Yard at four o'clock this morning. How many hours a day have you been working?"

"It varies. Between eighteen and twenty."

"Twenty!" Uncle Jan shook his head; the misgiving grew more perceptible on his face. It was difficult for the vice-admiral to adjust himself to the thought of failure in the Van Gogh family. "You should not need so many."

"I must get my work done, Uncle Jan."

Uncle Jan brought up his bushy eyebrows. "Be that as it may," he said, "I have promised your parents to take good care of you. So you will kindly get to bed, and in the future do not work so late."

Vincent pushed aside his exercises. He had no need for sleep; he had no need for love or sympathy or pleasure. He had need only to learn his Latin and Greek, his algebra and grammar, so that he might pass his examinations, enter the University, become a minister, and do God's practical work on earth.

5

By May, just a year after he came to Amsterdam, he began to realize that his unfitness for formal education, would finally conquer him. This was not a statement of fact, but an admission of defeat, and every time one portion of his brain threw the realization before him, he whipped the rest of his mind to drown the admission in weary labour.

If it had been a simple question of the difficulty of the work, and his manifest unfitness for it, he would not have been disturbed. But the question that racked him night and day was, "Did he want to become a clever, gentleman clergyman like his Uncle Stricker?" What would happen to his ideal of personal service to the poor, the sick, the downtrodden, if he thought only of declensions and formulae for five more years?

One afternoon, late in May, when he had finished his lesson with Mendes, Vincent said, "Mijnheer da Costa, could you find time to take a walk with me?"

Mendes had been sensitive to the growing struggle in Vincent; he divined that the younger man had reached a point where a decision was imminent.

"Yes, I had planned to go for a little stroll. The air is very clear after the rains. I should be glad to accompany you." He wrapped a wool scarf about his neck many times and put on a high collared, black coat. The two men went into the street, walked by the side of the same synagogue in which Baruch Spinoza had been excommunicated more than three centuries before, and after a few blocks passed Rembrandt's old home in the Zeestraat.

"He died in poverty and disgrace," said Mendes in an ordinary tone as they passed the old house.

Vincent looked up at him quickly. Mendes had a habit of piercing to the heart of a problem before one even mentioned it. There was a profound resilience about the man; things one said seemed to be plunged into fathomless depths for consideration. With Uncle Jan and Uncle Stricker, one's words hit a precise wall and bounced back fast to the tune of yes! or no! Mendes always bathed one's thought in the deep well of his mellow wisdom before he returned it.

"He didn't die unhappy, though," said Vincent.

"No," replied Mendes, "he had expressed himself fully and he knew the worth of what he had done. He was the only one in his time who did."

"Then did that make it all right with him, the fact that he knew? Suppose he had been wrong? What if the world had been right in neglecting him?"

"What the world thought made little difference. Rembrandt had to paint. Whether he painted well or badly didn't matter; painting was the stuff that held him together as a man. The chief value of art, Vincent, lies in the expression it gives to the artist. Rembrandt fulfilled what he knew to be his life purpose; that justified him. Even if his work had been worthless, he would have been a thousand times more successful than if

41

he had put down his desire and become the richest merchant in Amsterdam."

"I see."

"The fact that Rembrandt's work brings joy to the whole world today," continued Mendes, as though following his own line of thought, "is entirely gratuitous. His life was complete and successful when he died, even though he was hounded into his grave. The book of life closed then, and it was a beautifully wrought volume. The quality of his perseverance and loyalty to his idea is what was important, not the quality of his work."

They stopped to watch men working with sand carts near the Y, and then passed through many narrow streets with gardens full of ivy.

"But how is a young man to know he is choosing rightly, Mijnheer? Suppose he thinks there is something special he must do with his life, and afterwards he finds out he wasn't suited to that at all?"

Mendes drew his chin out of the collar of the coat, and his black eyes brightened. "Look, Vincent," he cried, "how the sunset is throwing a ruddy glow on those grey clouds."

They had reached the harbour. The masts of the ships and the row of old houses and trees on the waterfront were standing out against the colour and everything was reflected in the Zee. Mendes filled his pipe and passed the paper sack to Vincent.

"I am already smoking, Mijnheer," said Vincent.

"Oh yes, so you are. Shall we walk along the dyke to Zeeburg? The Jewish churchyard is there and we can sit for a moment where my people are buried."

They walked along in friendly silence, the wind carrying the smoke over their shoulders. "You can never be sure about anything for all time, Vincent," said Mendes. "You can only have the courage and strength to do what you think is right. It may turn out to be wrong, but you will at least have done it, and that is the important thing. We must act according to the best dictates of our reason, and then leave God to judge of its ultimate value. If you are certain at this moment that you want to serve Our Maker in one way or another, then that faith is the only guide you have to the future. Don't be afraid to put your trust in it."

"Suppose I am qualified?"

"To serve God?" Mendes looked at him with a shy smile.

"No, I mean qualified to become the sort of academic clergyman that the University turns out."

Mendes did not wish to say anything about Vincent's specific problem; he wanted only to discuss its more general phases and let the boy come to his own decision. By now they had reached the Jewish churchyard. It was very simple, full of old headstones with Hebrew inscriptions, and elderberry trees, and covered here and there with a high, dark grass. There was a stone bench near the plot reserved for the da Costa family, and here the two men sat down. Vincent put away his pipe. The churchyard was deserted at this hour of the evening; not a sound was to be heard.

"Every person has an integrity, a quality of character, Vincent," said Mendes, looking at the graves of his father and mother lying side by side, "and if he observes it, whatever he does will turn out well in the end. If you had remained an art dealer, the integrity that makes you the sort of man you are would have made you a good art dealer. The same applies to your teaching. Some day you will express yourself fully, no matter what medium you may choose."

"And if I do not remain in Amsterdam to become a professional minister?"

"It does not matter. You will return to London as an evangelist, or work in a shop, or become a peasant in the Brabant. Whatever you will do, you will do well. I have felt the quality of the stuff that goes to make you a man, and I know that it is good. Many times in your life you may think you are failing, but ultimately you will express yourself and that expression will justify your life."

"Thank you, Mijnheer da Costa. What you say helps me."

Mendes shivered a little. The stone bench under him was cold and the sun had gone down behind the sea. He rose. "Shall we go, Vincent?" he asked.

6.

The following day, as twilight was falling, Vincent stood at the window overlooking the Yard. The little avenue of poplars with their slender forms and thin branches stood out delicately against the grey evening sky.

"Because I am no good at formal studying," said Vincent to himself, "does that mean I can't be of any use in the world?

43

What, after all, have Latin and Greek to do with the love of our fellow men?"

Uncle Jan passed in the Yard below, making the rounds. In the distance Vincent could see the masts of the ships in the docks, in front the *Atjeh*, quite black, and the red and grey monitors surrounding it.

"The thing I wanted to do all along was God's practical work, not draw triangles and circles. I never wanted to have a big church and preach polished sermons. I belong with the humble and suffering *Now, Not Five Years From Now!*"

Just then the bell rang and the whole stream of workmen began pouring toward the gate. The lamplighter came to light the lantern in the Yard. Vincent turned away from the window.

He realized that his father and Uncle Jan and Uncle Stricker had spent a great deal of time and money on him in the past year. They would consider it entirely wasted if he gave up.

Well, he had tried honestly. He could not work more than twenty hours a day. He was obviously unfitted for the life of the study. He had begun too late. If he went out tomorrow as an evangelist, working for His people, would that be failure? If he cured the sick, comforted the weary, consoled the sinner, and converted the unbeliever, would that still be failure?

The family would say it was. They would say he could never succeed, that he was worthless and ungrateful, the black sheep of the Van Gogh family.

"Whatever you do," Mendes had said, "you will do well. Ultimately you will express yourself and that expression will justify your life."

Kay, who understood everything, had already surmised in him the seeds of a narrow-minded clergyman. Yes, that was what he would become if he remained in Amsterdam where the true voice grew fainter and fainter every day. He knew where his place was in the world, and Mendes had given him the courage to go. His family would scorn him, but that no longer seemed to matter. His own position was little enough to give up for God.

He packed his bag quickly and walked out of the house without saying good-bye.

The Belgian Committee of Evangelization, composed of the Reverends van den Brink, de Jong and Pietersen, was opening a new school in Brussels, where instruction was to be free and the students had to pay only a small sum for their board and lodging. Vincent visited the Committee and was accepted as a pupil.

"At the end of three months," said the Reverend Pietersen, "we will give you an appointment somewhere in Belgium."

"Providing he qualifies," said the Reverend de Jong heavily, turning to Pietersen. De Jong had lost a thumb in mechanical labour while a young man, and that had turned him to theology.

"What is wanted in evangelical work, Monsieur Van Gogh," said the Reverend van den Brink, "is the talent to give popular and attractive lectures to the people."

The Reverend Pietersen accompanied him out of the church in which the meeting had been held, and took Vincent's arm as they stepped into the glaring Brussels sunshine. "I am glad to have you with us, my boy," he said. "There is a great deal of fine work to be done in Belgium, and from your enthusiasm I should say that you are highly qualified to carry it on."

Vincent did not know which warmed him more, the hot sun or the man's unexpected kindness. They walked down the street between precipices of six-storey stone buildings, while Vincent struggled to find something to reply. The Reverend Pietersen stopped.

"This is where I turn off," he said. "Here, take my card, and when you have a spare evening, come to see me. I shall be happy to chat with you."

There were only three pupils including Vincent at the evangelical school. They were put in charge of Master Bokma, a small, wiry man with a concave face; a plumb line dropped from his brow to his chin would not have touched his nose or lips.

Vincent's two companions were country boys of nineteen. These two immediately became good friends, and to cement their friendship turned their ridicule on Vincent.

"My aim," he told one of them in an early, unguarded moment, "is to humble myself, *mourir à moi-même*." Whenever they found him struggling to memorize a lecture in French, or agonizing over some academic book, they would ask, "What are you doing, Van Gogh, dying within yourself?"

It was with Master Bokma that Vincent had his most difficult time. The master wished to teach them to be good speakers; each night at home they had to prepare a lecture to deliver the following day in class. The two boys concocted smooth, juvenile messages and recited them glibly. Vincent worked slowly over his sermons, pouring his whole heart into every line. He felt deeply what he had to say and when he rose in class the words would not come with any degree of ease.

"How can you hope to be an evangelist, Van Gogh," demanded Bokma, "when you cannot even speak? Who will listen to you?"

The climax of Bokma's wrath broke when Vincent flatly refused to deliver his lectures *extempore*. He laboured far into the night to make his compositions meaningful, writing out every word in painstaking, precise French. In class the following day the two boys spoke airily about Jesus Christ and salvation, glancing at their notes once or twice while Bokma nodded approval. Then it came Vincent's turn. He spread his lecture before him and began to read. Bokma would not even listen.

"Is that the way they teach you in Amsterdam? Van Gogh, no man has ever left my class who could not speak *extempore* at a moment's notice and move his audience!"

Vincent tried, but he could not remember in the proper sequence all the things he had written down the night before. His classmates laughed outright at his stumbling attempts and Bokma joined their merriment. Vincent's nerves were worn to a biting edge from the year in Amsterdam.

"Master Bokma," he declared, "I will deliver my sermons as I see fit. My work is good, and I refuse to submit to your insults!"

Bokma was outraged. "You will do as I tell you," he shouted, "or I will not allow you in my classroom!"

From then on it was open warfare between the two men. Vincent produced four times as many sermons as was demanded of him, for he could not sleep at night and there was little use in his going to bed. His appetite left him and he became thin and jumpy.

In November he was summoned to the church to meet with the Committee and get his appointment. At last all the obstacles in his way had been removed and he felt a tired gratification. His two classmates were already there when he arrived. The Reverend Pietersen did not look at him when he came in, but Bokma did, and with a glint in his eye.

The Reverend de Jong congratulated the boys on their successful work and gave them appointments to Hoogstraeten and Etiehove. The classmates left the room arm in arm.

"Monsieur Van Gogh," said De Jong, "the Committee has not been able to persuade itself that you are ready to bring God's work to the people. I regret to say that we have no appointment for you."

After what seemed a long time Vincent asked, "What was wrong with my work?"

"You refused to submit to authority. The first rule of our Church is absolute obedience. Further, you did not succeed in learning how to speak *extempore*. Your master feels you are not qualified to preach."

Vincent looked at the Reverend Pietersen but his friend was staring out the window. "What am I to do?" he asked of no one in particular.

"You may return to the school for another six months if you wish," replied van den Brink. "Perhaps at the end of that time . . ."

Vincent stared down at his rough, square-toed boots and noticed that the leather was cracking. Then, because he could think of absolutely no word to say, he turned and walked out in silence.

He passed quickly through the city streets and found himself in Laeken. Without knowing why he was walking, he struck out along the towpath with its busily humming workshops. Soon he left the houses behind and came to an open field. An old white horse, lean, emaciated, and tired to death by a life of hard labour, was standing there. The spot was lonely and desolate. On the ground lay a skull and at a distance in the background the bleached skeleton of a horse lying near the hut of a man who skinned horses.

Some little feeling returned to flood out the numbness, and Vincent reached forlornly for his pipe. He applied a match to the tobacco but it tasted strangely bitter. He sat down on a log in the field. The old white horse came over and rubbed his nose against Vincent's back. He turned and stroked the emaciated neck of the animal.

After a time there rose in his mind the thought of God, and he was comforted. "Jesus was calm in the storm," he said to

47

himself. "I am not alone, for God has not forsaken me. Someday, somehow, I will find a way to serve Him."

When he returned to his room he found the Reverend Pietersen waiting for him. "I came to ask you to have dinner at my home, Vincent," he said.

They walked along streets thronged with working people on their way to the evening meal. Pietersen chatted of casual things as though nothing had happened. Vincent heard every word he said with a terrible clarity. Pietersen led him into the front room, which had been turned into a studio. There were a few water-colours on the walls and an easel in one corner.

"Oh," said Vincent, "you paint. I didn't know."

Pietersen was embarrassed. "I'm just an amateur," he replied. "I draw a bit in my spare time for relaxation. But I shouldn't mention it to my *confrères* if I were you."

They sat down to dinner. Pietersen had a daughter, a shy, reserved girl of fifteen who never once lifted her eyes from the plate. Pietersen went on speaking of inconsequential things while Vincent forced himself, for politeness sake, to eat a little. Suddenly his mind became riveted to what Pietersen was saying; he had no idea how the Reverend had worked into the subject.

"The Borinage," his host said, "is a coal mining region. Practically every man in the district goes down into the *charbonnages*. They work in the midst of thousands of ever-recurring dangers, and their wage is hardly enough to keep body and soul together. Their homes are tumble-down shacks where their wives and children spend most of the year shivering with cold, fever, and hunger."

Vincent wondered why he was being told all this. "Where is the Borinage?" he asked.

"In the south of Belgium, near Mons. I recently spent some time there, and Vincent, if ever a people needed a man to preach to them and comfort them, it's the Borains."

A gulp came into Vincent's throat, barring the passage of food. He laid down his fork. Why was Pietersen torturing him?

"Vincent," said the Reverend, "why don't you go to the Borinage? With your strength and enthusiasm you could do a great deal of fine work."

"But how can I? The Committee . . ."

"Yes, I know. I wrote to your father the other day explaining the situation. I had an answer from him this afternoon. He

48

says he will support you in the Borinage until I can secure you a regular appointment."

Vincent jumped to his feet. "Then you will get me an appointment!"

"Yes, but you must give me a little time. When the Committee sees what splendid work you are doing it will surely relent. And even if it doesn't ... de Jong and van den Brink will come to me for a favour one of these fine days, and in return for that favour ... The poor people of this country need men like you, Vincent, and as God is my judge, any means is justified in getting you to them!"

8

As the train neared the South a group of mountains appeared on the horizon. Vincent gazed at them with pleasure and relief after the monotonous flat country of Flanders. He had been studying them only a few minutes when he discovered that they were curious mountains. Each one stood utterly by itself, rising out of the flat land with a precipitate abruptness.

"Black Egypt," he murmured to himself as he peered out of the window at the long line of fantastic pyramids. He turned to the man sitting next to him and asked, "Can you tell me how those mountains get there?"

"Yes," replied his neighbour, "they are composed of *terril*, the waste material that is brought up from the earth with the coal. Do you see that little car just about to reach the point of the hill? Watch it for a moment."

Just as he said this, the little car turned over on its side and sent a black cloud flying down the slope. "There," said the man, "that's how they grow. I've been watching them go up into the air a fraction of an inch every day for the past fifty years."

The train stopped at Wasmes and Vincent jumped off. The town was located in the hollow of a bleak valley; although an anaemic sun shone at an oblique angle, a substantial layer of coal smoke lay between Vincent and the heavens. Wasmes struggled up the side of the hill in two winding rows of dirty, red brick buildings, but before it reached the top, the bricks ran out and Petit Wasmes appeared.

As Vincent walked up the long hill he wondered why the village was so deserted. Not a man was to be seen anywhere;

an occasional woman stood in a doorway with a dull and stolid expression on her face.

Petit Wasmes was the miners' village. It could boast of only one brick building, the home of Jean-Baptiste Denis, the baker, which sat right on the crest of the hill. It was to this house Vincent made his way, for Denis had written to the Reverend Pietersen, offering to board the next evangelist to be sent to their town.

Madame Denis welcomed Vincent heartily, led him through the warm kitchen-bakery with its smell of rising bread, and showed him his room, a small space under the eaves, with a window facing the rue Petit Wasmes, and rafters coming down at an abrupt angle at the rear. The place had been scrubbed by Madame Denis's thick, competent hands. Vincent liked it immediately. He was so excited he could not even unpack his things, but rushed down the few rough, wooden stairs which led into the kitchen to tell Madame Denis that he was going out.

"You won't forget to come back to supper?" she asked. "We eat at five."

Vincent liked Madame Denis. He felt in her the nature that understands things without going to all the trouble of thinking about them. "I'll be here, Madame," he said. "I just want to look about a bit."

"We have a friend coming tonight whom you should meet. He is a foreman at Marcasse and can tell you many things you will want to know for your work."

It had been snowing heavily. As Vincent walked down the road he observed the thorn hedges around the gardens and fields that had been turned black from the smoke of the mine chimneys. On the east side of the Denis house was a steep ravine in which were located most of the miners' huts; on the other side was a great open field with a black *terril* mountain and the chimneys of the Marcasse *charbonnage*, where most of the Petit Wasmes miners descended. Across the field there was a hollow road grown over with thorn bushes and torn up by the roots of gnarled trees.

Although Marcasse was only one of a string of seven mines owned by the Charbonnages Belgique, it was the oldest and most dangerous pit in the Borinage. It had a bad reputation because so many men had perished in it, either in descending or ascending, by poison gas, explosion, flooding water, or by the collapse of old tunnels. There were two squat, brick buildings above the ground, in which the machinery was operated for bringing up the coal and where the coal was graded and dumped into cars. The tall chimneys, which once had been of yellow brick, spread tangible, black smoke over the neighbourhood twenty-four hours a day. Around Marcasse were poor miners' huts with a few dead trees, black from the smoke, thorn hedges, dunghills, ash dumps, heaps of useless coal, and towering above it all, the black mountain. It was a gloomy spot; at first sight everything looked dreary and desolate to Vincent.

"No wonder they call it the black country," he murmured.

After he had been standing there for some time the miners began to pour out of the gate. They were dressed in coarse, tattered garments with leather hats on their heads; the women wore the same outfit as the men. All were completely black and looked like chimney sweeps, the whites of their eyes presenting a strange contrast to the coal-dust covered faces. It was not without reason that they were called *gueules noires*. The glare of the feeble afternoon sunlight hurt their eyes after they had laboured in the darkness of the earth since before dawn. They stumbled out of the gate, half blinded, speaking among themselves in a swift unintelligible patois. They were small people with narrow, hunched-in shoulders and bony limbs.

Vincent understood now why the village had been deserted that afternoon; the real Petit Wasmes was not the small cluster of huts in the ravine, but the labyrinth city which existed underground at a depth of seven hundred metres, and in which almost the entire population spent the majority of its waking hours.

9

"Jacques Verney is a self-made man," Madame Denis told Vincent over the supper table, "but he has remained a friend to the miners."

"Don't all the men who get promoted stay friends with the workers?"

"No, Monsieur Vincent, it is not so. As soon as they move from Petit Wasmes to Wasmes they begin to look at things differently. For the sake of money they take the part of the owners and forget they once slaved in the mines. But Jacques is faithful and honest. When we have strikes he is the only one

51

with any influence over the miners. They will listen to nobody's advice but his. But, poor man, he hasn't long to live."

"What's the matter with him?" asked Vincent.

"The usual thing—lung trouble. Every man who goes down gets it. He probably won't last the winter out."

Jacques Verney came in a little later. He was short and stoop shouldered, with the deep set, melancholy eyes of the Borain. Antennae of hair shot out from his nostrils, from the ends of his eyebrows and from the concha of his ears. His head was bald. When he heard that Vincent was an evangelist come to better the lot of the miners, he sighed deeply. "Ah, monsieur," he said, "so many people have tried to help us. But life here goes on just as it always has."

"You think conditions bad in the Borinage?" asked Vincent.

Jacques was silent for a moment and then said, "For myself, no. My mother taught me to read a little, and through that I have become a foreman. I have a little brick house on the road leading down to Wasmes, and we are never in want of food. For myself I have nothing to complain . . ."

He was forced to interrupt himself for a violent fit of coughing; it seemed to Vincent that his flat chest would surely burst under the pressure. After walking to the front door and spitting into the road several times, Jacques again took his seat in the warm kitchen and gently pulled on the hairs of his ear, his nose, and his eyebrows.

"You see, Monsieur, I was already twenty-nine when I became a foreman. My lungs were gone by then. Nevertheless it has not been so bad for me these past few years. But the miners . . ." He glanced over at Madame Denis and asked, "What do you say? Shall I take him down to see Henri Decrucq?"

"Why not? It will do him no harm to hear the full truth."

Jacques Verney turned back to Vincent apologetically. "After all, Monsieur," he said, "I am a foreman and I owe some loyalty to 'Them'. But Henri, he will show you!"

Vincent followed Jacques out into the cold night and plunged immediately into the miners' ravine. The miners' huts were simple wooden hovels of one room. They had not been put up with any plan, but ran down the side of the hill haphazardly at crazy angles, creating a labyrinth of dirt-laden alleys, through which only the initiate could find their way. Vincent stumbled after Jacques, falling over rocks, logs, and heaps of refuse. About half-way down they came to Decrucq's shack. A light shone through the tiny window at the rear. Madame Decrucq answered the knock.

The Decrucqs' cabin was exactly the same as all the others in the ravine. It had an earthen floor, moss covered roof, and strips of burlap stuck between the planks to keep the wind out. In each of the rear corners there was a bed, one of them already occupied by three sleeping children. The furnishings consisted of an oval stove, a wooden table with benches, one chair, and a box nailed to the wall, containing a few pots and dishes. The Decrucqs, like most Borains, kept a goat and some rabbits so that they might have meat occasionally. The goat slept under the children's bed; the rabbits had a bit of straw behind the stove.

Madame Decrucq swung open the upper half of the door to see who was there and then bade the two men enter. She had worked in the same *couches* with Decrucq for many years before their marriage, pushing the little cars of coal down the track to the tally board. Most of the juice was gone out of her. She was faded, worn and aged, and she had not yet celebrated her twenty-sixth birthday.

Decrucq, who had been leaning his chair against the cold part of the stove, sprang up at the sight of Jacques. "Well!" he exclaimed. "It is a long time since you have been in my house. We are glad to have you here. And I bid your friend welcome."

It was Decrucq's boast that he was the only man in the Borinage whom the mines could not kill. "I shall die in my bed of old age," he often said. "They can't kill me, for I won't let them!"

On the right side of his head a large square of red scalp-skin glowed like a window through the thatch of his hair. That was a memento of the day when the cage in which he was descending had plunged a hundred metres like a stone in a well and killed his twenty-nine companions. When he walked he dragged one leg after him; it had been broken in four places when the timbers in his cell collapsed and imprisoned him for five days. His coarse, black shirt bulged on the right side over the mound of three broken ribs that had never been set after an explosion of fire-damp had hurled him against a coal car. But he was a fighter, a game-cock of a man; nothing could put him down. Because he always talked so violently against the company, he was given the very worst *couches,* where it was hardest to get out the coal and where the working conditions

53

were the most difficult. The more he took, the higher he flamed up against "them," the unknown and unseen but ever present enemy. A dimple, set just off centre in his stubby chin, made his short, compact face seem slightly askew.

"Monsieur Van Gogh," he said, "you have come to the right place. Here in the Borinage we are not even slaves, we are animals. We descend marcasse at three in the morning; for fifteen minutes we can rest while we eat our dinner, and then we work on until four in the afternoon. It is black down there, Monsieur, and hot. So we must work naked, and the air is full of coal-dust and poison gas, and we cannot breathe! When we take the coal from the *couche* there is no room to stand up; we must work on our knees and doubled in two. We begin to descend, boys and girls alike, when we are eight or nine. By twenty we have the fever and lung trouble. If we do not get killed by *grisou*, or in the cage (he tapped the red scalp-patch on his head), we may live until forty and then die of consumption! Do I tell lies, Verney?"

He spoke in such an excited patois that Vincent found difficulty in following him. The askew dimple gave his face an amused look, in spite of the fact that his eyes were black with anger.

"It is just so, Decrucq," said Jacques.

Madame Decrucq had gone to sit on her bed in the far corner. The faint glow of the kerosene lamp put her half in shadow. She listened to her husband while he spoke, even though she had heard the words a thousand times before. The years pushing coal cars, the birth of three children, and the succession of bitter winters in this burlap-stuffed hut had taken all the fight out of her. Decrucq dragged his bad leg from Jacques back to Vincent.

"And what do we get for all this, Monsieur? A one-room shack and just enough food to keep us swinging a pick. What do we eat? Bread, sour cheese, black coffee. Once or twice a year, perhaps, meat! If they cut off fifty centimes a day we would starve to death! We would not be able to bring up their *charbon*; that is the only reason they do not pay us less. We are on the margin of death, Monsieur, Every day of our lives! If we get sick we are put out without a franc, and we die like dogs while our wives and children are fed by the neighbours. From eight to forty, Monsieur, thirty-two years in the black earth, and then a hole in that hill across the way so we can forget it all."

54

10

Vincent found that the miners were ignorant and untaught, most of them being unable to read, but at the same time they were intelligent and quick at their difficult work, were brave and frank and of a very sensitive temperament. They were thin and pale from fever, and looked tired and emaciated. Their skin was pasty and sallow (they saw the sun only on Sundays), marked with thousands of tiny black pores. They had the deep-set, melancholy eyes of the oppressed who cannot fight back.

Vincent found them attractive. They were simple and good natured like the Brabant people in Zundert and Etten. The desolate feeling of the landscape was gone too, for he perceived that the Borinage had character and that things spoke to him.

After Vincent had been there a few days he held his first religious meeting in a rough shed in back of the Denis bakery. He cleaned the place thoroughly and then carried in benches for the people. The miners came at five with their families, long scarfs wrapped about their necks and little caps on their heads to keep out the cold. The only light was from a kerosene lamp which Vincent borrowed. The miners sat in the dark on the rough benches, watched Vincent hovering over his Bible and listened attentively, holding their hands under their armpits to keep them warm.

Vincent searched very hard to find the most appropriate message for his opening sermon. He finally selected Acts 16:9, "A vision appeared to Paul in the night: there stood a man of Macedonia and begged him saying, 'Come over into Macedonia and help us'."

"We must think of the Macedonian as a labourer, my friends," said Vincent, "a labourer with lines of sorrow and suffering and fatigue in his face. He is not without splendour or glamour, for he has an immortal soul, and he needs the food that does not perish, God's word. God wills that in imitation of Jesus Christ man should live humbly and go through life not reaching after lofty aims, but adapting himself to the lowly, learning from the gospel to be meek and simple of heart so that on the chosen day he may enter the heavenly Kingdom and find peace."

There were many sick people in the village and each day he

went the rounds like a doctor, bringing them whenever he could a bit of milk or bread, a warm pair of socks, or a cover to put over the bed. Typhoid and a malignant fever which the miners called *la sotte fièvre* descended upon the huts, giving the people bad dreams and making them delirious. The number of bedridden miners, emaciated, weak, and miserable, grew day by day.

The whole of Petit Wasmes called him Monsieur Vincent with affection, though still with a good bit of reserve. There was not a hut in the village to which he had not brought food and comfort, in which he had not nursed the sick and prayed with the miserable and brought God's light to the wretched. Several days before Christmas he found an abandoned stable near Marcasse, large enough to seat a hundred people. It was barren and cold and desolate, but the miners of Petit Wasmes filled it to the door. They listened to Vincent tell the story of Bethlehem and peace on earth. He had been in the Borinage only six weeks and had watched conditions grow more and more miserable with the passing of the days, but there, in an humble stable, lighted only by the smoky glow of a few small lamps, Vincent was able to bring Jesus Christ to the shivering blackjaws and warm their hearts with the promise of the Kingdom to Come.

There was only one flaw in his life, one factor to cause him any disturbance; his father was still supporting him. Each night he prayed for the time when he would be able to earn the few francs necessary for his humble needs.

The weather turned nasty. Black clouds overhung the whole region. Rain fell in torrents, making muddy creeks of the hollow roads and the earthen floors of the huts in the ravine. On New Year's day Jean-Baptiste walked down to Wasmes and returned with a letter for Vincent. The Reverend Pietersen's name was in the upper left-hand corner of the envelope. Vincent ran to his room under the eaves, trembling with excitement. The rain slashed away at the roof but he did not hear it. He tore open the envelope with clumsy fingers. The letter read:

Dear Vincent:

The Committee of Evangelization has heard about your splendid work and is therefore giving you a temporary nomination for six months, to begin the first of the year.

If at the end of June everything has gone well, your

appointment will be made permanent. In the meanwhile your salary will be fifty francs a month.

Write to me often and keep looking upwards.

Yours fondly,
Pietersen.

He threw himself flat on the bed, letter clutched tight in his hand, exultant. At last he was successful! He had found his work in life! This was what he had wanted all the time, only he had not had the strength and courage to go straight to it! He was to receive fifty francs a month, more than enough to pay for his food and lodging and he would never have to be dependent upon anyone again.

He sat down at the table and wrote a tumultuous, triumphant letter to his father telling him that he no longer needed his help, and that he meant from that time on to be a source of credit and gratification to the family. When he finished writing it was already twilight; thunder and lightning were smashing over Marcasse. He ran down the stairs, through the kitchen, and flung himself joyously into the rain.

Madame Denis came after him. "Monsieur Vincent! Where are you going? You've forgotten your hat and coat!"

Vincent did not stop to answer. He ran to a mound nearby. He could see in the distance a great part of the Borinage, with the chimneys, the mounds of coal, the little miners' cottages, and the scurrying to and fro like ants in a nest of the black figures that were just coming out of the *houillères*. In the distance there was a dark pine wood with little white cottages silhouetted against it, a church spire a long way off and an old mill. A haze hung over the whole scene. There was a fantastic effect of light and dark formed by the shadows of the clouds. For the first time since he had been in the Borinage it all reminded him of the pictures of Michel and of Ruysdael.

11

Now that he was an authorized evangelist, Vincent needed a permanent place to hold his meetings. After a good deal of searching he found at the very bottom of the ravine, on a little road through the pine woods, a rather large house that was called Salon du Bébe, where the children of the community had once been taught to dance. After Vincent put up all his prints the house took on an attractive air. Here every afternoon he gathered the children between the ages of four and eight, taught them how to read, and told them the elementary stories of the Bible. It was the only instruction most of them received in their entire lives.

"How are we going to get coal to heat the room?" Vincent demanded of Jacques Verney, who had helped him secure the Salon. "The children have to be kept warm and the meetings at night can last longer if the stove is going."

Jacques thought for a moment and then said, "Be here at noon tomorrow and I will show you how to get it."

When Vincent arrived at the Salon the next day he found a group of miners' wives and daughters awaiting him. They had on their black blouses, long black skirts and blue kerchiefs over their heads. All were carrying sacks.

"Monsieur Vincent, I have brought a sack for you," cried Verney's young daughter. "You must fill one, too."

They climbed through the maze of circuitous alleys formed by the miners' huts, passed the Denis bakery at the top of the hill, struck out across the field in the centre of which sat Marcasse, and skirted the walls of the buildings until they reached the black *terril* pyramid at the rear. Here they deployed, each one attacking the mountain from a different angle, climbing up its sides like tiny insects swarming over a dead log.

"You must go to the top before you will find any coal, Monsieur Vincent," said Mademoiselle Verney. "We have been picking the bottom of the heap clean for years. Come along, I'll show you which is the coal."

She scrambled up the black slope like a young goat, but Vincent had to go up most of the way on his hands and knees, for the stuff under his feet kept sliding away from him. Mademoiselle Verney scrambled on ahead, squatted on her haunches, and threw little pieces of caked mud at Vincent teasingly. She was a pretty girl with good colour in her cheeks and an alert, vivacious manner; Verney had been made a foreman when she was seven, and she had never seen the inside of a mine.

"Come along, Monsieur Vincent," she cried, "Or you will be the last to get your sack filled!" This was an excursion for her ; the company sold Verney fair coal at reduced rates.

They could not go altogether to the top for the little cars were dumping their loads of waste, first down one side, then down the other with mechanical regularity. It was no easy task to find coal on that pyramid. Mademoiselle Verney showed Vincent how to scoop up the *terril* in his hands and let the mud, rocks, clay and other foreign substances slip through his fingers. The amount of coal that escaped the company was negligible. The only thing the miners' wives ever found was a sort of shale composite which could not be sold in the commercial market. The *terril* was wet from the snow and rain, and soon Vincent's hands were scratched and cut, but he managed to get a quarter of a sackful of what he hoped was coal by the time the women had nearly filled theirs.

Each of the women left her sack at the Salon and rushed home to prepare the family supper, but not before promising to come to services that night and bring her family. Mademoiselle Verney invited Vincent home to share their supper, and he accepted with alacrity. The Verney house had two complete rooms; the stove, cooking equipment, and tableware in one room, the family beds in the other. Despite the fact that Jacques was fairly well off there was no soap in the house, for as Vincent had learned, soap was an impossible luxury for the Borains. From the time that the boy begins to descend the *charbonnage* and the girl begins to ascend the *terril* until the day they die, the Borains never completely get the coal-dust off their faces.

Mademoiselle Verney put a pan of cold water out in the street for Vincent. He scrubbed up as best he could. He did not know how well he had succeeded, but as he sat opposite the young girl and saw the black streaks from the coal-dust and smoke still lining her face, he realized that he must look as she did. Mademoiselle Verney chatted gaily all through the supper.

"You know, Monsieur Vincent," said Jacques, "you have been in Petit Wasmes almost two months now, and yet you really don't know the Borinage."

"It is true, Monsieur Verney," replied Vincent in all humility, "but I think I am slowly coming to understand the people."

"I don't mean that," said Jacques, plucking a long antenna out of his nose and looking at it with interest. "I mean you have only seen our life above ground. That is not important. We merely sleep above ground. If you would understand what our lives are like, you must descend one of the mines and see how we work from three in the morning until four in the afternoon."

"I am very eager to go down," said Vincent, "but can I get permission from the company?"

"I already have asked for you," replied Jacques, holding a cube of sugar in his mouth and letting the tepid, inky, bitter coffee pour over it and down his throat. "Tomorrow I descend Marcasse for safety inspection. Be in front of the Denis house at a quarter before three in the morning and I will pick you up."

The entire family accompanied Vincent to the Salon, but on the way over, Jacques, who had appeared so well and expansive in his warm house, shrivelled up with a violent cough and had to go home again. When Vincent arrived at the Salon he found Henri Decrucq already there, dragging his dead leg after him and tinkering with the stove.

"Ah, good evening, Monsieur Vincent," he cried with a smile as broad as his compact face would allow. "I am the only one in Petit Wasmes who can light this stove. I know it from old, when we used to have parties here. It is *méchant*, but I know all its tricks."

The content of the sacks was damp and only a small part of it was coal, but Decrucq soon had the bulging, oval stove sending out good warmth. As he hobbled about excitedly, the blood pounded to the bare spot on the scalp and turned the corrugated skin a dirty beet-red.

Nearly every miner's family in Petit Wasmes came to the Salon that night to hear Vincent preach the first sermon in his church. When the benches were filled, the neighbouring families brought in their boxes and chairs. Over three hundred souls crowded in. Vincent, his heart warmed by the kindness of the miners' wives that afternoon, and the knowledge that he was at last speaking in his own temple, preached a sermon so sincere and believing that the melancholy look on the Borains' faces fell away.

"It is an old belief and a good one," said Vincent to his blackjaw congregation, "that we are strangers on earth. Yet we are not alone, for our Father is with us. We are pilgrims; our life is a long journey from earth to Heaven.

"Sorrow is better than joy—and even in mirth the heart is sad. It is better to go to the house of mourning than to the house of feasts, for by sadness the countenance of the heart is made better.

"For those who believe in Jesus Christ there is no sorrow that is not mixed with hope. There is only a constantly being born again, a constantly going from darkness to light.

"Father, we pray Thee to keep us from evil. Give us neither poverty nor riches, but feed us with bread appropriate to us.

"Amen."

Madame Decrucq was the first to reach his side. There was a mist before her eyes and a quiver at the corner of her mouth. "Monsieur Vincent," she said, "my life was so hard that I had lost God. But you have given Him back to me. And I thank you for that."

When they were all gone, Vincent locked the Salon and walked thoughtfully up the hill to the Denises'. He could tell from the reception he had received that night that the reserve was completely gone from the attitude of the Borains, and that they trusted him at last. He was now fully accepted by the blackjaws as a Minister of God. What had caused the change? It could not have been because he had a new church; such things mattered not at all to the miners. They did not know about his evangelical appointment because he had not told them in the first place that he had no official position. And although he had preached a warm, beautiful sermon, he had delivered equally good ones in the wretched huts and in the abandoned stable.

The Denises had already gone to sleep in their little cubby-hole off the kitchen, but the bakery was still redolent of fresh, sweet bread. Vincent drew up some water from the deep well that had been enclosed in the kitchen, poured it out of the bucket into a bowl, and went upstairs to get his soap and mirror. He propped the mirror against the wall and looked at himself. Yes, his surmise had been correct; he had taken off only a small portion of the coal-dust at the Verneys'. His eyelids and jaws were still black. He smiled to himself as he thought of how he had consecrated the new temple with coal-dust all over his face, and how horrified his father and Uncle Stricker would have been if they could have seen him.

He dipped his hands into the cold water, worked up a lather from the soap he had brought with him from Brussels, and was just about to apply the suds vigorously to his face when something turned over in his mind. He poised his wet hands in mid-air. He looked into the mirror once again and saw the black coal-dust from the *terril* in the lines of his forehead, on the lids of his eyes, down the sides of his cheeks, and on the great ball of his chin.

"Of course!" he said aloud. "That's why they've accepted me. I've become one of them at last."

He rinsed his hands in the water and went to bed without touching his face. Every day that he remained in the Borinage he rubbed coal-dust on his face so that he would look like everyone else.

12

The following morning Vincent got up at two-thirty, ate a piece of dry bread in the Denis kitchen, and met Jacques in front of the door at a quarter to three. It had snowed heavily during the night. The road leading to Marcasse had been obliterated. As they struck out across the field toward the black chimneys and the *terril*, Vincent saw the miners scurrying over the snow from all directions, little black creatures hurrying home to their nest. It was bitterly cold ; the workers had their thin black coats tucked up around their chins, their shoulders huddled inward for warmth.

Jacques first took him into a room where many kerosene lamps were hanging on racks, each under a specific number. "When we have an accident down below," said Jacques, "we can tell which men are caught by the lamps that are missing."

The miners were taking their lamps hastily and rushing across a snow-covered yard to a brick building where the hoist was located. Vincent and Jacques joined them. The descending cage had six compartments, one above the other, in each of which a coal truck could be brought to the surface. A compartment was just large enough for two men to squat comfortably on their haunches while going down ; five miners were jammed into each of them, descending like a heap of coal.

Since Jacques was a foreman, only he and Vincent and one of his assistants crowded into the top compartment. They squatted low, their toes jammed up against the sides, their heads pushing against the wire top.

"Keep your hands straight in front of you, Monsieur Vincent," said Jacques. "If one of them touches the side wall, you will lose it."

A signal was given and the cage shot downwards on its two steel tracks. The free way through which it descended in the rock was only a fraction of an inch larger than the cage. An involuntary shudder ran through Vincent when he realized that the blackness fell away for half a mile beneath him and that if anything went wrong he would be plunged to death. It was a sort of horror he had never known before, this rocketing down a black hole into the abysmal unknown. He realized that he had little to fear, for there had not been an accident with the hoist in over two months, but the shadowy, flickering light of the kerosene lamps was not conducive to reasoning.

He spoke of his instinctive trembling to Jacques, who smiled sympathetically. "Every miner feels that," he said.

"But surely they get used to going down?"

"No, never! An unconquerable feeling of horror and fear for this cage stays with them until their dying day."

"And you, Monsieur . . .?"

"I was trembling inside of me, just as you were, and I have been descending for thirty-three years!"

At three hundred and fifty metres—half-way—the cage stopped for a moment, then hurtled downward again. Vincent saw streams of water oozing out of the side of the hole, and again he shuddered. Looking upward, he saw daylight about the size of a star in the sky. At six hundred and fifty metres they got out, but the miners continued on down. Vincent found himself in a broad tunnel with tracks cut through the rock and clay. He had expected to be plunged into an inferno of heat, but the passageway was fairly cool.

"This is not at all bad, Monsieur Verney!" he exclaimed.

"No, but there are no men working at this level. The *couches* were exhausted long ago. We get ventilation here from the top, but that does the miners down below no good."

They walked along the tunnel for perhaps a quarter of a mile, and then Jacques turned off. "Follow me, Monsieur Vincent," he said, "*mais doucement, doucement;* if you slip once, you will kill us."

He disappeared into the ground before Vincent's eyes. Vincent stumbled forward, found an opening in the earth, and groped for the ladder. The hole was just large enough to pass a thin man. The first five metres were not hard, but at the half-way point Vincent had to about-face in mid-air and descend in the opposite direction. Water began to ooze out of the rocks; mud slime covered the rungs of the ladder. Vincent could feel the water dripping over him.

At length they reached the bottom and crawled on their hands and knees through a long passage leading to *des caches* situated farthest from the exit. There was a long row of cells,

63

like partitions in a vault, supported by rough timbers. In each cell a unit of five miners worked, two digging out the coal with their picks, a third dragging it away from their feet, a fourth loading it into small cars, and a fifth pushing the cars down a narrow track.

The pickers worked in coarse linen suits, filthy and black. The shoveller was usually a young boy, stark naked except for a burlap loin-cloth, his body a dull black, and the miner pushing the car through the three foot passageway was always a girl, as black as the men, with a coarse dress covering the upper part of her body. Water was leaking through the roofs of the cells, forming a grotto of stalactites. The only light was from the small lamps whose wicks were turned down low to save fuel. There was no ventilation. The air was thick with coal-dust. The natural heat of the earth bathed the miners in rivulets of black perspiration. In the first cells Vincent saw that the men could work standing erect with their picks, but as he advanced down the passageway, the cells became smaller and smaller until the miners had to lie on the ground and swing their picks from the elbow. As the hours went on, the bodily heat of the miners raised the temperature of the cells, and the coal-dust thickened in the air until the men were gasping great mouthfuls of hot, black soot.

"These men earn two and a half francs a day," Jacques told Vincent, "providing the inspector at the checking post approves the quality of their coal. Five years ago they were earning three francs, but wages have been reduced every year since then."

Jacques inspected the timber proppings that stood between the miners and death. Then he turned to the pickers.

"Your propping is bad," he told them. "It is working loose and the first thing you know the roof will cave in."

One of the pickers, the leader of the gang, let forth a volley of abuse so fast that Vincent could catch only a few words.

"When they pay for propping," the man shouted, "we will prop! If we take the time off to prop, how will we get the coal out? We might as well die here under the rock as at home of starvation."

Beyond the last cell there was another hole in the ground. This time there was not even a ladder to descend. Logs had been shoved in at intervals to keep the dirt from pouring down and burying the miners below. Jacques took Vincent's lamp and hung it from his belt. "*Doucement*, Monsieur Vincent," he repeated. "Do not step on my head or you will send me crashing." They climbed down five metres more, foot following foot in the blackness, feeling for its timber to stand on while hands clutched the dirt in the sides, to keep from hurtling into oblivion.

At the next level there was another *couche*, but this time the miners did not even have cells to work in. The coal had to be picked out of a narrow angle in the wall. The men crouched on their knees, their backs pressed against the rock roof and threw their picks at the corner from which the coal was being taken. Vincent realized now that the cells above had been cool and comfortable; the heat at this lower level was like that of a blazing oven, thick enough to be cut with a blunt instrument. The men at work were panting like stricken animals, their tongues hanging out, thick and dry, and their naked bodies covered with a plaster of filth, grime and dust. Vincent, doing absolutely nothing, thought he could not bear the fierce heat and dust another minute. The miners were doing violent manual labour and their gorge was a thousand times higher than his, yet they could not stop to rest or cool off for a minute. If they did, they would not get out the requisite number of cars of coal and would not receive their fifty cents for the day's work.

Vincent and Jacques crawled on their hands and knees through the passageway connecting these beehive cells, flattening themselves against the wall every few seconds to let a car go by on the tiny tracks. This passage was smaller than the one above. The girls pushing the cars were younger, none of them over ten years of age. The coal cars were heavy and the girls had to fight and strain to get them along the tracks.

At the end of the passage there was a metal chute down which the cars were lowered on cables. "Come, Monsieur Vincent," said Jacques, "I will take you to the last level, seven hundred metres, and you will see something not to be found anywhere else in the world!"

They slid down the metal incline some thirty metres and Vincent found himself in a wide tunnel with two tracks. They walked for a half mile back in the tunnel; when it came to an end they pulled themselves up on a ledge, crawled through a *communiqué*, and lowered themselves on the other side into a freshly dug hole. "This is a new *couche*," said Jacques, "the hardest place of any mine in the world to get the coal."

Leading out of this excavation was a series of twelve minute black holes. Jacques shoved himself into one and shouted, "Follow me." The opening was just large enough to pass Vincent's shoulders. He jammed his way into it and crawled on his stomach like a snake, digging his way along with his fingernails and toes. He could not see Jacques's boots, three inches ahead of him. The tunnel through the rock was only a foot and a half high and two and a half feet wide. The hole from which the passageway started had almost no fresh air, but it was cool compared to this stope.

At the end of the crawl Vincent came into a little domelike hollow almost tall enough for a man to stand up. The place was pitch black and at first Vincent could see nothing; then he noticed four little blue glows along a wall. His body was wet with perspiration; the sweat from his brow brought the coal-dust down into his eyes, making them smart cruelly. He was panting for breath from the long crawl on his stomach and stood up with a feeling of relief to catch a little air. What he caught was fire, liquid fire that burned and choked him as it went down his lungs. This was the worst hole in all Màrcasse, a torture chamber worthy of the Middle Ages.

"*Tiens, tiens!*" cried a familiar voice, "*c'est Monsieur Vincent.* Have you come to see how we earn our fifty cents a day, Monsieur?"

Jacques went quickly to the lamps and inspected them. The arc of blue was eating up the light.

"He shouldn't have come down here!" Decrucq whispered in Vincent's ear, the whites of his eyes gleaming, "he will have a haemorrhage in that tunnel and then we will have to haul him out with blocks and a pulley."

"Decrucq," called Jacques, "have these lamps been burning this way all morning?"

"Yes," replied Decrucq carelessly, "this *grisou* is growing day by day. Once it will explode and then our troubles will be over."

"These cells were pumped out last Sunday," said Jacques.

"But it comes back, it comes back," said Decrucq scratching the black scar in his scalp with pleasure.

"Then you must lay off one day this week and let us clean it out again."

A storm of protest arose from the miners. "We have not enough bread now for the children! It is impossible to live on the wages, let alone give up a full day! Let them clean it out when we are not in here; we must eat like all the others!"

66

"It's all right," laughed Decrucq, "the mines can't kill me. They've tried it before. I shall die in my bed of old age. Speaking of food, what time is it, Verney?"

Jacques held his watch near the blue flame. "Nine o'clock."

"Good! We can eat our dinner."

The black, sweating bodies with the white eyeballs ceased their labours, and squatting on their haunches against the walls opened their kits. They could not crawl out into the slightly cooler hole to eat because they allowed themselves only fifteen minutes respite. The crawl going and coming would have taken almost that long. So they sat in the stagnant heat, took out two pieces or thick, coarse bread with sour cheese, and ate hungrily, the black soot from their hands coming off in great streaks on the white bread. Each man had a beer bottle of tepid coffee with which he washed down the bread. The coffee, the bread, and the sour cheese were the prize for which they worked thirteen hours a day.

Vincent had already been down six hours. He felt faint from lack of air and choking with the heat and dust. He did not think he could stand the torture very many more minutes. He was grateful when Jacques said they must go.

"Watch that *grisou*, Decrucq," said Jacques before he plunged into the hole. "If it gets bad, you'd better bring your gang out."

Decrucq laughed harshly. "And will they pay us our fifty cents for the day if we don't produce the coal?"

There was no answer to this question. Decrucq knew it as well as Jacques. The latter shrugged, and crawled on his stomach through the tunnel. Vincent followed him, completely blinded by the stinging, black sweat in his eyes.

After half an hour of walking they reached the *accrochage*, where the cage took coal and men to the surface. Jacques went into a cave in the rock, where the horses were kept, and coughed up black phlegm.

In the cage, shooting upward like a bucket in a well, Vincent turned to his friend and said, "Monsieur, tell me. Why do you people continue to go down into the mines? Why don't you all go elsewhere, find other employment?"

"Ah, my dear Monsieur Vincent, there is no other employment. And we cannot go elsewhere because we do not have the money. There is not a miner's family in the whole Borinage that has ten francs put away. But even if we could go, Monsieur, we would not. The sailor knows that all sorts of dangers await him aboard his ship, yet, ashore, he is homesick for the sea. So it is with us, Monsieur, we love our mines; we would rather be underground than above it. All we ask is a living wage, fair working hours, and protection against danger."

The cage reached the top. Vincent crossed the snow-covered yard, dazed by the feeble sunlight. The mirror in the wash-room showed him that his face was pitch black. He did not wait to wash. He plunged across the field, only half conscious, drinking in the fresh air and wondering if he had not suddenly caught the *sotte fièvre* and been suffering from nightmare. Surely God would not let His children work in such abominable slavery? Surely he must have dreamed all the things he had seen?

He passed the prosperous, comparatively well-to-do house of the Denises and without thinking stumbled down the filthy labyrinth of alleys in the ravine to Decrucq's hut. At first no one answered his knock. After a bit the six year old boy came. He was pale and anaemic and undersized, but he had some-thing of Decrucq's fighting courage about him. In two more years he would be descending Marcasse every morning at three, shovelling coal into cars.

"Mother went to the *terril*," said the boy in a high, thin voice. "You must wait, Monsieur Vincent; I am taking care of the babies."

Playing on the floor with some sticks and a piece of string were Decrucq's two infants with nothing on but little shirts. They were blue with the cold. The oldest boy fed *terril* to the stove but it gave off very little heat. Vincent watched them and shivered. Then he put the babies to bed and covered them up to the neck. He did not know why he had come to this miserable shack. He felt that he must do something, say something to the Decrucqs, help them in some way. He must let them know that he at least realized the full extent of their misery.

Madame Decrucq came home, her hands and face black. At first she did not recognize Vincent through his filth. She ran to the little box that hid her provisions, and put some coffee on the stove. It was colder than tepid when she handed it to him, black, bitter and woody, but he drank it to please the good woman.

"The *terril* is bad these days, Monsieur Vincent," she complained. "The company lets nothing through, not even

68

little grains. How am I to keep the babies warm? I have no clothes for them, only those little shirts and some sacking. The burlap gives them sores and rubs their skin off. If I keep them in bed all day, how will they grow?"

Vincent choked with unshed tears, but he could say nothing. He had never seen such abject personal misery. For the first time he wondered of what benefit prayers and the Gospel would be to this woman when her babies were freezing to death. Where was God in all this? He had a few francs in his pocket; he gave them to Madame Decrucq.

"Please buy woollen drawers for the children," he said.

It was a futile gesture, he knew; there were hundreds of other babies freezing in the Borinage. The Decrucq children would freeze again as soon as these drawers wore out.

He walked up the hill to the Denises'. The bakery kitchen was warm and cosy. Madame Denis heated him some water to wash in, and prepared him a nice lunch of the rabbit stew that had been left over from the night before. She saw that he was tired and overstrung from his experience so she put a trifle of butter out for his bread.

Vincent walked upstairs to his room. His stomach was warm and full. The bed was wide and comfortable; the sheets were clean, and on the pillow was a white pillow case. On the walls were prints by the great masters of the world. He opened his bureau and surveyed the rows of shirts, underclothes, socks, and vests. He went to the wardrobe and looked at his two extra pairs of shoes, his warm overcoat, and the suits of clothes hanging there. At last he realized that he was a liar and a coward. He preached the virtues of poverty to the miners but he himself lived in comfort and plenty. He was nothing more than a hypocritical slinger of words. His religion was an idle, useless thing. The miners ought to despise him and run him out of the Borinage. He pretended to share their lot, and here he had warm, beautiful clothes, a comfortable bed to sleep in, and more food in one meal than the miners had in a week. He did not even work for his ease and luxuries. He just went about telling glib lies and posing as a good man. The Borains ought not to believe a word he said; they ought not to come to his sermons or accept his leadership. His whole easy life gave the lie to his words. He had failed again, more miserably than ever before!

Well, he had only two choices; he could get out of the Borinage, run under the cover of night before they realized what a lying, weak-livered dog he was, or he could make use of the knowledge to which his eyes had been opened that day and really become a man of God.

He took all the clothes out of the bureau and packed them quickly into his bag. He also put in his suits, shoes, books, and prints, and closed the valise. He let it sit on the chair for the time being, and ran buoyantly out the front door.

At the bottom of the ravine there was a little creek. Just beyond that, the pine woods began the ascent of the other slope. In this woods there were scattered a few miners' cabins. After some inquiry, Vincent found one that was unoccupied. It was a board shanty without a window, built on a rather steep slope. The floor was the native earth trod down by long usage; the melting snow ran under the boards at the high end. Overhead there were rough beams holding the roof in place, and since the shack had not been used all winter, the knotholes and cracks between the boards let in icy blasts of air.

"Who owns this place?" Vincent demanded of the woman who had accompanied him.

"One of the business men in Wasmes."

"Do you know the rent?"

"Five francs a month."

"Very well, I'll take it."

"But Monsieur Vincent, you can't live here."

"Why not?"

"But ... but ... it is wretched. It is even worse than my place. It is the most wretched shack in Petit Wasmes!"

"That is exactly why I want it!"

He climbed up the hill again. A new feeling of peace had come into his heart. Madame Denis had gone to his room on some errand during his absence and had seen the packed valise.

"Monsieur Vincent," she cried when he came in, "what has gone wrong? Why are you going back to Holland so suddenly?"

"I am not going away, Madame Denise. I am staying in the Borinage."

"Then why ...?" A puzzled expression came over her face.

When Vincent explained, she said softly. "Believe me, Monsieur Vincent, you cannot live like that; you are not used to it. Times have changed since Jesus Christ; nowadays we must all live as best we can. The people know from your work that you are a good man."

Vincent was not to be dissuaded. He saw the merchant in
Wasmes, rented the shack, and moved in. When his first salary
cheque of fifty francs arrived a few days later, he bought
himself a little wooden bed and a second-hand stove. After
these expenditures he had just enough francs left to secure him
bread, sour cheese, and coffee for the rest of the month. He
piled dirt against the top wall of the cabin to keep the water
out, stuffed the cracks and knotholes with sacking. He now
lived in the same kind of house as the miners, ate the identical
food, and slept in the identical bed. He was one of them. He
had the right to bring them the Word of God.

13

The manager of the Charbonnages Belgique, which controlled
the four mines in the vicinity of Wasmes, was not at all the
sort of voracious animal that Vincent had been prepared to
find. True, he was a bit stoutish, but he had kindly, sympathetic eyes and the manner of one who had done a little
suffering on his own accord.

"I know, Monsieur Van Gogh," he said, after listening
attentively while Vincent poured out the tale of woe of the
miner. "It is an old story. The men think we are purposely
starving them to death so that we can earn greater profits. But
believe me, Monsieur, nothing could be farther from the truth.
Here, let me show you some charts from the International
Bureau of Mines in Paris."

He laid a large chart out on the table and indicated a blue
line at the bottom with his finger.

"Look, Monsieur," he said, "the Belgian coal mines are the
poorest in the world. The coal is so difficult for us to reach
that it is almost impossible to sell it in the open market for a
profit. Our operating expenses are the highest of any coal
mine in Europe, and our profits are the lowest! For you see,
we must sell our coal at the same price as the mines which
produce at the lowest ton cost. We are on the margin of
bankruptcy every day of our lives. Do you follow me?"

"I believe so."

"If we paid the miners one frank more a day our production
costs would rise above the market price of coal. We would
have to shut down altogether. And then they would really
starve to death."

"Couldn't the owners take a little less profit? Then there would be more for the workers."

The manager shook his head sadly. "No, Monsieur, for do you know what coal mines run on? Capital. Like every other industry. And capital must receive its return or it will go elsewhere. The stocks of the Charbonnages Belgique pay only three per cent dividends today. If they were reduced half of a percent the owners would withdraw their money. If they do that our mines will have to shut down, for we cannot operate without capital. And again the miners would starve. So you see, Monsieur, it is not the owners or managers who create this horrible condition in the Borinage. It is the unsatisfactory lay of the *couches*. And that condition, I suppose, we will have to blame on God!"

Vincent should have been shocked at this blasphemy. He was not. He was thinking of what the manager had told him.

"But at least you can do something about the working hours. Thirteen hours a day down there is killing off your whole village!"

"No, Monsieur, we cannot decrease the working hours because that would be equivalent to raising their wages. They would be turning out that much less coal for their fifty cents a day, and consequently our production cost per ton would be raised."

"There is one thing that certainly can be improved."

"You are going to speak of the dangerous working conditions?"

"Yes. At least you can decrease the number of accidents and deaths in the mines."

The manager shook his head patiently. "No, Monsieur, we cannot. We are unable to sell new stocks on the market because our dividends are too low. And we have absolutely no surplus of profits to invest in improvements.—Ah, Monsieur, it is a hopeless, vicious circle. I have gone around it many thousands of times. That is what has turned me from a firm, faithful Catholic to a bitter atheist. I cannot understand how a God in Heaven would purposely create such a condition and enslave a whole race of people in abject misery for century after century without one hour of providential mercy!"

Vincent could think of nothing to say. He walked home stunned.

14

The month of February was the most bitter one of the year. Naked winds swept through the valley and over the hilltop, making it almost impossible to walk through the streets. The miners' huts now needed the *terril* more than ever for warmth but the icy winds were so fierce that the women could not go out to the black mountain to search for it. They had nothing but their coarse skirts, blouses, cotton stockings, and kerchiefs to protect them against the biting winds.

The children had to stay in bed day after day to keep from freezing. Hot food was almost impossible to get because there was no coal for the stove. When the men came out of the blistering hot bowels of the earth they were plunged without a moment's preparation into the below zero weather, and had to struggle home across the snow-covered field in the cutting wind. Deaths from consumption and pneumonia occurred every day of the week. Vincent read a great many funeral services that month.

He had given up trying to teach the blue-faced children how to read, and was spending his days on the Marcasse mountain collecting what little coal he could, to be distributed among the huts where the misery was worst. He had no need to rub coal-dust on his face these days; he was never free from the mark of the miner. A stranger coming into Petit Wasmes would have called him " . . . just another blackjaw."

He had gathered almost half a sack of *terril* after many hours of work up and down the pyramid. The blue skin of his hands was torn by the ice-covered rock. At a little before four he decided to stop and take back what he had to the village so that at least a few wives might prepare hot coffee for their husbands. He reached the gate of Marcasse just as the miners began streaming out. Some of them recognized him and muttered a *bojou*, but the rest walked along with their hands in their pockets, shoulders caved inward, and eyes riveted to the ground.

The last one out of the gate was a little old man whose cough racked his whole body so badly that he scarcely could walk. His knees trembled, and when the freezing wind from the snow-covered fields hit him, he staggered as though from a smashing blow. He nearly fell on his face in the ice. After a moment he gathered courage and began to cross the field slowly, presenting his side to the blast. He had a piece of burlap sack wrapped around his shoulders, a sack he had somehow secured from a store in Wasmes. Vincent saw that something was printed on it. He strained his eyes to make out what it said and deciphered the letters: *FRAGILE.*

After leaving his *terril* at the miners' huts, Vincent went to his own shack and laid all his clothes out on the bed. He had five shirts, three suits of underwear, four pairs of socks, two pairs of shoes, two suits of clothes and an extra soldier's coat. He left one shirt, one pair of socks and one suit of underwear on the bed. Everything else he stuffed into the valise.

The suit of clothes he left with the old man who had *FRAGILE* written across his back. The underwear and shirts he left for the children, to be cut up and made into little garments. The socks were distributed among the consumptives who had to descend Marcasse. The warm coat he gave to a pregnant woman whose husband had been killed a few days before by a cave-in, and who had to take his place in the mine to support her two babies.

The Salon du Bébé was closed, as Vincent did not wish to take the *terril* away from the housewives. In addition, the families were afraid to tramp through the slush to get their feet wet. Vincent held little services at each hut and he made the rounds. As time went on, he found it necessary to devote himself to the practical duties of healing, washing, rubbing down, preparing hot drinks and medicines. At last he left his Bible at home because he never found time to open it. The Word of God had become a luxury that the miners could not afford.

The cold abated a little in March but fever set in to take its place. Vincent spent forty francs of his February salary for food and medicine for the sick, leaving himself on starvation rations. He was growing thinner from lack of food; his nervous, jumpy mannerisms became more exaggerated. The cold sapped his vitality; he began to walk around with a fever. His eyes became two great fire holes in their sockets, and his massive, Van Gogh head seemed to shrink. Hollows appeared in his cheeks and under his eyes, but his chin stuck out as firmly as ever.

The oldest Decrucq child contracted typhoid; a difficult situation set in over the beds. There were only two of them in the house; the parents occupied one and the three children the other. If the two babies remained in the same bed with the boy, they might catch the disease. If they were put on the floor

74

they would develop pneumonia. If the parents slept on the floor they would be unable to work the following day. Vincent realized immediately what must be done.

"Decrucq," he said when the miner came home from work, "will you help me a moment before you sit down to your supper?"

Decrucq was tired and ill from the pain in his scalp but he followed Vincent without question, dragging his dead leg after him. When they got to his hut Vincent threw one of the two blankets off the bed and said, "Take an end of this; we are going to move it up to your house for the boy."

Decrucq gritted his teeth. "We have three children," he said, "if God wills it so, we can lose one of them. But there is only one Monsieur Vincent to nurse the whole village, and I will not let him kill himself!"

He limped wearily out of the cabin. Vincent took the bed apart, loaded it on his shoulders, tramped to the Decrucq house and set it up. Decrucq and his wife looked at him over their supper of dry bread and coffee. Vincent transferred the child to his bed and nursed him.

Later that evening he went to the Denises' to ask if they had some straw he might take to his cabin to sleep on. Madame Denis was aghast when she heard what he had done.

"Monsieur Vincent," she exclaimed, "your old room is still unoccupied. You must come back here to live."

"You are very good, Madame Denis, But I cannot."

"I know, you are worrying about the money. But that does not matter. Jean-Baptiste and I make a good living. You can live here with us free, as a brother. Aren't you always telling us that all God's children are brothers?"

Vincent was cold, shivering cold. He was hungry. He was delirious with the fever he had been carrying about for weeks. He was weak from malnutrition, from lack of sleep. He was harassed and nearly insane with the cumulative grief and suffering of the village. The bed upstairs was warm and soft and clean. Madame Denis would give him food to wipe out that gnawing at the pit of his stomach; she would nurse his fever and fill him with hot, powerful drinks until the cold was driven from the marrow of his bones. He shivered, weakened, almost collapsed on the red tile floor of the bakery. Just in time he caught himself.

This was God's ultimate test. If he failed now, all the work he had done before would have been futile. Now that the

75

village was at its most horrible stage of suffering and deprivation, was he to backslide, to be a weak, contemptible coward and grasp comfort and luxury the first moment it was thrust under his nose?

"God sees your goodness, Madame Denis," he said, "and He will reward you for it. But you must not tempt me from my path of duty. If you do not find me some straw, I'm afraid I'll have to sleep on the ground. But don't bring anything else please, for I can't accept it."

He dumped the straw into one corner of his hut, over the damp ground, and covered himself with the thin blanket. He did not sleep all night; when morning came he had a cough, and his eyes seemed to have retreated even farther into his head. His fever had increased until he was only half conscious of his movements. There was no *terril* in the shack for the stove; he did not feel he could deprive the miners of even a handful of the stuff he collected from the black mountain. He managed to swallow a few mouthfuls of hard dry bread, and set out for his day's work.

15

March pushed its way wearily into April and conditions improved a bit. The winds disappeared, the slant of the sun became a little more direct, and at last the thaw came. With the melting of the snow the black fields became visible, the larks were heard, and in the woods the buds began to sprout on the elder trees. The fever died down and with the coming of warmer weather the women of the village were able to swarm over the Marcasse pyramid to get *terril*. Soon the cabins were blazing with cosy fires in their oval stoves; the children were able to stay out of bed during the day, and Vincent reopened the Salon. The entire village crowded in for the first sermon. A touch of a smile was coming back to the melancholy eyes of the miners; the people dared lift their heads just a little. Decrucq, who had appointed himself official fireman and janitor of the Salon, was cracking jokes over the stove and rubbing his scalp vigorously.

"Better times are coming," cried Vincent exultantly from his pulpit. "God has tried you and found you true. The worst of our suffering is over. The corn will ripen in the fields, and the sun will warm you as you sit before your homes after a good day's work. The children will run out to follow the lark and gather berries in the woods. Lift up your eyes to God, for the good things in life are in store for you. God is merciful. God is just. He will reward you for your faith and vigilance. Offer up thanks to Him, for better times are coming. Better times are coming."

The miners offered up fervent thanks. Cheerful voices filled the room and everyone kept saying to his neighbour, "Monsieur Vincent is right. Our suffering is over. The winter is gone. Better times are coming!"

A few days later, while Vincent and a group of the children were gathering *terril* behind Marcasse, they saw little black figures scurrying out of the building in which the hoist was located, and go running across the fields in all directions.

"What has happened?" exclaimed Vincent. "It can't be three o'clock yet. The sun isn't even in mid-heaven."

"There's been an accident!" shouted one of the older boys. "I've seen them run away like that before! Something's broken below!"

They scrambled down the black mountain as fast as they could, ripping their hands and clothes on the rocks. The field surrounding Marcasse was thick with black ants running to cover. By the time they all got down, the tide of movement had changed and the women and children were running across the field from the village, coming from every direction at a frightened speed, babies in their arms and infants tagging along behind.

When Vincent got to the gate he heard excited voices crying, 'Grisou! Grisou! The new *couche!* They're caught! They're trapped in!"

Jacques Verney, who had been laid up in bed during the intense cold, came dashing across the field at top speed. He had grown thinner, his chest more cavernous. Vincent caught him as he went by and said, "What is it? Tell me!"

"Decrucq's *couche!* Remember the blue lamps? I knew it would get them!"

"How many? How many are there? Can't we get at them?"

"Twelve cells. You saw them. Five men to a cell."

"Can't we save them?"

"I don't know. I'm taking a volunteer crew down immediately."

"Let me come along. Let me help."

"No. I need experienced men." He ran through the yard to the hoist.

77

The little cart with the white horse drew up to the gate, the same cart that had carried so many dead and injured to the cabins on the hillside. The miners who had run across the fields began returning with their families. Some of the women cried hysterically, others stared ahead of them, wide-eyed. The children whimpered and the foremen ran about, shouting at the tops of their voices, organizing rescue crews.

Suddenly the noise stopped. A little group came out of the hoist building and walked slowly down the stairs, carrying something wrapped in blankets. The hush was eloquent for a moment. Then everyone began shouting and crying at the same time.

"Who is it? Are they dead? Are they alive? For God's sake, tell us their names! Show them to us! My husband is down there! My children! Two of my babies are in that *couche!*"

The group stopped at the little cart with the white horse. One of the men spoke. "Three of the carriers who were dumping coal on the outside have been saved. But they are terribly burned."

"Who are they? For the love of Jesus tell us who they are! Show us! Show us! My baby is down there! My baby, my baby!"

The man lifted the blankets off the seared faces of two girls of about nine and a boy of ten. All three were unconscious. The families of the children fell upon them with mingled cries of lament and joy. The three blankets were laid in the cart with the white horse and driven across the hollow road of the field. Vincent and the families ran alongside like panting animals. From behind him Vincent heard the wail of fear and anguish mount ever higher and higher. He turned his head while he ran, and looked behind him, seeing the long line of *terril* mountains on the horizon.

"Black Egypt!" he cried aloud, giving vent to his pain. "Black Egypt, with the chosen people enslaved again! Oh, God, how could you? How could you?"

The children were burned almost to death. The skin and hair was seared off every part that had been exposed. Vincent went into the first cabin. The mother was wringing her hands in anguish. Vincent undressed the child and cried, "Oil, oil, quick!" The woman had a little oil in the house. Vincent applied it to the burns and then cried, "Now, bandage!"

The woman stood there staring at him, terror in her eyes.

78

Vincent became angry and shouted, "Bandages! Do you want your child to die?"

"We have nothing," she blubbered. "There is not a piece of white cloth in the house. There has not been all winter!"

The child stirred and moaned. Vincent grabbed off his coat and shirt, and tore his undershirt from his body. He replaced his coat, ripped the other garments to strips, and bandaged the child from head to foot. He took the can of oil and ran to the second child. He bandaged her as he had the first. When he reached the third child the shirt and undershirt had been used up. The ten year old boy was dying. Vincent took off his trousers and woollen drawers, replaced the trousers and cut the drawers into bandages.

He pulled his coat tightly over his bare chest and ran across the field to Marcasse. From far off he could hear the lament, the unending cry of the wife and mother.

The miners were standing about the gate. Only one relief crew could work down below at a time. The approach to the ledge was narrow. The men were waiting their turn. Vincent spoke to one of the assistant foremen.

"What are the chances?"

"They're dead by now."

"Can't we get to them?"

"They're buried under rock."

"How long will it take?"

"Weeks. Maybe months."

"But why? But why?"

"That's how long it took before."

"Then they're lost!"

"Fifty-seven men and girls!"

"Every one of them gone!"

"You'll never see them again!"

Crews relieved each other for thirty-six hours. The women who had husbands and children below could not be driven away. The men above kept telling them rescue was sure. The women knew they were lying. The miners' wives who had lost no one brought coffee and bread across the field. The stricken women would touch nothing. In the middle of the night Jacques Verney was brought up in a blanket. He had had a haemorrhage. He died the following day.

After forty-eight hours Vincent persuaded Madame Decrucq to return home with the children. For twelve days volunteer rescue crews worked without stopping. No mining went on. Since no coal was brought up, no wages were paid. The few francs surplus in the village was soon gone. Madame Denis went on baking bread and distributing it on credit. She exhausted her capital and had to shut down. The company contributed nothing. At the end of the twelfth day they told the rescue crews to stop. The men were ordered back to work. Petit Wasmes had not one centime between it and starvation.

The miners struck.

Vincent's wages for April arrived. He went down to Wasmes and bought fifty francs worth of food. He distributed it among the families. The village lived on it for six days. After that they went to the woods to collect berries, leaves, grass. The men went out of doors searching for things that lived: rats, gophers, snails, toads, lizards, cats, dogs. Anything that could be put into the stomach to stop the throbbing ache of hunger. At last there was nothing more to find. Vincent wrote to Brussels for help. No help came. The miners sat down to watch their wives and children starve under their eyes.

They asked Vincent to hold services for the fifty-seven lost souls in the mine, the ones who had gone before them. A hundred men, women and children packed into Vincent's tiny hut. Vincent had had nothing but coffee for days. He had had almost no solid food since the accident. He was too weak to stand on his feet. The fever and despair had returned to his heart. His eyes were just two black pin pricks, his cheeks had been sucked in, the circular bones under his eyes protruded, a dirty, red beard matted his face. He had rough sacking wrapped around his body to take the place of underwear. Only one lantern illuminated the shack. It hung from a broken rafter, giving but a flickering glow. Vincent lay on the straw in his corner, holding his head up on one elbow. The lantern flung fantastic, flickering shadows over the rough planks and the hundred mutely suffering souls.

He began speaking in a parched, feverish voice, every word filling the silence. The blackjaws, thin, emaciated, wracked by hunger and defeat, kept their eyes on him as they would on God. God was a long way off.

Strange, loud voices were heard outside the shack, lifted in indignation. The door was flung open and a child's voice cried, "Monsieur Vincent is in here, Messieurs."

Vincent stopped speaking. The hundred Borains turned their heads toward the door. Two well-dressed men stepped in.

The oil lamp flared up for a brief moment. Vincent saw horror and fear written across the strange faces.

"You are welcome, Reverend de Jong and Reverend van den Brink," he said without rising. "We are holding funeral services for the fifty-seven miners who were buried alive in Marcasse. Perhaps you will say a word of comfort to the people?"

It took the Reverends a long time to find their tongues.

"Shocking! Simply shocking!" cried de Jong, giving his protuberant stomach a resounding smack.

"You would think you were in the jungles of Africa!" said Van den Brink.

"Heaven only knows how much harm he's done."

"It may take years to bring these people back to Christianity."

De Jong crossed his hands on his paunch and exclaimed, "I told you not to give him an appointment in the first place."

"I know . . . but Pietersen . . . who could ever have dreamed of this? This chap is absolutely mad!"

"I suspected he was insane all the time. I never did trust him."

The reverend spoke in rapid, perfect French, not one word of which the Borains understood. Vincent was too weak and ill to realize the import of what they were saying.

De Jong stomached his way through the crowd and said to Vincent quietly but fiercely, "Send these filthy dogs home!"

"But the services! We haven't finished the . . ."

"Never mind the services. Send them away."

The miners filed out slowly, uncomprehending. The two Reverends faced Vincent. "What in the world have you done to yourself? What do you mean by holding services in a hole like this? What sort of a new barbarous cult have you started? Have you no sense of decency, of decorum? Is this conduct befitting a Christian minister? Are you utterly mad, that you behave like this? Do you wish to disgrace our Church?"

The Reverend de Jong paused for a moment, surveyed the mean, sordid shack, the bed of straw on which Vincent lay, the burlap wrapped around his body and his deep sunk, feverish eyes.

"It is a fortunate thing for the Church, Monsieur Van Gogh," he said, "that we have given you only a temporary appointment. You may now consider that appointment cancelled. You will never again be allowed to serve us. I find your

conduct disgusting and disgraceful. Your salary is ended and a
new man will be sent to take your place immediately. If I were
not charitable enough to think you entirely mad, I would call
you the worst enemy to Christianity that the Belgian Evangelical Church has ever had!"

There was a long silence. "Well, Monsieur Van Gogh, have
you nothing to say in your own defence?"

Vincent remembered the day in Brussels when they had
refused him an appointment. Now he could not even feel
anything, let alone speak.

"We may as well go, Brother de Jong," said the Reverend
van den Brink after a time. "There is nothing we can do here.
His case is quite hopeless. If we can't find a good hotel in
Wasmes, we'll have to ride back to Mons tonight."

16

The following morning a group of the older miners came to
Vincent. "Monsieur," they said "now that Jacques Verney is
gone, you are the only man we can trust. You must tell us
what to do. We do not wish to starve to death unless we have
to. Perhaps you can get 'them' to grant our wishes. After you
have seen them, if you tell us to go back to work, we will. And
if you tell us to starve, we will do that, too. We will listen to
you, Monsieur, and to no one else."

The offices of the Charbonnages Belgique had a funereal
air. The manager was glad to see Vincent and listened to him
in sympathy. "I know, Monsieur Van Gogh," he said, "that
the miners are outraged because we did not bore through to
the bodies. But what good would it have done? The company
has decided not to reopen that *couche*; it doesn't pay for
itself. We would have had to dig for perhaps a month, and
what would have been the result? Simply to take the men
from one grave and put them in another."

"Then what about the living? Can you do nothing to
improve conditions down below? Must they work in the face
of certain death every day of their lives?"

"*Oui*, Monsieur, they must. They must. The company has
no funds to invest in safety devices. The miners are on the
losing end of this quarrel; they cannot win because they have
iron-clad economic laws against them. What is worse, if they
don't return to work within another week, Marcasse will be

shut down permanently. Then God knows what will happen to them."

Vincent walked up the long winding road to Petit Wasmes, defeated. "Perhaps God knows," he said to himself bitterly. "And then again, perhaps He doesn't."

It was clearly evident that he was of no more use to the miners. He had to tell them to go back to work for thirteen hours a day in the consumption pits, for starvation rations, with sudden death staring half of them in the face and a slow, coughing death all the others. He had failed to help them in any way. Not even God could help them. He had come to the Borinage to put the Word of God into their hearts, but what could he say further when faced by the fact that the eternal enemy of the miners was not the owners, but the Almighty Father Himself?

The moment he told the miners to go back to work, to take up their slavery again, he ceased to be of any value to them. He could never preach another sermon—even if the Committee would allow him—for of what good was the Gospel now? God had turned a stone-deaf ear to the miners and Vincent had not been able to soften Him.

Then suddenly he realized something he had known for a long time. All this talk about God was childish evasion; desperate lies whispered by a frightened, lonely mortal to himself out in a cold, dark, eternal night. There was no God. Just as simply as that, there was no God. There was only chaos; miserable, suffering, cruel, tortuous, blind, endless chaos.

17

The miners returned to work. Theodorus Van Gogh, who heard from the Committee of Evangelization, wrote, enclosing money and asked Vincent to return to Etten. Instead Vincent went back to the Denises'. He made a farewell trip to the Salon, took all the prints off the wall and put them up in his room under the eaves.

It was bankruptcy once again, and time to take stock. Only there was no stock. There was no job, no money, no health, no strength, no ideas, no enthusiasms, no desires, no ambitions, no ideals, and worst of all, no pivot upon which to hang his life. He was twenty-six, five times a failure, without the courage to begin anew.

He looked at himself in the mirror. His reddish beard covered his face in whorls. His hair was thinning out, his rich, ripe mouth had been squeezed down to a narrow line, and his eyes were lost somewhere in dark caverns. The whole personality that was Vincent Van Gogh seemed to have shrivelled, grown cold, almost died within itself.

He borrowed a little soap from Madame Denis and scrubbed himself from head to foot, standing up in a basin of water. He looked down at what had been a massive, powerful body and saw that it was thin and emaciated. He shaved carefully and neatly, wondering where all the strange bones in his face had come from so suddenly. He combed his hair in its old design for the first time in months. Madame Denis brought him up a shirt and suit of underwear belonging to her husband. He dressed and descended to the cheerful bakery kitchen. He sat down to dinner with the Denises; solid cooked food passed his lips for the first time since the catastrophe at the mine. It seemed curious to him that he should bother to eat at all. The food in his mouth tasted like warm wood pulp.

Although he had not told the miners that he had been forbidden to preach again, they did not ask him to, nor did they seem to care about sermons. Vincent rarely spoke to them any more. He rarely spoke to anyone. He exchanged only a *bonjour* in passing. He never entered their huts or engaged in their daily lives or thoughts. By some profound understanding and tacit agreement the miners refrained from discussing him. They adopted his attitude of formality but they never condemned the change. Mutely they understood. And life went on in the Borinage.

A note from home informed him that Kay Vos's husband had died suddenly. He was at too low an ebb of emotional exhaustion to do more than store the fact in some remote corner of his mind.

The weeks passed. Vincent did nothing but eat, sleep, and sit in a daze. The fever was slowly being driven out of his body. He was gaining strength and weight. But his eyes were two glass openings to a corpse-filled coffin. Summer came; the black fields and chimneys and *terrils* glistened in the sun. Vincent walked through the country-side. He did not walk for exercise or for pleasure. He never knew where he was going or what he passed along the way. He walked because he was tired of lying, sitting, standing. And when he got tired of walking, he sat or lay or stood.

Shortly after his money ran out he received a letter from his brother Theo in Paris, begging him not to idle away his time in the Borinage but to use the enclosed banknotes to take a decisive step and re-establish himself. Vincent turned the money over to Madame Denis. He did not remain in the Borinage because he liked it; he stayed because there was no place else to go, and it would take so much effort to get there.

He had lost God and he had lost himself. Now he lost the most important thing on earth, the one and only person who had always been instinctively sympathetic, and who understood him as he hoped to be understood. Theo abandoned his brother. All during the winter he had written once and twice a week, long, loving letters of cheer and interest. Now the letters stopped altogether. Theo, too, had lost faith; had given up hope. And so Vincent was alone, utterly alone, without even his Maker, a dead man walking in a deserted world and wondering why he was still there.

18

Summer thinned into fall. With the death of the meagre vegetation something came to life within Vincent. He could not yet face his own life, so he turned to the lives of others. He returned to his books. Reading had always been his finest and most constant pleasure, and now in the stories of other people's triumphs and failures, sufferings and joys, he found surcease from the ever haunting spectre of his own fiasco.

When the weather permitted he went out into the fields and read for the entire day; when it rained he either lay on his bed under the eaves or leaned a chair against a wall in the Denis kitchen, and sat there for hours, engrossed. With the passing of the weeks he absorbed the life stories of hundreds of ordinary people like himself, who strove, succeeded a little, and failed a great deal; and through them he slowly got a proper perspective on himself. The theme that ran through his brain: "I'm a failure. I'm a failure. I'm a failure," gave way to "What shall I try now? What am I best fitted for? Where is my proper place in the world?" In every book he read, he looked for that pursuit which might give his life direction again.

Letters from home described his existence as *choquant*; his father insisted that he was violating all decent social conventions by leading the life of an idler. When did he plan to get a job again, to support himself, to become a useful member of society and contribute his share to the world's work?

Vincent would have liked to know the answer to that himself.

At length he reached the saturation point in reading and could no longer pick up a book. During the weeks that followed his debacle, he had been too stunned and ill to feel anything emotionally. Later he had turned to literature to drown out his feelings, and had succeeded. Now he was almost completely well, and the flood of emotional suffering that had been stored up for months broke like a raging torrent and engulfed him in misery and despair. The mental perspective he had gained seemed to do him no good.

He had reached the low point in his life and he knew it.

He felt that there was some good in him, that he was not altogether a fool and a wastrel, and that there was a small contribution he could make to the world. But what was that contribution? He was not fitted for the routine of business and he had already tried everything else for which he might have had an aptitude. Was he always doomed to fail and suffer? Was life really over for him?

The questions asked themselves, but they brought no answers. And so he drifted with the days that slurred into winter. His father would become disgusted and stop sending money; he would have to give up eating at the Denises' and go on short rations. Then Theo would feel a little prick of conscience and send a few notes through Etten. By the time Theo lost patience, his father would once again feel his responsibility. Between them Vincent managed to eat about half the time.

One clear November day Vincent wandered over to Marcasse empty handed, empty minded, and sat on a rusty, iron wheel outside the wall. An old miner came through the gate, his black cap forward over his eyes, shoulders hunched over, hands in pockets, and knees jerking out bonily. Something about the man, he could not tell exactly what, attracted Vincent. Idly, without particular interest, he reached into his pocket, pulled out the stub of a pencil and a letter from home, and on the back of the envelope quickly sketched the little figure tramping across the black field.

Vincent opened his father's letter and saw that the writing covered only one side. After a few moments another miner came out of the gate, a young chap about seventeen. He stood taller, more erect, and there was a cheerful lift to the line of his shoulders as he struck out along the high stone wall of Marcasse toward the railroad tracks. Vincent had several full minutes to sketch him before he disappeared.

19

At the Denises', Vincent found several sheets of clean, white paper and a thick pencil. He put his two rough sketches on the desk and began copying them. His hand was clumsy and stiff ; he could not get the line he had in mind on the paper. He used the eraser far more than the pencil, but kept plugging to reproduce his figures. He was so intent that he did not notice darkness creep across his room. He was startled when Madame Denis knocked on his door.

"Monsieur Vincent," she called, "supper is on the table."

"Supper!" exclaimed Vincent. "But it couldn't be that late already."

At the table he chatted animatedly with the Denises and there was a faint gleam in his eye. The Denises exchanged a significant look. After the light meal, Vincent excused himself and went immediately to his room. He lit the little lamp and pinned the two sketches on the wall, standing as far away from them as he could to get a perspective.

"They are bad," he said to himself with a curious grin, "very bad. But perhaps tomorrow I shall be able to do a little better."

He went to bed, placing the kerosene lamp on the floor beside him. He gazed at his two sketches without thinking about anything in particular; then his eyes saw the other prints he had on the wall. It was the first time he had actually seen them since that day, seven months ago, when he had taken them off the walls of the Salon. Suddenly he realized that he was homesick for the world of pictures. There once had been a time when he knew who Rembrandt was, who Millet, Jules Dupré, Delacroix and Maris were. He thought of all the lovely prints he had possessed at one time or another, the lithographs and etchings he had sent to Theo and his parents. He thought of all the beautiful canvases he had seen in the museums of London and Amsterdam, and in so thinking, he forgot to feel miserable, but fell into a deep, restful sleep. The kerosene lamp sputtered, burned bluely, and went out.

The following morning he awoke at two-thirty, thoroughly refreshed. He sprang lightly out of bed, dressed, took his big pencil and writing paper, found a piece of thin board in the bakery, and set out for Marcasse. He seated himself on the same rusty, iron wheel in the darkness and waited for the miners to begin coming in.

He sketched hastily and roughly, as he simply wanted to record his first impression of each personality. An hour later, when all the miners had gone down, he had five figures without faces. He walked briskly across the field, took a cup of coffee up to his room with him and when the light finally came, copied his sketches. He tried to put in all the strange little quirks of Borain appearance which his mind's eye knew so well, but which he had not been able to catch in the dark, with his models walking out from under him.

His anatomy was all wrong, his proportions were grotesque, and his drawing was so outlandish as to be funny. And yet the figures came out as Borains and could have been mistaken for nothing else. Vincent, amused at his own clumsiness and *gaucherie*, tore up the sketches. Then he sat on the edge of the bed, opposite the Allebé of the little old woman carrying hot water and coals on a wintry street, and tried to copy it. He managed to suggest the woman, but he couldn't get her into relation with either the street or the houses in the background. He crumpled up the sheet, flung it into a corner and sat his chair before the Bosboom study of a lone tree against a cloudy sky. It all looked so simple ; just a tree, a bit of loam, and clouds at the top. But Bosboom's values were precise and exquisite and Vincent learned that it is always the simplest piece of art which has practised the most rigid elimination and is therefore the most difficult to duplicate.

The morning passed outside the realm of time. When Vincent used up his last sheet of paper, he searched his belongings very thoroughly to see how much money he had. He found two francs, and believing he could get good paper and perhaps even a stick of charcoal in Mons, he set out to walk the twelve kilometres. As he went down the long hill between Petit Wasmes and Wasmes he saw a few miners' wives standing before their doors. He added a cordial *comment ça va?* to his usual automatic *bonjour*. At Paturages, a little town halfway to Mons, he noticed a pretty girl behind a bakery window. He went in to buy a five centime bun, just to look at her.

The fields between Paturages and Cuesmes were a bright shade of green from the heavy rains. Vincent decided to come back and sketch them when he could afford a green crayon. In Mons he found a pad of smooth yellow paper, some charcoal, and a heavy lead pencil. There was a bin of old prints in front of the store. Vincent pored over them for hours although he knew he could buy nothing. The owner joined him, and they commented on one print after another just as though they were two friends going through a museum.

"I must apologize that I haven't any money to buy one of your pictures," said Vincent, after they had spent a long time looking at them.

The owner brought his hands and shoulders up in an eloquent Gallic gesture and said, "It doesn't matter, Monsieur; come again another time even though you have no money."

He walked the twelve kilometres home in a leisurely fashion. The sun was setting over the pyramid-dotted horizon and lit up the outer fringe of some floating clouds with a delicate shell pink. Vincent noticed how the little stone houses of Cuesmes fell into natural etching designs, and how peaceful the green valley lay below him when he gained the top of a hill. He felt happy, and wondered why.

The following day he went to the *terril* behind Marcasse and sketched the girls and women as they leaned over the slope, digging specks of black gold out of the mountainside. After dinner he said, "Please do not leave the table for a moment, Monsieur, Madame Denis. I wish to do something."

He ran to his room, brought back the drawing pad and charcoal, and quickly planted a likeness of his friends on the paper. Madame Denis came around to look over his shoulder and exclaimed, "But Monsieur Vincent, you are an artist!"

Vincent was embarrassed. "No," he said, "I am only amusing myself."

"But it is nice," said Madame Denis. "It almost looks like me."

"Almost," laughed Vincent, "but not quite."

He did not write home to tell them what he was doing because he knew they would say, and rightly, "Oh, Vincent is at one of his fads again. When will he settle down and do something useful?"

Besides, this new activity had a curious special quality; it was his and nobody else's. He could not bring himself to talk or write about his sketches. He felt a reticence about them that he had not felt for anything before, a disinclination to let strange eyes see his work. They were, in some crude and incomprehensible way, sacred, even though they might be wretchedly amateurish in every last detail.

Once more he entered the miners' huts, but this time he carried drawing paper and crayon instead of a Bible. The miners were not any the less glad to see him. He sketched the children playing on the floor, the wives bending over their oval stoves, the family at supper when the day's work was done. He sketched Marcasse with its tall chimneys, the black fields, the pine woods across the ravine, the peasants plough-ing down around Paturages. If the weather was bad, he remained in his room, copying the prints on the walls and the rough drafts he had done the day before. When he went to bed at night, he felt that perhaps one or two of the things he had done that day were not so bad. He awakened the next morning to find he had slept off the intoxication of creative effort and that the drawings were wrong, all wrong. He threw them away without a qualm.

He had put down the beast of pain within him, and he was happy because he no longer thought of his unhappiness. He knew he ought to feel ashamed to keep on taking his father's and brother's money when he made no effort to support himself, but it did not seem to matter and he just went on sketching.

After a few weeks, when he had copied all the prints on the wall a great many times, he realized that if he was to make any progress he would have to have more to copy, and those of the masters. Despite the fact that Theo had not written to him for a year, he hid his pride under a pile of poor drawings and wrote to his brother.

Dear Theo:

If I am not mistaken you must still have "Les Travaux des Champs" by Millet. Would you be so kind as to lend them to me for a short time and send them by mail?

I must tell you that I am copying large drawings after Bosboom and Allebé. Well, perhaps if you saw them you would not be altogether dissatisfied.

Send me what you can and do not fear for me. If I can only continue to work, that will somehow or other set me right again.

I write to you while I am busy drawing and I am in a hurry to get back to it, so good night, and send me the prints as soon as possible.

With a hearty handshake in thought,
Vincent.

Slowly a new hunger grew upon him, the desire to talk to some artist about his work, and find out just where he was going right and where he was going wrong. He knew that his drawings were bad, but he was too close to them to see exactly why. What he needed was the ruthless eye of a stranger who was not blinded by the creative pride of the parent.

To whom could he go? It was a hunger more cogent than any he suffered the winter before when he had lived for days on dry bread. He simply had to know and feel that there were other artists in the world, men of his own kind who were facing the same technical problems, thinking in the same terms; men who would justify his efforts by showing their own serious concern with the elements of the painter's craft. There were people in the world, he remembered, men like Maris and Mauve, who gave their whole lives to painting. That seemed almost unbelievable here in the Borinage.

One rainy afternoon, as he was copying in his room, there flashed before his mind the picture of the Reverend Pietersen standing in his studio in Brussels and saying, "But don't tell my *confrères* about it!" He knew that he had his man at last. He looked over the original sketches he had done, selected the figures of a miner, a wife bending over her oval stove, and an old woman gathering *terril*. He set out for Brussels.

He had only a little over three francs in his pocket, so he could not afford to take a train. The distance on foot was some eighty kilometres. Vincent walked that afternoon, all that night, and most of the following day, getting within thirty kilometres of Brussels. He would have gone straight on except that his thin shoes had worn through and he had pushed his toes through the top of one of them. The coat he had used all the previous year in Petit Wasmes was covered with a layer of dust, and since he had not taken even a comb or change of shirt with him, he could do little more than throw cold water over his face the next morning.

He put cardboard inside the soles of his shoes and started out very early. The leather began to cut him where his toes stuck through at the top; soon his foot was covered with blood. The cardboard wore out, water blisters took its place, changed to blood blisters, and then broke. He was hungry, he was thirsty, he was tired, but he was as happy as a man could be.

He was actually going to see and talk to another artist!

He reached the outskirts of Brussels that afternoon without a centime in his pockets. He remembered very distinctly where Pietersen lived and walked rapidly through the streets. People moved aside quickly as he passed, and then stared after him, shaking their heads. Vincent did not even notice them, but made his way along as fast as his crippled feet would permit him.

The Reverend's young daughter answered the bell. She took one horrified look at Vincent's dirty, sweat-streaked face, his uncombed, matted hair, filthy coat, mud-caked trousers and black, bloody feet, and ran screaming down the hall. The Reverend Pietersen came to the door, peered at Vincent for a moment without recognizing him, and then broke into a hearty smile of recognition.

"Well, Vincent my son," he exclaimed, "how good it is to see you again. Come right in, come right in."

He led Vincent into the study and drew up a comfortable chair for him. Now that he had made his objective, the cable of will broke within Vincent, and all at once he felt the eighty kilometres that he had tramped in the last two days on bread and a little cheese. The muscles of his back relaxed, his shoulders slumped, and he found it curiously difficult to breathe.

"A friend of mine nearby has a spare room, Vincent," said Pietersen. "Wouldn't you like to clean up and rest after your journey?"

"Yes. I hadn't known I was so tired."

The Reverend took his hat and walked down the street with Vincent, oblivious to the stares of his neighbours.

"You will probably want to sleep tonight," he said, "but surely you will come to dinner tomorrow at twelve? We will have a great deal to talk about."

Vincent scrubbed, standing up in an iron basin, and although it was only six o'clock, went to sleep holding his empty stomach. He did not open his eyes until ten the next morning and only then because hunger was pounding implacably on some anvil within him. The man from whom the Reverend Pietersen rented the room lent Vincent a razor, a comb, and a clothes brush; he did what he could to make himself look neat and found everything repairable except the shoes.

Vincent was ravenous for food, and while Pietersen chatted lightly about the recent events in Brussels, piled it in unashamedly. After dinner the two men went into the study.

"Oh," said Vincent, "you've been doing a lot of work, haven't you? These are all new sketches on the walls."

"Yes," replied Pietersen, "I'm beginning to find a great deal more pleasure in painting than in preaching."

Vincent said smilingly, "And does your conscience prick you occasionally for taking so much time off your real work?"

Pietersen laughed and said, "Do you know the anecdote about Rubens? He was serving Holland as Ambassador to Spain and used to spend the afternoon in the royal gardens before his easel. One day a jaunty member of the Spanish Court passed and remarked, 'I see that the diplomat amuses himself sometimes with painting,' to which Rubens replied, 'No, the painter amuses himself sometimes with diplomacy!'"

Pietersen and Vincent exchanged an understanding laugh. Vincent opened his packet. "I have been doing a little sketching myself," he said, "and I brought along three figures for you to see. Perhaps you won't mind telling me what you think of them?"

Pietersen winced, for he knew that criticizing a beginner's work was a thankless task. Nevertheless he placed the three studies on the easel and stood a long way off looking at them. Vincent suddenly saw his drawings through his friend's eyes; he realized how utterly amateurish they were.

"My first impression," said the Reverend, after some time, "is that you must be working very close to your models. Are you?"

"Yes, I have to. Most of my work is done in the crowded miners' huts."

"I see. That explains your lack of perspective. Couldn't you manage to find a place where you can stand off from your subjects? You'll see them much more clearly, I'm sure."

"There are some fairly large miners' cabins. I could rent one for very little and fix it up as a studio."

"An excellent idea."

He was silent again and then said without effort, "Have you ever studied drawing? Do you block the faces on squared off paper? Do you take measurements?"

93

Vincent blushed. "I don't know how to do those things," he said. "You see, I've never had a lesson. I thought you just went ahead and drew."

"Ah, no," said Pietersen sadly. "You must learn your elementary technique first and then your drawing will come slowly. Here, I'll show you what's wrong with this woman."

He took a ruler, squared off the head and figure, showed Vincent how bad his proportions were, and then proceeded to reconstruct the head, explaining as he went along. After almost an hour of work he stepped back, surveyed the sketch, and said, "There. Now I think we have that figure drawn correctly."

Vincent joined him at the opposite end of the room and looked at the paper. There could be no doubt about it, the woman was now drawn in perfect proportion. But she was no longer a miner's wife, no longer a Borain picking up coal on the slope of her *terril*. She was just any perfectly drawn woman in the world, bending over. Without saying a word Vincent went to the easel, placed the figure of the woman bending over her oval stove beside the reconstructed drawing, and went back to join Pietersen.

"Hummmm," said the Reverend Pietersen. "Yes, I see what you mean. I've given her proportion and taken away character."

They stood there for a long time, looking at the easel. Pietersen said involuntarily, "You know, Vincent, that woman standing over her stove isn't bad. She isn't at all bad. The drawing is terrible, your values are all wrong and her face is hopeless. In fact she hasn't any face at all. But that sketch has got something. You caught something that I can't quite lay my finger on. What is it, Vincent?"

"I'm sure I don't know. I just put her down as I saw her."

This time it was Pietersen who walked quickly to the easel. He threw the sketch he had perfected into the wastebasket with a "You don't mind, do you, I've ruined it anyway," and placed the second woman there all by herself. He rejoined Vincent and they sat down. The Reverend started to speak several times but the words did not quite form. At last he said, "Vincent, I hate to admit it, but I really believe I almost like that woman. I thought she was horrible at first, but something about her grows on you."

"Why do you hate to admit it?" asked Vincent.

"Because I ought not to like it. The whole thing is wrong,

94

dead wrong! Any elementary class in art school would make you tear it up and begin all over again. And yet something about her reaches out at me. I could almost swear I have seen that woman somewhere before."

"Perhaps you have seen her in the Borinage," said Vincent artlessly.

Pietersen looked at him quickly to see if he was being clever and then said, "I think you're right. She has no face and she isn't any one particular person. Somehow she's just all the miners' wives in the Borinage put together. That something you've caught is the spirit of the miner's wife, Vincent, and that's a thousand times more important than any correct drawing. Yes, I like your woman. She says something to me directly."

Vincent trembled, but he was afraid to speak. Pietersen was an experienced artist, a professional; if he should ask for the drawing, really like it enough to . . .

"Could you spare her, Vincent? I would like very much to put her on my wall. I think she and I could become excellent friends."

20

When Vincent decided he had better return to Petit Wasmes, the Reverend Pietersen gave him a pair of his old shoes to replace the broken ones, and railroad fare back to the Borinage. Vincent took them in the full spirit of friendship which knows that the difference between giving and taking is purely temporal.

On the train Vincent realized two important things; the Reverend Pietersen had not once referred to his failure as an evangelist, and he had accepted him on equal terms as a fellow artist. He had actually liked a sketch well enough to want it for his own; that was the crucial test.

"He has given me my start," said Vincent to himself. "If he liked my work. other people will, too."

At the Denises' he found that "Les Travaux des Champs" had arrived from Theo, although no letter accompanied them. His contact with Pietersen had refreshed him, so he dug into Father Millet with gusto. Theo had enclosed some large sized sketch paper, and within a few days Vincent copied ten pages of "Les Travaux," finishing the first volume. Then, feeling that he needed work on the nude, and being quite certain he could never get anyone to pose for him that way in the Borinage, he wrote to his old friend Tersteeg, manager of the Goupil Galleries in The Hague, asking him if he would lend the "Exercises au Fusain" by Bargue.

In the meanwhile he remembered Pietersen's counsel and rented a miner's hut near the top of the rue Petit Wasmes for nine francs a month. This time the hut was the best he could find, not the worst. It had a rough plank floor, two large windows to let in light, a bed, table, chair, and stove. It was sufficiently large enough for Vincent to place his model at one end and get far enough away for complete perspective. There was not a miner's wife or child in Petit Wasmes who had not been helped in some way the winter before by Vincent, and no one ever turned down his request to come and pose. On Sundays the miners would throng to his cabin and let him make quick sketches of them. They thought it great fun. The place was always full of people looking over Vincent's shoulder with interest and amazement.

The "Exercises au Fusain" arrived from The Hague and Vincent spent the next two weeks copying the sixty studies, working from early morning to night. Tersteeg also sent the "Cours de Dessin" by Bargue; Vincent tackled this with tremendous vitality.

All five of the former failures were wiped completely from his mind. Not even serving God had brought such sheer ecstasy and constant, lasting satisfaction as creative art could give him. When for eleven days he had not one centime in his pocket and had to live off the few loaves he could borrow from Madame Denis, he did not once complain—even to himself—of his hunger. What did the hunger of his belly matter, when his spirit was being so well fed?

Every morning for a week he went to the gate of Marcasse at two-thirty and made a large drawing of the miners: men and women going to the shaft, through the snow by a path along a hedge of thorns; shadows that passed, dimly visible in the crepuscule. In the background he drew the large constructions of the mine, with the heaps of clinkers standing out vaguely against the sky. He made a copy of the sketch when it was finished and sent it in a letter to Theo.

Two full months passed this way, drawing from dawn to dark and then copying by the light of the lamp. Once again there came over him the desire to see and talk to another artist, to find out how he was getting on, for although he thought he had made some progress, achieved a little more plasticity of hand and judgment, he could not be sure. But this time he wanted a master, someone who would take him under his wing and teach him slowly and carefully the rudiments of the great craft. There was nothing he would not do in return for such instruction; he would black the man's boots and sweep the floor of his studio ten times a day.

Jules Breton, whose work he had admired since the early days, lived in Courrieres, a distance of a hundred and seventy kilometres. Vincent rode on the train until his money ran out, and then walked for five days, sleeping in hay ricks and begging his bread in exchange for a drawing or two. When he stood among the trees of Courrieres and saw that Breton had just built a fine new studio of red brick and generous proportion, his courage fled. He hung about the town for two days, but in the end, the chilly and inhospitable appearance of the studio defeated him. Then, weary, abysmally hungry, without a centime in his pocket, and the Reverend Pietersen's shoes wearing dangerously thin beneath him, he began the hundred and seventy kilometre walk back to the Borinage.

He arrived at the miner's cabin ill and despondent. There was no money or mail waiting for him. He went to bed. The miners' wives nursed him and gave him what tiny portions of food they could spare from the mouths of their husbands and children.

He had lost many pounds on the trip, the hollows were in his cheeks again, and fever ignited the bottomless pools of his green-black eyes. Sick as he was, his mind retained its clarity, and he knew that he had reached the point where a decision was imminent.

What was he to do with his life? Become a school teacher, book-seller, art dealer, mercantile clerk? Where was he to live? Etten, with his parents? Paris, with Theo? Amsterdam, with his uncles? Or just in the great void wherever chance might dump him down, working at whatever fortune dictated?

One day, when his strength had returned a little and he was sitting propped up in bed copying "Le Four dans les Landes" by Theodore Rousseau, and wondering how much longer he would have to indulge in this harmless little pastime of drawing, someone opened the door without knocking and walked in.

It was his brother Theo.

21

The passage of the years had improved Theo. Only twenty-three he was already a successful art dealer in Paris, respected by his *confreres* and family. He knew and practised all the social amenities of dress, manners and conversation. He wore a good black coat, crossing high on his chest with satin piping on the broad lapels, a high stiff collar, and a white tie with a huge knot.

He had the tremendous Van Gogh forehead. His hair was dark brown, his features delicate, almost feminine. His eyes were soft and wistful and his face tapered in a beautiful oval.

Theo leaned against the door of the shack and gazed at Vincent in horror. He had just left Paris a few hours before. In his apartment there was lovely Louis Philippe furniture to sit upon, a wash bowl with towels and soap, curtains on the windows, rugs on the floor, a writing desk, bookcases, soft lamps and pleasant wallpaper. Vincent was lying on a dirty, bare mattress, covered by an old blanket. The walls and floor were of rough plank, the only furnishings a battered table and chair. He was unwashed and unkempt, his coarse, red beard splashed all over his face and neck.

"Well, Theo," said Vincent.

Theo crossed hastily and leaned over the bed. "Vincent, what in God's name is wrong? What have you done to yourself?"

"Nothing. I'm all right now. I was sick a while."

"But this . . . this . . . hole! Surely you don't live here . . . this isn't your home?"

"Yes. What's the matter with it? I've been using it for a studio."

"Oh, Vincent!" He ran his hand over his brother's hair ; the lump in his throat prevented him from speaking.

"It's good to have you here, Theo."

"Vincent, please tell me what has been the matter with you. Why have you been sick? What was it?"

Vincent told him about Courrieres.

"You've exhausted yourself, that's what. Have you been eating properly since you're back? Have you been taking care of yourself?"

"The miners' wives have been nursing me."

"Yes, but what have you been eating?" Theo looked around him. "Where do you keep your stores? I don't see any."

"The women bring me in a little something every day. Whatever they can spare; bread, coffee, a little cheese, or rabbit."

"But, Vincent, surely you know you can't get your strength back on bread and coffee? Why don't you buy yourself some eggs and vegetables and meat?"

"Those things cost money here in the Borinage, the same as anywhere else."

Theo sat down on the bed.

"Vincent, for the love of God, forgive me! I didn't know. I didn't understand."

"That's all right, boy, you did all you could. I'm getting along fine. In a few days I'll be up and about again."

Theo ran his hand across his eyes as though to clear away some misty cobweb. "No. I didn't realize. I thought that you ... I didn't understand, Vincent, I just didn't understand."

"Oh, come. It's all right. How are things in Paris? Where are you bound for? Have you been to Etten?"

Theo jumped up. "Are there stores in this forsaken town? Can I buy things here?"

"Yes, there are places down the hill in Wasmes. But draw up that chair. I want to talk to you. Lord, Theo, it's been almost two years!"

Theo ran his fingers lightly over his brother's face, and said, "First of all I'm going to load you full of the best food I can find in Belgium. You've been starved, that's what's the matter with you. And then I'm going to give you a dose of something for that fever and put you to sleep on a soft pillow. It's a good thing I got here when I did. If I had only had the slightest idea ... Don't move until I get back."

He ran out of the door. Vincent picked up his pencil, looked at "Le Four dans les Landes," and went on copying. In a half hour Theo was back, two small boys following him. He had two sheets, a pillow, bundles of pots and dishes and packages of food. He put Vincent between the cool, white sheets and made him lie down.

"Now, how do you work this stove?" he asked, peeling off his beautiful coat and rolling up his sleeves.

"There's some paper and twigs. Light that first and then put in the coal."

Theo gazed at the *terril* and said, "Coal! Do you call this coal?"

"It's what we use. Here, let me show you how to work it."

He tried to get out of bed, but Theo was on him with a leap.

"Lie down, you idiot!" he cried, "and don't move again or I shall be forced to thrash you."

Vincent grinned for the first time in months. The smile in his eyes almost put the fever to rout. Theo put two eggs in one of his new pots, and cut up some string beans in another. In a third he warmed some fresh milk, and held a flat toaster over the fire, with white bread on it. Vincent watched Theo hovering above the stove in his shirt-sleeves, and the sight of his brother close to him once again did him more good than any food.

At length the meal was ready. Theo drew up the table alongside the bed and spread a clean, white towel from his bag. He put a nice cut of butter into the beans, broke the two soft boiled eggs into a dish, and picked up a spoon.

"All right, boy," he said, "open your mouth. You're going to have a square meal for the first time in Heaven knows how long."

"Oh, come off, Theo," said Vincent, "I can feed myself."

Theo filled the spoon with egg and held it up for Vincent. "Open your mouth, young fellow," he said, "or I'll pour it in your eye."

When Vincent finished, he put his head back on the pillow with a deep sigh of contentment. "Food tastes good," he said. "I had forgotten."

"You're not going to forget again in a hurry."

"Now tell me, Theo, everything that's been happening. How are things at Goupils? I'm starved for news of the outside world."

"Then you'll have to stay starved for a little while longer. Here's something to put you to sleep. I want you to be quiet and give that food a chance to work."

"But, Theo, I don't want to sleep. I want to talk. I can sleep any time."

"Nobody asked you what you wanted. You're taking orders. Drink this down like a good fellow. And when you wake up, I have a nice steak and potatoes that will set you right on your feet."

Vincent slept until sundown, and awoke feeling greatly refreshed. Theo was sitting under one of the windows, looking at Vincent's drawings. Vincent watched him for a long time before he made a sound, a feeling of peace in his heart.

When Theo saw that he was awake, he jumped up with a broad smile.

"Well! And how do you feel now? Better? You certainly were sleeping."

"What did you think of the sketches? Did you like any of them?"

"Wait until I put that steak on. I have the potatoes all peeled, ready to boil." He attended to things at the stove and brought back a basin of warm water to the bedside. "Shall I use my razor, Vincent, or yours?"

"Can't I eat the steak without getting shaved?"

"No, sir. Nor without getting your neck and ears washed, and your hair neatly combed. Here, tuck this towel under your chin."

He gave Vincent a clean shave, washed him thoroughly, combed his hair, and put him into one of the new shirts he was carrying in his bag.

"There!" he exclaimed, backing away to survey the job he had done. "You look like a Van Gogh now."

"Theo, quick! The steak's burning!"

Theo set the table and put out the meal of boiled potatoes and butter, a thick, tender steak, and milk.

"My word, Theo, you don't expect me to eat that whole steak?"

"I certainly do not. Half of it belongs to me. Well, let's pitch in. All we would have to do would be to close our eyes, and we could imagine we were home at Etten."

After dinner Theo loaded Vincent's pipe with some tobacco from Paris. "Smoke up," he said. "I oughtn't to allow you to do this, but I guess real tobacco will do you more good than harm."

Vincent smoked in contentment, occasionally rubbing the warm, slightly moist stem of his pipe against his smooth cheek. Theo looked over the bowl of his pipe, through the rough boards, and all the way back to his childhood in the Brabant. Vincent had always been the most important person in the world to him, far more important than either his mother or father. Vincent had made his childhood sweet and good. He had forgotten that the last year in Paris; he ought never to forget it again. Life without Vincent was somehow incomplete for him. He felt that he was a part of Vincent, and that Vincent was a part of him. Together they had always understood the world; alone it somehow baffled him. Together they had found the meaning and purpose of life, and valued it; alone he often wondered why he was working and being successful. He had to have Vincent to make his life full. And Vincent needed him, for he was really only a child. He had to be taken out of this hole, put on his feet again. He had to be made to realize that he had been wasting himself, and be jerked into some rejuvenating action.

"Vincent," he said, "I'm going to give you a day or two to get your strength back, and then I'm taking you home to Etten."

Vincent puffed in silence for many minutes. He knew that this whole affair had to be thrashed out, and that unfortunately they had no medium but words. Well, he would have to make Theo understand. After that, everything would come all right.

"Theo, what would be the good of my going home? Involuntarily I have become in the family a kind of impossible and suspect person, at least somebody whom they do not trust. That's why I believe the most reasonable thing for me to do is to keep at a distance, so that I cease to exist for them.

"I am a man of passions, capable of doing foolish things. I speak and act too quickly when it would have been better to wait patiently. This being the case, must I consider myself a dangerous man, incapable of doing anything? I do not think so. But the question is to try to put these selfsame passions to a good use. For instance, I have an irresistible passion for pictures and books, and I want continually to instruct myself, just as I want to eat my bread. You certainly will understand that."

"I do understand, Vincent. But looking at pictures and reading books at your age is only a diversion. They have nothing to do with the main business of life. It is almost five years now that you have been without employment, wandering here and there. And during that time you have been going down hill, deteriorating."

Vincent poured some tobacco in his hand, rubbed it between his palms to make it moist, and stuffed it into his pipe. Then he forgot to light it.

"It is true," he said, "that now and then I have earned my crust of bread, now and then a friend has given it to me in charity. It is true that I have lost the confidence of many, that my financial affairs are in a sad state, and that my future is only too sombre. But is that necessarily deterioration? I must continue, Theo, on the path I have taken. If I don't study, if I don't go on seeking any longer, then I am lost."

"You're evidently trying to tell me something, old boy, but I'm blessed if I can gather what it is."

Vincent lit his pipe, sucking in the flame of the match. "I remember the time," he said, "when we walked together near the old mill at Ryswyk ; then we agreed in many things."

"But, Vincent, you have changed so much."

"That is not quite true. My life was less difficult then ; but as to my way of looking at things and thinking, that has not changed at all."

"For your sake I would like to believe that."

"Theo, you must not think that I disavow things. I am faithful in my unfaithfulness, and my only anxiety is, how can I be of use in the world? Cannot I serve some purpose and be of some good?"

Theo rose, struggled with the kerosene lamp, and finally lit it. He poured out a glass of milk. "Here, drink this. I don't want you to exhaust yourself."

Vincent drank it down too quickly, almost choking on its richness. Without even waiting to wipe the cream off his eager lips, he went on. "Our inward thoughts, do they ever show outwardly? There may be a great fire in our soul and no one comes to warm himself by it. The passers-by see only a bit of smoke coming through the chimney and continue on their way. Now look here, what must be done? Mustn't one tend that inward fire, have faith in oneself, wait patiently for the hour when somebody will come and sit near it?"

Theo got up and sat on the bed. "Do you know the picture that just flashed into my mind?" he asked.

"No."

"The old mill at Ryswyk."

"It was a nice old mill, wasn't it?"

"Yes."

"And our childhood was nice, too."

"You made my childhood pleasant, Vincent. My first memories are always of you."

There was a long silence.

"Vincent, I do hope you realize that the accusations I have made come from the family and not from me. They persuaded me to come here and see if I couldn't shame you into returning to Holland and a job."

"It's all right, Theo, the words they say are perfectly true.

It's just that they don't understand my motives and don't see the present in relation to my whole life. But if I have come down in the world, you, on the contrary, have risen. If I have lost sympathies, you have gained them. That makes me very happy. I say it in all sincerity, and it will always be so. But I should be very glad if it were possible for you to see in me something else than an idle man of the worst type."

"Let's forget those words. If I have not written to you all year, it was through negligence, not disapproval. I've believed in you and had implicit faith in you since the earliest days when I used to take your hand through the high, grass fields at Zundert. And I haven't any less faith now. I need only to be near you to know that everything you do will eventually come right."

Vincent smiled, a broad, happy, Brabantine smile. "That was good of you, Theo."

Theo suddenly became the man of action.

"See here, Vincent, let's settle this thing right here and now. I have a suspicion that behind all these abstractions you've been dealing in, there is something you want to do, something that you feel is ultimately right for you and that will finally bring you to happiness and success. Well, old boy, just name it. Goupil and Company have raised my wages twice during the past year and a half, and I have more money than I know what to do with. Now if there is something you want to do, and you will need help right at first, simply tell me that you have at last found your real life work, and we'll form a partnership. You'll supply the work and I'll supply the funds. After we've put you on a paying basis, you can return the investment with dividends. Now confess, haven't you something in mind? Hadn't you decided long ago that there was something you wanted to do with the rest of your life?"

Vincent looked over at the pile of sketches Theo had been studying under the window. A grin of amazement, incredulity, and at last awareness spread across his face. His eyes opened wide, his mouth opened, his whole personality seemed to burst open like a *tournesol* in the sun.

"Well I'll be blessed!" he murmured. "That's what I've been trying to say all along, and I didn't know it."

Theo's eyes followed his to the sketches. "I thought so," he said.

Vincent was quivering with excitement and joy; he seemed to have suddenly awakened from some profound sleep.

"Theo, you knew it before I did! I wouldn't let myself think about it. I was afraid. Of course there's something I must do. It's the thing I've pointed towards all my life, and I never suspected it. I felt a tremendous urge to sketch, to put down what I saw on paper while I was studying in Amsterdam and Brussels. But I wouldn't allow myself to. I was afraid it would interfere with my real work. *My real work!* How blind I was! Something has been trying to push itself out of me all these years and I wouldn't let it. I beat it back. Here I am, twenty-seven, with nothing accomplished. What an idiot, an utterly blind and stupid idiot I've been."

"It doesn't matter, Vincent. With your strength and determination you'll be able to accomplish a thousand times as much as any other beginner. And you've got a long life ahead of you."

"I have ten years anyway. I'll be able to turn out some good work in that time."

"Of course you will! And you can live wherever you like; Paris, Brussels, Amsterdam, The Hague. Just take your choice and I'll send you money to live on each month. I don't care if it takes you years, Vincent, I'll never give up hope if you don't."

"Oh, Theo, all these bitter months I've been working toward something, trying to dig the real purpose and meaning out of my life, and I didn't know it! But now that I do know, I'll never be discouraged again. Theo, do you realize what it means? After all these wasted years I have found myself at LAST! I'm going to be an artist. Of course I'm going to be an artist. I've got to be. That's why I failed at all my other jobs, because I wasn't meant for them. But now I've got the one thing that can never fail. Oh, Theo, the prison is open at last, and you're the one who unbarred the gates!"

"Nothing can ever estrange us! We're together again, aren't we, Vincent?"

"Yes, Theo, for life."

"Now, just you rest and get well. In a few days, when you're better, I'll take you back to Holland, or Paris, or wherever you want to go."

Vincent sprang out of bed with a leap that carried him halfway across the cabin.

"In a few days, hell!" he cried. "We're going right now. There's a train for Brussels at nine o'clock."

He began pulling on his clothes with furious speed.

"But Vincent, you can't travel tonight. You're sick."

"Sick! That's ancient history. I never felt better in my life. Come on, Theo, boy, we've got about ten minutes to make that railway station. Throw those nice white sheets into your bag and let's be on our way!"

BOOK TWO

ETTEN

1

Theo and Vincent spent a day together in Brussels, and then Theo returned to Paris. Spring was coming, the Brabantine countryside called, and home seemed like a magic haven. Vincent bought himself a workman's suit of rough black velvet, of the material known as *veloutine,* some unbleached, muslin coloured Ingres paper for sketching, and caught the next train home to Etten and the family parsonage.

Anna Cornelia disapproved of Vincent's life because she felt it brought him more pain than happiness. Theodorus disapproved on objective grounds; if Vincent had been someone else's son, he would have had nothing to do with him. He knew that God did not like Vincent's evil way of living, but he had a suspicion that He would like even less the casting off of a son by his father.

Vincent noticed that his father's hair had grown whiter and that the right lid drooped still lower over his eye. Age seemed to be shrinking his features; he grew no beard to make up for the loss, and the expression on his face had changed from "This is me," to "Is this me?"

In his mother Vincent found greater strength and attractiveness than before. Age built her up rather than tore her down. The smile engraved in curved lines between her nostrils and chin forgave one's errors before they were committed; the broadness and wideness and goodness of her face were an eternal "Yea" to the beauty of life.

For several days the family stuffed Vincent with revivifying food and affection, ignoring the fact that he had no fortune and no future. He walked on the heath among the cottages

106

with the thatched roofs, watched the woodcutters who were busy on a piece of ground where a pine wood had been cut down, strolled leisurely on the road to Roozendaal, past the Protestant barn with the mill right opposite in the meadow and the elm trees in the churchyard. The Borinage receded, his health and strength came back with a rush, and within a short time he was eager to begin his work.

One rainy morning Anna Cornelia descended to the kitchen at an early hour to find the stove already glowing red, and Vincent sitting before it, his feet propped up on the grate, with a half finished copy after "Les Heures de la Journée" in his lap.

"Why son, good morning," she exclaimed.

"Good morning, Mother." He kissed her broad cheek fondly.

"What makes you get up so early, Vincent?"

"Well, Mother, I wanted to work."

"Work?"

Anna Cornelia looked at the sketch in his lap, then at the glowing stove. "Oh, you mean get the fire started. But you mustn't get up for that."

"No, I mean my drawing."

Once again Anna Cornelia glanced over her son's shoulder at the copy. It looked to her like a child's efforts to reproduce something from a magazine during a play hour.

"You are going to work at drawing things, Vincent?"

"Yes."

He explained his decision and Theo's efforts to help him. Contrary to his expectations, Anna Cornelia was pleased. She walked quickly into the living room and returned with a letter.

"Our cousin, Anton Mauve, is a painter," she said, "and he makes a great deal of money. I had this letter from my sister only the other day—Mauve married her daughter Jet, you know—and she writes that Mijnheer Tersteeg at Goupils sells everything Anton does for five and six hundred guilders."

"Yes, Mauve is becoming one of our important painters."

"How long does it take to make one of those pictures, Vincent?"

"That depends, Mother. Some canvases take a few days, some a few years."

"A few years! Oh, my!"

Anna Cornelia thought for a moment and then asked, "Can you draw people so that it looks like them?"

"Well, I don't know. I have some sketches upstairs. I'll show them to you."

When he returned, his mother had on her white kitchen cap and was placing kettles of water on the broad stove. The shining blue and white tiles of the wall gave the room a cheerful air.

"I'm fixing your favourite cheese bake, Vincent," said Anna Cornelia. "Do you remember?"

"Do I remember! Oh, Mother!" He threw his arm about her shoulder roughly. She looked up at him with a wistful smile. Vincent was her eldest child and her favourite; his unhappiness was the only thing in life that grieved her.

"Is it good to be home with your mother?" she asked.

He pinched her fresh, wrinkled cheek playfully.

"Yes, sweetheart," he answered.

She took the sketches of the Borains and studied them carefully.

"But Vincent, what has happened to their faces?"

"Nothing. Why?"

"They haven't any."

"I know. I was only interested in the figure."

"But you can draw people's faces, can't you? I'm sure lots of women here in Etten would like to have their portraits painted. There's a living in that."

"Yes, I suppose so. But I'll have to wait until my drawing is right."

His mother was breaking eggs into a pan of sour cheese she had strained the day before. She paused with half the shell of an egg in each hand and turned from the stove.

"You mean you have to make your drawing right so the portraits will be good enough to sell?"

"No," replied Vincent, sketching rapidly with his pencil, "I have to make my drawing right so that my drawing will be right."

Anna Cornelia stirred the yolks into the white cheese thoughtfully and then said, "I'm afraid I don't understand that, son."

"Neither do I," said Vincent, "but anyway it's so."

Over the fluffy golden cheese bake at breakfast, Anna Cornelia broke the news to her husband. They had been doing a great deal of uneasy speculating about Vincent in private.

"Is there a future in that, Vincent?" asked his father. "Will you be able to support yourself?"

"Not just at first. Theo is going to help me until I get on my feet. After my drawing becomes accurate, I should be able to make money. Draftsmen in London and Paris earn from ten to fifteen francs a day, and the men who do illustrations for the magazines make good money."

Theodorus was relieved to find that Vincent had something—anything in mind, and was not going to drift idly as he had all these years.

"I hope, if you begin this work, Vincent, you will keep on with it. You'll never get anywhere changing from pillar to post."

"This is the end, Father. I'll not change again."

2

After a time the rain stopped and warm weather set in. Vincent took his drawing material and easel out of doors and began exploring the country. He liked best to work on the heath, near Seppe, though he often went to a big swamp in the Passievaart to draw the water lilies. Etten was a small, closely knit town and its people looked at him askance. The black velvet suit was the first of its kind to be seen in the village; never before had the natives known a full grown man to spend his days in the open fields with nothing but pencil and drawing paper. He was courteous to his father's parishioners in a rough, disinterested sort of way, but they wanted to have nothing to do with him. In this tiny, provincial settlement he was a freak, a sport; everything about him was bizarre; his clothes, his manner, his red beard, his history, the fact that he did not work, his incessant sitting in the fields and looking at things. They mistrusted and were afraid of him because he was different, even though he did them no harm and asked only to be let alone. Vincent had no idea the people did not like him.

He was doing a large study of the pine wood that was being cut down, concentrating on a lone tree at the border of a creek. One of the labourers who was clearing away would come and watch him draw, looking over his shoulder with a vacant grin, and occasionally breaking into a loud snigger. The sketch took Vincent some time. Each day the peasant's guffaws grew louder. Vincent decided to find out just what amused the man.

"You find it funny," he asked politely, "that I draw a tree?"

The man roared. "Yes, yes, it is so funny. You must be *fou!*"

Vincent deliberated for a moment and then asked, "Would I be *fou* if I planted a tree?"

The peasant sobered up instantly. "Oh, no, certainly not."

"Would I be *fou* if I tended the tree and took care of it?"

"No, of course not."

"Would I be *fou* if I picked the fruit off?"

"*Vous vous moquez de moi!*"

"Well then, would I be *fou* if I chopped the tree down, just as they have done here?"

"Oh, no, trees must be cut down."

"Then I can plant a tree, tend it, pick it, and cut it down, but if I draw one I am *fou*. Is that right?"

The peasant broke into his broad grin again. "Yes, you must be *fou* to sit there like that. All the village says so."

In the evenings he sat with the rest of the family in the living room. Around the immense wooden table the entire family gathered, sewing, reading, writing letters. His young brother Cor was a quiet child who rarely spoke. Of his sisters, Anna had married and moved away. Elizabeth disliked him so thoroughly that she did her best to pretend he had never come home. Willemien was sympathetic; she posed for Vincent whenever he asked her, and gave him an uncritical friendship. But their relationship was tied to earthly things.

Vincent worked at the table too, comfortable in the light of the huge yellow lamp which sat impartially in the centre. He copied his exercises or the sketches he had made in the fields that day. Theodorus watched him do one figure over a dozen times and always throw away the finished product with dissatisfaction; at last the dominie could contain himself no longer.

"Vincent," he said, leaning across the broad expanse of table, "don't you ever get them right?"

"No," replied Vincent.

"Then I wonder if you aren't making a mistake?"

"I'm making a great many, Father. Which one do you refer to?"

"It seems to me that if you had any talent, if you were really cut out to be an artist, those sketches would come right the first time."

Vincent glanced down at his study of a peasant kneeling

before a bag in which he was putting potatoes. He could not seem to catch the line of the beggar's arm.

"Perhaps so, Father."

"What I mean is, you shouldn't have to draw those things a hundred times without ever getting them right. If you had any natural ability, they would come to you without all this trying."

"Nature always begins by resisting the artist, Father," he said, without putting down his pencil, "but if I really take my work seriously, I won't allow myself to be led astray by that resistance. On the contrary, it will be a stimulus the more to fight for victory."

"I don't see that," said Theodorus. "Good can never grow out of evil, nor can good work grow out of bad."

"Perhaps not in theology. But it can in art. In fact, it must."

"You're wrong, my boy. An artist's work is either good or bad. And if it's bad, he's no artist. He ought to have found that out for himself at the beginning and not have wasted all his time and effort."

"But what if he has a happy life turning out bad art? What then?"

Theodorus searched his theological training, but he could find no answer to this question.

"No," said Vincent, rubbing out the bag of potatoes and leaving the man's left arm suspended stiffly in mid-air. "At bottom, nature and a true artist agree. It may take years of struggling and wrestling before she becomes docile and yielding, but in the end, the bad, very bad work will turn into good work and justify itself."

"What if at the end the work remains poor? You've been drawing that fellow kneeling down for days and he's still wrong. Suppose you go on drawing him for years and years and he keeps on being wrong?"

Vincent shrugged. "The artist takes that gamble, Father."

"Are the rewards worth the gamble?"

"Rewards? What rewards?"

"The money one gets. And the position in society."

Vincent looked up from his paper for the first time and examined his father's face, feature by feature, as though he were looking at some strange being.

"I thought we were discussing good and bad art," he said.

111

3

He worked night and day at his craft. If he thought of the future at all, it was only to bring closer in fancy the time when he would no longer be a burden on Theo, and when the finished product of his work would approximate perfection. When he was too tired to sketch, he read. When he was too tired to do either, he went to sleep.

Theo sent Ingres paper, pictures from a veterinary school of the anatomy of a horse, a cow, and a sheep, some Holbeins in "The Models from the Artists," drawing pencils, quill pens, the reproduction of a human skeleton, sepia, as many francs as he could spare, and the admonition to work hard and not become a mediocre artist. To this advice Vincent replied, "I shall do what I can, but mediocre in its simple signification I do not despise at all. And one certainly does not rise above that mark by despising what is mediocre. But what you say about hard work is entirely right. 'Not a day without a line!' as Gavarni warns us."

More and more he had the feeling that the drawing of the figure was a good thing, and that indirectly it had a good influence on the drawing of landscape. If he drew a willow tree as if it were a living being—and it really was so after all—then the surroundings followed in due course, if only he concentrated all his attention on that same tree and did not give up until he had brought some life into it. He loved landscape very much, but ten times more he loved those studies from life, sometimes of startling realism, which had been drawn so well by Gavarni, Daumier, Doré, De Groux and Felicien Rops. By working on types of labourers, he hoped eventually to be able to do illustrations for the magazines and newspapers; he wanted to support himself completely during the long hard years in which he would perfect his technique and go on to higher forms of expression.

One time his father, who thought he read for entertainment, said, "Vincent, you are always talking about how hard you must work. Then why do you waste your time on all those silly French books?"

Vincent placed a marking finger in "Le Père Goriot" and looked up. He kept hoping that some day his father might understand him when he spoke of serious things.

"You see," he said slowly, "not only does the drawing of figures and scenes from life demand a knowledge of the handicraft of drawing, but it demands also profound studies of literature."

"I must say I don't gather that. If I want to preach a good sermon, I don't spend my time in the kitchen watching your mother pickle tongues."

"Speaking of tongues," said Anna Cornelia, "those fresh ones ought to be ready by tomorrow breakfast."

Vincent did not bother to upset the analogy.

"I can't draw a figure," he said, "without knowing all about the bones and muscles and tendons that are inside it. And I can't draw a head without knowing what goes on in that person's brain and soul. In order to paint life one must understand not only anatomy, but what people feel and think about the world they live in. The painter who knows his own craft and nothing else will turn out to be a very superficial artist."

"Ah, Vincent," said his father, sighing deeply, "I'm afraid you're going to develop into a theorist!"

Vincent returned to "Le Père Goriot."

Another time he became greatly excited at the arrival of some books by Cassagne which Theo sent to correct the trouble with his perspective. Vincent ran through them lovingly and showed them to Willemien.

"I know of no better remedy for my ailment," he said to her. "If I am cured of it, I shall have these books to thank."

Willemien smiled at him with her mother's clear eyes.

"Do you mean to tell me, Vincent," asked Theodorus, who was distrustful of everything that came from Paris, "that you can learn to draw correctly by reading ideas about art in books?"

"Yes."

"How very odd."

"That is to say, if I put into practice the theory they contain. However, practice is a thing one cannot buy at the same time with the books. If that were so there would be a larger sale of them."

The days passed busily and happily into summer, and now it was the heat that kept him off the heath, and not the rain. He sketched his sister Willemien in front of the sewing machine, copied for a third time the exercises after Bargue, drew five times over a man with a spade, *Un Bécheur,* in different positions, twice a sower, twice a girl with a broom. Then a

113

woman with a white cap who was peeling potatoes, a shepherd leaning on his staff, and finally an old, sick farmer sitting on a chair near the hearth, with his head in his hands and his elbows on his knees. Diggers, sowers, ploughers, male and female, that was what he felt he must draw continually; he must observe and put down everything that belonged to country life. He did not stand altogether helpless before nature any longer; that gave him an exaltation unlike any he had ever known before.

The townspeople still thought him queer and kept him at arm's length. Although his mother and Willemien—and even his father in his own way—heaped kindness and affection upon him, in those innermost recesses to which no one in Etten or the parsonage could ever possibly penetrate, he was frightfully alone.

In time the peasants grew to like and trust him. He found in their simplicity something akin to the soil in which they were hoeing or digging. He tried to put that into his sketches. Often his family could not tell where the peasant ended and the earth began. Vincent did not know how his drawings came out that way but he felt they were right, just so.

"There should be no strict line between," he said to his mother who asked about this one evening. "They are really two kinds of earth, pouring into each other, belonging to each other; two forms of the same matter, indistinguishable in essence."

His mother decided that since he had no wife, she had better take him in hand and help him become successful.

"Vincent," she said one morning, "I want you to be back in the house by two o'clock. Will you do that for me?"

"Yes, Mother. What is it you wish?"

"I want you to come with me to a tea party."

Vincent was aghast. "But Mother, I can't be wasting my time that way!"

"Why will it be wasting your time, son?"

"Because there's nothing to paint at a tea party."

"That's just where you're wrong. All the important women of Etten will be there."

Vincent's eyes went to the kitchen door. He almost made a bolt for it. After an effort he controlled himself and tried to explain; the words came slowly and painfully.

"What I mean, Mother," he said, "is that the women at a tea party have no character."

114

"Nonsense! They all have splendid characters. Never a word has been breathed against one of them."

"No, dear," he said, "of course not. What I mean is, they all look alike. The pattern of their lives has fitted them to a specific mould."

"Well, I'm sure I can tell one from the other without any difficulty."

"Yes, sweetheart, but you see, they've all had such easy lives that they haven't anything interesting carved into their faces."

"I'm afraid I don't understand, son. You draw every labourer and peasant you see in the fields."

"Ah, yes."

'But what good will that ever do you? They're all poor, and they can't buy anything. The women of the town can pay to have their portraits painted."

Vincent put his arms about her and cupped her chin in his hand. The blue eyes were so clear, so deep, so kind and loving. Why did they not understand?

"Dear," he said quietly, "I beg you to have a little faith in me. I know how this job has to be done, and if you will only give me time I will succeed. If I keep working hard on the things that look useless to you now, eventually I will be able to sell my drawings and make a good living."

Anna Cornelia wanted to understand just as desperately as Vincent wished to be understood. She brushed her lips against her boy's rough, red beard and in her mind travelled back to that day of apprehension and fear when this strong, hard man body she held in her arms had been torn from her in the Zundert parsonage. Her first baby had been still-born, and when Vincent announced himself by yelling lustily and long, her thankfulness and joy knew no bounds. In her love for him there was always mingled a touch of sorrow for the first child that had never opened its eyes, and of gratitude for all the others that had followed.

"You're a good boy, Vincent," she said. "Go your own way. You know what is best. I only wanted to help you."

Instead of working in the fields that day, Vincent asked Piet Kaufman, the gardener, to pose for him. It took a little persuasion, but Piet finally consented.

"After dinner," he agreed. "In the garden."

When Vincent went out later he found Piet carefully dressed in his stiff Sunday suit, hands and face scrubbed. "One moment," he cried excitedly, "until I get a stool. Then I'll be ready."

He placed a little stool beneath him and sat down, rigid as a pole, all set to have his daguerreotype taken. Vincent had to laugh in spite of himself.

"But, Piet," he said, "I can't draw you in those clothes."

Piet looked down at his suit in astonishment. "What's the matter with them?" he demanded. "They're new. I only wore them a few Sunday mornings to meeting."

"I know," said Vincent. "That's why. I want to sketch you in your old working clothes, bending over a rake. That's the way your lines come through. I want to see your elbows and knees and omoplate. I can't see anything now except your suit."

It was the word omoplate that decided Piet.

"My old clothes are dirty and patched. If you want me to pose, you'll have to do me as I am."

And so Vincent went back to the fields and did the diggers bending over the soil. The summer passed and he realized that for the moment at least he had exhausted the possibilities of his own instruction. Once again he had the keen desire to enter into relation with some artist and continue his study in a good studio. He began to feel it absolutely necessary to have access to things well done, to see artists at work, for then he could tell what he lacked, and learn how to do better.

Theo wrote, inviting him to come to Paris, but Vincent understood that he was not yet ripe for that great venture. His work was still too raw, too clumsy, too amateurish. The Hague was only a few hours away, and there he could get help from his friend, Mijnheer Tersteeg, manager of Goupil and Company, and from his cousin, Anton Mauve. Perhaps it would be better for him to settle in The Hague during the next stage of his slow apprenticeship. He wrote, asking Theo's advice, and his brother replied with the railroad fare.

Before moving permanently, Vincent wished to find out whether Tersteeg and Mauve would be friendly and help him ; if not, he would have to go elsewhere. He carefully wrapped up all his sketches—with a change of linen this time—and set out for the capital of his country in the true tradition of all young provincial artists.

Mijnheer Herman Gijsbert Tersteeg was the founder of The
Hague school of painting, and the most important art dealer in
Holland. People from all over the country came to him for
advice on what pictures they should buy ; if Mijnheer Tersteeg
said a canvas was good, his opinion was considered as defini-
tive.

When Mijnheer Tersteeg succeeded Uncle Vincent Van
Gogh as manager of Goupil and Company, the rising young
Dutch artists were scattered all over the country. Anton
Mauve and Josef lived in Amsterdam, Jacob and Willem
Maris were in the provinces, and Josef Israels, Johannes
Bosboom and Blommers were wandering about from town to
town without any permanent headquarters. Tersteeg wrote to
each one in turn and said,

"Why should we not all join forces here in The Hague and
make it the capital of Dutch art? We can help each other, we
can learn from each other, and by our concerted effort we can
bring Dutch painting back to the world eminence it enjoyed in
the age of Frans Hals and Rembrandt."

The response of the painters was slow, but in the course of
the years every young artist whom Tersteeg picked out as
having ability settled in The Hague. There was at this time
absolutely no demand for their canvases. Tersteeg had chosen
them, not because they were selling, but because he saw in
their work the possibility of future greatness. He bought
canvases from Israels, from Mauve, and Jacob Maris six years
before he could persuade the public to see anything in them.

Year after year he went on buying patiently the work of
Bosboom, Maris and Neuhuys, turning their canvases to the
wall at the rear of his shop. He knew that these had to be
supported while they struggled toward their maturity ; if the
Dutch public was too blind to recognize its own native genius,
he, the critic and dealer, would see that these fine young men
were not lost to the world forever through poverty, neglect,
and discouragement. He bought their canvases, criticized their
work, brought them into contact with their fellow painters,
and encouraged them through the hard years. Day after day
he fought to educate the Dutch public, to open its eyes to the
beauty and expression of its own men.

By the time Vincent went to visit him at The Hague, he had
succeeded. Mauve, Neuhuys, Israels, Jacob and Willem Maris,

Bosboom, and Blommers not only had everything they painted sold at high prices by Goupil and Company, but they were in a fair way to becoming classics.

Mijnheer Tersteeg was a handsome man in the Dutch tradition; he had strong, prominent features, a high forehead, brown hair combed straight back, a flat, beautifully rounded, full-face beard, and eyes as pellucid as a Dutch lake sky. He wore a full black jacket in the Prince Albert manner, wide, striped trousers that fell over his shoes, a high, single collar and ready made, black, bow ties that his wife attached for him every morning.

Tersteeg had always liked Vincent, and when the latter was transferred to the London branch of Goupil and Company, he had penned a warm note of commendation about the boy to the English manager. He had sent Vincent the "Exercises au Fusain" to the Borinage and had included the "Cours de Dessin Bargue" because he knew it would be helpful. While it was true that Goupil and Company in The Hague was owned by Uncle Vincent Van Gogh, Vincent had every reason to believe that Tersteeg was fond of him for his own sake. Tersteeg was not the man to cater.

Goupil and Company was located at number 20, Plaats, the most aristocratic and expensive square in all The Hague. Only a stone's throw away was the S'Graven Haghe castle which had been the beginning of the city, with its medieval court-yard, the moat that had been turned into a beautiful lake, and at the far end the Mauritshuis where hung Rubens, Hals, Rembrandt, and all the little Dutch masters.

Vincent walked from the station along the narrow, winding busy Wagenstraat, cut through the Plein and Binnenhof of the castle, and found himself in the Plaats. It was eight years since he had last walked out of Goupils; the tide of suffering he had gone through in that short space of time welled over his body and mind, stunning him.

Eight years ago. Everybody had liked him and been proud of him. He had been his Uncle Vincent's favourite nephew. It was common knowledge that he would not only be his uncle's successor but his heir as well. He could have been a powerful and wealthy man by now, respected and admired by everyone he met. And in time he would have owned the most important string of art galleries in Europe.

What had happened to him?

He did not take the time to answer the question, but crossed

118

the Plaats and entered Goupil and Company. The place was beautifully decorated; he had forgotten. He suddenly felt cheap and shoddy in his workingman's suit of rough black velvet. The street level of the gallery was a long salon hung in rich beige drapes; three steps above that was a smaller salon with a glass roof, and to the rear of that, a few steps higher still, a tiny, intimate exhibition room for the initiate. There was a broad staircase leading to the second floor where Tersteeg had his office and living quarters. The walls going up were pyramided with pictures.

The gallery smacked of great wealth and culture. The clerks were well-groomed men with polished manners. The canvases on the walls were hung in expensive frames, set against costly hangings. Thick, soft rugs sank under Vincent's feet and the chairs, set so modestly in the corners, he remembered as priceless antiques. He thought of his drawings of the tattered miners coming out of the shaft, of their wives bent over the *terril*, of the diggers and sowers of the Brabant. He wondered if his simple drawings of poor, humble people would ever be sold in this great palace of art.

It did not seem very likely.

He stood gazing in awkward admiration at a sheep's head by Mauve. The clerks who were chatting softly behind a table of etchings took one look at his clothes and posture and did not even bother to ask if there was something he wished. Tersteeg, who had been in the intimate gallery arranging an exhibition, came down the steps into the main salon. Vincent did not see him.

Tersteeg stopped at the bottom of the few steps and studied his former clerk. He took in the short cropped hair, the red stubble on his face, the peasant's boots, the workingman's coat buttoned up around his neck with no necktie concealed beneath it, the clumsy bundle he was carrying under his arm. There was something so altogether *gauche* about Vincent; it showed up cruelly, in high relief in this elegant gallery.

"Well, Vincent," said Tersteeg, walking noiselessly across the soft rug. "I see you are admiring our canvases."

Vincent turned. "Yes, they are fine, aren't they? How are you, Mijnheer Tersteeg? I bring you compliments from my mother and father."

The two men shook hands across the unbridgeable chasm of eight years.

119

"You are looking very well, Mijnheer. Even better than when I last saw you."

"Ah, yes, living agrees with me, Vincent. It keeps me young. Won't you come up to my office?"

Vincent followed him up the broad staircase, stumbling all over himself because he could not tear his eyes from the paintings on the wall. It was the first time he had seen good work since that brief hour in Brussels with Theo. He was in a daze. Tersteeg opened the door of his office and bowed Vincent in.

"Will you sit down, Vincent?" he asked.

Vincent had been gawking at a canvas by Weissenbruch, whose work he had never seen before. He sat down, dropped his bundle, picked it up again, and then crossed to Tersteeg's highly polished desk.

"I've brought back the books you so kindly lent me, Mijnheer Tersteeg."

He unwrapped his bundle, pushed a shirt and pair of socks to one side, took out the series of "Exercises au Fusain," and laid them on the table.

"I worked on the drawings very hard, and you have done me a great service by lending them to me."

"Show me your copies," said Tersteeg, getting to the point.

Vincent shuffled about in the pile of papers and extricated the first series he had drawn in the Borinage. Tersteeg maintained a stony silence. Vincent then quickly showed the second copies he had made when he settled at Etten. This group elicited an occasional "Hummmm" but nothing more. Vincent then showed the third copies, the ones he had finished shortly before leaving. Tersteeg was interested.

"That's a good line," he said once. "I like the shading," he contributed another time. "You almost got that!"

"I felt it wasn't bad, myself," said Vincent.

He finished the pile and turned to Tersteeg for judgement.

"Yes, Vincent," said the older man, laying his long, thin hands out flat on the desk, with the fingers tapering upward, "you have made a little progress. Not much, but a little. I was afraid when I looked at your first copies . . . Your work shows at least that you have been struggling."

"Is that all? Just struggle? No ability?"

He knew he shouldn't have asked that question, but he could not keep it down.

"Isn't it too early for us to speak of that, Vincent?"

"Perhaps so. I've brought some of my original sketches along. Would you care to see them?"

"I should be delighted."

Vincent laid out some of his sketches of the miners and peasants. Immediately that awful silence fell, the silence famous all over Holland for having broken the indisputable news to hundreds of young artists that their work was bad. Tersteeg looked over the entire lot without even a "Hummmm" escaping his lips. Vincent felt sick. Tersteeg sat back, looked out the window and over the Plaats at the swans in the lake. Vincent knew from experience that if he did not speak first, the silence would go on forever.

"Don't you see any improvement at all, Mijnheer Tersteeg?" he asked. "Don't you think my Brabant sketches better than the ones from the Borinage?"

"Well," replied Tersteeg, turning back from the view, "they are better. But they are not good. There is something fundamentally wrong with them. Just what it is, I can't say offhand. I think you had better keep to your copying for a time. You're not ready to do original work yet. You must get a better grasp of elementals before you turn to life."

"I would like to come to The Hague to study. Do you think that a good idea. Mijnheer?"

Tersteeg did not wish to assume any obligations toward Vincent. The whole situation looked very peculiar to him.

"The Hague is a nice place," he said. "We have good galleries and a number of young painters. But whether it is any better than Antwerp, Paris, or Brussels, I'm sure I don't know."

Vincent left, not altogether discouraged. Tersteeg had seen some progress, and his was the most critical eye in all Holland. At least he was not standing still, He knew that his sketches from life were not all that they should have been, but he was confident that if he worked hard and long they would come right in the end.

5

The Hague is perhaps the cleanest and most well-bred city in all Europe. It is, in the true Holland manner, simple, austere and beautiful. The immaculate streets are lined with full-bosomed trees, the houses are of neat and fastidious brick, with tiny, lovingly kept gardens of roses and geraniums in front. There are no slums, poverty stricken districts, or careless eyesores; everything is kept up with that efficient asceticism of the Dutch.

Many years before, The Hague had adopted the stork as its official emblem. The population had grown by leaps and bounds ever since.

Vincent waited until the following day before calling on Mauve at his home Uileboomen 198. Mauve's mother-in-law was a Carbentus, a sister of Anne Cornelia, and since family ties were strong in those circles, he received Vincent warmly.

Mauve was a powerfully built man with sloping but tremendous shoulders and a large chest. His head, like that of Tersteeg and most of the Van Gogh family, was a more important factor in his appearance than the features of his face. He had luminous eyes, somewhat sentimental, a strong, straight bridged nose springing bonily from his brow without any declivity, a high square forehead, flat ears, and salt-grey beard which concealed the perfect oval of his face. His hair was combed on the extreme right side, a great swash of it lying across the skull and parallel to his forehead.

Mauve was a man full of an energy which he did not dissipate. He painted, and when he got tired doing that he went on painting, and when that fatigued him he painted some more. By that time he would be refreshed and could go back to his painting again.

"Jet isn't home, Vincent," said Mauve. "Shall we go out to the atelier? I think we'll be more comfortable there."

"Yes, let's." He was eager to see the studio.

Mauve led him out to his large wooden atelier in the garden. The entrance was on the side near the house, but some little distance from it. The garden was walled in by hedges, giving Mauve complete isolation for his work.

A delicious smell of tobacco smoke, old pipes, and varnish greeted Vincent as he stepped in. The atelier was quite large, with pictures on easels standing about on a thick Deventer rug. The walls were warm with studies; in one corner was an antique table, and before it a small Persian rug. The north wall was half window. Books were scattered about, and on every available inch of flat space could be found the painter's tools. In spite of the life and fullness of the studio, Vincent could feel the definite orderliness that emanated from Mauve's character and dominated the place.

The formalities of family compliments engaged them only a

122

few seconds; immediately they plunged into the only subject in the world that either of them cared a tinker's dam about. Mauve had been avoiding other painters assiduously for some time (he always maintained that a man could either paint or talk about painting, but he could not do both) and was full of his new project, a misty landscape in a minor key of twilight. He did not discuss it with Vincent, he simply poured it out to him.

Madame Mauve came home and insisted that Vincent remain for supper. He sat before the fireplace and chatted with the children after the pleasant meal, and thought of how fine it would be if he could only have a little home of his own, with a wife who loved him and believed in him, and children around to pronounce him Emperor and Lord by the simple title of father. Would that happy day never come for him?

It was not long before the two men were back in the studio again, pulling contentedly at their pipes. Vincent took out his copies. Mauve looked them over with the quick, discerning eye of the professional.

"They're not badly done," he said, "for exercises. But of what importance are they?"

"Importance? I don't . . ."

"You've only been copying, Vincent, like a schoolboy. The real creating had already been done by other men."

"I thought they might give me the feel of things."

"Nonsense. If you want to create, go to life. Don't imitate. Haven't you any sketches of your own?"

Vincent thought of what Tersteeg had said about his original studies. He debated whether or not to show them to Mauve. He had come to The Hague to ask Mauve to be his teacher. And if all he could show was inferior work . . .

"Yes," he replied, "I have been doing character studies right along."

"Good!"

"I have some sketches of the Borain miners and the peasants in the Brabant. They're not very well done, but . . ."

"Never mind all that," said Mauve. "Let me see them. You ought to have caught some real spirit there."

Vincent laid out his sketches to the accompaniment of a furious beating in his throat. Mauve sat down and ran his left hand along the great swash of hair, smoothing the grain of it on his head again and again. Soft chuckles escaped from behind his salt and pepper beard. Once he rammed his hand against the swash of hair, left it standing in a bush, and threw a quick look of disapproval at Vincent. A moment later he took the study of a labourer, rose and held it alongside of a rough draft figure on his new canvas.

"Now I see where I went wrong!" he exclaimed.

He picked up a drawing pencil, adjusted the light and made a few rapid strokes, his eyes on Vincent's sketch all the time.

"That's better," he said stepping back. "Now the beggar looks as though he belongs on the land."

He walked to Vincent's side and put his hand on his cousin's shoulder.

"It's all right," he said. "You're on the road. Your sketches are clumsy, but they're authentic. They have a certain vitality and rhythm I haven't found very often. Throw away your copy books, Vincent; buy yourself a paint box. The sooner you begin working in colour, the better it will be for you. Your drawing is only half bad now, and you can keep improving it as you go along."

Vincent thought the moment auspicious.

"I am going to move to The Hague, cousin Mauve," he said, "and continue my work. Would you be kind enough to help me sometimes? I need help from a man like you. Just little things, such as you showed me about your studies this afternoon. Every young artist needs a master, Cousin Mauve, and I will be grateful if you will let me work under you."

Mauve looked carefully at all the unfinished canvases in his studio. Whatever little time he took away from his work he liked to spend with the family. The warm aura of praise in which he had engulfed Vincent evaporated. In its place came withdrawal. Vincent, always highly sensitive to the changes in people's attitude, felt it instantly.

"I'm a busy man, Vincent," said Mauve, "and I have little opportunity to help others. An artist must be selfish; he must guard every second of his working time. I doubt if I could teach you much."

"I don't ask for a great deal," said Vincent. "Just let me work with you here sometimes and watch you build up a canvas. Talk to me about your work as you did this afternoon, so I'll see how a whole project is completed. And occasionally, when you are resting, you might look over my drawings and point out my mistakes. That's all I ask."

"You think you are asking only a little. But believe me, it is a serious matter, to take an apprentice."

"I wouldn't be a burden to you, I can promise that."

Mauve considered for a long time. He had never wanted an apprentice; he disliked having people about when he worked. He did not often feel communicative about his own creations, and he had never received anything but abuse for the advice he offered beginners. Still, Vincent was his cousin, Uncle Vincent Van Gogh and Goupils bought his canvases, and there was something about the crude, intense passion of the boy—the same crude, intense passion he had felt in the drawings—that appealed to him.

"Very well, Vincent," he said, "we'll have a try at it."

"Oh, Cousin Mauve!"

"I'm not promising anything, mind you. It may turn out very badly. But when you settle in The Hague, you come to the studio and we'll see if we can help each other. I am going to Drenthe for the fall; suppose you come at the beginning of winter."

"That is just when I wanted to come. I still need a few months more of work in the Brabant."

"Then it is settled."

A crooning voice sang inside of Vincent all the way home on the train. "I have a master. I have a master. In a few months I shall be studying with a great painter, and then I shall learn to paint, too. I will work, oh how I will work during the next few months, and then he shall see what progress I have made."

When he got home to Etten he found Kay Vos there.

6

Kay's great grief had spiritualized her. She had loved her husband devotedly and his death had killed something within her. The tremendous vitality of the woman, her high spirits, her enthusiasm and verve were completely gone. Even her warm, live hair seemed to have lost its sparkle. Her face had tapered down to an ascetic oval, her blue eyes had deep pools of brooding blackness in them, and the superb lustre of her skin had paled to a monotone. If she had less vitality than when Vincent knew her in Amsterdam, she now had in its place a more mellow beauty, a seasoned sadness which gave her depth and substance.

"It's nice to have you here at last, Kay," said Vincent.

"Thank you, Vincent."

It was the first time they had called each other by their Christian names without attaching the "Cousin." Neither knew quite how it had happened, nor for that matter did they even think about it.

"You've brought Jan with you, of course?"

"Yes, he's in the garden."

"It's the first time you've visited the Brabant. I'm glad I'm here to show it to you. We must take long walks over the heath."

"I would like that, Vincent."

She spoke kindly, but without enthusiasm. He noticed that her voice had deepened, become more vibrant. He remembered how sympathetic she had been to him in the house on the Keizersgracht. Should he speak to her about the death of her husband, offer his condolence? He knew that it was his duty to say something but he felt it would be more delicate not to throw her grief into her face again.

Kay appreciated his tact. Her husband was sacred to her and she could not discuss him with people. She, too, remembered those pleasant winter evenings on the Keizersgracht when she had played cards with Vos and her parents by the fire, while Vincent sat under a lamp in a far corner. Mute pain welled up within her and a mistiness covered her now black eyes. Vincent put his hand softly over hers and she looked up at him with a deeply pulsating gratitude. He saw how exquisite suffering had made her. Before, she had been only a happy girl; now she was a passionately suffering woman with all the richness that emotional misery can bring. Once again there flashed into his mind the old saying:

"From out of pain, beauty."

"You'll like it here, Kay," he said quietly. "I spend all day out in the fields sketching; you must come with me and bring Jan."

"I would only be in your way."

"Oh, no! I enjoy company. I can show you many interesting things as we walk."

"Then I'll be happy to come."

"It will be good for Jan. The air will make him sturdy."

She pressed his hand ever so lightly.

"And we'll be friends, won't we, Vincent?"

"Yes, Kay."

She released his hand and stared across the road at the Protestant Church, without seeing it.

Vincent went out into the garden, placed a bench nearby for Kay, and helped Jan make a little house of sand. He forgot for the moment the great news he had brought home from The Hague.

At dinner that night he told the family that Mauve had accepted him as a pupil. Ordinarily he would not have repeated any word of praise that either Tersteeg or Mauve might have given him, but the presence of Kay at the table made him want to appear in his best light. His mother was greatly pleased.

"You must do everything Cousin Mauve tells you," she said. "He is a successful man."

The following morning, Kay, Jan, and Vincent set out very early for the Liesbosch, where Vincent wanted to sketch. Although he never bothered to take anything with him to eat at midday, his mother packed a nice lunch for the three of them. She had an idea that it was some sort of picnic. On the way they passed a magpie's nest in the high acacia in the churchyard; Vincent promised to find an egg for the excited boy. They walked through the pine woods with its crunchy bed of needles, then across the yellow, white, and grey sand of the heath. At one spot Vincent saw an abandoned plough and wagon standing in the field. He set up his small easel, lifted Jan into the wagon, and made a quick sketch. Kay stood a little way off to one side, watching Jan romp. She was silent. Vincent did not wish to intrude upon her; he was glad enough just to have her company. He had never known it could be so pleasant to have a woman at his side while he worked.

They passed a number of cottages with thatched roofs, and then came to the road to Roozendaal. At length Kay spoke.

"You know, Vincent," she said, "seeing you before your easel reminded me of something I used to think about you in Amsterdam."

"What was that, Kay?"

"You're sure you won't be hurt?"

"Not at all."

"Then, to tell you the truth, I never did think you were cut out to be a clergyman. I knew you were wasting your time all along."

"Why didn't you tell me?"

"I didn't have the right to do that, Vincent."

She pushed several strands of red-gold hair under her black

bonnet; a crooked furrow in the road threw her against Vincent's shoulder. He put his hand under her arm to help her regain her balance, and forgot to take it away.

"I knew you would have to work things out for yourself," she said. "No amount of telling would have done any good."

"Now I remember," said Vincent. "You warned me against becoming a narrow-minded clergyman. That was a queer thing for a minister's daughter to say."

He smiled at her eagerly, but her eyes went sad.

"I know. But you see, Vos taught me a great many things I might not otherwise have understood."

Vincent dropped his hand to his side. The mention of Vos's name put a queer, intangible barrier between them.

After an hour's walk they reached the Liesbosch, and once again Vincent set up his easel. There was a bit of swamp he wanted to catch. Jan played in the sand and Kay sat behind him on a little stool he had brought along. She held a book in her hand but she did not read. Vincent sketched rapidly, with a certain *élan*. The study sprang up under his hand with more vigour than he had known before. He could not tell whether it was because of Mauve's compliments or Kay's presence, but his pencil had a surety of touch. He did several sketches in quick succession. He did not turn to look at Kay, nor did she speak to interrupt him, but her nearness gave him a glow of well-being. He wanted his work to be particularly good that day so Kay would admire it.

At lunch time they walked a short way to an oak grove. Kay spread the contents of the basket under a cool tree. The air was utterly still. The smell of the water lilies in the swamp mingled with the faint oak fragrance above them. Kay and Jan sat on one side of the basket, Vincent on the other. Kay served him. The picture of Mauve and his family, sitting about the homely supper table, came to his mind.

As he looked at Kay he thought he had never seen anyone so beautiful. The thick, yellow cheese was delicious and his mother's bread had its usual sweet tang, but he could not eat. A new and formidable hunger was awakening within him. He could not tear his gaze from Kay's delicate skin, the chiselled oval, the brooding, night-pool eyes, the full, sweet mouth that had been robbed momentarily of its ripeness, but which he knew would blossom again.

After lunch Jan went to sleep with his head pillowed in his mother's lap. Vincent watched her stroke the child's light hair, gazing down searchingly into the innocent face. He knew that she was seeing the face of her husband reflected in the child, that she was in their house on the Keizersgracht with the man she loved, and not on the Brabant heath with her Cousin Vincent.

He sketched all afternoon, part of the time with Jan on his lap. The boy had taken a liking to him. Vincent let him mark up several sheets of Ingres paper with black smudges. He laughed and shouted and ran about in the yellow sand, constantly returning to Vincent with questions, with things he had found, with demands that he be entertained. Vincent did not mind; it was good to have a warm, live little animal climbing over him affectionately.

Fall was coming on and the sun set very early. On the way home they stopped at the frequent pools to watch the sunset colourings settle on the water with butterfly wings, darken slowly, and disappear in the dusk. Vincent showed Kay his drawings. She saw them only slightly, and what she did see, she thought crude and clumsy. But Vincent had been good to Jan, and she knew only too well the nature of pain.

"I like them, Vincent," she said.

"Do you, Kay?"

Her praise released a locked flood-gate within him. She had been so sympathetic in Amsterdam; she would understand all the things he was trying to do. Somehow, she seemed the only one in the world who would. He could not talk to his family about his projects because they did not even know the vocabulary; with Mauve and Tersteeg he had to assume a beginner's humility which he did not always feel.

He poured out his heart in hurried, incoherent words. As his enthusiasm increased, he quickened his pace, and Kay had difficulty in keeping up with him. When he was feeling anything deeply, his poise fled and in its place came the old violent, jerky manner. Gone was the mannered gentleman of the afternoon; the provincial boor startled and frightened her. She felt his outburst to be so ill-bred, so immature. She did not know that he was paying her the rarest, the most valuable compliment that man can pay to woman.

He poured out to her all those feelings that had been bottled up within him since Theo had departed for Paris. He told her of his aims and ambitions, of the spirit with which he was trying to imbue his work. Kay wondered why he was getting so excited. She did not interrupt him, nor did she listen. She lived in the past, always in the past, and she found it slightly distasteful that anyone should live with so much joy and vigour in the future. Vincent was feeling his own effervescence too keenly to sense her withdrawal. He went on gesticulating until a name he spoke caught Kay's attention.

"Neuhuys? Do you mean the painter who lived in Amsterdam?"

"He used to. He's at The Hague now."

"Yes. Vos was his friend. He brought him home several times."

Vincent stopped her.

Vos! Always Vos! Why? He was dead. He had been dead over a year. It was time she forgot him. He belonged to the past, just as Ursula did. Why did she always have to bring the conversation back to Vos? Even in the Amsterdam days he had never liked Kay's husband.

Fall deepened. The carpet of pine needles in the woods turned to a crinkly rust-brown. Every day Kay and Jan accompanied Vincent into the fields while he worked. A touch of colour came into her cheeks from the long walks across the heath, and her step became more firm and confident. She took her sewing basket with her now and kept her fingers as busy as Vincent's. She began speaking more freely and liberally about her childhood, about the books she had read, and interesting people she had known in Amsterdam.

The family looked on with approval. Vincent's company was giving her an interest in life. Her presence in the house made Vincent far more amiable. Anna Cornelia and Theodorus thanked God for the opportune arrangement, and did everything they could to throw the two young people together.

Vincent loved everything about Kay; the slender, fragile figure encased so sternly in the long black dress; the perky, black bonnet she wore when she went into the fields; the natural perfume of her body in his nostrils when she bent in front of him; the way she puckered her mouth when she spoke rapidly; the probing glance of her deep blue eyes; the touch of her vibrant hand on his shoulder or arm when she took Jan from him; her throaty, enharmonic voice that shook him to the very depths of his nature, and which he heard singing in his head after he had gone to sleep; the live lustre of her skin, in which he burned to bury his famished lips.

He knew now that for many years he had been living only

partially, that great funds of affection and tenderness in him had been dried up, the clear, cooling waters of love been refused to his parched palate. He was happy only when Kay was near him; her presence seemed to reach out and embrace him gently. When she went with him to the fields, he worked rapidly and with a flair; when she stayed at home, each line was drudgery. In the evenings he sat across the great wooden table from her in the sitting room, and although he copied his sketches, her delicate face was always between him and his paper. If occasionally he glanced up to see her sitting in the pale light of the huge yellow lamp and caught her eye, she would smile at him with a sweet passive melancholy. Often he felt he could not stay away from her for another moment, that he would have to spring up before the whole family and crush her to him fiercely, burying his hot, dry lips in the well of her cool mouth.

It was not only her beauty he loved, but her whole being and manner; her quiet walk, her perfect poise and bearing, the good breeding that she expressed with every slight gesture.

He had not even suspected how lonely he had been in the seven long years since he had lost Ursula. In all his life he had never heard a woman say one caressing word, look at him with the mist of tender affection in her eyes, run her fingers lightly over his face, and follow their trail with kisses.

No woman had ever loved him. That was not life, that was death. It had not been so bad when he had loved Ursula, for then—in his adolescence—he had only wanted to give, and it was the giving that had been refused. But now, in his mature love, he wanted to give and receive equally. He knew that life would be impossible unless his new hunger could be fed by Kay's warm response.

One night he was reading Michelet and he ran across the phrase, "*il faut qu'une femme souffle sur toi pour que tu sois homme.*"

Michelet was always right. He had not been a man. Although he was twenty-eight, he was still unborn. The fragrance of Kay's beauty and love had been breathed upon him and he had become a man at last.

As a man, he wanted Kay. He wanted her desperately and passionately. He loved Jan, too, for the child was part of the woman he loved. But he hated 'Vos, hated him with all his strength, because nothing he could do seemed to drive the dead man from the foreground of Kay's mind. He did not

131

regret her former love and marriage any more than he regretted the years of suffering that his love for Ursula had caused him. They both had been hammered on the forge of pain, and their love would be the purer for it.

He knew that he could make Kay forget this man who belonged to the past. He could make his love so burning in the present that the past would be wiped out. He was going to The Hague soon, to study under Mauve. He would take Kay with him, and they would set up a *ménage* like the one he had seen on the Uileboomen. He wanted Kay for his wife, to have her near him always. He wanted a home, and children who would bear the stamp of his features upon their faces. He was a man now, and it was time he stopped wandering. He needed love in his life; it would take the roughness out of his work, round off the crude edges, quicken it with the consciousness of reality that had been lacking. He had never known before how much of him had been dead without love; if he had known, he would have loved passionately the first woman he had come upon. Love was the salt of life; one needed it to bring out the flavour of the world.

He was glad now that Ursula had not loved him. How superficial his love had been then, how deep and rich it was now. If he had married Ursula he would never have known the meaning of true love. He would never have been able to love Kay! He realized for the first time that Ursula had been a shallow, empty-headed child, with no fineness or quality. He had spent years of suffering over a *poupon!* One hour with Kay was worth a lifetime with Ursula. The road had been hard but it had led him to Kay, and that was its justification. Life would be good from now on; he would work, he would love, and he would sell his drawings. And they would be happy together. Every human life had its pattern that had to be worked out slowly to its ultimate conclusion.

In spite of his impulsive nature and impassioned state of mind, he managed to control himself. A thousand times, when he was alone with Kay in the fields and they were speaking of things that mattered not at all, he wanted to exclaim, "See here, let us drop all this pretence and casualness. I want to hold you in my arms, and kiss your lips over and over and over again! I want you to be my wife and stay with me forever! We belong to each other, and in our aloneness we need each other·desperately!"

By some miracle he managed to restrain himself. He could

not suddenly speak of love out of a clear sky; it would have been too crude. Kay never gave him the slightest opening. She always avoided the subjects of love and marriage. How and when was he to speak? He felt that he must soon, for winter was approaching and he had to go to The Hague.

At last he could bear it no longer; his will broke. They had taken the road toward Breda. Vincent had spent the morning sketching diggers at work. They ate their lunch by a little brook in the shadow of some elm trees. Jan was asleep on the grass. Kay was sitting beside the basket. Vincent knelt down to show her some drawings. While he spoke, rapidly, without knowing a word that he said, he could feel Kay's warm shoulder burning into his side; it was this contact that fired him beyond control. The sketches fell out of his hand, he caught Kay to him suddenly, fiercely, and a great wave of rough, passionate words broke from his lips.

"Kay, I can't bear not to tell you for another moment! You must know that I love you, Kay, better than I do myself! I've always loved you, from the first time I saw you in Amsterdam! I've got to have you near me always! Kay, tell me that you love me just a little. We'll go to The Hague to live, all by ourselves. We'll have our home, and we'll be happy. You love me, don't you, Kay? Say you'll marry me, Kay dear."

Kay had made no effort to free herself. Horror and revulsion had sent her mouth all awry. She did not hear the words he said, but she caught their import, and a great terror arose within her. Her blue-black eyes stared at him cruelly and she raised a hand to mute the cry at her lips.

"*No, never, never!*" she breathed fiercely.

She wrenched herself free from his grasp, snatched up the sleeping child, and ran wildly across the field. Vincent pursued her. Terror lent speed to her legs. She fled before him. He could not understand what had happened.

"Kay! Kay!" he called out. "Don't run away."

The sound of his voice drove her on even faster. Vincent ran, waving his arms madly, his head bobbing about on his shoulders. Kay stumbled and fell in the soft furrow of the field. Jan whimpered. Vincent flung himself on his knees in the dirt before her and grasped her hand.

"Kay, why do you run away from me when I love you so? Can't you see, I've got to have you. You love me too, Kay. Don't be frightened. I'm only saying that I love you. We'll forget the past, Kay, and begin a new life."

The look of horror turned to hatred in Kay's eyes. She wrenched her hand away from him. Jan was now fully awake. The fierce, impassioned look on Vincent's face frightened the child, and the tumultuous words pouring from the strange man's lips put him into a terror. He flung his arms about his mother's neck and began to cry.

"Kay, dear, can't you say that you love me just a little bit?"

"No, never, never!"

Once again she ran across the field towards the road. Vincent sat there in the soft sand, stunned. Kay gained the road and disappeared. Vincent picked himself up and dashed after her, calling her name at the top of his voice. When he got to the road, he saw her a long way down, still running, the child clasped to her bosom. He stopped. He watched them vanish at a turning. He stood there quietly for a long time. Then he recrossed the field. He picked up his sketches from the ground. They were slightly dirty. He put the lunch things into the basket, strapped his easel to his back, and trudged wearily home.

The parsonage was thick with tension; Vincent felt it the moment he entered the door. Kay had locked herself in her room with Jan. His mother and father were alone in the sitting room. They had been talking, but stopped abruptly when he entered; he could feel half a sentence suspended in mid-air. He closed the door behind him. He saw that his father must be frightfully angry, for the lid of his right eye was almost closed.

"Vincent, how could you?" wailed his mother.

"How could I what?" He was not sure precisely what they were reproaching him for.

"Insult your cousin that way!"

Vincent could think of no answer to this. He unstrapped the easel from his back and placed it in a corner. His father was still too wrought up to speak.

"Did Kay tell you exactly what happened?" he asked.

His father loosened the high collar that was cutting into the red flesh of his neck. His right hand gripped the edge of the table.

"She told us that you threw your arms about her and raved like a madman."

"I told her I loved her," said Vincent quietly. "I don't quite see how that's an insult."

"Is that all you told her?" His father's tone was icy.

"No. I asked her to be my wife."

134

"Your wife!"

"Yes. What is so astonishing about that?"

"Oh, Vincent, Vincent," said his mother, "how could you even think of such a thing?"

"Surely you must have been thinking too . . ."

"But how could I ever dream you would fall in love with her?"

"Vincent," said his father, "do you realize that Kay is your first cousin?"

"Yes. What of it?"

"You can't marry your first cousin. That would be . . . that would be . . ."

The dominie couldn't even bring himself to pronounce the word. Vincent went to the window and stared out over the garden.

"What would it be?"

"Incest!"

Vincent controlled himself with an effort. How dare they muck over his love with second-hand words?

"That is sheer nonsense, Father, and completely unworthy of you."

"I tell you it would be incest!" shouted Theodorus. "I won't allow that sinful relation in the Van Gogh family."

"I hope you don't think you're quoting the Bible, Father? Cousins have always been allowed to marry."

"Oh, Vincent, my dear," said his mother, "if you did love her, why didn't you wait? Her husband is dead only a year. She still loves him devoutly. And you know you have no money to support a wife."

"I consider what you have done," said his father, "as distinctly premature and indelicate."

Vincent recoiled. He fumbled for his pipe, held it in his hand for a moment, and then put it back.

"Father, I must ask you firmly and decidedly not to use such expressions any more. My love for Kay is the finest thing that has ever happened to me. I won't have you calling it indelicate and premature."

He snatched up his easel and went to his room. He sat on the bed and asked himself, "What has happened? What have I done? I told Kay that I loved her and she ran away. Why? Doesn't she want me?"

"No, never, never!"

He spent the night tormenting himself by going over and

135

over the scene. Always he ended at the same spot. That little sentence sounded in his ears like his death knell and his doom.

It was late the following morning before he could bring himself to go downstairs. The air of tension had been cleared away. His mother was in the kitchen. She kissed him when he came in, and patted his cheek sympathetically for a moment.

"Did you sleep, dear?" she asked.

"Where is Kay?"

"Father drove her to Breda."

"Why?"

"To catch a train. She's going home."

"To Amsterdam?"

"Yes."

"I see."

"She thought it would be better, Vincent."

"Did she leave a message for me?"

"No, dear. Won't you sit down to your breakfast?"

"No word at all? About yesterday? Was she angry with me?"

"No, she just thought she'd go home to her parents."

Anna Cornelia decided it would be better not to repeat the things Kay had said ; instead she put an egg on the stove.

"What time does that train leave Breda?"

"At ten-twenty."

Vincent glanced at the blue kitchen clock.

"It's that time now," he said.

"Yes."

"Then there's nothing I can do about it."

"Come sit down here, dear. I have some nice fresh tongue this morning."

She cleared away a space at the kitchen table, laid a napkin and spread breakfast for him. She hovered over him, urging him to eat ; she had the feeling that if only he would put enough into his stomach, everything would come all right.

Vincent saw it pleased her, so he swallowed everything she placed on the table. But the taste of "No, never, never" was in his mouth to make bitter every sweet bite he ate.

7

He knew that he loved his work far better than he did Kay. If he had been forced to choose between one and the other, there would have been not the slightest doubt in his mind. Yet his drawing suddenly went flat. He could no longer work with any interest. He looked over the sketches of the Brabant types on the wall and saw that he had made progress since his love for Kay had awakened. He knew that there was still something harsh and severe in his drawings, but he felt Kay's love could soften that. His love was serious and passionate enough not to be chilled by many "No, never, nevers;" he considered her refusal as a block of ice that he would press to his heart to thaw.

It was the little germ of doubt in his mind that prevented him from working. Suppose he could never change her decision? She seemed to have conscientious scruples even at the idea of a possible new love. He wanted to cure her of the fatal disease of burying herself too much in the past. He wanted to join his draftsman's fist with her lady's hand, and work for their daily bread and happiness.

He spent his time in his room, writing passionate, imploring messages to Kay. It was several weeks before he learned she did not even read them. He wrote almost daily letters to Theo, his confidant, strengthening himself against the doubt in his own heart and the concerted attacks of his parents and the Reverend Stricker. He suffered, suffered bitterly, and he was not always able to hide it. His mother came to him with a face full of pity and many comforting words.

"Vincent," she said, "you are only smashing your poor head against a stone dyke. Uncle Stricker says her 'No!' is quite decisive."

"I'll not take his word for anything."

"But she told him, dear."

"That she doesn't love me?"

"Yes, and that she will never change her mind."

"We shall see about that."

"It's all so hopeless. Vincent. Uncle Stricker says that even if Kay loved you, he would not consent to the marriage unless you earned at least a thousand francs a year. And you know you are a long way from that."

"Well, Mother, he who loves lives, he who lives works, and he who works has bread."

"Very pretty, my dear, but Kay was brought up in luxury. She has always had nice things."

"Her nice things don't make her happy now."

"If you two were sentimental and married, great misery

137

would come of it; poverty, hunger, cold, illness. For you know the family would not help with a single franc."

"I've been through all those things before, Mother, and they don't frighten me. It still would be better for us to be together than not to be together."

"But my child, *if Kay doesn't love you!*"

"If only I could go to Amsterdam, I tell you I could change that 'No!' to 'Yes!'"

He considered it one of the worst *petites miseres de la vie humaine* that he could not go to see the woman he loved, that he could not earn a single franc to pay his railroad fare. His impotence put him in a rage. He was twenty-eight; for twelve years he had been working hard and denying himself everything but the bare necessities of life, yet in all the world, he had no way to command the pitifully small sum to buy a ticket to Amsterdam.

He considered walking the hundred kilometres, but he knew he would arrive dirty, hungry and worn. He did not mind the strain of it all, but if he should enter the Reverend Stricker's house as he entered the Reverend Pietersen's . . .! After he had sent Theo a long letter in the morning, he sat down again in the evening and wrote another:

Dear Theo:

I am in desperate need of money for the trip to Amsterdam. If I have just enough I go.

I send along a few drawings; now tell me why they do not sell, and how I can make them salable. For I must earn some money for a railroad ticket to go and fathom that "No, never, never."

As the days went on he felt new, healthy energy arise. His love made him resolute. He had driven out the germ of doubt, and in his own mind he now knew that if he could only see Kay, help her to understand the sort of person he really was inside, he could change that "No, never, never" to "Yes! for ever, for ever!" He went back to his work with a new verve; although he knew that his draftsman's fist was still unwieldy, he felt a powerful confidence that time would wipe that out, just as it would Kay's refusal.

The following evening he sent a letter to the Reverend Stricker, stating his case clearly. He did not mince his words, and he grinned as he thought of the expletive that would be wrenched from his uncle's lips. His father had forbidden him to write the letter; a real battle was preparing in the par-

sonage. Theodorus saw life in terms of strict obedience and
strict behaviour; he knew nothing of the vicissitudes of
human temperament. If his son could not fit himself to the
mould, then it was his son who was wrong, and not the mould.

"It's all the fault of those French books you read," said
Theodorus across the evening table. "If you keep company
with thieves and murderers, how can anyone expect you to
behave like an obedient son and a gentleman?"

Vincent looked up from his Michelet in mild astonishment.

"Thieves and murderers? Do you call Victor Hugo and
Michelet thieves?"

"No, but that's what they write about. Their books are full
of evil."

"Nonsense, Father; Michelet is as pure as the Bible itself."

"I want none of your blaspheming here, young man!"
shouted Theodorus in a righteous rage. "Those books are
immoral. It's your French ideas that have ruined you."

Vincent rose, walked around the table, and placed "L'Amour
et la Femme" before Theodorus.

"There is only one way for you to be convinced," he said.
"Just read a few pages for yourself. You will be impressed.
Michelet only wants to help us solve our problems and our
little miseries."

Theodorus swept "L'Amour et la Femme" onto the floor
with the gesture of a good man casting away sin.

"I don't need to read it!" he fumed. "We have a great-uncle
in the Van Gogh family who was infected with French ideas
and he took to drink!"

"Mille pardons, Father Michelet," murmured Vincent,
picking up the book.

"And why Father Michelet, if I may ask?" said Theodorus
icily. "Are you trying to insult me?"

"I hadn't thought of any such thing," said Vincent. "But I
must tell you frankly that if I needed advice I would sooner go
to Michelet than to you. It would be more likely to be in
season."

"Oh, Vincent," implored his mother, "why must you say
such things? Why must you break up family ties?"

"Yes, that's what you're doing," exclaimed Theodorus.
"You're breaking up family ties. Your conduct is unpardon-
able. You had better leave this house and go elsewhere to
live."

Vincent walked up to his studio room and sat down on the

bed. He wondered idly why it was that whenever he received a tremendous blow he sat on the bed instead of a chair. He looked around the walls of his room at the diggers, the sowers, the labourers, the seamstress and the cleaning girl, the wood-choppers and the drawings from Heike. Yes, he had made progress. He was going forward. But his work was not finished here yet. Mauve was in Drenthe and would not return for another month. He did not wish to leave Etten. He was comfortable; living elsewhere would be more expensive. He wanted time to crash through his clumsy expression and catch the true spirit of the Brabant types before he went away forever. His father had told him to leave the house, had actually cursed at him. But it had all been said in anger. If they really said "Go!" and meant it ... Was he really so bad that he had to be driven from his father's house?

The next morning he received two letters in the mail. The first was from the Reverend Stricker, an answer to his registered letter. There was also a note enclosed from the Reverend's wife. They summed up Vincent's career in no uncertain terms, told him that Kay loved someone else, that the other man was wealthy, that they wished his outlandish attacks upon their daughter to cease instantly.

"There are really no more unbelieving, hard hearted and worldly people alive than clergymen," observed Vincent to himself, crushing the Amsterdam letter in his hand with as much savage pleasure as though it had been the Reverend himself.

The second letter was from Theo.

"The drawings are well expressed. I will do my utmost to sell them. In the meanwhile I am enclosing twenty francs for that trip to Amsterdam. Good luck, old boy."

8

When Vincent left the Central railway station, night was beginning to close in. He walked rapidly up the Damrak to the Dam, past the King's Palace and the post office and cut across to the Keizersgracht. It was the hour when all the stores and offices were being emptied of their clerks and salesmen.

He crossed the Singel, and stopped for a moment on the bridge of the Heerengracht to watch the men of a flower barge eat their dinner of bread and herring at an open table. He turned left on the Keizersgracht, passed the long row of narrow Flemish dwellings, and found himself in front of the short, stone steps and black railing of the Reverend Stricker's house. He remembered the first time he had stood there, at the beginning of his Amsterdam adventure, and he realized that there are some cities in which men are forever ill-fated.

He had rushed all the way up the Damrak and across the Centre at top speed; now that he arrived he felt a fear and hesitancy about entering. He looked upward and noticed the iron hook sticking out above the attic window. He thought what an excellent opportunity it afforded for a man to hang himself.

He traversed the wide, red brick pavement and stood on the curb, looking down into the canal. He knew that the next hour would determine the whole course of his external life. If he could only see Kay, talk to her, make her understand, everything would work out. But the father of a young girl possessed the key to the front door. Supposed the Reverend Stricker refused to admit him.

A sand barge came slowly upstream, being pushed to its nightly anchorage. There was a trail of moist yellow sand over the black side where the cargo had been shovelled out of the hollow. Vincent noticed that there was no wash strung from stern to prow, and idly wondered why. A thin, bony man stuck the side of his chest to the pole, and leaning against it heavily, pushed his way down the catwalk while the thick, clumsy boat slipped upstream from under him. A woman in a dirty apron sat at the stern, like a piece of water-carved stone, the hand behind her guiding the clumsy tiller. A little boy, a girl, and a filthy white dog stood on top of the cabin and gazed at the houses along the Keizersgracht wistfully.

Vincent mounted the five stone steps and rang the bell. After a moment the maid came. She peered at Vincent standing in the shadows, recognized him and thrust her adequate bulk into the doorway.

"Is the Reverend Stricker at home?" asked Vincent.

"No. He's out." She had received her orders.

Vincent heard voices inside. He pushed the woman aside brusquely.

"Get out of my way," he said.

The maid followed him and tried to bar his entrance.

"The family is at dinner," she protested. "You can't go in."

Vincent walked down the long hall and stepped into the dining room. As he did so he saw the very end of a familiar

141

black dress disappear through the other door. The Reverend Stricker, his Aunt Wilhelmina, and the two younger children were at the table. Five places had been laid. At the place where the empty chair was pushed back at a crooked angle, there was a plate of broiled veal, whole potatoes, and string beans.

"I couldn't stop him, sir," said the maid. "He just pushed his way in."

There were two silver candlesticks on the table, with tall white candles giving off the only light. Calvin, hanging on the wall, looked eerie in the yellow glow. The silver service from the carved sideboard gleamed in the darkness, and Vincent noticed the little high window under which he had first spoken to Kay.

"Well, Vincent," said his uncle, "you seem to have less manners every day."

"I want to speak to Kay."

"She's not here. She's visiting with friends."

"She was sitting in this place when I rang the bell. She had begun her dinner."

Stricker turned to his wife. "Take the children out of the room."

"Now, Vincent," he said, "you are causing a great deal of trouble. Not only I, but everyone else in the family has completely lost patience with you. You're a tramp, an idler, a boor, and as far as I can see, an ungrateful, vicious character. How dare you even presume to love my daughter? It is an insult to me."

"Let me see Kay, Uncle Stricker. I want to talk to her."

"She doesn't want to talk to you. She never wants to lay eyes on you again!"

"Kay said that?"

"Yes."

"I don't believe it."

Stricker was aghast. It was the first time he had been accused of lying since he had been ordained.

"How dare you say that I am not telling the truth!"

"I'll never believe that until I hear it from her own lips. And even then I won't."

"When I think of all the precious time and money I wasted on you here in Amsterdam."

Vincent sank wearily into the chair Kay had just vacated, and rested both his arms on the table.

"Uncle, listen to me a moment. Show me that even a

142

clergyman can have a human heart under his triple steel armour. I love your daughter. I love her desperately. Every hour of the day and night I think of her and long for her. You work for God, then for God's sake show me a little mercy. Don't be so cruel to me. I know that I'm not successful yet, but if you'll give me a little time, I will be. Give me a chance to show her my love. Let me help her to understand why she must love me. Surely you must have been in love once, Uncle, and you know what agony a man can suffer. I've suffered enough ; let me find a little happiness for once. Just give me a chance to win her love, that's all I ask. I can't bear this aloneness and misery another day!"

The Reverend Stricker looked down at him for a moment and then said, "Are you such a weakling and a coward that you can't stand a little pain? Must you be forever whimpering about it?"

Vincent sprang to his feet violently. All the softness was gone from him now. Only the fact that they were standing across the table from each other, separated by two tall candles in silver candlesticks, kept the younger man from hitting the minister. A bruising silence hummed in the room while the two men stood staring at the sparkling points of light in each other's eyes.

Vincent did not know how much time passed. He raised his hand and placed it near the candle.

"Let me speak to her," he said, "for just as long as I can hold my hand in this flame."

He turned his hand over and placed the back of it in the flame. The light in the room dimmed. The carbon from the candle instantly made his flesh black. Within a few seconds it turned to a raw, burning red. Vincent did not flinch or take his eyes from his uncle. Five seconds passed. Ten. The skin on the back of his hand began to puff. The Reverend Stricker's eyes were wide with horror. He seemed paralysed. Several times he tried to speak, to move, but he could not. He was held in the grip of Vincent's cruel, probing eyes. Fifteen seconds passed. The puffed skin cracked open but the arm did not even tremble. The Reverend Stricker at last brought himself to consciousness with a violent jerk.

"You crazy man!" he shouted at the top of his voice. "You insane fool!"

He threw himself across the table, snatched the candle from under Vincent, and crushed the light with his fist. Then he leaned down to the candle nearest and blew it out with a great puff.

The room was in utter darkness. The two men stood leaning on their palms, across the table from each other, peering into the darkness, unable to see, yet seeing each other only too clearly.

"You're mad!" cried the Reverend. "And Kay despises you with all her heart! Get out of this house and never dare to come back!"

Vincent picked his way slowly along the dark street and found himself somehow on the outskirts of the town. The familiar and pleasantly fetid odour of still water assailed his nostrils as he stood staring down into a brackish, dead canal. The gas lamp at the corner cast a light on his left hand—some deep instinct had kept his drawing hand at his side—and he saw that there was a black hole in the skin. He passed over a series of tiny waterways smelling faintly of a long forgotten sea. At last he found himself near the house of Mendes da Costa. He squatted down on the bank of a canal. He dropped a pebble on the heavy green blanket of *kroos*. It sank without even showing that there was water beneath.

Kay was gone from his life. The "No, never, never" had been wrung from the depths of her soul. Her cry had now become transposed, had become his property. It pounded through his head, repeating, "No, never, never shall you see her again. Never shall you hear the lilting croon of her voice, the smile in her deep blue eyes, the feel of her warm skin on your cheek. Never shall you know love, for it cannot live, no, not even for as long as you can hold your flesh in the burning crucible of pain!"

A great inarticulate surge of grief welled up in his throat. He raised his left hand to his mouth to stifle the cry, that Amsterdam and all the world might never know that he had been judged, and deemed unworthy. On his lips he tasted the bitter, bitter ash of unrequited desire.

BOOK THREE

THE HAGUE

1

Mauve was still in Drenthe. Vincent searched the neighbourhood of the Uileboomen, and found a little place behind the Ryn station for fourteen francs a month. The studio—it had been known as a room until Vincent took it—was fairly large, with an alcove for cooking and a large window facing the south. There was a stove squatting low in one corner with a long black pipe disappearing in the wall up by the ceiling. The wallpaper was a clean, neutral shade; out of the window Vincent could see the lumber yard belonging to the owner of the house, a green meadow, and then a vast stretch of dune. The house was located on the Schenkweg, the last street between The Hague and the meadows to the southeast. It was covered with black soot from the engines that banged in and out of the Ryn station.

Vincent bought a strong kitchen table, two kitchen chairs, and a blanket to throw over himself while he slept on the floor. These expenditures exhausted his small fund of money, but the first of the month was not far off and Theo would send the hundred francs that had been agreed upon as his monthly allowance. The cold January weather would not permit him to work out of doors: since he had no money to pay models he had to sit by and wait for Mauve to return.

Mauve came back to the Uileboomen. Vincent went at once to his cousin's studio. Mauve was setting up a big canvas excitedly, the swash of hair across his forehead falling into his eyes. He was about to begin the big project of the year, a canvas for the Salon, and had chosen for his subject a fishing smack being drawn up on the beach at Scheveningen by horses. Mauve and his wife Jet had thought it extremely doubtful that Vincent would ever come to The Hague; they knew that nearly everyone has a vague prompting to become an artist at some time or other during his life.

"So you've come to The Hague after all. Very well, Vincent, we shall make a painter of you. Have you found a place to live?"

145

"Yes, I'm over at 138 Schenkweg, just behind the Ryn station."

"That's close by. How are you fixed for funds?"

"Well, I haven't the money to do a great deal. I bought a table and a couple of chairs."

"And a bed," said Jet.

"No, I've been sleeping on the floor."

Mauve said something in an undertone to Jet who went into the house and returned in a moment with a wallet. Mauve took out a hundred guilder note. "I want you to take this as a loan, Vincent," he said. "Buy yourself a bed; you must rest well at night. Is your rent paid?"

"Not yet."

"Then get it off your mind. How about the light?"

"There's plenty of it, but the only window has a southern exposure."

"That's bad; you had better get it fixed. The sun will change the light on your models every ten minutes. Buy yourself some drapes."

"I don't like to borrow money from you, Cousin Mauve. It's enough that you should be willing to teach me."

"Nonsense. Vincent; it happens once in every man's life that he has to set up housekeeping. In the long run it's cheaper to have things of your own."

"Yes, that's so. I hope to be able to sell a few drawings soon and then I'll pay you back."

"Tersteeg will help you. He bought my things when I was younger and just learning. But you must begin to work in water-colour and oil. There is no market for simple pencil sketches."

Mauve, in spite of his bulk, had a nervous manner of darting about at great speed. As soon as his eyes lighted on something he was looking for he thrust one shoulder out before him and flung himself in that direction.

"Here, Vincent," he said, "here's a painting box with some water-colours, brushes, palette, palette knife, oil, and turpentine. Let me show you how to hold that palette and stand before your easel."

He showed Vincent a few elements of technique. Vincent picked up the ideas very quickly.

"Good!" said Mauve. "I used to think you were a dullard, but I see it is not so. You may come here in the mornings and work on water-colours. I'll propose your name for a special membership of *Pulchri*; you can draw there several evenings a week from the model. Besides, it will give you some intercourse with painters. When you begin to sell you can take out a regular membership."

"Yes, I want to work from the model. I shall try to hire one to come in every day. Once I get the human figure, everything else will come of its own accord."

"That's so," agreed Mauve. "The figure is the hardest to get, but once you have it, trees and cows and sunsets are simple. Men who neglect the figure do so because they find it too hard."

Vincent bought a bed, drapes for the window, paid his rent, and tacked the Brabant sketches on the wall. He knew they were unsalable and he easily saw their defects, but there was something of nature in them; they had been made with a certain passion. He could not have pointed out just where the passion was, nor how it got there; he did not even realize its full value until he became friends with De Bock.

De Bock was a charming man. He was *bien élevé*, had pleasant manners and a permanent income. He had been educated in England. Vincent met him at Goupils. De Bock was the exact antithesis of Vincent in every way; he took life casually, nothing ruffled or excited him, and his entire make-up was delicate. His mouth was exactly as long as his nostrils were wide.

"Won't you come have a pot of tea with me?" he asked Vincent. "I'd like to show you some of my recent things. I think I have a new flair since Tersteeg has been selling me."

His studio was located in Willemspark, the aristocratic section of The Hague. He had his walls draped off in neutral velvets. Lounging divans with luxurious cushions filled every corner. There were smoking tables, amply filled bookcases, and oriental rugs. When Vincent thought of his own studio, he felt like an anchorite.

De Bock lit the gas under a Russian samovar and sent his housekeeper for some cakes. Then he took a canvas out from a closet and placed it on the easel.

"This is my latest," he said. "Will you have a cigar while you're looking? It may help the picture; you never can tell."

He spoke in a light, amused tone. Since Tersteeg had discovered him, his self-confidence had gone sky high. He knew Vincent would like the picture. He took out one of the

147

long Russian cigarettes for which he was famous in The Hague, and studied Vincent's face for a passing judgement.

Vincent scrutinized the canvas through the blue smoke of De Bock's expensive cigar. He felt in De Bock's attitude that horrible moment of suspense when the artist shows one of his creations to strange eyes for the first time. What was he to say? The landscape was not bad, but neither was it good. It was too much like De Bock's character: casual. He remembered how furious and ill it made him when some young upstart dared condescend to his work. Although the picture was the sort that could be seen in its entirety with one glance, he continued to study it.

"You have a feeling for landscape, De Bock," he said. "And you certainly know how to put charm in it."

"Oh, thanks," said De Bock, pleased at what he thought was a compliment. "Won't you have a cup of tea?"

Vincent clutched the teacup with both hands, fearing that he might spill it on the rich rug. De Bock went to the samovar and drew himself a cup. Vincent wished desperately not to say anything against De Bock's work. He liked the man and wanted him for a friend. But the objective craftsman arose within him and he could not put down his criticism.

"There's only one thing I'm not sure I like about this canvas."

De Bock took the tray from his housekeeper and said, "Have a cake, old fellow."

Vincent refused because he did not see how he was going to eat a cake and hold a cup of tea on his lap at the same time.

"What was it you didn't care for?" asked De Bock lightly.

"Your figures. They don't seem authentic."

"You know," confided De Bock, stretching out leisurely on a comfortable divan, "I've often meant to plug away at the figure. But I never seem to get around to it. I take a model and work a few days, and then I suddenly become interested in some landscape or other. After all, landscape is very definitely my medium, so I needn't let the figure bother me much, need I?"

"Even when I do landscapes," said Vincent, "I hope to get something of the figure into them. Your work is years ahead of mine; besides, you're an accepted artist. But will you permit me to offer just one word of friendly criticism?"

"Love to have you."

"Well then, I should say your painting lacks passion."

148

"Passion?" inquired De Bock, cocking one eye at Vincent as he leaned over the samovar. "Which one of the numerous passions are you referring to?"

"It's rather hard to explain. But your sentiment seems a trifle vague. In my opinion it could stand a little more intensity."

"But see here, old chap," said De Bock, straightening up and regarding one of his canvases closely. "I can't spew emotion all over the canvas just because people tell me to, can I? I paint what I see and feel. If I don't feel any bloody passion, how am I to get it on my brush? One can't buy it at the greengrocer's by the pound, now can one?"

Vincent's studio looked almost mean and sordid after De Bock's, but he knew there were compensations for its austerity. He pushed the bed back into one corner and hid his cooking utensils; he wanted the place to be a painter's studio, not living quarters. Theo's money for the month had not yet arrived but he still had a few francs left from Mauve's loan. He used them to hire models. He had been in his studio only a short time when Mauve came to visit him.

"It took me only ten minutes to walk over," he said, looking about. "Yes, this will do. You should have north light, but this will do. It will make a favourable impression on those people who have suspected you of amateurism and idleness. I see you've been working from the model today?"

"Yes. Every day. But it's expensive."

"And the cheapest way in the end. Are you short of funds, Vincent?"

"Thank you, Cousin Mauve. I can get along."

He did not think it wise to become a financial burden on Mauve. He had just a franc left in his pocket, enough to eat on for a day, but he wanted Mauve to give freely of his instruction; money was not really important.

Mauve spent an hour showing him how to daub in watercolours, and how to wash out again. Vincent made rather a mess of things.

"Don't let that disturb you," said Mauve cheerfully. "You will spoil at least ten drawings before you come to handle the brush well. Let me see some of your latest Brabant sketches."

Vincent brought them out. Mauve was such a master of technique that he could penetrate to the essential weakness of a piece of work in a very few words. He never said, "This is wrong," and then stopped. He always added "Try it this way."

Vincent listened closely, for he knew that Mauve spoke to him just as he would have spoken to himself if he had gone wrong in one of his own canvases.

"You can draw," said Mauve. "That year with your pencil will be of great value to you. I shouldn't be surprised to see Tersteeg buying your water-colours in a short time."

This magnificent consolation did Vincent little good two days later when he had not a centime in his pocket. It was already several days past the first of the month and the hundred francs had not yet arrived from Theo. What could be wrong? Was Theo angry with him? Could it be possible that Theo would go back on him now, at the very moment when he was on the threshold of a career? He found a stamp in his coat pocket; that enabled him to write to his brother and beg him to send on at least a part of the allowance so that he might eat and hire a model occasionally.

For three days he went without a bite of food, working at water-colours at Mauve's in the morning, sketching in the soup kitchens and third-class waiting rooms in the afternoons, and going either to *Pulchri* or Mauve's to work again at night. He was afraid that Mauve would discover his situation and become discouraged with him. Vincent realized that although Mauve had come to like him, his cousin would cast him aside without a second thought if his troubles began to have an effect upon Mauve's painting. When Jet invited him to dinner, he refused.

The low, dull ache at the pit of his stomach turned his mind back to the Borinage. Was he to be hungry all his life? Was there never to be a moment of comfort or peace for him anywhere?

The next day he swallowed his pride and went to see Tersteeg. Perhaps he could borrow ten francs from the man who supported half the painters of The Hague.

Tersteeg was in Paris on business.

Vincent developed a fever and could no longer hold the pencil. He went to bed. The following day he dragged himself back to the Plaats and found the dealer in. Tersteeg had promised Theo that he would look after Vincent. He lent him twenty-five francs.

"I have been meaning to look in at your studio for some time, Vincent," he said. "I shall drop around shortly."

It was all Vincent could do to answer politely. He wanted to get away and eat. He had thought on his way to Goupils, "If only I can get some money, I will be all right again." But now that he had the money he was more miserable than ever. He felt utterly and forlornly alone.

"Dinner will cure all that," he said to himself.

Food removed the pain in his stomach but not the pain of aloneness that lodged in some intangible spot within him. He bought some cheap tobacco, went home, stretched out on the bed and smoked his pipe. The hunger for Kay came back to him with terrific force. He felt so desperately miserable he could not breathe. He jumped up from the bed, opened the window and stuck his head out into the snow covered January night. He thought of the Reverend Stricker. A chill ran through him, as though he had been leaning too long against the cold stone wall of a church. He closed the window, snatched up his hat and coat, and ran out to a wine café that he had seen in front of the Ryn station.

2

The wine café had an oil lamp hanging at the entrance and another over the bar. The middle of the shop was in semi-darkness. There were a few benches against the wall with mottled, stone topped tables before them. It was a working-man's shop with faded walls and a cement floor; a place of refuge rather than joy.

Vincent sat down at one of the tables. He leaned his back against the wall wearily. It was not so bad when he was working, when there was money for food and models. But to whom could he turn for simple companionship, for a casual and friendly word about the time of day? Mauve was his master, Tersteeg a busy and important dealer, De Bock a wealthy man of society. Perhaps a glass of wine would help him over the bad spot. Tomorrow he would be able to work, and things would look better.

He sipped the sour red wine slowly. There were few people in the shop. Opposite him sat a labourer of some sort. In the corner near the bar sat a couple, the woman in gaudy clothes. At the table next to him was a woman alone. He did not look at her.

The waiter came by and said to the woman roughly, "More wine?"

"Haven't a sou," she replied.

151

Vincent turned. "Won't you have a glass with me?" he asked.

The woman looked at him for an instant. "Sure."

The waiter brought the glass of wine, took the twenty centimes and went away. The tables were close together.

"Thanks," said the woman.

Vincent surveyed her closely. She was not young, not beautiful, slightly faded, one over whom life had passed. Her figure was slender but well formed. He noticed her hand as it clasped the glass of wine; it was not a lady's hand like Kay's, but the hand of one who worked much. She reminded him, in the half light, of some curious figure by Chardin or Jan Steen. She had a crooked nose that bulged in the middle, and a shadowy moustache on her upper lip. Her eyes were melancholy but there was, none the less, a touch of spirit in them.

"Not at all," he replied. "I'm grateful for your company."

"My name is Christine," she said. "What's yours?"

"Vincent."

"Do you work here at The Hague?"

"Yes."

"What do you do?"

"I'm a painter."

"Oh. That's a hell of a life too, ain't it?"

"Sometimes."

"I'm a laundress. When I have strength enough to work. But that ain't always."

"What do you do then?"

"I was on the streets for a long time. I go back to it when I'm too sick to work."

"Is it hard to be a laundress?"

"Yes. They work us twelve hours. And they don't pay nothing. Sometimes, after I washed all day, I got to find a man to earn food for the kids."

"How many children have you, Christine?"

"Five. I'm carrying another one now."

"Your husband is dead?"

"I got them all from strangers."

"That made it difficult, didn't it?"

She shrugged. "Jesus Christ. A miner can't refuse to go down because he might get killed, can he?"

"No. Do you know who any of the fathers are?"

"Only the first son of a bitch. I never even knew their names."

"What about the one you're carrying now?"

"Well, I can't be sure. I was too sick to wash then, so I was on the streets a lot. But it don't matter."

"Will you have another glass of wine?"

"Make it gin and bitters." She reached into her purse, took out the butt of a rough, black cigar and lit it. "You don't look prosperous," she said. "Do you sell any paintings?"

"No, I'm just beginning."

"You look pretty old to be beginning."

"I'm thirty."

"You look forty. How do you live then?"

"My brother sends me a little money."

"Well, it's no goddam worse than being a laundress."

"With whom do you stay, Christine?"

"We're all at my mother's."

"Does she know you go on the streets?"

The woman laughed uproariously but without mirth. "Christ yes! She sent me there. That's what she did all her life. It's how she got me and my brother."

"What does your brother do?"

"He's got a woman at the house. He pimps for her."

"That can't be very good for your five children."

"It don't matter. They'll all be doing the same some day."

"It's all a rum go, isn't it, Christine?"

"Ain't no good crying about it. Can I have another glass of gin and bitters? What did you do to your hand? You got a big black sore."

"I burned it."

"Oh, that must have hurt awful." She picked up his hand tenderly.

"No, Christine, it was all right. I wanted to."

She dropped his hand. "Why did you come in here all alone? Ain't you got no friends?"

"No. My brother, but he's in Paris."

"Makes a guy feel lonesome, don't it?"

"Yes, Christine, horribly."

"I get like that, too. There's all the kids at home, and my mother and brother. And all the men I pick up. But you live alone anyhow, don't you? It ain't people that count. It's having someone you really like."

"Hasn't there ever been anyone you cared for, Christine?"

"The first fellow. I was sixteen. He was rich. Couldn't marry

153

me 'count of his family. But he paid for the baby. Then he died, and I was left without a centime."

"How old are you?"

"Thirty-two. Too old to have kids. The doctor at the free ward said this one will kill me."

"It won't if you have proper medical attention."

"Where in hell am I going to get it? I ain't got nothing saved up. The doctors at the free ward don't care; they got too many sick women."

"Have you no way at all of getting a little money?"

"Sure. If I stay on the streets all night for a couple of months. But that'll kill me quicker than the kid."

They were silent for several moments. "Where are you going when you leave here, Christine?"

"I been at the tubs all day and I come in here to get a glass because I'm dead. They were supposed to pay me a franc and a half, but they put me off 'till Saturday. I got to get two francs for food. I thought I'd rest before I found a man."

"Will you let me come with you, Christine? I'm very much alone. I'd like to."

"Sure. Saves me the trouble. Besides, you're kind of nice."

"I like you too, Christine. When you picked up my burned hand ... that was the first kind word a woman has said to me in I can't remember how long."

"That's funny. You ain't bad to look at. You got a nice way."

"I'm just unlucky in love."

"Yes, that's how it is, ain't it? Can I have another glass of gin and bitters?"

"Listen, you and I need not make ourselves drunk to feel something for each other. Just put in your pocket what I can spare. I'm sorry it isn't more."

"You look like you need it worse than me. You can come anyway. After you go, I'll find some other guy for the two francs."

"No. Take the money. I can spare it. I borrowed twenty-five francs from a friend."

"All right. Let's get out of here."

On their way home, threading their way through the dark streets, they chatted easily, like old friends. She told him of her life, without sympathy for herself, without complaint.

"Have you ever posed as a model?" Vincent asked her.

"When I was young."

154

"Then why not pose for me? I can't pay you much. Not even a franc a day. But after I begin selling, I'll pay you two francs. It will be better than washing clothes."

"Say, I'd like that. I'd bring my boy. You can paint him for nothing. When you get tired of me you can have my mother. She'd like to make an extra franc now and then. She's a charwoman."

At length they reached her house. It was a rough stone building of one floor and a court. "You don't got to see anyone," said Christine. "My room's in front."

It was a modest, simple little room in which she lived; the plain paper on the wall gave it a quiet, grey tone, like a picture by Chardin, thought Vincent. On the wooden floor there was a mat and a piece of old crimson carpet. An ordinary kitchen stove was in one corner, a chest of drawers in another, and in the centre a large bed. It was the interior of a real working woman's home.

When Vincent awoke in the morning and found himself not alone, but saw there in the twilight a fellow creature beside him, it made the world look so much more friendly. The pain and aloneness were gone from him and in their place had come a deep feeling of peace.

3

In the morning post he received a note from Theo with the hundred francs enclosed. Theo had been unable to send it until several days after the first. He rushed out, found a little old woman digging in her front garden nearby, and asked if she wouldn't come and pose for him for fifty centimes. The old woman assented gladly.

In the studio he placed the woman against a drowsy background, sitting next to the chimney and stove with a little tea-kettle off to one side. He was seeking tone; the old woman's head had a great deal of light and life in it. He made three fourths of the water-colour in a green soap style. The corner where the woman sat he treated tenderly, softly, and with sentiment. For some time his work had been hard, dry, brittle; now it flowed. He hammered his sketch on the paper and expressed his idea well. He was grateful to Christine for what she had done for him. Lack of love in his life could bring him infinite pain, but it could do him no harm; lack of sex

155

could dry up the well springs of his art and kill him.

"Sex lubricates," he murmured to himself as he worked with fluidity and ease. "I wonder why Papa Michelet never mentioned that."

There was a knock on the door. Vincent admitted Mijnheer Tersteeg. His striped trousers were creased painstakingly. His round, brown shoes were as bright as a mirror. His beard was carefully barbered, his hair parted neatly on the side, and his collar was of impeccable whiteness.

Tersteeg was genuinely pleased to find that Vincent had a real studio and was hard at work. He liked to see young artists become successful; that was his hobby as well as his profession. Yet he wanted that success to be arrived at through systematic and preordained channels; he found it better for a man to work through the conventional means and fail, than break all the rules and succeed. For him the rules of the game were far more important than the victory. Tersteeg was a good and honourable man; he expected everyone else to be equally good and honourable. He admitted no circumstancs which could change evil into good or sin into salvation. The painters who sold their canvases to Goupils knew that they had to toe the mark. If they violated the dictates of genteel behaviour Tersteeg would refuse to handle their canvases even though they might be masterpieces.

"Well, Vincent," he said, "I am glad to surprise you at work. That is how I like to come in on my artists."

"It is good of you to come all this way to see me, Mijnheer Tersteeg."

"Not at all. I have been meaning to see your studio ever since you moved here."

Vincent looked about at the bed, table, chairs, stove, and easel.

"It isn't much to look at."

"Never mind, pitch into your work and soon you'll be able to afford something better. Mauve tells me that you're beginning water-colours; there is a good market for those sketches. I should be able to sell some for you, and so should your brother."

"That's what I'm working toward, Mijnheer."

"You seem in rather better spirits than when I saw you yesterday."

"Yes, I was ill. But I recovered last night."

He thought of the wine, the gin and bitters, and Christine;

156

he shivered at what Tersteeg would say if he knew about them. "Will you look at some of my sketches, Mijnheer? Your reaction would be valuable to me."

Tersteeg stood before the old woman in her white apron, standing out from the green soap background. His silence was not so eloquent as Vincent remembered it from the Plaats. He leaned on his walking stick for some moments, then hung it on his arm.

"Yes, yes," he said, "you're coming along. Mauve will make a water-colourist out of you, I can see that. It will take some time, but you will get there. You must hurry, Vincent, so that you can earn your own living. It is quite a strain on Theo to have to sent you a hundred francs a month ; I saw that when I was in Paris. You must support yourself as quickly as possible. I should be able to buy some of the small sketches very soon now."

"Thank you, Mijnheer. It is good of you to take an interest."

"I want to make you successful, Vincent. It means business for Goupils. As soon as I begin to sell your work, you will be able to take a better studio, buy some good clothes, and go out a bit into society. That is necessary if you want to sell your oils, later. Well, I must run onto Mauve's. I want to see that Scheveningen thing he is doing for the Salon."

"You'll look in again, Mijnheer?"

"Yes, of course. In a week or two. Mind you work hard and show me some improvement. You must make my visits pay, you know."

He shook hands and departed. Vincent pitched into his work once more. If only he could make a living, the very simplest living out of his work. He asked for nothing more. He could be independent. He would not have to be a burden on anyone. And best of all there would be no hurry; he could let himself feel his way slowly and surely toward maturity and the expression he was seeking.

In the afternoon mail there was a note from De Bock, on pink stationery.

Dear Van Gogh:

I'm bringing Artz's model to your studio tomorrow morning so that we can sketch together.

De B.

Artz's model proved to be a very beautiful young girl who charged one franc-fifty for posing. Vincent was delighted, as he would never have been able to hire her. There was a roaring fire in the little stove and the model undressed by it to keep warm. Only the professional models would pose naked in The Hague. This exasperated Vincent; the bodies he wanted to draw were those of old men and women, bodies that had tone and character.

"I've brought along my tobacco pouch," said De Bock, "and a little lunch that my housekeeper put up. I thought we might not want to disturb ourselves to go out."

"I'll try some of your tobacco. Mine is a trifle strong for the morning."

"I'm ready," said the model. "Will you pose me?"

"Sitting or standing, De Bock?"

"Let's try the standing first. I have some erect figures in my new landscape." They sketched for about an hour and a half, and then the model tired.

"Let's do her sitting down," said Vincent. "The figure will be more relaxed."

They worked until noon, each bent over his own drawing board, exchanging only an occasional grunt about the light or tobacco. Then De Bock unpacked the lunch, and all three gathered about the stove to eat it. They munched the thin slices of bread, cold meats and cheese, and studied their morning's sketches.

"Queer, what an objective view you can get of your own work once you begin to eat," remarked De Bock.

"May I see what you've done?"

"With pleasure."

De Bock had put down a good likeness of the girl's face, but there was not even a faint suggestion of the individual nature of her body. It was just a perfect body.

"I say," exclaimed De Bock, looking at Vincent's sketch, "what's that thing you've got instead of her face? Is that what you mean by putting passion into it?"

"We weren't doing a portrait," replied Vincent. "We were doing a figure."

"That's the first time I ever heard a face doesn't belong on a figure."

"Take a look at your stomach," said Vincent.

"What's the matter with it?"

"It looks as though it were filled with hot air. I can't see an inch of bowels."

"Why should you? I didn't notice any of the poor girl's entrails hanging out."

The model went on eating without even a smile. She thought all artists were crazy, anyhow. Vincent placed his sketch alongside of De Bock's.

"If you will notice," he said, "my stomach is full of guts. You can tell just by looking at it that many a ton of food has wended its weary way through the labyrinth."

"What's that got to do with painting?" demanded De Bock. "We're not specialists in viscera, are we? When people look at my canvases, I want them to see the mist in the trees, and the sun setting red behind the clouds. I don't want them to see guts."

Every morning Vincent went out bright and early to find a model for the day. Once it was a blacksmith's boy, once an old woman from the insane asylum on the Geest, once a man from the peat market, and another time a grandmother and child from the Paddemoes, or Jewish quarter. Models cost him a great deal of money, money that he knew he ought to be saving for food for the end of the month. But of what good was it for him to be at The Hague, studying under Mauve, if he could not go full speed ahead? He would eat later, when he became established.

Mauve continued to instruct him patiently. Every evening Vincent went to the Uileboomen to work in the busy, warm studio. Sometimes he became discouraged because his water-colours were thick, muddy and dull. Mauve only laughed.

"Of course they're not right yet," he said. "If your work were transparent *now*, it would possess only a certain chic and would probably become heavy later on. Now you are pegging away at it and it becomes heavy, but afterwards it will go quickly and become light."

"That's true, Cousin Mauve, but if a man must earn money from his drawing, what is he to do?"

"Believe me, Vincent, if you try to arrive too soon, you will only kill yourself as an artist. The man of the day is usually the man of a day. In things of art the old saying is true, 'Honesty is the best policy!' It is better to take more trouble on a serious study than to develop a kind of chic that will flatter the public."

"I want to be true to myself, Cousin Mauve, and express severe, true things in a rough manner. But when there is the necessity of making one's living ... I have done a few things I thought Tersteeg might ... of course I realize ..."

"Let me see them," said Mauve.

He glanced at the water-colours and tore them into a thousand pieces. "Stick to your roughness, Vincent," he said, "and don't run after the amateurs and dealers. Let those who like come to you. In due time you shall reap."

Vincent glanced down at the scraps of paper. "Thank you, Cousin Mauve," he said. "I needed that kick."

Mauve was having a little party that night, and a number of artists drifted in; Weissenbruch, known as the "merciless sword" for his fierce criticism of other men's work; Breitner, De Bock, Jules Bakhuyzen and Neuhuys, Vos's friend.

Weissenbruch was a little man with an enormous spirit. Nothing could ever conquer him. What he disliked—and that was nearly everything—he destroyed with a single lash of his tongue. He painted what he pleased and how he pleased, and made the public like it. Tersteeg had once objected to something in one of his canvases, so he refused to sell anything more through Goupil. Yet he sold everything he painted; nobody knew how or to whom. His face was as sharp as his tongue; his head, nose, and chin cutting. Everyone feared him and coveted his approbation. He had become a national character by the simple expedient of despising things. He got Vincent off into the corner by the fire, spat into the flames at frequent intervals to hear the pleasant sound of the hiss, and fondled a plaster foot.

"I hear you're a Van Gogh," he said. "Do you paint as successfully as your uncles sell pictures?"

"No. I don't do anything successfully."

"And a damn good thing for you. Every artist ought to starve until he's sixty. Then perhaps he would turn out a few good pieces of canvas."

"Tosh! You're not much over forty, and you're doing good work."

Weissenbruch liked that "Tosh!" It was the first time anyone had had the courage to say it to him for years. He showed his appreciation by lighting into Vincent.

"If you think my painting is any good, you better give up and become a *concierge*. Why do you think I sell it to the fool public? Because it's junk! If it was any good, I'd keep it for myself. No, my boy, I'm only practising now. When I'm sixty I shall really begin painting. Everything I do after that I shall

160

keep by my side; when I die I'll have it buried with me. No artist ever lets go of anything he thinks is good, Van Gogh. He only sells his garbage to the public."

De Bock tipped Vincent a wink from the other side of the room, so Vincent said, "You've missed your profession, Weissenbruch ; you ought to be an art critic."

Weissenbruch laughed and called out, "This cousin of yours isn't half as bad as he looks, Mauve. He's got a tongue in his head." He turned back to Vincent and said cruelly, "What in hell do you go round in those dirty rags for? Why don't you buy yourself some decent clothes?"

Vincent was wearing an old suit of Theo's that had been altered for him. The operation had not been successful, and, in addition, Vincent had been wearing it over his water-colours every day.

"Your uncles have enough money to clothe the whole population of Holland. Don't they give you anything?"

"Why should they? They agree with you that artists should starve."

"If they don't believe in you they must be right. The Van Goghs are supposed to be able to smell a painter a hundred kilometres away. You're probably rotten."

"And you can go to hell!"

Vincent turned away angrily, but Weissenbruch caught him by the arm. He was smiling broadly.

"That's the spirit!" he cried. "I just wanted to see how much abuse you would take. Keep your courage up, my boy. You've got the stuff."

Mauve enjoyed doing imitations for his guests. He was the son of a clergyman, but there was room for only one religion in his life: painting. While Jet passed around tea and cookies and cheese balls, he preached the sermon about the fishing bark of Peter. Had Peter received or inherited that bark? Had he bought it on the instalment plan? Had he, oh horrible thought, stolen it? The painters filled the room with their smoke and laughter, gulping down cheese balls and cups of tea with amazing rapidity.

"Mauve has changed," mused Vincent to himself.

He did not know that Mauve was undergoing the metamorphosis of the creative artist. He began a canvas lethargically, working almost without interest. Slowly his energy would pick up as ideas began to creep into his mind and become formulated. He would work a little longer, a little harder each day. As objects appeared clearly on the canvas, his demands upon himself became more exacting. His mind would flee from his family, from his friends and other interests. His appetite would desert him and he would lie awake nights thinking of things to be done. As his strength went down his excitement went up. Soon he would be living on nervous energy. His body would shrink on its ample frame and the sentimental eyes become lost in a hazy mist. The more he became fatigued, the more desperately he worked. The nervous passion which possessed him would rise higher and higher. In his mind he knew how long it would take him to finish ; he set his will to last until that very day. He was like a man ridden by a thousand demons ; he had years in which to complete the canvas, but something forced him to lacerate himself every hour of the twenty-four. In the end, he would be in such a towering passion and nervous excitement that a frightful scene ensued if anyone got in his way. He hurled himself at the canvas with every last ounce of his strength. No matter how long it took to finish, he always had will enough to the last drop of paint. Nothing could have killed him before he was completely through.

Once the canvas was delivered, he collapsed in a heap. He was weak, ill, delirious. It took Jet many days to nurse him back to health and sanity. His exhaustion was so complete that the very sight or smell of paint made him nauseated. Slowly, very slowly, his strength would return. In its wake would come his interest. He would begin to potter about the studio cleaning up things. He would walk in the fields, at first seeing nothing. In the end some scene would strike his eye. And so the cycle began all over again.

When Vincent had first come to The Hague, Mauve was just beginning the Scheveningen canvas. But now his pulse was rising day by day, and soon the mad, magnificent, most devastating of all deliriums would set in, that of artistic creation.

4

Christine knocked at Vincent's door a few nights later. She was dressed in a black petticoat and dark blue camisole, with a black cap over her hair. She had been standing at the washtub all day. Her mouth usually hung a little open when she was extremely fatigued ; the pock-marks seemed to be wider and deeper than he had remembered them.

"Hello, Vincent," she said. "Thought I'd come see where you lived."

"You're the first woman to call on me, Christine. I bid you welcome. May I take your shawl?"

She sat down by the fire and warmed herself. After a moment she looked about the room.

"This ain't bad," she said. " 'Cept that it's empty."

"I know. I haven't any money for furniture."

"Well, I guess it's all you need."

"I was just going to fix supper, Christine. Will you join me?"

"Why don't you call me Sien? Everyone does."

"All right, Sien."

"What was you having for supper?"

"Potatoes and tea."

"I made two francs today. I'll go buy a little beef."

"Here, I have money. My brother sent me some. How much do you want?"

"I guess fifty centimes is all we can eat."

She returned in a few moments with a paper of meat. Vincent took it from her and attempted to prepare dinner.

"Here, you sit down. You don't know nothing about cooking. I'm a woman."

As she leaned over the stove, the heat sent a warm glow to her cheek. She looked rather pretty. It was so natural and homelike to see her cutting potatoes into a pot, putting the meat in with them to stew and simmer. Vincent leaned a chair against the wall and watched her, a feeling of warmth in his heart. It was his home, and here was a woman preparing dinner for him with loving hands. How often he had dreamed of this picture with Kay as his companion. Sien glanced about at him. She saw the chair leaning against the wall at a perilous angle.

"Here, you damn fool," she said, "you sit up straight. Was you wanting to break your neck?"

Vincent grinned. Every woman with whom he had ever lived in the same house—his mother, sisters, aunts and cousins—every last one of them had said, "Vincent, sit up straight on that chair. You'll break your neck."

"All right, Sien," he said. "I'll be good."

As soon as her back was turned, he leaned the chair against the wall again and smoked his pipe contentedly. Sien put the dinner on the table. She had bought two rolls while she was out; when they finished eating the beef and potatoes, they mopped up the gravy with their bread.

"There," said Sien, "I bet you can't cook like that."

"No, Sien, when I cook, I can't tell whether I'm eating fish, fowl, or the devil."

Over their tea Sien smoked one of her black cigars. They chatted animatedly. Vincent felt more at home with her than he did with Mauve or De Bock. There was a certain fraternity between them that he did not pretend to understand. They spoke of simple things, without pretence or competition. When Vincent spoke, she listened; she was not eager for him to get through so that she could talk about herself. She had no ego that she wished to assert. Neither of them wished to impress the other. When Sien spoke of her own life, its hardships and miseries, Vincent had only to substitute a few words to make her stories describe perfectly his own. There was no challenge in their words, no affectation in their silences. It was the meeting of two souls unmasked, stripped of all class barrier artifice and distinction.

Vincent got up. "What are you going to do?" she asked.

"The dishes."

"Sit down. You don't know how to do dishes. I'm a woman."

He tipped his chair against the stove, filled his pipe, and puffed contentedly while she leaned over the basin. Her hands were good with the soap suds on them, the veins standing out, the intricate network of wrinkles speaking of the labour they had done. Vincent got pencil and paper and sketched them.

"It's nice here," she said when she finished the dishes. "If only we had some gin and bitters . . ."

They spent the evening sipping the bitters, while Vincent sketched Sien. She seemed content to rest quietly in a chair by the warm stove, hands in her lap. The glow of the heat and the pleasure of talking to someone who understood gave her vivacity and alertness.

"When do you finish with your washing?" he asked.

"Tomorrow. And a good thing. I couldn't stand much more."

"Have you been feeling badly?"

"No, but it's coming, it's coming. The goddam kid wiggles in me now and again."

"Then you'll begin posing for me next week?"

"Is this all I got to do, just sit?"

164

"That's all. Sometimes you'll have to stand or pose naked."

"That ain't so bad. You do all the work and I get paid."

She looked out the window. It was snowing.

"Wish I was home," she said. "It's cold and I ain't got nothing but my shawl. It's a long walk."

"Do you have to come back to this neighbourhood again tomorrow morning?"

"Six o'clock. It's still dark then."

"You can stay here if you like, Sien. I'd be glad to have company."

"Won't I be in your way?"

"Not a bit. It's a wide bed."

"Can two sleep there?"

"Easily."

"Then I'll stay."

"Good."

"It's nice of you to ask me, Vincent."

"It's nice of you to stay."

In the morning she fixed him coffee, made the bed, and swept out the studio. Then she left him to go to her tubs. The place seemed suddenly empty when she was gone.

5

Tersteeg looked in again that afternoon. His eyes were bright and his cheeks red from the walk in the glowing cold.

"How does it go, Vincent?"

"Very well, Mijnheer Tersteeg. It is good of you to come again."

"Perhaps you have something interesting to show me? That is what I came for."

"Yes, I have some new things. Won't you sit down?"

Tersteeg looked at the chair, reached for his kerchief to dust it off, and then decided it might not be good manners. He sat down. Vincent brought him three or four small water-colours. Tersteeg glanced at them all hurriedly, as though he were skimming a long letter, then went back to the first and studied it.

"You're coming along," he said after a time. "These aren't right yet, they're a bit crude, but you show progress. You should have something for me to buy very soon, Vincent."

"Yes, Mijnheer."

165

"You must think about earning your living, my boy. It is not right to live on another man's money."

Vincent took the water-colours and looked at them. He supposed they were crude, but like every other artist, he was unable to see the imperfections in his own work.

"I would like nothing better than to support myself, Mijnheer."

"Then you must work harder. You must speed things up. I would like to have you do some things soon that I can buy."

"Yes, Mijnheer."

"At any event, I am glad to see you happy and at work. Theo has asked me to keep an eye on you. Do some good work, Vincent ; I want to establish you in the Plaats."

"I try to make good things. But my hand doesn't always obey my will. However, Mauve complimented me on one of these."

"What did he say?"

"He said, 'It almost begins to look like a water-colour.' "

Tersteeg laughed, wrapped his wool scarf about his neck, said "Plug on, Vincent, plug on ; that is how great pictures are produced," and was gone.

Vincent had written to his Uncle Cor that he was established in The Hague, and had invited his uncle to visit him. Uncle Cor came often to The Hague to buy supplies and pictures for his art shop, which was the most important one in Amsterdam. One Sunday afternoon Vincent gave a party for some children with whom he had become acquainted. He had to keep them amused while he sketched, so he bought a bag of sweets and told them stories as he bent over his drawing board. When he heard a sharp knock on the door and a deep, booming voice, he knew that his uncle had arrived.

Cornelius Marinus Van Gogh was well known, successful and wealthy. For all that, there was a touch of melancholy about his wide, dark eyes. His mouth was a little less full than the other Van Gogh mouths. He had the family head; square across the wide, high brow, square across the strong jawbones, with a huge, rounded chin and a powerful nose.

Cornelius Marinus took in every last detail of the studio while giving the impression that he had not even glanced at it. He had probably seen the inside of more artists' studios than any man in Holland.

Vincent gave the children the rest of the sweets and sent them home.

"Will you have a cup of tea with me, Uncle Cor? It must be very cold out."

"Thank you, Vincent."

Vincent served him and marvelled at how unconcernedly his uncle balanced the cup on his knee while chatting lightly about news of the day.

"So you are going to be an artist, Vincent," he said. "It's about time we had one in the Van Gogh family. Hein and Vincent and I have been buying canvases from strangers for the past thirty years. Now we'll be able to keep a little of the money in the family!"

Vincent smiled. "I have a running start," he said, "with three uncles and a brother in the picture selling business. Will you have a bit of cheese and bread, Uncle Cor? Perhaps you're hungry?"

C.M. knew that the easiest way to insult a poor artist was to refuse his food. "Yes, thank you," he said. "I had an early breakfast."

Vincent put several slices of thick, black bread on a chipped plate and then took out some coarse cheese from a paper. C.M. made an effort to eat a little.

"Tersteeg tells me that Theo is sending you a hundred francs a month?"

"Yes."

"Theo is young, and he should save his money. You ought to be earning your own bread."

Vincent's gorge was still high from what Tersteeg had said on the subject only the day before. He answered quickly, without thinking.

"Earn bread, Uncle Cor? How do you mean that? Earn bread ... or deserve bread? Not to deserve one's bread, that is to say, to be unworthy of it, that certainly is a crime, for every honest man is worthy of his bread. But unluckily, not being able to earn it, though deserving it, that is a misfortune, and a great one."

He toyed with the black bread before him, rolling a piece of the inside into a round, hard pill.

"So, if you say to me, Uncle Cor, 'You are unworthy of your bread,' you insult me. But if you make the rather just remark that I do not earn it always, that certainly is so. But what is the use in making the remark? It certainly does not get me any further, if you say no more than that."

C.M. spoke no more about earning bread. They got along

pleasantly enough until, quite by chance, Vincent mentioned the name of De Groux in speaking about expression.

"But don't you know, Vincent," said C.M., "that in private life De Groux has no good reputation?"

Vincent could not sit there and hear that said of the brave Father De Groux. He knew it would be far better to "Yes" his uncle, but he never seemed able to find a "Yes" when he was with the Van Goghs.

"It has always seemed to me, Uncle Cor, that when an artist shows his work to the public he has the right to keep to himself the inward struggle of his own private life, which is directly and fatally connected with the peculiar difficulties involved in producing a work of art."

"Just the same," said C.M. sipping the tea for which Vincent had offered him no sugar, "the mere fact that a man works with a paint brush, instead of a plough or a salesbook, does not give him the right to live licentiously. I don't think we ought to buy the pictures of artists who don't behave properly."

"I think it even more improper for a critic to dig up a man's private life, when his work is beyond reproach. The work of an artist and his private life are like a woman in childbirth and her baby. You may look at the child, but you may not lift her chemise to see if it is blood-stained. That would be very indelicate."

C.M. had just put a small bit of bread and cheese into his mouth. He spat it out hastily into the cup of his hand, rose, and flung it into the stove.

"Well, well," he commented. "Well well well well!"

Vincent was afraid that C.M. was going to be angry, but luckily things took a turn for the better. Vincent brought out his portfolio of smaller sketches and studies. He placed a chair by the light for his uncle. C.M. did not say anything at first, but when he came to a little drawing of the Paddemoes as seen from the peat market, that Vincent had sketched at twelve o'clock one night while strolling about with Breitner, he stopped.

"This is rather good," he remarked. "Could you make me more of these views of the city?"

"Yes, I make them for a change sometimes when I am tired of working from the model. I have some more. Would you care to see them?"

He leaned over his uncle's shoulder and searched through

the uneven papers. "This is the Vleersteeg ... this the Geest. This one is the fish market."

"Will you make twelve of them for me?"

"Yes, but this is business, so we must set a price."

"Very well, how much do you ask?"

"I have fixed the price for a small drawing of this size, either in pencil or pen, at two-francs-fifty. Do you think that unreasonable?"

C.M. had to smile to himself. It was such a humble sum.

"No, but if they turn out well, I will ask you to make twelve of Amsterdam. Then I shall fix the price myself so that you will get a little more for them."

"Uncle Cor, this is my first order! I can't tell you how happy it makes me!"

"We all want to help you, Vincent. Just bring your work up to standard, and between us we'll buy everything you make." He took up his hat and gloves. "Give my compliments to Theo when you write."

Intoxicated with his success, Vincent snatched up his new water-colour and ran all the way to the Uileboomen. Jet answered the door. She seemed rather worried.

"I wouldn't go into the studio if I were you, Vincent. Anton is in a state."

"What's the trouble? Is he ill?"

Jet sighed. "The usual thing."

"Then I don't suppose he'll want to see me."

"You'd better wait until another time, Vincent. I'll tell him you were here. When he calms down a bit he'll come round to see you."

"You won't forget to tell him?"

"I won't forget."

Vincent waited many days, but Mauve did not come. In his place came Tersteeg, not once but twice. Each time the report was the same.

"Yes, yes, you have made a little progress, perhaps. But they are not right yet. I still could not sell them in the Plaats. I'm afraid you don't work hard enough or fast enough, Vincent."

"My dear, Mijnheer, I get up at five o'clock and work until eleven and twelve at night. The only time I stop is for a bite of food now and then."

Tersteeg shook his head uncomprehendingly. He looked at the water-colours again. "I don't understand it. The same element of roughness and crudeness that I saw the first time you came to the Plaats is still in your work. You ought to be getting over that by now. Hard work usually does it, if a man has any ability at all."

"Hard work!" said Vincent.

"Goodness knows I want to buy your things, Vincent. I want to see you begin earning your own living. I don't think it right that Theo should have to ... But I can't buy until your work is right, now can I? You're not looking for charity."

"No."

"You must hurry, that's all, you must hurry. You must begin to sell and make your own living."

When Tersteeg repeated this formula for the fourth time Vincent wondered if the man were playing some game on him. "You must earn your own living ... but I can't buy anything!" How in the devil was he going to earn his living if no one would buy?

He met Mauve on the street one day. Mauve was walking at a furious clip with his head down, going nowhere, shoving his right shoulder out in front of him as he walked. He almost seemed not to recognize Vincent.

"I have not seen you for a long time, Cousin Mauve."

"I've been busy." Mauve's voice was cool, indifferent.

"I know ; the new canvas. How is it coming?"

"Oh ..." He made a vague gesture.

"May I drop into your studio some time for a moment? I'm afraid I'm not making progress with my water-colours."

"Not now! I'm busy, I tell you. I can't be wasting my time."

"Won't you come in to see me some time when you're out for a walk? Just a few words from you would set me right."

"Perhaps, perhaps, but I'm busy now. I must be going!"

He darted forward, thrusting his body before him, nervously propelling himself down the street. Vincent stood staring after him.

What in the world had happened? Had he insulted his cousin? Had he in some way estranged him?

He was utterly amazed a few days later to have Weissenbruch walk into his studio. Weissenbruch never bothered with the younger painters, or for that matter the accepted ones, except to give their work a hearty damning now and then.

"Well, well," he said, looking about, "this certainly is a palace. You'll be doing portraits of the King and Queen here pretty soon."

"If you don't like it," growled Vincent, "you can get out."

"Why don't you give up painting, Van Gogh? It's a dog's life."

"You seem to thrive under it."

"Yes, but I'm successful. You'll never be."

"Perhaps not. But I'll paint far better pictures than you ever will."

Weissenbruch laughed. "You won't but you'll probably come closer to it than anyone in The Hague. If your work is anything like your personality . . ."

"Why didn't you say so?" demanded Vincent, taking out his portfolio. "Want to sit down?"

"I can't see when I'm sitting."

He pushed the water-colours aside with a "This is not your medium ; water-colours are too insipid for the things you've got to say," and concentrated on the pencil sketches of the Borains, the Brabantines, and the old people Vincent had drawn since coming to The Hague. He chuckled to himself gaily as he gazed at one figure after another. Vincent prepared for a stiff volley of abuse.

"You draw confoundedly well, Vincent," said Weissenbruch, his sharp eyes twinkling. "I could work from these drawings myself!"

Vincent had set himself to catch a heavy weight ; Weissenbruch's words were so light they almost broke his back. He sat down abruptly.

"I thought you were called the 'merciless sword.' "

"So I am. If I saw no good in your studies, I would tell you so."

"Tersteeg has scolded me about them. He says they are too rough and crude."

"Nonsense! That's where their strength lies."

"I want to go on with those pen sketches, but Tersteeg says I must learn to see things as water-colours."

"So they can sell, eh? No, my boy, if you see things as pen drawings, you must put them down as pen drawings. And above all, never listen to anybody—not even me. Go your own way."

"It looks like I'll have to."

'When Mauve said you were a born painter, Tersteeg said no, and then Mauve took your part against him. I was there. If it happens again, I will take your part also, now that I have seen your work."

"Mauve said I was a born painter?"

171

"Don't let that turn your head. You'll be lucky if you die one."

"Then why has he been so cool to me?"

"He treats everyone the same, Vincent, when he's finishing a picture. Don't let it worry you; when the Scheveningen canvas is done he'll come round. In the meanwhile you may drop in at my studio if you want any help."

"May I ask you one question, Weissenbruch?"

"Yes."

"Did Mauve send you here?"

"Yes."

"Why did he do that?"

"He wanted to hear my opinion about your work."

"But why should he want that? If he thinks I'm a born ..."

"I don't know. Perhaps Tersteeg put a doubt in his mind about you."

6

If Tersteeg was losing faith in him and Mauve was growing cooler every day, Christine was taking their place, and bringing into his life the simple companionship for which he longed. She came to the studio early every morning, and brought with her a sewing basket so that her hands might keep company with his. Her voice was rough and her choice of words unfortunate, but she spoke quietly, and Vincent found it easy not to hear her when he wanted to concentrate. For the most part, she was content to sit quietly by the stove, looking out the window or sewing little things for the new baby. She was a clumsy model and learned slowly, but she was eager to please. She soon fell into the habit of preparing his dinner before she went home.

"You mustn't bother about that, Sien," he told her.

"It ain't no bother. I can do it better than you."

"Then of course you'll join me?"

"Sure. Mother's taking care of the kids. I like to stay here."

Vincent gave her a franc every day. He knew it was more than he could afford, but he liked her company; the thought that he was saving her from the tubs pleased him. Sometimes, if he had to go out during the afternoon, he would sketch her until late at night, and then she would not bother to go home at all. He enjoyed waking to the smell of fresh coffee and the sight of a friendly woman hovering over the stove. It was the first time he had ever had a *ménage;* he found it very comfortable.

"Sometimes Christine would stay over for no reason at all. "I think I'll sleep here tonight, Vincent," she would say. "Can I?"

"Of course, Sien. Stay as often as you like. You know I'm glad to have you."

Although he never asked her to do anything, she acquired the habit of washing his linen, mending his clothes, and doing his little marketing.

"You don't know how to take care of yourselves, you men," she said. "You need a woman around. And I'm sure they cheat you at the market."

She was by no means a good housekeeper; the many years of sloth in her mother's house had destroyed most of the will to cleanliness and order. She took care of things sporadically, in sudden bursts of energy and determination. It was the first time she was keeping house for anyone she liked, and she enjoyed doing things ... when she remembered them. Vincent was delighted to find that she wanted to do anything at all; he never even thought of reproving her. Now that she was no longer dead tired day and night, her voice lost some of its roughness; the vile words dropped out of her vocabulary one by one. She had learned to exercise very little control over her emotions, and when something displeased her, she would fly into a passionate rage, dropping back into her rough voice and using obscene words that Vincent had not heard since he was a young boy at school.

At such moments he saw Christine as a caricature of himself; he sat by quietly until the storm subsided. Christine was equally tolerant. When his drawing went all wrong, or she forgot everything he had taught her and posed awkwardly, he would burst into a fit of rage that fairly shook the walls. She let him speak his piece; in a very few moments calm was restored. Fortunately they never became angry at identical moments.

After he had sketched her often enough to become familiar with the lines of her body, he decided to do a real study. It was a sentence from Michelet that set him on the track: *Comment se fait-il qu'il y ait sur la terre une femme seule désespérée?* He posed Christine naked on a low block of wood near the stove. He turned the block of wood into a tree stump, put in a little vegetation, and transposed the scene to the out-of-doors.

173

Then he drew Christine, gnarled hands on her knees, the face buried in the scraggy arms, the thin hair covering the spine a short way down, the bulbous breasts drooping to meet the lean shanks, the flat feet insecurely on the ground. He called it *Sorrow*. It was the picture of a woman from whom had been squeezed all the juice of life. Under it he wrote the line from Michelet.

The study took a week and exhausted his supply of money; there were still ten days to go until the first of March. There was enough black bread in the house to last for two or three days. He would have to stop working from the model altogether and that would set him back some more.

"Sien," he said, "I'm afraid I can't have you any more until after the first of the month."

"What's the matter?"

"I have no more money."

"You mean for me?"

"Yes."

"I ain't got nothing else to do. I'll come anyway."

"But you must have money, Sien."

"I can get some."

"You can't do any washing, if you're here all day."

". . . well . . . don't worry . . . I'll get some."

He let her come for three more days, until his bread ran out. It was still a week to the first. He told Sien that he was going to Amsterdam to visit his uncle and that he would call at her house when he got back. He did some copying in his studio for three days on water without feeling much pain. On the third afternoon he went to De Bock's, hoping to be served tea and cake.

"Hello, old fellow," said De Bock, standing at his easel, "make yourself comfortable. I'm going to work straight through until my dinner engagement. There are some magazines over on the table. Just dig in."

But not a word about tea.

He knew Mauve would not see him, and he was ashamed to beg from Jet. He would rather have died of starvation than ask Tersteeg for anything after the latter had spoken against him to Mauve. No matter how desperate he became, it never occurred to him that he might earn a few francs at some craft other than his own. His old foe the fever came up, his knees developed rickets and he stayed in bed. Though he knew it was impossible, he kept hoping for the miracle that would send Theo's hundred francs a few days early. Theo did not get paid until the first.

Christine walked in the afternoon of the fifth day without knocking. Vincent was asleep. She stood over him, looking at the furrowed lines in his face, the paleness of the skin under his red beard, the parchment roughness of his lips. She placed a hand lightly on his forehead and felt the fever. She searched the shelf on which the supplies were usually kept. She saw that there was not a crumb of dry, black bread or a lone bean of coffee. She went out.

About an hour later Vincent began having dreams of his mother's kitchen in Etten and the beans she used to prepare for him. He awakened to find Christine mixing things in pots over the stove.

"Sien," he said.

She went over to the bed and put her cool hand on his cheek ; the red beard was on fire. "Don't be proud no more," she said. "And don't tell no more lies. If we're poor, it ain't our fault. We got to help each other. Didn't you help me the first night we met down the wine cellar?"

"Sien," he said.

"Now you lay there. I went home and got some potatoes and string beans. They're all ready."

She mashed the potatoes on the plate, put some green beans alongside, sat on his bed and fed him. "Why did you give me your money every day if you didn't have enough? It ain't no good if you go hungry."

He could have stood the privation until Theo's money arrived, even if it had been weeks. It was always the unexpected piece of kindness that broke his back. He decided to see Tersteeg. Christine washed his shirt, but there was no iron to smooth it with. The next morning she gave him a little breakfast of bread and coffee. He set out to walk to the Plaats. One heel was off his muddy boots, his trousers were patched and dirty. Theo's coat was many sizes too small. He had an old necktie askew at the left side of his neck. On his head was one of the outlandish caps that he had a perfect genius for picking up, no one knew where.

He walked along the Ryn railroad tracks, skirted the edge of the woods and the station where the steam cars left for Scheveningen, and made for town. The feeble sun made him sensitive to his own anaemia. At the Plein he caught sight of himself in the window glass of a shop. In one of his rare moments of clarity he saw himself as the people of The Hague saw him: a dirty, unkempt tramp, belonging nowhere, wanted by no one, ill, weak, uncouth and *déclassé*.

The Plaats opened on a broad triangle to meet the Hofvijver alongside of the castle. Only the richest shops could afford to keep establishments there. Vincent was afraid to venture into the sacred triangle. He had never before realized how many millions of miles of caste he had put between himself and the Plaats.

The clerks in Goupils were dusting. They stared at him with unabashed curiosity. This man's family controlled the art world of Europe. Why did he go about so foully?

Tersteeg was at his desk in the upstairs office. He was opening mail with a jade handled paper knife. He noticed Vincent's small, circular ears that came below the line of his eyebrows, the oval of his face that tapered down through the jaws and then flattened out at the square chin, the head that was going smooth of hair above the left eye, the green-blue eyes that stared through him so probingly and yet without comment, the full, red mouth made redder by the beard and moustache in which it was set. He could never make up his mind whether he thought Vincent's face and head ugly or beautiful.

"You're the first customer in the shop this morning, Vincent," he said. "What can I do for you?"

Vincent explained his predicament.

"What have you done with your allowance?"

"I've spent it."

"If you have been improvident, you can't expect me to encourage you. There are thirty days to each month: you should not spend more than the proper share each day."

"I have not been improvident. Most of the money has gone for models."

"Then you should not hire them. You can work more cheaply by yourself."

"To work without models is the ruin of a painter of the figure."

"Don't paint figures. Do cows and sheep. You don't have to pay them."

"I can't draw cows and sheep, Mijnheer, if I don't feel cows and sheep."

"You ought not to be drawing people, anyway; you can't sell those sketches. You ought to be doing water-colours and nothing else."

"Water-colour is not my medium."

"I think your drawing is a kind of narcotic which you take in order not to feel the pain it costs you not to be able to make water-colours."

There was a silence. Vincent could think of no possible answer to this.

"De Bock doesn't use models, and he's wealthy. Yet I think you will agree with me that his canvases are splendid; the prices are going up steadily. I have been waiting for you to get some of his charm into your work. But somehow it doesn't come. I am really disappointed, Vincent; your work remains uncouth and amateurish. Of one thing I am sure, you are no artist."

Vincent's cutting hunger of the past five days suddenly severed the sinews in his knees. he sat down weakly on one of the hand carved Italian chairs. His voice was lost somewhere in his empty bowels, and he could not find it.

"Why do you say that to me, Mijnheer?" he asked, after a pause.

Tersteeg took out a spotless handkerchief, wiped his nose, the corners of his mouth, and his chin beard. "Because I owe it to both you and your family. You ought to know the truth. There is still time for you to save yourself, Vincent, if you act quickly. You are not cut out to be an artist; you ought to find your right niche in life. I never make a mistake about painters."

"I know," said Vincent.

"One great objection for me is that you started too late. If you had begun as a boy, you might have developed some quality in your work by now. But you are thirty, Vincent, and you ought to be successful. I was at your age. How can you ever hope to succeed if you have no talent? And worse yet, how can you justify yourself in taking charity from Theo?"

"Mauve once said to me, 'Vincent, when you draw you are a painter.' "

"Mauve is your cousin; he was being kind to you. I am your friend, and believe me, my kindness is of the better sort. Give it up before you find that your whole life has slipped out from under you. Some day, when you have found your real work and are successful, you will come back to thank me."

"Mijnheer Tersteeg, I have not had a centime in my pocket for a piece of bread in five days. But I would not ask you for money if it were only for myself. I have a model, a poor, sick woman. I have not been able to pay her the money I owe. She needs it. I beg you to lend me ten guilders until the money arrives from Theo. I will pay it back."

Tersteeg rose and stared out the window at the swans in the pond, all that was left of the original court water works. He wondered why Vincent had come to The Hague to settle, when his uncles owned art shops in Amsterdam, Rotterdam, Brussels, and Paris.

"You think it would be a favour if I lent you ten guilders," he said without turning about, his hands clasped behind his Prince Albert coat. "But I'm not sure it wouldn't be a greater favour to refuse you."

Vincent knew how Sien had earned the money for those potatoes and string beans. He could not let her go on supporting him.

"Mijnheer Tersteeg, no doubt you are right. I am no artist and I have no ability. It would be very unwise for you to encourage me with money. I must begin earning my own living immediately and find my niche in life. But for the sake of our old friendship I ask you to lend me ten guilders."

Tersteeg took a wallet from the inside of his Prince Albert, searched for a ten guilder note, and handed it to Vincent without a word.

"Thank you," said Vincent. "You are very kind."

As he walked home along the well kept streets with the neat little brick houses speaking to him eloquently of security, comfort, and peace, he murmured to himself, "One cannot always be friends; one must quarrel sometimes. But for six months I will not go to see Tersteeg again, or speak to him, or show him my work."

He dropped in at De Bock's to find out just what this salable thing was, this charm that De Bock had, but he had not. De Bock was sitting with his feet up on a chair, reading an English novel.

"Hello," he said, "I'm in the doldrums. Can't draw a line. Pull up a chair and amuse me. Is it too early in the morning for a cigar? Have you heard any good stories lately?"

"Let me see some of your canvases again, will you, De Bock? I want to find out why your work sells and mine doesn't."

178

"Talent, old fellow, talent," said De Bock, getting up lazily. "It's a gift. Either you have it or you haven't. I couldn't tell you what it is myself, and I paint the blasted things."

He brought in half a dozen canvases still on their frames, and chatted lightly about them while Vincent sat there, poking holes through the thin paint and thin sentiment with burning eyes.

"Mine are better," he said to himself. "Mine are truer, deeper. I say more with a carpenter's pencil than he says with a whole paint box. What he expresses is obvious. When he gets all through he has said nothing. Why do they give him praise and money and refuse me the price of black bread and coffee?"

When he made his escape, Vincent murmured to himself, "There is a consumptive atmosphere in that house. There is something blasé and insincere about De Bock that oppresses me. Millet was right: *'J'aimerais mieux ne rien dire que de me' exprimer faiblement.'*

"De Bock can keep his charm and his money. I'll take my life of reality and hardship. That is not the road on which one perishes."

He found Christine mopping the wooden floor of the studio with a wet rag. Her hair was tied up in a black kerchief and a faint dew of perspiration glistened in the pock holes of her face.

"Did you get the money?" she asked, looking up from the floor.

"Yes. Ten francs."

"Ain't it wonderful to have rich friends?"

"Yes. Here are the six francs I owe you."

Sien got up and wiped her face on the black apron.

"You can't give me nothing now," she said. "Not till your brother sends that money. Four francs won't help you much."

"I can get along. Sien. You need this money."

"So do you. Tell you what we'll do. I'll stay here till you get a letter from your brother. We'll eat out of the ten francs like it belonged to both of us. I can make it last longer than you."

"What about the posing? I won't be able to pay you anything for that."

"You'll give me my bed and board. Ain't that enough? I'm glad enough to stay here where it's warm and I don't got to go to work and make myself sick."

Vincent took her in his arms and smoothed back the thin, coarse hair from her forehead.

"Sien, sometimes you almost perform a miracle. You almost make me believe there is a God!"

7

About a week later he went to call on Mauve. His cousin admitted him to the studio but threw a cloth over his Scheveningen canvas hastily before Vincent could see it.

"What is it you want?" he asked, as though he did not know.

"I've brought a few water-colours. I thought you might be able to spare a little time."

Mauve was cleaning a bunch of brushes with nervous, preoccupied movements. He had not been into his bedroom for three days. The broken snatches of sleep he had managed on the studio couch had not refreshed him.

"I'm not always in a mood to show you things, Vincent. Sometimes I am too tired and then you must for goodness' sake await a better moment."

"I'm sorry, Cousin Mauve," said Vincent, going to the door. "I didn't mean to disturb you. Perhaps I may drop in tomorrow evening?"

Mauve had taken the cloth off his easel and did not even hear him.

When Vincent returned the following evening, he found Weissenbruch there. Mauve was verging on hysterical exhaustion. He seized upon Vincent's entrance to amuse himself and his friend.

"Weissenbruch," he cried, "this is how he looks."

He went off into one of his clever impersonations, screwing up his face in rough lines and sticking his chin forward eagerly to look like Vincent. It was a good caricature. He walked over to Weissenbruch, peered up at him through half shut eyes and said, "This is the way he speaks." He went off into a nervous sputtering of words in the rough voice that often came out of Vincent. Weissenbruch howled.

"Oh, perfect, perfect," he cried. "This is how others see you, Van Gogh. Did you know you were such a beautiful animal? Mauve, stick your chin out that way again and scratch your beard. It's really killing."

Vincent was stunned. He shrank into a corner. A voice came

180

out of him that he did not recognize as his own. "If you had spent rainy nights on the streets of London, or cold nights in the open of the Borinage, hungry, homeless, feverish, you would also have ugly lines in your face, and a husky voice!"

After a few moments, Weissenbruch left. As soon as he was gone from the room, Mauve stumbled to a chair. The reaction from his little debauch made him quite weak. Vincent stood perfectly still in the corner; at last Mauve noticed him.

"Oh, are you still here?" he said.

"Cousin Mauve," said Vincent impetuously, screwing up his face in the manner that Mauve had just caricatured, "what has happened between us? Only tell me what I have done. Why do you treat me this way?"

Mauve got up wearily and pushed the swash of hair straight upward.

"I do not approve of you, Vincent. You ought to be earning your own living. And you ought not go about disgracing the Van Gogh name by begging money from everyone."

Vincent thought a moment and then said, "Has Tersteeg been to see you?"

"No."

"Then you don't care to teach me any more?"

"No."

"Very well, let us shake hands and not feel any bitterness or animosity toward each other. Nothing could ever alter my feeling of gratitude and obligation to you."

Mauve did not answer for a long time. Then he said, "Do not take it to heart, Vincent. I am tired and ill. I will help you all I can. Have you some sketches with you?"

"Yes. But this is hardly the time . . ."

"Show them to me."

He studied them with red eyes and remarked, "Your drawing is wrong. Dead wrong. I wonder that I never saw it before."

"You once told me that when I drew, I was a painter."

"I mistook crudity for strength. If you really want to learn, you will have to begin all over again at the beginning. There are some plaster casts over in the corner by the coal bin. You can work on them now if you like."

Vincent walked to the corner in a daze. He sat down before a white plaster foot. For a long time he was unable to think or move. He drew some sketching paper from his pocket. He

181

could not draw a single line. He turned about and looked at Mauve standing before his easel.

"How is it coming, Cousin Mauve?"

Mauve flung himself on the little divan, his bloodshot eyes closing instantly. "Tersteeg said today that it's the best thing I've done."

After a few moments, Vincent remarked aloud, "Then it was Tersteeg!"

Mauve was snoring lightly and did not hear him.

After a time the pain numbed a little. He began sketching the plaster foot. When his cousin awoke a few hours later, Vincent had seven complete drawings. Mauve jumped up like a cat, just as though he had never been asleep, and darted to Vincent's side.

"Let me see," he said. "Let me see."

He looked at the seven sketches and kept repeating, "No! No! No!"

He tore them all up and flung the pieces on the floor. "The same crudity the same amateurishness! Can't you draw that cast the way it looks? Are you unable to make a positive statement about a line? Can't you make an exact duplicate for once in your life?"

"You sound like a teacher at a drawing academy, Cousin Mauve."

"If you had gone to more academies, you might know how to draw by now. Do that foot over again. And see if you can make it a foot!"

He went through the garden into the kitchen to get something to eat, and returned to work on his canvas by lamplight. The hours of the night went by. Vincent drew foot after foot. The more he drew, the more he detested the poisonous piece of plaster sitting before him. When dawn sneaked gloomily in the north window, he had a great number of copies before him. He rose, cramped and sick at heart. Once again Mauve looked at his sketches and crumpled them in his hand.

"They're no good," he said, "no good at all. You violate every elemental rule of drawing. Here, go home and take this foot with you. Draw it over and over and over again. And don't come back until you get it right!"

"I'll be damned if I will!" shouted Vincent.

He flung the foot into the coal bin, shattering it to a thousand pieces. "Do not speak to me again about plaster, for

182

I cannot stand it. I will draw from casts only when there are no more hands and feet of living people to draw from."

"If that's the way you feel about it," said Mauve icily.

"Cousin Mauve, I will not allow myself to be governed by a cold system, yours or anyone else's. I've got to express things according to my own temperament and character. I must draw things the way I see them, not the way you see them!"

"I care to have nothing more to do with you," said Mauve in the tone of a doctor speaking to a corpse.

When Vincent awoke at noon, he found Christine in the studio with her eldest son, Herman. He was a pale faced child of ten with fish-green, frightened eyes and a negligible chin. Christine had given him a piece of paper and pencil to keep him quiet. He had not been taught to read or write. He came to Vincent shyly, for he was wary of strangers. Vincent showed him how to hold the pencil and draw a cow. He was delighted and soon became friendly. Christine put out a little bread and cheese, and the three of them lunched at the table.

Vincent thought of Kay and beautiful little Jan. A lump arose in his throat.

"I ain't feeling so good today, so you can draw Herman instead."

"What's the matter, Sien?"

"I dunno. My insides is all twisted."

"Have you felt like this with all the other children?"

"I been sick, but not like this. This is worse."

"You must see a doctor."

"It ain't no use seeing the doctor at the free ward. He only gives me medicine. Medicine don't do no good."

"You ought to go to the state hospital at Leyden."

". . . I guess I ought."

"It's only a short ride on the train. I'll take you there tomorrow morning. People go from all over Holland to that hospital."

"They say it's good."

Christine stayed in bed all day. Vincent sketched the boy. At dinner time he walked Herman home to Christine's mother and left him. Early in the morning they took the train to Leyden.

"Of course you've been feeling sick," said the doctor after he had examined Christine and asked her innumerable questions. "The child is not in position."

"Can anything be done, doctor?" asked Vincent.

183

"Oh, yes, we can operate."

"Would that be serious?"

"Not at this time. The child would simply have to be turned with the forceps. However, that takes a little money. Not for the operation, but for the hospital expenses." He turned to Christine. "Have you anything saved up?"

"Not a franc."

The doctor almost allowed himself a sigh. "That's usually the way," he said.

"How much would it cost, doctor?" said Vincent.

"Not more than fifty francs."

"And if she doesn't have the operation?"

"There's not a chance in the world of her pulling through."

Vincent thought for a moment. The twelve water-colours for his Uncle Cor were almost done; that would be thirty francs. He would take the other twenty francs off Theo's April allowance.

"I'll take care of the money, doctor," he said.

"Good. Bring her back on Saturday morning and I'll operate myself. Now just one thing more; I don't know what the relationship is between you two and I don't care to be told. That's not part of the doctor's business. But I think you ought to be informed that if this little lady ever goes back to walking the streets, she will be dead within six months."

"She'll never return to that life, doctor. I give you my word."

"Splendid. Then I'll see you on Saturday morning."

A few days later Tersteeg came in. "I see you are still at it," he said.

"Yes, I am at work."

"I received the ten francs you sent back in the mail. You might at least have come in to thank me for the loan personally."

"It was a long walk, Mijnheer, and the weather was bad."

"The walk was not too long when you wanted the money, eh?"

Vincent did not answer.

"It is just such lack of manners, Vincent, that turns me against you. It is why I have no faith in you and cannot buy your work."

Vincent sat himself on the edge of the table and prepared for another struggle. "I should think that your buying would be a thing quite apart from personal disputes and difference," he said. "I should think it would depend not on me but on my work. It is not exactly fair to let personal antipathy influence your judgement."

"Certainly not. If you could only make something salable, with some charm in it, I would be only too glad to sell it in the Plaats."

"Mijnheer Tersteeg, work on which one has plodded hard and into which one has put some character and sentiment, is neither unattractive nor unsalable, I think it is perhaps better for my work not to try to please everyone at first."

Tersteeg sat down without unbuttoning his topcoat or taking off his gloves. He sat with both hands resting on the knob of his cane.

"You know, Vincent, I sometimes suspect that you prefer not to sell ; that you would much rather live off someone else."

"I would be very happy to sell a drawing, but I am happier still when a real artist like Weissenbruch says about a piece of work which you call unsalable, 'That is true to nature ; I could work from that myself.' Although money is of great value to me, especially now, the principal thing is for me to make something serious."

"That might apply to a rich man like De Bock, but it certainly does not apply to you."

"The fundamentals of painting, my dear Mijnheer, have very little to do with a man's income."

Tersteeg put his stick across his knees and leaned back in his chair. "Your parents have written to me, Vincent, and asked me to do what I can to help you. Very well. If I cannot in full conscience buy your drawings I can at least give you a little practical advice. You are ruining yourself by going about in those unspeakable rags. You must buy yourself some new clothes and try to keep up appearances. You forget that you are a Van Gogh. Again, you should try to associate with the better people of The Hague, and not always go about with working people and the lower classes. You somehow have a penchant for the sordid and ugly ; you have been seen in the most questionable of places and with the most questionable of companions. How can you ever hope to arrive at success if you behave that way?"

Vincent got off the corner of the table and stood over Tersteeg. If there was any chance to win back the man's friendship, this was the time and place. He searched about within himself to find a soft and sympathetic voice.

185

"Mijnheer, it is good of you to try to help me, and I will answer as sincerely and truthfully as I know how. How can I dress better when I have not a single franc to spare for clothes, and no way of earning one?

"To stroll on wharves, and in alleys and markets, in waiting rooms and even saloons, that is not a pleasant pastime, *except for an artist*! As such, one would rather be in the dirtiest place, where there is something to draw, than at a tea party with charming ladies. The searching for subjects, the living among working people, the drawing from nature on the very spot is a rough work, even a dirty work at times. The manners and dress of a salesman are not suitable for me, or for anyone else who does not have to talk with fine ladies and rich gentlemen to sell them expensive things and make money.

"My place is drawing diggers in a hole on the Geest, as I have been doing all day. There, my ugly face and shabby coat perfectly harmonize with the surroundings, and I am myself and work with pleasure. When I wear a fine coat, the working people I want to sketch are afraid of me and distrust me. The purpose of my drawing is to make people see things worth observing and which not everyone knows. If I sometimes have to sacrifice social manners to get my work done, am I not justified? Do I lower myself by living with the people I draw? Do I lower myself when I go into the houses of labourers and poor people, and when I receive them in my studio? I think my profession requires it. Is that what you call ruining myself?"

"You are very headstrong, Vincent, and will not listen to older men who can help you. You failed before, and you will fail again. It will be the same story all over."

"I have a draftsman's fist, Mijnheer Tersteeg, and I cannot stop drawing no matter how much you advise me! I ask you, since the day I began to draw, have I ever doubted or hesitated or wavered? I think you know quite well that I pushed onward, and that little by little I am growing stronger in the battle."

"Perhaps. But you are battling for a lost cause."

He rose, buttoned the glove on his wrist, and placed the high silk hat on his head. "Mauve and I will take care that you do not receive any more money from Theo. That is the only way to bring you around to your senses."

Vincent felt something crash in his breast. If they attacked him from the side of Theo, he was lost.

"My God!" he cried. "Why should you do this to me? What have I done to you that you should want to destroy me? Is it honest to kill a man just because he differs from your opinions? Can't you let me go my own way? I promise never to bother you again. My brother is the only soul I have left in the world. How can you take him from me?"

"It is for your own good, Vincent," said Tersteeg, and went out.

Vincent grabbed up his money purse and ran all the way downtown to buy a plaster foot. Jet answered the doorbell at the Uileboomen. She was surprised to see him.

"Anton isn't at home," she said. "He's frightfully angry at you. He said he doesn't ever want to see you again. Oh, Vincent, I'm so unhappy that this has happened!"

Vincent put the plaster foot in her hand. "Please give this to Anton," he said, "and tell him that I am deeply sorry."

He turned away and was about to go down the steps when Jet put a sympathetic hand on his shoulder.

"The Scheveningen canvas is finished. Would you care to see it?"

He stood in silence before Mauve's painting, a large picture of a fishing smack being drawn up on the beach by horses. He knew that he was looking at a masterpiece. The horses were nags, poor, ill-treated old nags, black, white and brown ; they were standing there, patient and submissive, willing, resigned and quiet. They still had to draw the heavy boat up the last bit of the way ; the job was almost finished. They were panting, covered with sweat, but they did not complain. They had got over that long ago, years and years ago. They were resigned to live and work somewhat longer, but if tomorrow they had to go to the skinner, well, be it so, they were ready.

Vincent found a deep, practical philosophy in the picture. It said to him, *"Savoir souffrir sans se plaindre, ça c'est la seule chose partique, c'est la grande science, la leçon à apprendre, la solution du problème de la vie."*

He walked away from the house, refreshed and ironically amused that the man who struck him the very worst of all blows should be the one to teach him how to bear it with resignation.

8

Christine's operation was successful, but it had to be paid for. Vincent sent off the twelve water-colours to his Uncle Cor and waited for the thirty francs payment. He waited many, many days; Uncle Cor sent the money at his leisure. Since the doctor at Leyden was the same one who was going to deliver Christine, they wished to keep in his good graces. Vincent sent off his last twenty francs many days before the first. The same old story began all over again. First coffee and black bread, then just black bread, then plain water, then fever, exhaustion, and delirium. Christine was eating at home, But there was nothing left over to bring to Vincent. When he reached the end of his rope, he crawled out of bed and floated somehow or other through a burning fog to Weissenbruch's studio.

Weissenbruch had plenty of money but he believed in living austerely. His atelier was four flights up, with a huge skylight on the north. There was nothing in the workshop to distract the man; no books, no magazines, no sofa or comfortable chair, no sketches on the walls, no window to look out of, nothing but the bare implements of his trade. There was not even an extra stool for a guest to sit down; that kept people away.

"Oh, it's you, is it?" he growled, without putting down his brush. He did not mind interrupting people in their own studios, but he was about as hospitable as a trapped lion when anyone bothered him.

Vincent explained what he had come for.

"Oh, no, my boy!" exclaimed Weissenbruch. "You've come to the wrong person, the very last man in the world. I wouldn't lend you a ten centime piece."

"Can't you spare the money?"

"Certainly I can spare it! Do you think I'm a goddam amateur like you and can't sell anything? I've got more money in the bank right now than I can spend in three lifetimes."

"Then why won't you lend me twenty-five francs? I'm desperate! I haven't even a crumb of stale bread in the house."

Weissenbruch rubbed his hands in glee. "Fine! Fine! That's exactly what you need! That's wonderful for you. You may be a painter yet."

Vincent leaned against the bare wall; he did not have the strength to stand up without support. "What is there so wonderful about going hungry?"

"It's the best thing in the world for you, Van Gogh. It will make you suffer."

"Why are you so interested in seeing me suffer?"

Weissenbruch sat on the lone stool, crossed his legs, and pointed a red-tipped brush at Vincent's jaw.

"Because it will make a real artist of you. The more you suffer, the more grateful you ought to be.That's the stuff out of which first-rate painters are made. An empty stomach is better than a full one, Van Gogh, and a broken heart is better than happiness. never forget that!"

"That's a lot of rot, Weissenbruch, and you know it."

Weissenbruch made little stabs in Vincent's direction with his brush. "The man who has never been miserable has nothing to paint about, Van Gogh. Happiness is bovine; it's only good for cows and tradesmen. Artists thrive on pain; if you're hungry, discouraged and wretched, be grateful. God is being good to you!"

"Poverty destroys."

"Yes, it destroys the weak. But not the strong! If poverty can destroy you, then you're a weakling and ought to go down."

"And you wouldn't raise a finger to help me?"

"Not even if I thought you the greatest painter of all time. If hunger and pain can kill a man, then he's not worth saving. The only artists who belong on this earth are the men whom neither God nor the devil can kill until they've said everything they want to say."

"But I've gone hungry for years, Weissenbruch. I've gone without a roof over my head, walking in the rain and snow with hardly anything on, ill and feverish and abandoned. I have nothing more to learn from that sort of thing."

"You haven't scratched the surface of suffering yet. You're just a beginner. I tell you, pain is the only infinite thing in this world. Now run on home and pick up your pencil. The hungrier and more miserable you get, the better you will work."

"And the quicker I'll have my drawings rejected."

Weissenbruch laughed heartily. "Of course they'll be rejected! They ought to be. That's good for you, too. It will make you even more miserable. Then your next canvas will be better than the one before. If you starve and suffer and have your work abused and neglected for a sufficient number of years, you may eventually—notice I say you may, not you will—you may eventually turn out one painting that will be fit to hang alongside of Jan Steen or ..."

"... or Weissenbruch!"

"Just so. Or Weissenbruch. If I gave you any money now I would be robbing you of your chances for immortality."

"To hell with immortality! I want to draw here and now. And I can't do that on an empty stomach."

"Nonsense, my boy. Everything of value that has been painted has been done on an empty stomach. When your intestines are full, you create at the wrong end."

"It doesn't seem to me that I've heard you suffering so much."

"I have creative imagination. I can understand pain without going through it."

"You old fraud!"

"Not at all. If I had seen that my work was insipid, like De Bock's, I would have thrown my money away and lived like a tramp. It just so happens that I can create the perfect illusion of pain without a perfect memory of it. That's why I'm a great artist."

"That's why you're a great humbug. Come along, Weissenbruch, be a good fellow and lend me twenty-five francs."

"Not even twenty-five centimes! I tell you, I'm sincere. I think too highly of you to weaken your fabric by lending you money. You will do brilliant work some day, Vincent, providing you carve out your own destiny; the plaster foot in Mauve's dustbin convinced me of that. Now run along, and stop at the soup kitchen for a bowl of free broth."

Vincent stared at Weissenbruch for a moment, turned and opened the door.

"Wait a minute!"

"You don't mean to tell me you're going to be a coward and weaken?" asked Vincent harshly.

"Look here, Van Gogh, I'm no miser; I'm acting on principle. If I thought you were a fool, I'd give you twenty-five francs to get rid of you. But I respect you as a fellow craftsman. I'm going to give you something you couldn't buy for all the money in the world. And there's not another man in The Hague, except Mauve, that I'd give it to. Come over here. Adjust that curtain on the skylight. That's better. Have a look at this study. Here's how I'm going to work out the design and apportion my material. For Christ's sake, how do you expect to see it if you stand in the light?"

An hour later Vincent left, exhilarated. He had learned more in that short time than he could have in a year at art school. He walked some distance before he remembered that he was hungry, feverish, and ill, and that he had not a centime in the world.

9

A few days later he encountered Mauve in the dunes. If he had any hopes of a reconciliation, he was disappointed.

"Cousin Mauve, I want to beg your pardon for what happened in your studio. It was stupid of me. Can't you see your way clear to forgive me? Won't you come and see my work some time and talk things over?"

Mauve refused point blank. "I will certainly not come to see you, that is all over."

"Have you lost faith in me so completely?"

"Yes. You have a vicious character."

"If you will tell me what I have done that is vicious, I will try to mend my ways."

"I am no longer interested in what you do."

"I have done nothing but eat and sleep and work as an artist. Is that vicious?"

"Do you call yourself an artist?"

"Yes."

"How absurd. You never sold a picture in your life."

"Is that what being an artist means—selling? I thought it meant one who was always seeking without absolutely finding. I thought it means the contrary from 'I know it, I have found it.' When I say I am an artist, I only mean 'I am seeking, I am striving, I am in it with all my heart.' "

"Nevertheless, you have a vicious character."

"You suspect me of something—it is in the air—you think I am keeping something back. 'Vincent is hiding something that cannot stand the light.' What is it, Mauve? Speak to me frankly."

Mauve went back to his easel and began applying paint. Vincent turned away and walked slowly over the sand.

He was right. There *was* something in the air. The Hague had learned about his relation to Christine. De Bock was the one to break the news. He blew in with a naughty smile on his bud-like mouth. Christine was posing, so he spoke in English.

"Well, well, Van Gogh," he said, throwing off his heavy black overcoat and lighting a long cigarette. "It's all over town that you've taken a mistress. I heard it from Weissenbruch, Mauve and Tersteeg. The Hague is up in arms about it."

"Oh," said Vincent, "so that's what it's all about."

"You should be more discreet, old fellow. Is she some model about town? I thought I knew all the available ones."

Vincent glanced over at Christine knitting by the fire. There was a homely sort of attractiveness about her as she sat there, sewing in her merino and apron, her eyes upon the little garment she was making. De Bock dropped his cigarette to the floor and jumped up.

"My God!" he exclaimed, "You don't mean to tell me *that's* your mistress?"

"I have no mistress, De Bock. But I presume that's the woman they're talking about."

De Bock wiped some imaginary perspiration from his forehead and looked Christine over carefully. "How the devil can you bring yourself to sleep with her?"

"Why do you ask that?"

"My dear old chap, She's a hag! The commonest sort of a hag! What can you be thinking about? No wonder Tersteeg was shocked. If you want a mistress, why don't you pick up one of the neat little models about town? There are plenty of them around."

"As I told you once before, De Bock, this woman is not my mistress."

"Then what ...?"

"She's my wife!"

De Bock closed his tiny lips over his teeth with the gesture of a man tucking a buttonhole around a button.

"Your wife!"

"Yes. I intend to marry her."

"My God!"

De Bock threw one last look of horror and repulsion at Christine, and fled without even putting on his coat.

"What were you saying about me?" asked Christine.

Vincent crossed and looked down at her for a moment. "I told De Bock that you are going to be my wife."

Christine was silent for a long time, her hands working busily. Her mouth hung slightly open and her tongue would dart quickly, like the tongue of a snake, to moisten the rapidly drying lips.

"You would really marry me, Vincent? Why?"

"If I don't marry you, it would have been kinder of me to let you alone. I want to go through the joys and sorrows of domestic life in order to paint it from my own experience. I was in love with a woman once, Christine. When I went to her

192

house, they told me I disgusted her. My love was true and honest and strong, Christine, and when I came away I knew it had been killed. But after death there is a resurrection; you were that resurrection."

"But you can't marry me! What about the children? And your brother may stop sending the money."

"I respect a woman who is a mother, Christine. We'll keep the new baby and Herman here with us, the others can stay with your mother. As for Theo ... yes ... he may cut off my head. But when I write him the full truth I do not think he will abandon me."

He sat on the floor by her feet. She was looking so much better than when he had first met her. There was a little touch of happiness in her melancholy brown eyes. A new spirit of life had come to her whole personality. Posing had not been easy for her, but she had worked hard and patiently. When he first met her, she had been coarse and ill and miserable; now her whole manner was more quiet. She had found new health and life. As he sat there looking up into her crude, marked face into which a slight note of sweetness had come, he thought once again of the line from Michelet: *"Comment se fait-il qu'il y ait sur la terre une femme seule désespérée?"*

"Sien, we'll skimp and be as saving as possible, won't we? I fear there will come a time when I shall be quite without means. I shall be able to help you until you go to Leyden, but when you come back I don't know how you will find me, with or without bread. What I have I will share with you and the child."

Christine slipped off the chair, on to the floor beside him, put her arms about his neck and laid her head on his shoulder.

"Just let me stay with you, Vincent. I don't ask for much. If there's nothing but bread and coffee, I don't complain. I love you, Vincent. You're the first man's ever been good to me. You don't got to marry me if you don't want. I'll pose and work hard and do whatever you tell me. Only let me stay with you! It's the first time I ever been happy, Vincent. I don't want things. I'll just share what you have and be happy."

He could feel the swelling child against him, warm and living. He ran his fingertips gently over her homely face, kissing the scars one by one. He let her hair fall down her back, smoothing out the thin strands with tender strokes of his hand. She laid her flushed, happy cheek on his beard and rubbed softly against the grain.

"You do love me, Christine?"

"Yes, Vincent, I do."

"It's good to be loved. The world may call it wrong if it likes."

"To hell with the world," said Christine, simply.

"I will live as a labourer; that suits me. You and I understand each other and we do not need to mind what anybody says. We do not have to pretend to keep up a social standing. My own class cast me out long ago. I would rather have a crust of bread at my own hearth, however poor it may be, than live without marrying you."

They sat on the floor, warmed by the red glow of the stove, entwined in each other's arms. It was the postman who broke the spell. He handed Vincent a letter from Amsterdam. It read:

Vincent:

Have just heard of your disgraceful conduct. Kindly cancel my order for the six drawings. I will take no further interest in your work.

C. M. Van Gogh.

His whole fate now rested with Theo. Unless he could make Theo understand the full nature of his relationship with Christine, he too would be justified in cutting off the hundred francs a month. He could do without his master, Mauve; he could do without his dealer, Tersteeg; he could do without his family, friends, and *confrères* as long as he had his work and Christine. But he could not do without that hundred francs a month!

He wrote long, passionate letters to his brother, explaining everything, begging Theo to understand and not desert him. He lived from day to day with a dark fear of the worst. He did not dare to order more drawing material than he could pay for, or undertake any water-colours or push on.

Theo offered objections, many of them, but he did not condemn. He offered advice too, but not once did he infer that if his advice were not taken he would stop sending the money. And in the end, although he did not approve, he assured Vincent that his help would go on just as before.

It was now early May. The doctor at Leyden had told Christine she would be confined sometime in June. Vincent decided that it would be wiser if she did not move in with him until after the confinement, at which time he hoped to rent the

194

vacant house next door on the Schenkweg. Christine spent most of her time at the studio, but her possessions still remained at her mother's. They were to be officially married after her recovery.

He went to Leyden for Christine's confinement. The child did not move from nine in the evening until half past one. It had to be taken with the forceps, but it was not injured at all. Christine suffered a great deal of pain, but she forgot it all when she saw Vincent.

"We will soon begin to draw again," she said.

Vincent stood looking down at her with tears in his eyes. It did not matter that the child belonged to another man. It was his wife and baby, and he was happy with a taut pain in his chest.

When he returned to the Schenkweg he found the landlord and owner of the lumber yard in front of the house.

"What about taking that other house, Mijnheer Van Gogh? It is only eight francs a week. I'll have it all painted and plastered for you. If you will pick out the kind of wallpaper you like, I will put it on for you."

"Not so fast," said Vincent. "I would like the new house for when my wife comes home, but I must write to my brother first."

"Well, I must put on some wallpaper, so pick the one you like best, and if you can't take the house, it won't matter."

Theo had been hearing about the house next door for several months. It was much larger, with a studio, living room, kitchen alcove, and an attic bedroom. It was four francs a week more than the old place, but with Christine, Herman, and the baby all coming to the Schenkweg, they needed the new space. Theo replied that he had received another raise in salary and that Vincent could rely upon receiving a hundred and fifty francs a month for the present. Vincent rented the new house immediately. Christine was coming home in a week and he wanted her to find a warm nest upon her arrival. The owner lent him two men from the yard to carry his furniture next door to the new studio. Christine's mother came there to straighten things.

10

The new studio looked so real, with plain greyish-brown paper, scrubbed wooden floors, studies on the walls, an easel at each end, and a large, white deal working table. Christine's mother put up white muslin curtains at the windows. Adjoining the studio was an alcove where Vincent kept all his drawing boards, portfolios and woodcuts; in a corner was a closet for his bottles, pots, and books. The living room had a table, a few kitchen chairs, an oil stove, and a large wicker chair for Christine near the window. Beside it he put a small iron crib with a green cover, and above it the etching by Rembrandt of the two women by the cradle, one of them reading from the Bible by the light of a candle.

He secured everything that was strictly necessary for the kitchen; when Christine came back she could prepare dinner in ten minutes. He bought an extra knife, fork, spoon, and plate against the day when Theo should come to visit them. Up in the attic he put a large bed for himself and his wife, and the old one with all the bedding in good order for Herman. He and Christine's mother got straw, seaweed, bedticking, and filled the mattresses themselves in the attic.

When Christine left the hospital, the doctor who treated her, the nurse of the ward, and the head nurse all came to say good-bye. Vincent realized more fully than before that she was a person for whom serious people might have sympathy and affection. "She has never seen what is good," he said to himself, "so how can she be good?"

Christine's mother and her boy Herman were at the Schenkweg to greet her. It was a delightful homecoming, for Vincent had told her nothing about the new nest. She ran about touching things; the cradle, the easy chair, the flower pot he had placed on the sill outside her window. She was in high spirits.

"The professor was awfully funny," she cried. "He said, 'I say, are you fond of gin and bitters? And can you smoke cigars?' 'Yes,' I answered him. 'I only asked it,' he said, 'to tell you that you need not give it up. But you must not use vinegar, pepper, or mustard. And you should eat meat at least once a week.' "

Their bedroom looked a good deal like a hold of a ship, for it had been wainscotted. Vincent had to carry the iron cradle upstairs every night and down again to the living room in the morning. He had to do all the housework for which Christine was still too weak; making the beds, lighting the fire, lifting and carrying and cleaning. He felt as though he had been together with Christine and the children for a long time, and that he was in his element. Although she still suffered from the operation, there was a renewing and a reviving in her.

Vincent went back to work with a new peace in his heart. It was good to have a hearth of one's own, to feel the bustle and organization of a family about one. Living with Christine gave him courage and energy to go on with his work. If only Theo did not desert him he was certain that he could develop into a good painter.

In the Borinage he had slaved for God; here he had a new and more tangible kind of God, a religion that could be expressed in one sentence: that the figure of a labourer, some furrows in a ploughed field, a bit of sand, sea and sky were serious subjects, so difficult, but at the same time so beautiful, that it was indeed worth while to devote his life to the task of expressing the poetry hidden in them.

One afternoon, coming home from the dunes, he met Tersteeg in front of the Schenkweg house.

"I am glad to see you, Vincent," said Tersteeg. "I thought I would come and inquire how you are getting on."

Vincent dreaded the storm that he knew would break once Tersteeg got upstairs. He stood chatting with him a few moments on the street in order to gather strength. Tersteeg was friendly and pleasant. Vincent shivered.

When the two men entered, Christine was nursing the baby in her wicker chair. Herman was playing by the stove. Tersteeg gaped at them for a long, long time. When he spoke, it was in English.

"What is the meaning of that woman and child?"

"Christine is my wife. The child is ours."

"You have actually married her?"

"We haven't gone through the ceremony yet, if that's what you mean."

"How can you think of living with a woman . . . and children who . . ."

"Men usually marry, do they not?"

"But you have no money. You're being supported by your brother."

"Not at all. Theo pays me a salary. Everything I make belongs to him. He will get his money back some day."

"Have you gone mad, Vincent? This is certainly a thing that comes from an unsound mind and temperament."

"Human conduct, Mijnheer, is a great deal like drawing. The whole perspective changes with the shifted position of the

197

eye, and depends not on the subject, but on the man who is looking."

"I shall write to your father, Vincent. I shall write and tell him of the whole affair."

"Don't you think it would be ridiculous if they received an indignant letter from you, and soon after, a request from me to come and visit here at my expense?"

"You intend to write, yourself?"

"Can you ask that? Of course I will. But you must admit that now is a very untimely moment. Father is being moved to the vicarage at Neunen. My wife's condition is such that any anxiety or strain now would be murder."

"Then of course I shan't write. My boy, you're as foolish as the man who wants to drown himself. I only want to save you from it."

"I don't doubt your good intentions, Mijnheer Tersteeg, and that is why I try not to be angry at your words. But this conversation is very disagreeable to me."

Tersteeg went away, a baffled look on his face. It was Weissenbruch who delivered the first real blow from the outside world. He drifted in nonchalantly one afternoon to see if Vincent was still alive.

"Hello," he said. "I notice you managed to get along without that twenty-five francs."

"Yes."

"Now aren't you glad I didn't coddle you?"

"I believe about the first thing I said to you, that night at Mauve's, was 'Go to hell!' I repeat my invitation."

"If you keep this up, you'll become another Weissenbruch; you've got the making of a real man in you. Why don't you introduce me to your mistress. I've never had the honour."

"Bait me all you like, Weissenbruch, but leave her alone."

Christine was rocking the iron cradle with its green cover. She knew that she was being ridiculed, and looked up at Vincent with pain in her face. Vincent crossed to the mother and child and stood by their side, protectively. Weissenbruch glanced at the group, then at the Rembrandt over the cradle.

"I say," he exclaimed, "you make a corking motif. I'd like to do you. I'd call it *Holy Family!*"

Vincent sprang after Weissenbruch with an oath, but the latter got out the door safely. Vincent went back to his family. There was a bit of mirror hung on the wall beside the

Rembrandt. Vincent glanced up, caught the reflection of the three of them and in one horrible, devastating instant of clarity saw through the eyes of Weissenbruch . . . the bastard, the whore, and the charity monger.

"What did he call us?" asked Christine.

"The Holy Family."

"What's that?"

"A picture of Mary, Jesus, and Joseph."

Tears sprang to her eyes and she buried her head in the baby's clothes. Vincent went on his knees beside the iron cradle to comfort her. Dusk was creeping in the north window and threw a quiet shadow over the room. Once again Vincent was able to detach himself and see the three of them, just as though he were not a member of the group. This time he saw through the eyes of his own heart.

"Don't cry, Sien," he said. "Don't cry, darling. Lift up your head and dry your tears. *Weissenbruch was right!*"

11

Vincent discovered Scheveningen and oil painting at about the same time. Scheveningen was a little fishing village lying in a valley of two protective sand dunes on the North Sea. On the beach there were rows of square fishing barks with one mast and deep-coloured, weather beaten sails. They had rude, square rudders behind, fishing nets spread out ready for the sea, and a tiny rust-red or sea-blue triangular flag aloft. There were blue wagons on red wheels to carry the fish to the village; fisherwives in white oilskin caps fastened at the front by two round gold pins; family crowds at the tide's edge to welcome the barks; the Kurzaal flying its gay flags, a pleasure house for foreigners who liked the taste of salt on their lips, but not choked down their throats. The sea was grey with whitecaps at the shore and ever deepening hues of green fading into a dull blue; the sky was a cleaning grey with patterned clouds and an occasional design of blue to suggest to the fishermen that a sun still shines over Holland. Scheveningen was a place where men worked, and where the people were indigenous to the soil and the sea.

Vincent had been doing a good many street scenes in water-colour and he found that medium satisfactory for a quick impression. But water-colour did not have the depth, the

199

thickness, the character to express the things he needed to say. He yearned for oil, but he was afraid to tackle it because he had heard of so many painters being ruined by going to oil before they learned to draw. Then Theo came to The Hague.

Theo was now twenty-six and a competent art dealer. He travelled frequently for his house, and was everywhere known as one of the best young men in the business. Goupil and Company had sold out in Paris to Boussod, Valadon (known as *les Messieurs*) and although they had retained Theo in his former position, the art business was not what it had been under Goupil and Uncle Vincent. Pictures were now sold for the highest price obtainable—regardless of merit—and only the successful painters were patronized. Uncle Vincent, Tersteeg, and Goupil had considered it the very first duty of an art dealer to discover and encourage new and young artists; now only the old and recognized painters were solicited. The newcomers in the field, Manet, Monet, Pissarro, Sisley, Renoir, Berthe Morisot, Cezanne, Degas, Guillaumin, and even younger men, Toulouse-Lautrec, Gauguin, Seurat and Signac, were trying to say something different from what Bouguereau and the academicians were repeating endlessly, but no one would listen to them. None of these revolutionists had ever had a canvas exhibited or offered up for sale under the roof of *les Messieurs*. Theo had developed a profound distaste for Bouguereau and the academicians; his sympathies were all with the young innovators. Every day he did what he could to persuade *les Messieurs* to exhibit the new paintings and educate the public to buy. *Les Messieurs* thought the innovators mad, childish, and completely without technique. Theo thought them the future masters.

Christine remained upstairs in the attic bedroom while the brothers met in the studio. When their first greetings were over, Theo said, "I had to come on business, too, but I must confess that my primary purpose in The Hague is to dissuade you from establishing any permanent relationship with this woman. First of all, what is she like?"

"Do you remember our old nurse at Zundert, Leen Verman?"

"Yes."

"Sien is that kind of person. She is just an ordinary woman of the people, yet for me she has something sublime. Whoever loves one ordinary, commonplace person, and is loved by her, is already happy, notwithstanding the dark side of life. It was

200

the feeling of being of some use that brought me to myself again and made me revive. I did not seek for it, but it found me. Sien puts up with all the worries and troubles of a painter's life, and is so willing to pose that I think I shall become a better artist with her than if I had married Kay."

Theo walked about the studio and finally spoke while staring intently at a water-colour. "The only thing I can't understand is how you could fall in love with this woman while you were so desperately in love with Kay."

"I didn't fall in love, Theo, not immediately. Because Kay turned me down, should all my human feelings be extinguished? When you come here you do not find me discouraged and melancholy, but you come into a new studio and a home in full swing; no mysterious studio, but one that is rooted in real life—a studio with a cradle and a baby's high chair—where there is no stagnation, but where everything pushes and urges and stirs to activity. To me it is as clear as day that one must feel what one draws, that one must live in the reality of family life if one wishes to express intimately that family life."

"You know I never draw class distinctions, Vincent, but do you think it wise . . .?"

"No, I don't think I've lowered or dishonoured myself," interrupted Vincent, "because I feel my work lies in the heart of the people, that I must keep close to the ground, grasp life to the quick, and make progress through many cares and troubles."

"I don't dispute all that." Theo crossed swiftly and stood looking down at his brother. "But why does it necessitate a marriage?"

"Because there is a promise of marriage between her and me. I don't want you to consider her as a mistress, or as somebody with whom I am having a liaison without caring for the consequences. That promise of marriage is twofold; firstly a promise of civil marriage as soon as circumstances will permit, but secondly, it is a promise meanwhile to help each other, to cherish each other as if we were already married, to share everything together."

"But surely you will wait a bit before you go into the civil marriage?"

"Yes, Theo, if you ask me. We will postpone it until I earn a hundred and fifty francs by selling my work, and your help will no longer be necessary. I promise you I shall not marry

her until my drawing has progressed so far that I'm independent. By degrees, as I begin to earn, you can send me less
each month, and at last I will not need your money any longer.
Then we will talk about a civil marriage."

"That sounds like the wisest thing to do."

"Here she comes, Theo. For my sake, try to think of her
only as a wife and mother! For that's what she really is."

Christine came down the stairs at the rear of the studio. She
had on a neat black dress, her hair was carefully combed back,
and the touch of colour in her face almost obliterated the
pock marks. She had become pretty in a homely sort of way.
Vincent's love had surrounded her with an aura of confidence
and well being. She shook hands with Theo quietly, asked if he
wouldn't have a cup of tea, and insisted that he remain for
supper. She sat in her easy chair by the window, sewing and
rocking the cradle. Vincent ran excitedly back and forth
across the studio, showing charcoal figures, street scenes in
water-colour, group studies hammered on with a carpenter's
pencil. He wanted Theo to see the progress of his work.

Theo had faith that some day Vincent would become a
great painter, but he was never quite sure he liked the things
Vincent had done ... as yet. Theo was a discriminating
amateur, carefully trained in the art of judging, but he never
could make up his mind just what he thought of his brother's
work. For him, Vincent was always in a state of becoming,
never in the state of having arrived.

"If you begin to feel the need to work in oil," he said, after
Vincent had shown him all his studies and spoken of his
craving, "why don't you begin? What are you waiting
for?"

"For the assurance that my drawing is good enough. Mauve
and Tersteeg say I don't know how ..."

"... and Weissenbruch says you do. You're the one who
must be the final judge. If you feel that you've got to express
yourself in deeper colour now, the time is ripe. Jump in!"

"But, Theo, the expense! Those confounded tubes cost their
weight in gold."

"Meet me at my hotel tomorrow morning at ten. The
sooner you begin sending me oil canvases, the quicker I'll get
my money out of this investment."

During supper Theo and Christine chatted animatedly.
When Theo left, he turned to Vincent on the stairs and said in
French, "She's nice, really nice. I had no idea!"

They made a strange contrast, walking up the Wagenstraat the following morning; the younger brother carefully groomed, his boots polished, linen starched, suit pressed, necktie neatly in place, black bowler hat at a jaunty angle, soft brown beard carefully trimmed, walking along with a well poised, even pace; and the other, with worn out boots, patched trousers that did not match the tight coat, no necktie, an absurd peasant's cap stuck on the top of his head, beard scrambling out in furious red whorls, hitching along with jerky, uneven steps, waving his arms and making excited gestures as he talked.

They were not conscious of the picture they made.

Theo took Vincent to Goupils to buy the tubes of paint, brushes, and canvas. Tersteeg respected and admired Theo; he wanted to like and understand Vincent. When he heard what they had come for, he insisted upon finding all the material himself and advising Vincent on the merits of the various pigments.

Theo and Vincent tramped the six kilometres across the dunes to Scheveningen. A fishing smack was just coming in. Near the monument there was a little wooden shed in which a man sat on the lookout. As soon as the boat came in view the fellow appeared with a large flag. He was followed by a crowd of children. A few minutes after he had waved his flag, a man on an old horse arrived to go and fetch the anchor. The group was joined by a number of men and women who came pouring over the sand hill from the village to welcome the crew. When the boat was near enough, the man on horseback went into the water and returned with the anchor. Then the fishermen were brought ashore on the backs of fellows with high rubber boots, and with each arrival there was a great cheer of welcome. When they were all ashore and the horses had dragged the bark up on the beach, the whole troop marched home over the sand hill in caravan style, with the man on the horse towering over them like a tall spectre.

"This is the sort of thing I want to do with my paints," said Vincent.

"Let me have some canvases as soon as you become satisfied with your work. I might be able to find purchasers in Paris."

"Oh, Theo, you must! You must begin to sell me!"

12

When Theo left, Vincent began experimenting with his pigments. He did three oil studies; one a row of pollard willows behind the Geest bridge, another of a cinder path, and a third of the vegetable gardens of Meerdervoort where a man in a blue smock was picking up potatoes. The field was of white sand, partly dug up, still covered with rows of dried stalks with green weeds between. In the distance there were dark green trees and a few roofs. When he looked at his work in the studio, he was elated; he was certain that no one could possibly know they were his first efforts. The drawing, the backbone of painting and the skeleton that supported all the rest, was accurate and true to life. He was surprised a little because he had thought his first things would be failures.

He was busy painting a sloping ground in the woods, covered with moldered, dry beech leaves. The ground was light and dark reddish brown, made more so by the shadows of trees which threw streaks over it and sometimes half blotted it out. The question was to get the depth of colour, the enormous force and solidness of the ground. While painting, he perceived for the first time how much light there was still in that darkness. He had to keep that light, and keep at the same time the depth of rich colour.

The ground was a carpet of deep reddish brown in the glow of an autumn evening sun, tempered by the trees. Young birches sprang up, caught light on one side, and were sparkling green there, the shadowy sides of the stems were warm, deep black-green. Behind the saplings, behind the brownish red soil was a very delicate sky, bluish grey, warm, hardly blue, all aglow. Against it was a hazy border of green and a network of little stems and yellowish leaves. A few figures of wood gatherers were wandering around like dark masses of mysterious shadow. The white cap of a woman, who was bending to reach a dry branch, stood out brusquely against the deep red-brown of the ground. A dark silhouette of a man appeared above the underbrush; moulded against the sky, the figure was large and full of poetry.

While painting he said to himself, "I must not go away before there is something of an autumn evening feeling in it, something mysterious, something serious." But the light was fading. He had to work quickly. The figures he painted in at once by a few strong strokes with a resolute brush. It struck him how firmly the little tree stems were rooted in the ground. He tried to paint them in, but the ground was already so sticky that a brush stroke was lost in it. He tried again and again, desperately, for it was getting darker. At last he saw he was defeated; no brush could suggest anything in that rich loam-brown of the earth. With a blind intuition he flung the brush away, squeezed the roots and trunks on the canvas from the tubes of paint, picked up another brush, and modelled the thick, coloured oil with the handle.

"Yes," he exclaimed, as night finally claimed the woods, "now they stand there, rising from the ground, strongly rooted in it. I have said what I wanted to say!"

Weissenbruch looked in that evening. "Come along with me to *Pulchri*. We're having some tableaux and charades."

Vincent had not forgotten his last visit. "No, thanks, I don't care to leave my wife."

Weissenbruch walked over to Christine, kissed her hand, asked after her health, and played with the baby quite jovially. He evidently had no recollection of the last thing he had said to them.

"Let me see some of your new sketches, Vincent."

Vincent complied only too gladly. Weissenbruch picked out a study of Monday's market, where they were pulling down the stands; another of a line waiting in front of the soup kitchen; another of three old men at the insane asylum; another of a fishing smack at Scheveningen with the anchor raised, and a fifth that Vincent had made on his knees, in the mud of the dunes during a driving rain storm.

"Are these for sale? I'd like to buy them."

"Is this another of your poor jokes, Weissenbruch?"

"I never joke about painting. These studies are superb. How much do you want?"

Vincent said, "Name your own price," numbly, afraid that he was going to be ridiculed at any moment.

"Very well, how about five francs apiece? Twenty-five for the lot."

Vincent's eyes shot open. "That's too much! My Uncle Cor only paid me two and a half francs."

"He cheated you, my boy. All dealers cheat you. Some day they will sell for five thousand francs. What do you say, is it a deal?"

"Weissenbruch, sometimes you're an angel and sometimes you're a fiend!"

"That's for variety, so my friends won't get tired of me."

He took out a wallet and handed Vincent twenty-five francs. "Now come along with me to *Pulchri*. You need a little entertainment. We're having a farce by Tony Offermans. It will do you good to laugh."

So Vincent went along. The hall of the club was crowded with men all smoking cheap and strong tobacco. The first tableau was after an etching by Nicholas Maes, *The Stable at Bethlehem*, very good on tone and colour, but decidedly off in expression. The other was after Rembrandt's *Isaac Blessing Jacob*, with a splendid Rebecca looking on to see if her trick would succeed. The close air gave Vincent a headache. He left before the farce and went home, composing the sentences of a letter as he walked.

He told his father as much about the story of Christine as he thought expedient, enclosed Weissenbruch's twenty-five francs, and asked Theodorus to come to The Hague as his guest.

A week later his father arrived. His blue eyes were fading, his step becoming slower. The last time they had been together, Theodorus had ordered his oldest son from the house. In the interim they had exchanged friendly letters. Theodorus and Anna Cornelia had sent several bundles of underwear, outer clothing, cigars, homemade cake, and an occasional ten franc note. Vincent did not know how his father would take to Christine. Sometimes men were understanding and generous, sometimes they were blind and vicious.

He did not think his father could remain indifferent and raise objections—near a cradle. A cradle was not like anything else; there was no fooling with it. His father would have to forgive whatever there might have been in Christine's past.

Theodorus had a large bundle under his arm. Vincent opened it, drew out a warm coat for Christine, and knew that everything was all right. After she had gone upstairs to the attic bedroom, Theodorus and Vincent sat together in the studio.

"Vincent," said his father, "there was one thing you did not mention in your letter. Is the baby yours?"

"No. She was carrying it when I met her."

"Where is its father?"

"He deserted her." He did not think it necessary to explain the child's anonymity.

"But you will marry her, Vincent, won't you? It's not right to live this way."

"I agree. I want to go through the legal ceremony as soon as possible. But Theo and I decided that it would be better to wait until I am earning a hundred and fifty francs a month through my drawing."

Theodorus sighed. "Yes, perhaps that would be the best. Vincent, your mother would like you to come home for a visit sometime. And so should I. You will enjoy Nuenen, son; it is one of the most lovely villages in all the Brabant. The little church is so tiny, and looks like an Eskimo's igloo. It seats less than a hundred people, imagine! There are hawthorn hedges around the parsonage, Vincent, and behind the church is a flower filled yard with sand mounds and old wooden crosses."

"With wooden crosses!" said Vincent. "White ones?"

"Yes. The names are in black, but the rain is washing them away."

"Is there a nice tall steeple on the church, Father?"

"A delicate, fragile one, Vincent, but it goes way, way up into the sky. Sometimes I think it almost reaches God."

"Throwing a thin shadow over the graveyard." Vincent's eyes were sparkling. "I'd like to paint that."

"There's a stretch of heath and pine woods close by, and peasants digging in the fields. You must come home soon for a visit, son."

"Yes, I must see Nuenen. The little crosses, and the steeple and the diggers in the field. I guess there will always be something of the Brabant about me."

Theodorus returned home to assure his wife that things were not so bad with their boy as they had imagined. Vincent plunged into his work with an even greater zeal. More and more he found himself going back to Millet: *"L'art c'est un combat; dans l'art il faut y mettre sa peau"*. Theo believed in him, his mother and father did not disapprove of Christine, and no one in The Hague disturbed him any more. He was completely free to go ahead with his work.

The owner of the lumber yard sent him as models all the men who came for work and could not get it. As his pocketbook emptied his portfolio filled. He drew the baby in the cradle by the stove many, many times. When the fall rains came he worked outdoors on oil torchon and captured the effects he wanted. He quickly learned that a colourist is one who, seeing a colour in nature, knows at once how to analyse it and say. "That grey-green is yellow with black, and hardly any blue."

Whether he was drawing the figure or landscape, he wished to express not sentimental melancholy but serious sorrow. He wanted to reach out so far that people would say of his work, "He feels deeply, he feels tenderly."

He knew that in the eyes of the world he was a good-for-nothing, an eccentric and disagreeable man, someone who had no position in life. He wanted to show in his work just what there was in the heart of such an eccentric man, of such a nobody. In the poorest huts, in the dirtiest corners, he saw drawings and pictures. The more he painted, the more other activities lost their interest. The more he got rid of them the quicker his eye grasped the picturesque qualities of life. Art demanded persistent work, work in spite of everything, and a continuous observation.

The only difficulty was that oil pigments were so frightfully expensive, and he laid his colour on so thick. When he squeezed it out of the tube on to the canvas in rich deep masses, it was like pouring francs into the Zuider Zee. He painted so fast that his canvas bill was enormous; he did at one sitting an oil that would have taken Mauve two months. Well, he could not paint thin, and he could not work slowly; his money evaporated and his studio became filled with pictures. As soon as his allowance arrived from Theo—who had arranged to send fifty francs on the first, tenth, and twentieth—he would rush down to the dealer and buy large tubes of ochre, cobalt, and Prussian blue, and smaller tubes of Naples yellow, *terra sienna*, ultramarine, and gamboge. Then he would work happily until the paints and the francs were exhausted, usually five or six days after the allowance arrived from Paris, and his troubles set in again.

He was amazed to find that so many things had to be bought for the baby; that Christine had to have constant medicines, new garments, special foods; that Herman had to buy books and supplies for the school he was sent to; and that the household was a bottomless pit into which he was forever pouring lamps, pots, blankets, coal and wood, curtains, rugs, candles, sheets, silverware, plates, furniture, and an endless stream of food. It was hard to know just how to apportion the fifty francs between his painting and the three people who were dependent upon him.

"You look like a labourer rushing off to the wine shop the minute he gets paid," remarked Christine one time when

Vincent snatched the fifty francs out of Theo's envelope and began gathering up empty tubes.

He built a new perspective instrument with two long legs that would stand up in the sand of the dunes, and had the blacksmith make iron corners for the frame. Scheveningen, with the sea, the sand dunes, the fisherfolk, the barks and horses and nets, lured him most. He trudged across the dunes every day, loaded down with his heavy easel and perspective instrument, to catch the changing nature of the sea and sky. As fall deepened and other artists began to hug their studio fires, he went out to paint in the wind, the rain, the mist and the storm. In the roughest of weather his wet paint often became covered with blowing sand and salt water. The rain drenched him, the mist and wind chilled him, the sand got into his eyes and nose . . . and he loved every last minute of it. Nothing but death could stop him now.

One night he showed Christine a new canvas. "But Vincent," she exclaimed, "how do you make it look so real?"

Vincent forgot he was speaking to an illiterate woman of the people. He might have been talking to Weissenbruch or Mauve.

"I don't know myself," he said. "I sit down with a white board before the spot that strikes me, and I say, 'That white board must become something!' I work for a long time, I come back home dissatisfied, I put it away in the closet. When I have rested a little I go to look at it with a kind of fear. I am still dissatisfied because I have too clearly in my mind the splendid original to be content with what I have made of it. But after all, I find in my work an echo of what struck me. I see that nature has told me something, has spoken to me, and that I have put it down in shorthand. In my shorthand there may be words that cannot be deciphered, there may be mistakes or gaps, but there is something in it of what the woods or beach or figure has told me. Do you understand?"

"No."

13

Christine understood very little of what he was doing. She thought his hunger to paint things a sort of costly obsession. She knew it was the rock upon which his life was built, however, and made no attempt to oppose him; the purpose, the slow progress and painful expression of his work were completely lost upon her. She was a good companion for ordinary domestic purposes, but only a very small part of Vincent's life was domestic. When he wished to express himself in words, he was forced to write to Theo; he poured out a long passionate letter almost every night, telling of all the things he had seen, painted, and thought during the day. When he wished to enjoy the expression of others, he turned to novels: French, English, German and Dutch. Christine shared only a fraction of his life. But he was satisfied; he did not regret his decision to take Christine to wife, nor did he attempt to force upon her the intellectual pursuits for which she was manifestly unqualified.

All this was very well during the long months of the summer, autumn, and fall, when he left the house as early as five and six o'clock in the morning, to be gone until the light of day failed completely and he had to trudge home across the dunes in the cool dusk. But when a terrific snow-storm served to celebrate the first anniversary of their meeting in the wine shop opposite the Ryn station, and Vincent had to work at home from morning until night, it became more difficult to maintain a satisfactory relationship.

He went back to drawing, and saved money on paints, but the models ate him out of house and home. People who would gladly work for next to nothing at the worst kind of menial labour would demand a large sum just to come and sit for him. He asked permission to sketch at the insane asylum, but the authorities declared they had no precedent for it, and besides they were laying new floors so he could not work there except on visiting days.

His only hope lay in Christine. As soon as she was well and strong he expected her to pose for him, work as hard as she had before the baby came. Christine had different ideas. At first she would say, "I'm not strong enough. Wait a bit. You ain't in any hurry." When she was completely well again, she thought herself too busy.

"It's not the same now as it was, Vincent," she would say."I got to nurse the baby. And I got to keep a whole house clean. There's four people to cook for."

Vincent arose at five in the morning to do the housework so that she would be free to pose during the day. "But I ain't a model no more," she protested. "I'm your wife."

"Sien, you must pose for me! I can't afford to hire models every day. That's one of the reasons you're here."

Christine flared up into one of the unrestrained fits of

210

temper that had been so common when she first met Vincent.
"That's all you took me in for! So you could save money out
of me! I'm just a goddam servant to you! If I don't pose
you'll throw me out again!"

Vincent thought for a moment and then said, "You heard
all those things at your mother's. You didn't think of them for
yourself."

"Well, and what if I did? They're true, ain't they?"

"Sien, you'll have to stop going there."

"Why? I guess I love my mother, don't I?"

"But they're ruining things between us. The first thing you
know they'll have you back in their way of thinking. Then
where will our marriage be?"

"Ain't you the one tells me go there when there's no food in
the house? Make some more money and I won't have to go
back."

When he finally did get her to pose, she was useless. She
committed all the errors he had worked so hard to eradicate
the year before. Sometimes he suspected that she wiggled,
made awkward gestures purposely so that he would become
disgusted and not bother her to pose any more. In the end he
had to give her up. His expense for outside models increased.
Along with it, the number of days that they were without
money for food also increased, and so did the amount of time
that Christine was forced to spend at her mother's. Each time
she came back from there he perceived a slight change in her
bearing and attitude. He was caught in a vicious circle; if he
used all his money for living, Christine would not go back to
the influence of her mother; he could maintain their relationship on a wholesome plane. But if he did that, he would have
to give up his work. Had he saved her life just to kill himself?
If she did not go to her mother's several times a month, she
and the children would starve; if she did go she would
eventually destroy their home. What was he to do?

Christine ill and carrying a child, Christine in the hospital,
Christine recovering from the confinement, was one sort of
person; a woman abandoned, *désespérée*, on the verge of a
miserable death, intensely grateful for a single kind word or
helpful action; a woman who knew all the pain in the world
and would do anything for a moment's surcease, who would
make all sorts of fervent and heroic promises to herself and
life. Christine well again, her body and face filled out with
good food, medicine, and care, was another sort of woman.

The memory of pain was receding, the resolution to be a good housewife and mother weakening; the thoughts and habits of her earlier life were coming back again slowly. She had lived loosely and on the streets, amid liquor, black cigars, vile language, and coarse men for fourteen years. With the strength of her body returning, the fourteen years of sloth overbalanced the one year of care and gentle love. An insidious change began to steal upon her. Vincent could not understand it at first; then slowly a consciousness of what was happening came over him.

It was just about this time, the beginning of the new year, that he received a curious letter from Theo. His brother had met on the streets of Paris a woman, alone, ill, despairing. She suffered from an ailment of the foot and could not work. She had been ready to kill herself. Vincent had taught Theo the way; he followed his master. He found a place for the woman in the home of some old friends. He secured a doctor and had examinations made. He paid for all the expenses of the woman's life. In his letters he called her his patient.

"Should I marry my patient, Vincent? Is that the best way for me to serve her? Should I go through the legal ceremony? She suffers much; she is unhappy; she was deserted by the only person she loved. What must I do to save her life?"

Vincent was deeply touched, and he wrote of his sympathy. But every day Christine was becoming more difficult. When there was only bread and coffee, she grumbled. She insisted that he leave off having models and use his money for the house. When she could not have a new dress, she neglected the old one and let it become covered with food and dirt. She stopped mending his clothes and linen. She fell once again under the influence of her mother, who persuaded her that Vincent would either run away or throw her out. Since a permanent relationship was impossible, what was the good of bothering about the temporary one?

Could he advise Theo to marry his patient? Was legal marriage the best way to save these women? Or was the most important thing a roof over their heads, good food to build their health, and kindness to bring them back to a love of life?

"Wait!" he cautioned his brother. "Do all you can for her; it is a noble cause. But the ceremony will help you not at all. If a love grows between you, then a marriage will grow, too. But see first if you can save her."

212

Theo was sending fifty francs three times a month. Now that Christine was growing careless in her housekeeping, the money did not last as long as it had before. Vincent was avaricious for models so that he could collect enough studies for some real canvases. He regretted every franc that had to be taken away from his drawing and sunk into the house. She begrudged every franc that had to be taken away from the house and sunk into the drawing. It was a struggle for their lives. The hundred and fifty francs a month could just have supplied him with food, shelter and materials; the attempt to make it provide for four people was heroic but impossible. He began owing money to the landlord, to the shoemaker, the grocer, the baker, and the colour dealer. To cap the climax, Theo went short on funds.

Vincent wrote imploring letters. "If you can please send the money just a little before the twentieth, at least not later. I have only two sheets of paper in the house and one last crumb of crayon. I have not a franc for models or food." Three times a month he wrote such letters; when the fifty francs arrived, he already owed it all to the tradesmen and had nothing to live on for the next ten days.

Theo's "patient" had to be operated on for tumor of the foot. Theo had her taken to a good hospital. At the same time he was sending money home to Nuenen, for the new congregation was small, and Theodorus's income was not always sufficient to meet the needs of the family. Theo was supporting himself and his patient, Vincent, Christine, Herman, Antoon, and the family at Nuenen. He was pushed to the last centime of his salary and could not send Vincent an extra franc.

At last it came about, in early March, that Vincent was left with one franc, a torn note that had already been refused by a tradesman. There was not a mouthful of food left in the house. The next money could not arrive from Theo for at least nine days. He was desperately afraid to put Christine into the hands of her mother for that length of time.

"Sien," he said, "we can't starve the children. You had better take them home to your mother's until Theo's letter arrives."

They looked at each other for a moment, thinking the same thoughts, but without the courage to utter them.

"Yes," she said, "I guess I got to."

The grocer gave him a loaf of black bread and some coffee

213

for the torn bill. He brought models into the house and owed them their money. He became increasingly nervous. His work went hard and dry. He had been starving his body. The incessant financial worries were telling on him. He could not go on without working, yet every hour of work showed him that he was losing ground.

At the end of nine days, promptly on the thirtieth, the letter arrived from Theo with fifty francs. His "patient" had recovered from the operation and he had put her in a private home. The financial strain was telling on him, too, and he had grown despondent. He wrote, "I am afraid I cannot assure you of anything in the future."

That sentence almost drove Vincent out of his mind. Did Theo mean simply that he would not be able to send any more money? That in itself would not be so bad. But did it mean that from the almost daily sketches Vincent sent him to show the progress of his work, his brother had come to the conclusion that he was without talent and could hope for nothing in the future?

He lay awake at night worrying about it, wrote incessant letters to Theo begging for an explanation, and cast about desperately for some means of making his own livelihood. There were none.

14

When he went for Christine he found her in the company of her mother, brother, brother's mistress, and a strange man. She was smoking a black cigar and drinking gin. She did not seem at all pleased at the thought of going back to the Schenkweg.

The nine days at her mother's house had brought back the old habits, the destroying ways of life.

"I can smoke cigars if I want!" she cried. "You ain't got no right to stop me if I get them myself. The doctor at the hospital said I could drink all the gin and bitters I wanted."

"Yes, as medicine . . . to improve your appetite."

She broke into a raucous laugh. "Medicine! What a————— you are!" It was an expression she had not used since the very first days of their acquaintanceship.

Vincent was in a ragged state of sensitivity. He flew into uncontrollable rages. Christine followed his example. "You ain't taking care of me no more!" she shouted. "You don't

214

even give me something to eat. Why don't you make more money? What in hell kind of man are you, anyway?"

As the hard winter slipped into a grudging spring, Vincent's condition went from bad to worse. His debts increased. Because he could not give his stomach the right food, it went back on him. He could not swallow a bite. The ills of his stomach went to his teeth. He lay awake at night with the pain. The ache from his teeth went to his right ear, and all day it twitched jumpily.

Christine's mother began coming to the house, smoking and drinking with her daughter. She no longer thought Christine fortunate to be married. Once Vincent found her brother there, but he dodged out of the door as soon as Vincent entered.

"Why did he come here?" demanded Vincent. "What does he want of you?"

"They say you are going to throw me out."

"You know I'll never do that, Sien. Not as long as you want to stay."

"Mother wants me to leave. She says it ain't good for me to stay here without something to eat."

"Where would you go?"

"Home, of course."

"And take the children into that house?"

"It's better than starving here. I can work and earn my own living."

"What would you work at?"

"Well . . . something."

"As a charwoman? At the tubs?"

". . . I guess."

He saw immediately that she was lying.

"So that's what they're trying to persuade you to do!"

"Well . . . it ain't so bad . . . you make a living."

"Listen, Sien, if you go back to that house you're lost. You know your mother will send you on the streets again. Remember what the doctor at Leyden said. If you go back to that life, it will kill you!"

"It ain't going to kill me. I feel all right now."

"You feel well because you have been living carefully! But if you go back . . .!"

"Jesus Christ, who's going back? Unless you send me."

He sat on the arm of her wicker chair and put his hand on her shoulder. Her hair was uncombed. "Then believe me, Sien,

215

I will never abandon you. As long as you are willing to share what I have, I will keep you with me. But you must stay away from your mother and brother. They'll destroy you! Promise me, for your own sake, that you won't see them any more."

"I promise."

Two days later, when he came back from sketching at the alms house, the studio was empty. There was no sign of supper. He found Christine at her mother's, drinking.

"I told you I love my mother," she protested when they got home. "I guess I can see her all I want. You don't own me. I got a right to do as I please."

She fell into all the familiar, slovenly habits of her former life. When Vincent tried to correct them and explain that she was estranging herself from him, she would answer, "Yes, I know it quite well, you don't want me to stay with you." He showed her how dirty the house was, and how neglected. She answered, "Well, I am lazy and good-for-nothing; I always was that way and it can't be helped." If he tried to show her to what ultimate end her slothfulness was taking her she would reply, "I'm nothing but an outcast, that's true, and I'll end up by throwing myself in the river!"

The mother came to the studio nearly every day now, and took from Vincent the companionship he had so valued in Christine. The house fell into chaos. Meals became fitful. Herman was allowed to go around ragged and dirty, and stay away from school. The less Christine did, the more she smoked and drank her gin. She would not tell Vincent where she got the money for these things.

Summer came. Vincent went out of doors to paint again. This meant new outlays for paints, brushes, canvas, frames, bigger easels. Theo reported improved condition on his "patient," but serious problems in his relationship with her. What was he to do with the woman, now that she was better?

Vincent shut his eyes to everything in his personal life and continued to paint. He knew that his house was crashing about his ears, that he was being drawn into the abysmal sloth that had recaptured Christine. He tried to bury his despair in his work. Each morning when he set out on a new project, he hoped that this canvas would be so beautiful and perfect that it would sell immediately and establish him. Each night he returned home with the sad realization that he was still many years from the mastery he longed for.

His only relief was Antoon, the child. He was a miracle

216

of vitality, and swallowed all kinds of eatables with much laughing and cooing. He often sat with Vincent in the studio, on the floor in a corner. He would crow at Vincent's drawings and then sit quietly looking at the sketches on the walls. He was growing up to be a pretty and vivacious child. The less attention Christine paid to the baby, the more Vincent loved him. In Antoon he saw the real purpose and reward for his actions of last winter.

Weissenbruch looked in only once. Vincent showed him some of the sketches of the year before. He had become frightfully dissatisfied with them.

"Don't feel that way," said Weissenbruch. "After a good many years you will look back on these early pieces of work and realize that they were sincere and penetrating. Just plug on, my boy, and don't let anything stop you."

What finally did stop him was a smash in the face. During the spring he had taken a lamp to the crockery man to have it repaired. The merchant had insisted that Vincent take some new dishes with him.

"But I have no money to pay for them."

"It doesn't matter. There is no hurry. Take them and pay me when you get the money."

Two months later he banged on the door of the studio. He was a burly chap with a neck as thick as his head.

"What do you mean by lying to me?" he demanded. "What do you take my goods for and not pay me when you got money all the time?"

"At the moment I am absolutely flat. I will pay you as soon as I receive money."

"That's a lie! You just gave money to my neighbour, the shoemaker."

"I am at work," said Vincent, "and I don't care to be disturbed. I'll pay you when I get the money. Please get out."

"I'll get out when you give me that money, and not before!"

Vincent indiscreetly pushed the man toward the door. "Get out of my house," he commanded.

That was just what the tradesman was waiting for. As soon as he was touched, he smashed over his right fist into Vincent's face and sent him crashing into the wall. He struck Vincent again, knocked him to the floor, and walked out without another word.

Christine was at her mother's. Antoon crawled across the

floor and patted Vincent's face, crying. After a few minutes Vincent came back to consciousness, dragged himself up the stairs to the attic and lay over the bed.

The blows had not hurt his face. He felt no pain. He had not injured himself when he had fallen heavily to the floor. But those two blows had broken something within him and defeated him. He knew it.

Christine came back. She went upstairs to the attic. There was neither money nor dinner in the house. She often wondered how Vincent managed to keep alive. She saw him lying across the bed, head and arms dangling over one side, feet over the other.

"What's the matter?" she asked.

After a long time he found the strength to twist about and put his head on the pillow. "Sien, I've got to leave The Hague."

"...yes...I know."

"I must get away from here. Out to the country somewhere. To Drenthe, maybe. Where we can live cheaply."

"You want me to come with you? It's an awful hole, Drenthe. What will I do when you ain't got no money and we don't eat?"

"I don't know, Sien. I guess you won't eat."

"Will you promise to use the hundred and fifty francs to live on? Not to spend it on models and paints?"

"I can't, Sien. Those things come first."

"Yes, to you!"

"But not to you. Why should they?"

"I got to live too, Vincent. I can't live without eating."

"And I can't live without painting."

"Well, it's your money ... you come first ... I understand. Have you a few centimes? Let's go over to the wine café across from the Ryn station."

The place smelled of sour wine. It was late afternoon, but the lamps had not yet been lit. The two tables where they had first sat near each other were empty. Christine led the way to them. They each ordered a glass of sour wine. Christine toyed with the stem of her glass. Vincent remembered how he had admired her worker's hands when she made that identical gesture at the table almost two years before.

"They told me you'd leave me," she said in a low voice. "I knew it, too."

· "I don't want to desert you, Sien."

"It ain't desertion, Vincent. You never done me nothing but good."

"If you are still willing to share my life, I'll take you to Drenthe."

She shook her head without emotion. "No, there ain't enough for two of us."

"You understand, don't you, Sien? If I had more, I'd give you anything. But when I must choose between feeding you and feeding my work . . ."

She laid her hand over his; he could feel the rough parchment of her skin. "It's all right. You don't got to feel bad about it. You done all you could for me. I guess it's just time we was through . . . that's all."

"Do you want us to be, Sien? If it will make you happy, I'll marry you and take you with me."

"No. I belong with my mother. We all got to live our own lives. It'll be all right; my brother's going to take a new house for his girl and me."

Vincent drained his glass, tasting the bitter dregs at the bottom.

"Sien, I've tried to help you. I loved you and gave you all the kindness I had in me. In return I want you to do one thing for me, just one thing."

"What?" she asked dully.

"Don't go back on the streets again. It will kill you! For the sake of Antoon, don't go back to that life."

"Have we enough left for another glass of wine?"

"Yes."

She swallowed half the contents in a single gulp and then said, "I only know that I can't earn enough, 'specially when I got to pay for all the children. So if I walk the street it will be because I must, not because I want to."

"If you get enough work you'll promise me, won't you, not to go back to that?"

"Sure, I promise."

"I'll send you money, Sien, every month. I'll always pay for the baby. I want you to give the little fellow a chance."

"He'll be all right . . . same as the rest."

Vincent wrote to Theo of his intention to go to the country and sever his connection with Christine. Theo answered by return mail with an extra hundred franc note to pay off his debts, and a strong word of approval. "My patient disap-

219

peared the other night," he wrote. "She's completely well now, but we couldn't seem to find any relationship to fit ourselves into. She took everything with her and left me no address. It's better that way. Now you and I are both unencumbered."

Vincent stored all the furniture in the attic. He wanted to come back to The Hague sometime. The day before he was to leave for Drenthe he received a letter and a package from Nuenen. In the package was some tobacco, and one of his mother's cheese cakes wrapped in oil paper.

"When are you coming home to paint those wooden crosses in the churchyard?" his father asked.

He knew at once that he wanted to go home. He was ill, starved, desperately nervous, fatigued and discouraged. He would go home to his mother for a few weeks and recover his health and spirits. A feeling of peace that he had not known for many months came over him when he thought of his Brabant countryside, the hedges and dunes and diggers in the field.

Christine and the two children accompanied him to the station. They all stood on the platform, unable to speak. The train came in and Vincent boarded it. Christine stood there with the baby at her breast, holding Herman by the hand. Vincent watched them until his train pulled out into the glaring sunlight, and the woman was lost forever in the grimy blackness of the station.

BOOK FOUR

NUENEN

1

The vicarage at Nuenen was a two-storey, whitewashed, stone building with a tremendous garden in the back. There were elms, hedges, flower beds, a pond, and three pollard oaks. Although Nuenen had a population of twenty-six hundred, only one hundred of them were Protestant. Theodorus's church was tiny; Nuenen was a step down from the prosperous little market town of Etten.

Nuenen was in reality only a small cluster of houses that lined both sides of the road from Eindhoven, the metropolis of the district. Most of the people were weavers and peasants whose huts dotted the heath. They were God fearing, hard working people who lived according to the manners and customs of their ancestors.

On the front of the vicarage, over the door, were the black iron figures A° 1764. The entrance door led straight off the road and admitted to a wide hall which split the house in two. On the left-hand side, dividing the dining room and kitchen, was a rude stairway which led up to the bedrooms. Vincent shared the one over the living room with his brother Cor. When he awoke in the morning he could see the sun rise over the fragile tower of his father's church, and gently lay pastel shades on the pool. At sunset, when the tones were deeper than at dawn, he would sit in a chair by the window and watch the colour being thrown over the pool like a heavy blanket of oil, and then slowly dissolving into the dusk.

Vincent loved his parents; his parents loved him. All three made desperate resolves that the relationship was to be kept friendly and agreeable. Vincent ate a great deal, slept a great deal, walked sometimes on the heath. He talked, painted, and read not at all. Everyone in the house was elaborately courteous to him, as he was to them. It was a self-conscious relationship; before they spoke they had to say to themselves, "I must be careful! I don't want to disrupt the harmony!"

The harmony lasted as long as Vincent's illness. He could not be comfortable in the same room with people who did not think as he thought. When his father remarked, "I am going to read Goethe's 'Faust.' It has been translated by the Reverend Ten Kate, so it cannot be so very immoral," Vincent felt his gorge rise.

He had come home only for a two week vacation, but he loved the Brabant and wanted to stay on. He wished to paint simply and quietly from nature, trying to say nothing but what he saw. He had no other desire than to live deep in the heart of the country, and paint rural life. Like good Father Millet, he wanted to live with, understand, and paint the peasants. He had the firm conviction that there were a few people who, having been drawn into the city and bound up there, yet retained unfading impressions of the country, and remained homesick all their lives for the fields and the peasants.

He had always known that he would come back to the Brabant some day and remain for ever. But he could not stay in Nuenen if his parents did not want him.

"A door must be either open or shut," he said to his father. "Let us try to come to an understanding."

"Yes, Vincent, I want that very much. I see that your painting is going to come to something after all, and I am pleased."

"Very well, tell me frankly whether you think we can all live here in peace. Do you want me to stay?"

"Yes."

"For how long?"

"As long as you wish. This is your home. Your place is with us."

"And if we disagree?"

"Then we must not get upset about it. We must try to live calmly and abide with each other."

"But what am I to do about a studio? You don't want me working in the house."

"I have been thinking about that. Why not take the wrangle room, out in the garden? You can have it all to yourself. No one need bother you."

The wrangle room was just off the kitchen, but there was no connecting door. It was a cubicle of a room, with one small window, high up, looking out on to the garden. The floor was of clay, always damp in winter.

"We'll light a big fire in here, Vincent, and dry the place out. Then we'll put down a plank floor so that you can be perfectly comfortable. What do you say?"

Vincent looked about. It was a humble room, very much like the peasants' huts on the heath. He could turn it into a real rural studio.

"If that window is too small," said Theodorus, "I have a little spare money now and we can make it larger."

"No, no, it's perfect just as it is. I'll get the same amount of light on the model that I would get if I were doing him in his own hut."

They brought in a perforated barrel and lit a big fire. When all the dampness had dried out of the walls and roof, and the clay floor was hard, they laid down the wooden planks. Vincent carried in his little bed, a table, a chair and his easels. He tacked up his sketches, brushed a rough GOGH into the whitewashed wall next to the kitchen, and settled down to become a Dutch Millet.

2

The most interesting people around Nuenen were the weavers. They dwelt in little thatched, clay and straw huts, generally of two rooms. In the one room, with a tiny patch of window letting in just a sliver of light, the family lived. There were square recesses in the walls, about three feet off the ground, for beds; a table, a few chairs, a peat stove, and a rough cabinet for the dishware and pots. The floor was of uneven clay, the walls of mud. In the adjoining room, about a third the size of the living room, and with half its height cut off by sloping eaves, was the loom.

A weaver who worked steadily could weave a piece of sixty yards in a week. While he weaved, a woman had to spool for him. On that piece of cloth the weaver made a net profit of four and a half francs a week. When he took it to the manufacturer, he often got the message that not before one or two weeks had passed could he take another piece home. Vincent found that they had a different spirit from the miners of the Borinage; they were quiet, and nowhere was there to be heard anything resembling rebellious speeches. But they looked as cheerful as cab horses, or the sheep transported by steamer to England.

Vincent quickly made friends with them. He found the weavers to be simple souls, asking only for enough work to earn the potatoes, coffee, and occasional strip of bacon on which they lived. They did not mind his painting while they worked; he never came without a bit of sweet for the child of the family, or a bag of tobacco for the old grandfather.

He found a loom of old, greenish-brown oak, in which the date 1730 was cut. Near the loom, before a little window which looked out on a green plot, stood a baby chair. The baby in it sat gazing for hours at the flying shuttle. It was a miserable little room with a clay floor, but in it Vincent found a certain peace and beauty which he tried to capture on his canvas.

He arose early in the morning and spent the entire day in the fields, or in the huts of the peasants and weavers. He felt at home with the people of the field and the loom. It had not been in vain that he had spent so many evenings with the miners, the peat diggers, and peasants, musing by the fire. By witnessing peasant life continually, at all hours of the day, he had become so absorbed in it that he hardly thought of anything else. He was searching for *ce qui ne passe pas dans ce qui passe*.

He went back to his love of drawing from the figure, but along with it he now had another love; colour. The half-ripe corn fields were of a dark golden tone, ruddy and gold bronze, raised to a maximum of effect by contrast to the broken cobalt tone of the sky. In the background were women's figures, very rough, very energetic, with sunbronzed faces and arms, with dusty, coarse, indigo clothes, and black bonnets in the form of berets on their short hair.

When he came swinging vigorously along the main road, easel strapped to his back, and wet canvas under his arm, the blinds of every house would open just a crack from the bottom, and he would run the gauntlet of curious and scandalized feminine eyes. At home he found that the old saying, "A door must either be open or shut," was not altogether true when applied to family relationships. The door of domestic felicity at the parsonage had a habit of remaining in some mysterious position that was very definitely neither open nor shut. His sister Elizabeth loathed him; she was afraid his eccentricities would ruin her marriage chances in Nuenen. Willemien liked him but thought him a bore. It was not until later that he became friends with his younger brother Cor.

Vincent ate his dinner, not at the family table, but in one corner, his plate on his lap, and the sketches of the day propped up on a chair before him, scrutinizing his work with piercing eyes, ripping it to pieces for imperfections and poor values. He never spoke to the family. They rarely addressed him. He ate his bread dry because he did not want to get in the habit of indulging himself. Occasionally, if the name of some writer whom he liked came up for discussion at the table, he would turn to them and speak for a moment. But on the whole he found that the less they had to say to each other, the better off they all were.

3

He had been painting in the fields for about a month when he began to have the very curious feeling that he was being watched. He knew that the people of Nuenen stared at him, that the peasants in the field used to rest on their hoes occasionally and gaze at him in wonder. But this was something different. He had a sense that he was not only being

224

watched, but followed. For the first few days he tried to shake it off, impatiently, but he could not get rid of the sensation that a pair of eyes was staring holes through his back. Many times he searched the field about him with his glance, but he could see nothing. Once he thought he saw the white skirt of a woman disappear behind a tree when he turned suddenly. Another time, as he came out of a weaver's house, a figure scurried quickly down the road. Still a third time, when he was painting in the woods, he left his easel and walked to the pond for a drink. When he returned, he found fingerprints in the wet paint.

It took him almost two weeks to catch the woman. He was sketching diggers on the heath; there was an old abandoned wagon not far from him. The woman stood behind it while he worked. He picked up his canvas and easel suddenly, and pretended that he was making for home. The woman ran on ahead. He followed without arousing her suspicion, and saw her turn in at the house next to the parsonage.

"Who lives next door on the left, Mother?" he asked as they all sat down to dinner that night.

"The Begeman family."

"Who are they?'

"'We don't' know much about them. There are five daughters and a mother. The father evidently died some time ago.'

"What are they like?'

"It's hard to tell; they're rather secretive."

"Are they Catholic?"

"No, Protestant. The father was a dominie."

"Are any of the girls unmarried?"

"Yes, all of them. Why do you ask?"

"I just wondered. Who supports the family?"

"No one. They seem to be wealthy."

"You don't know any of the girls' names, I suppose?"

His mother looked at him curiously. "No."

The following day he went back to the same spot in the fields. He wanted to catch the blue of the peasant figures in the ripe corn or against the withered leaves of a beech hedge. The people wore a coarse linen which they wove themselves, warp black, woof blue, the result of which was a black and blue, striped pattern. When this faded and became somewhat discoloured by wind and weather, it was an infinitely quiet, delicate tone which just brought out the flesh colours.

About the middle of the morning he felt the woman behind

him again. Out of the corner of his eye he caught a sight of her dress in a copse behind the abandoned wagon. ·

"I'll catch her today," he murmured to himself, "even if I have to stop in the middle of this study."

He was getting more and more into the habit of *dashing a thing off*, getting down his impression of the scene before him in one great splurge of passionate energy. What had struck him most about the old Dutch pictures was that they had been painted quickly, that the great masters dashed off a thing from the first stroke and did not retouch it. They had painted in a grand rush to keep intact the purity of their first impression, of the mood in which the motif had been conceived.

He forgot about the woman, in the heat of his creative passion. When he happened to glance around an hour later, he noticed that she had left the woods and was now standing behind the wagon. He wanted to jump up and catch her, ask her why she had been following him all this time, but he could not tear away from his work. After a while he turned around again and noted to his surprise that she was standing in front of the wagon, gazing at him steadily. It was the first time she had come out into the open.

He went on working at a fever pitch. The harder he worked, the closer the woman seemed to come. The more passion he poured out on the canvas, the hotter the eyes became that were staring through his back. He turned his easel a fraction to get the light and saw that she was standing in the middle of the field, half-way between the wagon and himself. She looked like a woman mesmerized, walking in her sleep. Step by step she came closer and closer, pausing each time, trying to hold back, coming steadily forward, impelled toward him by some power beyond her control. He felt her at his back. He whirled about and gazed into her eyes. There was a frightened, feverish expression on her face ; she seemed caught up in some baffling emotion which she could not master. She did not look at Vincent, but at his canvas. He waited for her to speak. She remained silent. He turned back to his work and in a final burst of energy, finished. The woman did not move. He could feel her dress touching his coat.

It was late afternoon. The woman had been standing in the field for many hours. Vincent was exhausted, his nerves worked up to a fine edge by the excitement of creation. He got up and turned to the woman.

Her mouth went dry. She moistened the upper lip with her

tongue, then the lower lip with the upper one. The slight
moisture vanished instantly and her lips became parched. She
had a hand at her throat and seemed to have difficulty in
breathing. She tried to speak, but could not.

"I am Vincent Van Gogh, your neighbour," he said. "But I
suppose you know that."

"Yes." It was a whisper, so faint he could hardly hear it.

"Which one of the Begeman sisters are you?"

She swayed a little, caught him by the sleeve and steadied
herself. Again she tried to moisten her lips with a dry tongue,
and made several attempts to speak before she succeeded.

"Margot."

"And why have you been following me, Margot Begeman?
I've known about it for several weeks."

A muted cry escaped her lips. She dug her nails into his arms
to support herself, then fell to the ground in a faint.

Vincent went on his knees, put his arm under her head, and
brushed the hair back from her brow. The sun was just setting
red over the fields and the peasants were trudging their weary
way home. Vincent and Margot were alone. He looked at her
carefully. She was not beautiful. She must have been well on in
her thirties. Her mouth stopped abruptly at the left corner,
but on the right a thin line continued down almost to the jaw.
There were circles of blue with little flesh freckles under the
eyes. The skin seemed just on the point of going wrinkled.

Vincent had a little water with him in a canteen. He
moistened Margot's face with one of the rags he used to wipe
off paint. Her eyes shot open suddenly, and he saw that they
were good eyes, a deep brown, tender, almost mystical. He
took a little water on the end of his fingers and ran them over
Margot's face. She shivered against his arm.

"Are you feeling better, Margot?" he asked.

She lay there for a brief instant, looking into his green-blue
eyes, so sympathetic, so penetrating, so understanding. Then,
with a wild sob that seemed wrenched from her inmost core,
she flung her arms about his neck and buried her lips in his
beard.

4

The following day they met at an appointed place some
distance from the village. Margot had on a charming, high
necked, white cambric dress and was carrying a summer hat in

227

her hand. Although still nervous in his company, she seemed more self-possessed than she had been the day before. Vincent laid down his palette when she came. She had not even a fraction of Kay's delicate beauty, but compared to Christine, she was a very attractive woman.

He rose from his stool, not knowing what to do. Ordinarily he was prejudiced against women who wore dresses; his territory was more those who wore jackets and petticoats. The so-called respectable class of Dutch women was not particularly attractive to paint or look at. He preferred the ordinary servant girls; they were often very Chardin-like.

Margot leaned up and kissed him, simply, possessively, as though they had been sweethearts for a long time, then held herself to him, trembling for a moment. Vincent spread his coat on the ground for her. He sat on his stool; Margot leaned against his knee and looked up at him with an expression that he had never seen before in the eyes of a woman.

"Vincent," she said, just for the pure joy of uttering his name.

"Yes, Margot." He did not know what to do or say.

"Did you think bad things of me last night?"

"Bad things? No. Why should I have?"

"You may find it difficult to believe, but, Vincent, when I kissed you yesterday, it was the first time I had ever kissed a man."

"But why? Have you never been in love?"

"No."

"What a pity."

"Isn't it?" She was silent for a moment. "You have loved other women, haven't you?"

"Yes."

"Many of them?"

"No. Just ... three."

"And did they love you?"

"No, Margot, they didn't."

"But they must have."

"I've always been unfortunate in love."

Margot moved closer to him and rested her arm on his lap. She ran the fingers of her other hand over his face playfully, touching his high ridged, powerful nose, the full, open mouth, the hard, rounded chin. A curious shiver ran through her; she took her fingers away.

"How strong you are," she murmured. "Everything about

228

you; your arms and chin and beard. I've never known a man like you before."

He cupped her face in his hands roughly. The love and excitement that throbbed there made it appealing.

"Do you like me a little?" she asked anxiously.

"Yes."

"And will you kiss me?"

He kissed her.

"Please don't think ill of me, Vincent. I couldn't help myself. You see, I fell in love ... with you ... and I couldn't keep away."

"You fell in love with me? You really fell in love with me? But why?"

She leaned up and kissed him on the corner of the mouth. "That's why," she said.

They sat quietly. A little way off was the Cimetière des Paysans. For ages the peasants had been laid to rest in the very fields which they dug up when alive. Vincent was trying to say on his canvas what a simple thing death was, just as simple as the falling of an autumn leaf, just a bit of earth dug up, a wooden cross. The fields around, where the grass of the churchyard ended beyond the little wall, made a last line against the sky, like the horizon of the sea.

"Do you know anything about me, Vincent?" she asked softly.

"Very little."

"Have they ... has anyone told you ... my age?"

"No."

"Well, I'm thirty-nine. In a very few months I shall be forty. For the last five years I have been telling myself that if I did not love someone before I left my thirties, I should kill myself."

"But it is easy to love, Margot."

"Ah, you think so?"

"Yes. It's only being loved in return that is difficult."

"No. In Nuenen it is very hard. For over twenty years I have wanted desperately to love someone. And I never have been able to."

"Never?"

She glanced away. "Once ... when I was a girl ... I liked a boy."

"Yes?"

"He was a Catholic. They drove him away."

229

"They?"

"My mother and sisters."

She rose to her knees in the deep loam of the field, soiling her pretty white dress. She placed both elbows on his thighs and rested her face in her hands. His knees touched her sides, gently.

"A woman's life is empty if she has no love to fill it, Vincent."

"I know."

"Every morning, when I awakened, I said to myself, 'Today, surely, I shall find someone to love! Other women do, so why shouldn't I?' Then night would come and I would be alone and miserable. An endless row of empty days, Vincent. I have nothing to do at home—we have servants—and every hour was filled up with longing for love. With each night I said to myself, 'You might just as well have been dead today, for all that you have lived.' I kept bolstering myself up with the thought that some day, somehow, a man must come along whom I could love. My birthdays passed, the thirty-seventh, and eighth, and ninth. I could not have faced forty without ever having loved. Then you came along, Vincent. *Now I too have loved at last!*"

It was a cry of triumph, as though she had gained a great victory. She leaned up, holding her mouth to be kissed. He stroked her soft hair back from her ears. She flung her arms about his neck and kissed him in a thousand wandering nibbles. Sitting there on his little painter's stool, his palette at his side, and the Cimetière des Paysans just in front, holding the kneeling woman close to him, and engulfed in the flow of her welled-up passion, Vincent felt for the first time in his life the luscious, healing balm of a woman's outpoured love. And he trembled, for he knew that he was on sacred ground.

Margot sat on the earth between his legs, her head back on his knee. There was colour in her cheeks and lustre in her eyes; she was breathing deeply and with effort. In the flush of her love she looked not more than thirty. Vincent, unable to feel anything at all, ran his fingers over the soft skin of her face until she clasped his hand, kissed it, and held the palm against her burning cheek. After a time she spoke.

"I know that you don't love me," she said quietly. "That would be asking too much. I only prayed to God to let me fall in love. I never even dreamed it would be possible for anyone

230

to love me. It's loving that's important, isn't it, Vincent, not being loved."

Vincent thought of Ursula and Kay. "Yes," he replied.

She rubbed the back of her head against his knee, looking up at the blue sky. "And you'll let me come with you? If you don't want to talk, I'll just sit by quietly and never say a word. Only let me be near you; I promise not to disturb you or interfere with your work."

"Of course you can come. But tell me, Margot, if there were no men in Nuenen, why didn't you go away? At least for a visit? Didn't you have the money?"

"Oh, yes, I have plenty of money. My grandfather left me a good income."

"Then why didn't you go to Amsterdam or The Hague? You would have met some interesting men."

"They didn't want me to."

"None of your sisters are married, are they?"

"No, dear, all five of us are single."

A flash of pain went through him. It was the first time a woman had ever called him dear. He had known before how miserable it was to love and not be loved in return, but he had never suspected the utter sweetness of having a good woman love him with the whole of her being. He had looked upon Margot's love for him as a sort of curious accident to which he was no party. That one, simple word, spoken so quietly and fondly by Margot, changed his entire mental state. He gathered Margot to him and held her quivering body against his.

"Vincent, Vincent," she murmured, "I love you so."

"How queer that sounds, to hear you say you love me so."

"I don't mind now that I've had to go all these years without love. You were worth waiting for, my very own dear. In all my dreams of love I never imagined that I could feel about anyone the way I do about you."

"I love you too, Margot," he said.

She drew away from him slightly. "You don't have to say that, Vincent. Maybe after a while you will come to like me a little. But now all I ask is that you let me love you!"

She slipped out of his arms, put his coat off to one side, and sat down. "Go to work, dear," she said. "I must not get in your way. And I love to watch you paint."

231

Nearly every day Margot accompanied him when he went out to paint. Oftentimes he would walk ten kilometres to reach the exact spot on the heath that he wanted to work with, and they would both arrive tired and exhausted by the heat. But Margot never complained. The woman had undergone a startling metamorphosis. Her hair, which had been a mouse brown, took on a live blonde tint. Her lips had been thin and parched; now her mouth went full and red. Her skin had been dry and almost wrinkled; now it was smooth and soft and warm. Her eyes seemed to grow larger, her breasts swelled out, her voice took on a new lilt, and her step became strong and vigorous. Love had opened some strange spring within her, and she was constantly being bathed in its elixir of love. She brought surprise lunches to please him, sent to Paris for some prints that he had mentioned with admiration, and never intruded on his work. When he painted, she sat perfectly still at his side, bathing in the same luxuriant passion that he flung at his canvases.

Margot knew nothing about painting, but she had a quick and sensitive intelligence, and a faculty for saying the right thing at the right moment. Vincent found that, without knowing, she understood. She gave him the impression of a Cremona violin that had been spoiled by bungling repairers.

"If I had only met her ten years ago!" he said to himself.

One day she asked him, as he was preparing to attack a new canvas, "How can you be sure that the spot you choose will come out right on the canvas?"

Vincent thought for a moment and then replied, "If I want to be active, I must not be afraid of failures. When I see a blank canvas staring at me with a certain imbecility, I just dash something down."

"You certainly do dash. I never saw anything grow as fast as your canvases."

"Well, I have to. I find paralysing the stare of a blank canvas which says to me, 'You don't know anything!' "

"You mean it's a sort of challenge?"

"Exactly. The blank canvas stares at me like an idiot, but I know that it is afriad of the passionate painter who dares, who once and for all has broken the spell of that 'you cannot.' Life itself turns towards a man an infinitely vacant, discouraging, hopelessly blank side on which nothing is written, Margot, no more than on this blank canvas."

"Yes, doesn't it."

"But the man of faith and energy is not frightened by that blankness; he steps in, he acts, he builds up, he creates, and in the end the canvas is no longer blank but covered with the rich pattern of life."

Vincent enjoyed having Margot in love with him. She never looked upon him with critical eyes. Everything he did she thought right. She did not tell him that his manners were crude, that his voice was rough, that there were harsh lines in his face. She never condemned him for not earning money, or suggested that he do anything but paint. Walking home through the quiet dusk, his arm about her waist, his voice soft from her sympathy, he told her all of the things he had done, of why he preferred painting the *rouwboerke* (peasant in mourning) to the Mayor, why he thought a peasant girl, in her dusty and patched blue petticoat and bodice, more beautiful than a lady. She questioned nothing and accepted everything. He was what he was, and she loved him completely.

Vincent was unable to get used to his new position. Every day he waited for the relationship to break, for Margot to become unkind and cruel, and confront him with his failures. Her love increased with the ripening of the summer; she gave him that fullness of sympathy and adoration which only a mature woman can bestow. Unsatisfied that she did not turn against him of her own accord, he tried to goad her into condemnation by painting his failures as black as he could. She saw them not as failures, but as simple accounts of why he did what he had to do.

He told her the story of his fiasco in Amsterdam and the Borinage. "Surely that was a failure," he said. "Everything I did there was wrong, now wasn't it?"

She smiled up at him indulgently. "The king can do no wrong."

He kissed her.

Another day she said to him, "My mother tells me you are a wicked man. She has heard that you lived with loose women in The Hague. I told them it was vicious scandal."

Vincent related the tale of Christine. Margot listened with some of the brooding melancholy in her eyes that had been there before love dissipated it.

"You know, Vincent, there's something Christ-like about you. I'm sure my father would have thought so, too."

"And that's all you can find to say to me when I tell you I lived for two years with a prostitute?"

"She wasn't a prostitute; she was your wife. Your failure to save her was not your fault, any more than was your failure to save the Borains. One man can do very little against a whole civilization."

"It's true, Christine was my wife. I told my brother Theo, when I was younger, 'If I cannot get a good wife, I shall take a bad one. Better a bad one than none at all.'"

There was a slightly strained silence; the subject of marriage had not come up between them. "There is only one thing I regret about the Christine affair," said Margot. "I wish I could have had those two years of your love for myself."

He gave up trying to break her love for him, and accepted it. "When I was younger, Margot," he said, "I thought that things depended on chance, on small accidents or misunderstandings that had no reason. But getting older, I begin to see deeper motives. It is the plight of most people that by a kind of fatality they have to seek a long time for light."

"As I had to seek for you!"

They had reached the low door of a weaver's house. Vincent pressed her hand warmly. She gave him a smile of such sweet surrender that he wondered why fate had seen fit to keep love from him all these years. They entered the thatched hut. Summer had passed into fall and the days were growing dark. A suspension lamp hung over the loom. A piece of red cloth was being woven. The weaver and his wife were arranging the threads; dark, bent figures against the light, standing out against the colour of the cloth, casting big shadows on the laths and beams of the loom. Margot and Vincent exchanged an understanding smile; he had taught her to catch the underlying beauty in ugly places.

By November and the *chute des feuilles*, when all the leaves on the trees fell off in a few days, the whole of Nuenen was talking about Vincent and Margot. The village liked Margot; it distrusted and feared Vincent. Margot's mother and four sisters tried to break off the affair, but she insisted that it was only a friendship, and what harm could there be in walking in the fields together? The Begemans knew Vincent to be a drifter, and confidently expected him to leave any day. They were not greatly worried. The village was; it said over and over again that no good could come from that queer Van Gogh man, and that the Begeman family would regret it if they did not keep their daughter out of his hands.

Vincent could never understand why the people of the town disliked him so. He interfered with no one, injured no one. He did not realize what a strange picture he made in this quiet hamlet, where life had not changed in one word or custom for hundreds of years. It was not until he found that they thought him an idler that he gave up hope of making them like him. Dien van den Beek, a small shopkeeper, hailed him as he was passing one day, and threw down the gage for the village.

"Fall has come now and the nice weather is over, eh?" he asked.

"Yes."

"A man supposes you'll be going to work soon, eh?"

Vincent shifted the easel on his back to a more comfortable position. "Yes, I'm just on my way out to the heath."

"No, I mean work," said Dien. "Real work that you do all year."

"Painting is my work," said Vincent quietly.

"A man means work that you get paid for ; a job."

"Going to the fields as you see me now is my job, Mijnheer van den Beek, just as selling goods is yours."

"Yes, but I sell goods! Do you sell what you make?"

Every soul to whom he had spoken in the village had asked that identical question. He was getting heartily sick of it.

"I sell sometimes. My brother is a dealer and he buys."

"You should go to work, Mijnheer. It is not good for you to idle this way. A man will grow old and he will have nothing."

"Idle! I work twice as long as you keep this store open."

"You call that work? Sitting and daubing? That's only play for children. Keep a store; plough in the fields; that's a real man's work. You're getting too old to be wasting your time."

Vincent knew that Dien van den Beek merely voiced the opinion of the village, and that to the provincial mind the words artist and worker were mutually exclusive. He gave up caring what the people thought, and ceased to see them when he passed them on the street. When their distrust of him had come to a positive climax, an accident happened that put him back in favour.

Anna Cornelia broke her leg on getting out of the train at Helmond. She was rushed home immediately. Although the

235

doctor did not tell the family so, he feared for her life. Vincent threw aside his work without a second thought. His experience in the Borinage had made him an excellent nurse. The doctor watched him for a half hour and then said, "You are better than a woman; your mother will be in excellent hands."

The people of Nuenen, who could be as kind in times of a crisis as they could be cruel in times of boredom, came to the vicarage with dainties and books and comforting thoughts. They stared at Vincent in utter amazement; he changed the bed without moving his mother, bathed and fed her, took care of the cast on her leg. At the end of two weeks, the village had completely revised its opinion of him. He spoke to them in their own language when they came; they discussed how best to avoid bed sores, what foods a sick person should eat, how warm the room should be kept. Talking to him thus and understanding him, they decided that he was a human being after all. When his mother felt a little better and he could go out to paint for a short time each day, they addressed him with a smile, and by name. He no longer felt the blinds go up a tiny fraction from the bottom, one by one, as he walked through the town.

Margot was at his side at all times. She was the only one who was not amazed at his gentleness. They were speaking in whispers in the sick room one day, when Vincent happened to remark, "The key to many things is the thorough knowledge of the human body, but it decidedly costs money to learn it. There is a very beautiful book, 'Anatomy for Artists,' by John Marshall, but it is very expensive."

"Haven't you the money to spare?"

"No, and I shan't have until I sell something."

"Vincent, it would make me so happy if you would let me lend you some. You know I have a regular income, and I never manage to spend it."

"It's good of you, Margot, but I couldn't."

She did not press her point, but a couple of weeks later handed him a package from The Hague. "What is it?" he asked.

"Open it and see."

There was a little note tied on the cord. The package contained Marshall's book; the note read FOR THE HAPPIEST BIRTHDAY OF THEM ALL.

"But this isn't my birthday!" he exclaimed.

"No," laughed Margot, "it's mine! My fortieth, Vincent.

You gave me a present of my life. Do be good and take it, dear. I'm so happy today, and I want you to be, too."

They were in his studio in the garden. No one was about, only Willemien who was sitting with her mother in the house. It was late afternoon, and the falling sun pasted a slight patch of light on the whitewashed wall. Vincent fingered the book tenderly; it was the first time anyone but Theo had been so happy to help him. He threw the book on the bed and took Margot in his arms. Her eyes were slightly misty with the love of him. During the past few months they had done very little caressing in the fields; they were afraid of being seen, Margot always gave herself to his caresses so whole-heartedly, with such generous surrender. It was five months now since he had left Christine; he was a little nervous about trusting himself too far. He wanted to do nothing to injure Margot or her love for him.

He looked down into her kind brown eyes as he kissed her. She smiled at him, then closed her eyes and opened her lips slightly to receive his. They held each other tightly, their bodies fitting from mouth to toe. The bed was only a step away. Together, they sat down. In that locked embrace each forgot the loveless years that had made their lives so stark.

The sun sank and the square of light on the wall went out. The wrangle room was bathed in a mellow dusk. Margot ran her hand over Vincent's face, strange sounds coming from her throat in the language of love. Vincent felt himself sinking into the abyss from which there is only one precipitate return. He tore himself from Margot's arms and jumped up. He went to his easel and crumpled a piece of paper on which he had been working. There was no sound but the call of the magpie in the acacias and the tinkling bells of the cows coming home. After a moment Margot spoke, quietly and simply.

"You can if you want, dear," she said.

"Why?" he asked, without turning about.

"Because I love you."

"It wouldn't be right."

"I told you before, Vincent, the king can do no wrong!"

He dropped on one knee. Her head lay on the pillow. He noticed again the line on the right side of her mouth, that ran down to her jaw, and kissed it. He kissed the too narrow bridge of her nose, the two full nostrils, and ran his lips over the skin of her face that had gone ten years younger. In the dusk, lying receptively with her arms about his neck, she looked again the beautiful girl she must have been at twenty.

"I love you, too, Margot," he said. "I didn't know it before, but now I do."

"It's sweet of you to say that, dear." Her voice was gentle and dreamy. "I know you like me a little. And I love you with all my heart. That satisfies me."

He did not love her as he had loved Ursula and Kay. He did not even love her as he had loved Christine. But he felt something very tender for this woman lying so passively in his arms. He knew that love included nearly every human relationship. Something within him ached at the thought that he could feel so little for the only woman in the world who loved him unrestrainedly, and he remembered the agony he had undergone because Ursula and Kay had not returned his love. He respected Margot's overwhelming love for him, yet in some inexplicable way he found it a trifle distasteful. Kneeling on the plank floor of the dark wrangle room, with his arms under the head of the woman who loved him just as he had loved Ursula and Kay, he at last understood why the two women had fled him.

"Margot," he said, "my life is a poor one, but I should be very happy if you would share it with me."

"I want to share it with you, dear."

"We could stay right here in Nuenen. Or would you rather go away after we're married?"

She rubbed her head against his arm, caressingly. "What is it that Ruth said? 'Whither thou goest, I will go.'"

6

They were in no way prepared for the storm that arose the next morning when they broke the news to their respective families. With the Van Goghs the problem was simply one of money. How could he take a wife when Theo was supporting him?

"First you must earn money and make your life straight; then you can marry," said his father.

"If I make my life straight by wrestling with the naked truth of my craft," replied Vincent, "the earning of money will come in due time."

"Then you must also marry in due time. But not now!"

238

The disturbance in the vicarage was only a little squall compared to what was going on next door in the house of women. With five sisters, all unmarried, the Begemans could face the world in a solid front. Margot's marriage would be a living proof to the village of the failure of the other girls. Madame Begeman thought it better that four of her daughters be kept from further unhappiness than that one of them be made happy.

Margot did not accompany him to the weavers that day. Late in the afternoon she came to the studio. Her eyes were puffy and swollen; she looked more her forty years than ever before. She held him close for a moment in a sort of desperate embrace.

"They've been abusing you frightfully all day," she said. "I never knew a man could be so many bad things and still live."

"You should have expected that."

"I did. But I had no idea they would attack you so viciously."

He put his arm about her gently and kissed her cheek. "Just leave them to me," he said. "I'll come in tonight after supper. Perhaps I can persuade them that I'm not such an awful person."

As soon as he set foot in the Begeman house he knew that he was in strange, alien territory. There was something sinister about the atmosphere created by six women, an atmosphere never broken by a masculine voice or footstep.

They led him into the parlour. It was cold and musty. There had not been people in it for months. Vincent knew the four sisters' names, but he had never taken the trouble to attach the names to the faces. They all seemed like caricatures of Margot. The eldest sister, who ran the household, took it upon herself to manage the inquisition.

"Margot tells us that you wish to marry her. May one presume to ask what has happened to your wife in The Hague?"

Vincent explained about Christine. The atmosphere of the parlour went several degrees colder.

"How old are you, Mijnheer Van Gogh?"

"Thirty-one."

"Has Margot told you that she is . . ."

"I know Margot's age."

"May one presume to ask how much money you earn?"

"I have a hundred and fifty francs a month."

239

"What is the source of that income?"

"My brother sends it to me."

"You mean your brother supports you?"

"No. He pays me a monthly salary. In return he gets everything I paint."

"How many of them does he sell?"

"I really couldn't say."

"Well, I can. Your father tells me he has never sold one of your pictures yet."

"He will sell them later. They will bring him in many times as much as they would now."

"That is problematical, to say the least. Suppose we discuss the facts."

Vincent studied the hard, unbeautiful face of the elder sister. He could expect no sympathy from that quarter.

"If you don't earn anything," she continued, "may one be allowed to ask how you expect to support a wife?"

"My brother chooses to gamble a hundred and fifty francs a month on me; that's his affair, not yours. For me it remains a salary. I work very hard to earn it. Margot and I could live on that salary if we managed carefully."

"But we wouldn't have to!" cried Margot. "I have enough to take care of myself."

"Be quiet, Margot!" commanded her eldest sister.

"Remember, Margot," said her mother, "I have the power to stop that income if you ever do anything to disgrace the family name!"

Vincent smiled. "Would marrying me be a disgrace?" he asked.

"We know very little about you, Mijnheer Van Gogh, and that little is unfortunate. How long have you been a painter?"

"Three years."

"And you are not successful yet. How long will it take you to become successful?"

"I don't know."

"What were you before you took up painting?"

"An art dealer, teacher, book-seller, divinity student and evangelist."

"And you failed at all of them?"

"I gave them up."

"Why?"

"I was not suited to them."

"How long will it take you to give up painting?"

"He'll never do that!" exclaimed Margot.

"It seems to me, Mijnheer Van Gogh," said the old sister, "that you are presumptuous in wanting to marry Margot. You're hopelessly *declassé*, you haven't a franc to your name, nor any way of earning one, you are unable to stick to any sort of job, and you drift about like an idler and a tramp. How could we dare to let our sister marry you?"

Vincent reached for his pipe, then put it back again. "Margot loves me and I love her. I can make her happy. We would live here for another year or so and then go abroad. She will never receive anything but kindness and love from me."

"You'll desert her!" cried one of the other sisters who had a shriller voice. "You'll get tired of her and desert her for some bad woman like the one in The Hague!"

"You just want to marry her for her money!" said another.

"But you won't get it," announced the third. "Mother will turn the allowance back into the estate."

Tears came to Margot's eyes. Vincent rose. He realized that there was no use wasting time on these viragoes. He would simply have to marry Margot in Eindhoven and leave for Paris immediately. He did not want to go away from the Brabant yet; his work was not finished there. But he shuddered when he thought of leaving Margot alone in that house of barren women.

Margot suffered in the days that followed. The first snow fell and Vincent was forced to work in his studio. The Begemans would not allow Margot to visit him. From the moment she got out of bed in the morning until she was permitted to feign sleep, she was forced to listen to tirades against Vincent. She had lived with her family for forty years; she had known Vincent only a few months. She hated her sisters, for she knew they had destroyed her life, but hatred is one of the more obscure forms of love and sometimes breeds a stronger sense of duty.

"I don't understand why you won't come away with me,' Vincent told her, "or at least marry me here without their consent."

"They wouldn't let me."

"Your mother?"

"My sisters. Mother merely sits back and agrees."

"Does it matter what your sisters say?"

"Do you remember I told you that when I was young I almost fell in love with a boy?"

241

"Yes."

"They stopped that. My sisters. I don't know why. All my life they've stopped the things I wanted to do. When I decided to visit relatives in the city, they wouldn't let me go. When I wished to read, they wouldn't allow the better books in the house. Every time I invited a man to the house, they would rip him to pieces after he left so that I could never look at him again. I wanted to do something with my life; become a nurse, or study music. But no, I had to think the same things they thought, and live exactly as they lived."

"And now?"

"Now they won't let me marry you."

Much of the newly acquired life had gone out of her voice and carriage. Her lips were dry, and the tiny flesh freckles under her eyes stood out.

"Don't worry about them, Margot. We will marry and that will be the end of it. My brother has often suggested that I come to Paris. We could live there."

She did not answer. She sat on the edge of the bed and stared down at the floor planking. Her shoulders turned in a crescent. He sat beside her and took her hand.

"Are you afraid to marry me without their consent?"

"No." Her voice was without strength or conviction. "I'll kill myself, Vincent, if they take me away from you. I couldn't stand it. Not after having loved you. I'll kill myself, that's all."

"They wouldn't have to know. Do it first and tell them afterwards."

"I can't go against them. They're too many for me. I can't fight them all."

"Well, don't bother fighting them. Just marry me and that will be the end of it."

"It wouldn't be the end. It would be the beginning. You don't know my sisters."

"Nor do I want to! But I'll have another try at them tonight."

He knew it was futile, the moment he entered the parlour. He had forgotten the chilling air of the place.

"We've heard all that before, Mijnheer Van Gogh," said the sister, "and it neither convinces nor impresses us. We have made up our minds about this matter. We want to see Margot happy, but we don't want her to throw her life away. We have decided that if at the end of two years you still want to marry, we will withdraw our objections."

"Two years!" said Vincent.

"I won't be here in two years," said Margot quietly.

"Where will you be?"

"I'll be dead. I'll kill myself if you don't let me marry him."

During the flood of, "How dare you say such things!" and "You see the sort of influence he's had on her!" Vincent escaped. There was nothing more he could do.

The years of maladjustment had told on Margot. She was not nervously strong, nor was her health of the best. Under the frontal attack of the five determined women, her spirits sank lower and lower with each passing day. A girl of twenty might have fought her way out unscathed, but Margot had had all the resistance and will beaten out of her. The wrinkles showed on her face, the old melancholy returned to her eyes, her skin went sallow and rough. The line on the right side of her mouth deepened.

The affection Vincent had felt for Margot evaporated with her beauty. He never really loved her or wanted to marry her; now he wanted to less than ever. He was ashamed of his callousness; that made him all the more ardent in his love making. He did not know whether she divined his true feelings.

"Do you love them more than you do me, Margot?" he asked one day when she managed to escape to his studio for a few minutes.

She shot him a look of surprise and reproach. "Oh, Vincent!"

"Then why are you willing to give me up?"

She cuddled into his arms like a tired child. Her voice was low and lost. "If I thought you loved me as I love you, I would go against the whole world. But it means so little to you ... and so much to them ..."

"Margot, you're mistaken, I love you ..."

She laid her finger gently on his lips. "No, dear, you would like to ... but you don't. You mustn't feel badly about it. I want to be the one who loves the most."

"Why don't you break away from them and be your own master?"

"It's easy for you to say that. You're strong; you can fight anyone. But I'm forty ... I was born in Neunen ... I've never

243

been farther away than Eindhoven. Don't you see, dear, I've never broken with anyone or anything in my life."

"Yes, I see."

"If it was something *you* wanted, Vincent, I would fight for you with all my strength. But it's only something I want. And after all, it comes so late . . . my life is gone now . . ."

Her voice sank to a whisper. He raised her chin with his first finger and held it with his thumb. There were unshed tears in her eyes.

"My dear girl," he said. "My very dear Margot. We could live a whole life together. All you need to say is the word. Pack your clothes tonight while your family is asleep. You can hand them to me out the window. We'll walk to Eindhoven and catch the early morning train to Paris."

"It's no use, dear. I'm part of them and they're part of me. But in the end I'll have my way."

"Margot, I can't bear to see you unhappy this way."

She turned her face to him. The tears went away. She smiled. "No, Vincent, I'm happy. I got what I asked for. It's been wonderful loving you."

He kissed her, and on her lips he tasted the salt from the tears that had rolled down her cheek.

"It has stopped snowing," she said a little later. "Are you going to sketch in the fields tomorrow?"

"Yes, I think so."

"Where will you be? I'll come to you in the afternoon."

He worked late the next day, a fur cap on his head and the linen blouse drawn tightly around his neck. The evening sky was of lilac with gold, over dark silhouettes of the cottages, between the masses of ruddy-coloured brushwood. Above, the spare black poplars rose; the foreground was of a faded and bleached green, varied by strips of black earth and pale dry reeds along the ditch edges.

Margot came walking rapidly across the field. She was wearing the same white dress in which he had first met her, with a scarf thrown over her shoulders. He noticed a faint touch of colour in her cheeks. She looked like the woman who had bloomed so beautifully under love only a few weeks back. She was carrying a small work-basket in her hands.

She flung her arms about his neck. He could feel her heart beating wildly against him. He tipped her head back and looked into the brownness of her eyes. The melancholy was gone.

244

"What is it?" he asked. "Has something happened?"

"No, no," she cried, "it's ... it's just that I'm happy ... to be with you again ..."

"But why have you come out in this light dress?"

She was silent for a moment and then said, "Vincent, no matter how far away you go, I want you always to remember one thing about me."

"What, Margot?"

"That I loved you! Always remember that I loved you more than any other woman in your whole life."

"Why are you trembling so?"

"It's nothing. I was detained. That's why I was late. Are you nearly finished?"

"In a few moments."

"Then let me sit behind you while you work, just as I used to. You know, dear, I never wanted to be in your way, or hinder you. I only wanted you to let me love you."

"Yes, Margot." He could think of nothing else to say.

"Then go to work, my darling, and finish ... so that we can go home together." She shivered a little, drew the scarf about her, and said, "Before you begin, Vincent, kiss me just once more. The way you kissed me ... that time ... in your studio ... when we were so happy in each other's arms."

He kissed her tenderly. She drew her dress about her and sat behind him. The sun disappeared and the short winter gloaming fell over the flat land. The quiet of the country evening engulfed them.

There was the clink of a bottle. Margot rose to her knees with a half stifled cry, then sank to the earth in a violent spasm. Vincent jumped up and flung himself before her. Her eyes were closed; across her face was spread a sardonic smile. She went through a series of quick convulsions; her body went rigid and arched backwards, with the arms flexed. Vincent bent over the bottle that was lying in the snow. A white, crystalline residue had been left just inside the mouth of the bottle. It was odourless.

He picked Margot up in his arms and ran madly across the fields. He was a kilometre away from Nuenen. He was afraid she would die before he could get her back to the village. It was just before the supper hour. People were sitting out in front of their doors. Vincent came in the far side of town and had to run through the full length of the village with Margot in his arms. He reached the Begeman house, kicked the door open with a smash of his boot, and laid Margot on the sofa in the parlour. The mother and sisters came running in.

"Margot took poison!" he cried. "I'll get the doctor!"

He ran for the village doctor and dragged him away from his supper table. "You are sure it was strychnine?" the medical man demanded.

"It looked that way."

"And she was still alive when you got her home?"

"Yes."

Margot was writhing on the divan when they got there. The doctor bent over her.

"It was strychnine, all right," he said, "but she took something along with it to kill the pain. Smells to me like laudanum. She didn't realize it would act as an antidote."

"Then she will live, doctor?" demanded the mother.

"She has a chance. We must get her to Utrecht immediately. She will have to be kept under close observation."

"Can you recommend a hospital in Utrecht?"

"I don't think a hospital advisable. We had better take her to a *maison de santé* for a time. I know a good one. Order your carriage. We must make that last train out of Eindhoven."

Vincent stood in a dark corner, silent. The carriage was brought around to the front of the house. The doctor wrapped Margot in a blanket and carried her out. Her mother and five sisters followed. Vincent brought up the rear. His family was standing next door, on the porch of the vicarage. The whole village had gathered before the Begeman house. A hard silence fell when the doctor came out with Margot in his arms. He lifted her into the carriage. The women got in. Vincent stood beside it. The doctor picked up the reins. Margot's mother turned, saw Vincent, and screamed:

"You did this! You killed my daughter!"

The crowd looked at Vincent. The doctor flicked the horses with the whip. The carriage disappeared down the road.

7

Before his mother had broken her leg, the villagers were unfriendly toward Vincent because they mistrusted him and could not understand his way of life. But they had never actively disliked him. Now they turned against him violently, and he could feel their hatred surrounding him on all sides.

246

Backs were turned when he approached. No one spoke to him or saw him. He became a pariah.

He did not mind for his own sake—the weavers and peasants in their huts still accepted him as their friend—but when people stopped coming to the parsonage to see his parents, he realized that he would have to move.

Vincent knew that the best thing for him to do was to get out of the Brabant altogether and leave his parents in peace. But where was he to go? The Brabant was his home. He wanted to live there always. He wished to draw the peasants and weavers; in that he found the only justification for his work. He knew that it was a good thing in the winter to be deep in the snow, in the autumn deep in the yellow leaves, in the summer among the ripe corn, and in spring amid the grass; that it was a good thing to be always with the mowers and peasant girls, in summer with a big sky overhead, in winter by the fireside, and to feel that it always had been so and always would be.

For him Millet's *Angelus* was the closest man had ever come to creating anything divine. In the crudeness of peasant life he found the only true and lasting reality. He wanted to paint out of doors, on the spot itself. There he would have to wipe off hundreds of flies, battle the dust and sand, and get the canvases scratched as he carried them for hours across the heath and hedges. But when he returned he would know that he had been face to face with reality and had caught something of its elemental simplicity. If his peasant pictures smelled of bacon, smoke, and potato steam, that was not unhealthy. If a stable smelled of dung, that belonged to a stable. If the fields had an odour of ripe corn or of guano or manure, that too was healthy—especially for people from the city.

He solved his problem in a very simple manner. A short distance down the road was the Catholic church, and next to it the house of the caretaker. Johannus Schafrath was a tailor; he followed that trade when he was not taking care of the church. His wife Adriana was a good soul. She rented Vincent two rooms, with a sort of pleasure at being able to do something for the man against whom the whole village had turned.

The Schafrath house was divided in the middle by a large hallway; on the right, as one entered, were the quarters of the family. On the left was a large sitting room overlooking the road, and a smaller room behind it. The sitting room became

247

Vincent's studio, the one behind it his storeroom. He slept upstairs in the beamed attic, one half of which was used for hanging out the Schafrath wash. In the other half was a high bed with a *veeren bed*, and a chair. When night came, Vincent would throw his clothes over the chair, jump into bed, smoke a bowl of tobacco, watch the glow fade into the darkness, and fall asleep.

In the studio he put up his drawings in water-colour and chalk ; heads of men and women whose Negro-like, turned up noses, projecting jawbones, and large ears were strongly accentuated. There were weavers and weaver's looms, women driving the shuttle, peasants planting potatoes. He made friends with his brother Cor ; together they built a cupboard and collected at least thirty different birds' nests, all kinds of moss and plants from the heath, shuttles, spinning wheels, bed warmers, peasants' tools, old caps and hats, wooden shoes, dishes, and everything connected with country life. They even put a small tree in one of the rear corners.

He settled down to work. He found that bistre and bitumen, which most painters were abandoning, made his colouring ripe and mellow. He discovered that he had to put little yellow in a colour to make it seem very yellow, if he placed it next to a violet or lilac tone.

He also learned that isolation is a sort of prison.

In March his father, who had walked a great distance over the heath to visit a sick parishioner, fell in a heap on the back steps of the parsonage. When Anna Cornelia got to him he was already dead. They buried him in the garden near the old church. Theo came home for the funeral. That night they sat in Vincent's studio, talking first of family affairs, then of their work.

"I have been offered a thousand francs a month to leave Goupils and go with a new house," said Theo.

"Are you going to take it?"

"I think not. I have an idea their policy will be purely commercial."

"But you've been writing me that Goupils . . ."

"I know, *les Messieurs* are also after the big profits. Still, I have been with them for twelve years. Why should I change for a few more francs? Some day they may put me in charge of one of their branches. If they do, I shall begin selling the Impressionists."

"Impressionists? I think I've seen that name in print some-where. Who are they?"

"Oh, just the younger painters around Paris; Edouard Manet, Degas, Renoir, Claude Monet, Sisley, Courbet, Lautrec, Gauguin, Cezanne, Seurat."

"Where did they get their name?"

"From the exhibition of 1874 at Nadar's. Claude Monet had a canvas there which he called *Impression; Soleil Levant*. A newspaper critic by the name of Louis Leroy called it an exhibition of *Impressionistes* and the name has stuck."

"Do they work in light or dark colours?"

"Oh, light! They despise dark colours."

"Then I don't think I could work with them. I intend to change my colouring, but I shall go darker instead of lighter."

"Perhaps you will think differently when you come to Paris."

"Perhaps so. Are any of them selling?"

"Durand-Rel sells an occasional Manet. That's about all."

"Then how do they live?"

"Lord only knows. On their wits, mostly. Rousseau gives violin lessons to children; Gauguin borrows from his former stock exchange friends; Seurat is supported by his mother; Cezanne by his father. I can't imagine where the others get their money."

"Do you know them all, Theo?"

"Yes, I'm getting acquainted slowly. I've been persuading *les Messieurs* to give them a smaller corner for exhibition at Goupils, but they wouldn't touch an Impressionist canvas with a ten foot pole."

"Those fellows sound like the sort I ought to meet. See here, Theo, you do absolutely nothing to procure me some distrac-tion by meeting other painters."

Theo went to the front window of the studio and stared out over the tiny grass plot that separated the caretaker's house from the road to Eindhoven.

"Then come to Paris and live with me," he said. "You're sure to end up there eventually."

"I'm not ready yet. I have some work to finish here, first."

"Well, if you remain in the provinces you can't hope to associate with your own kind."

"That may be true. But, Theo, there is one thing I cannot understand. You have never sold a single drawing or painting for me; in fact you have never even tried. Now have you?

249

"No."

"Why not?"

"I've shown your work to the connoisseurs. They say ..."

"Oh, the connoisseurs!" Vincent shrugged his shoulders. "I'm well acquainted with the banalities in which most connoisseurs indulge. Surely, Theo, you must know that their opinions have very little to do with the inherent quality of a piece of work."

"Well, I shouldn't say that. Your work is almost salable, but ..."

"Theo, Theo, those are the identical words you wrote to me about my very first sketches from Etten."

"They are true, Vincent; you seem constantly on the verge of coming into a superb maturity. I pick up each new sketch eagerly, hoping that at last it has happened. But so far ..."

"As for being salable or unsalable," interrupted Vincent, knocking out his pipe on the stove, "that is an old saw on which I do not intend to blunt my teeth."

"You say you have work here. Then pitch in and finish it. The sooner you get to Paris, the better it will be for you. But if you want me to sell in the meantime, send me pictures instead of studies. Nobody wants studies."

"Well, it's rather difficult to say just where a study leave off and a picture begins. Let us paint as much as we can, Theo, and be ourselves with all our faults and qualities. I say 'us' because the money from you, which I know costs you trouble enough to procure for me, gives you the right to consider half of it your own creation."

"Oh, as for that ..." Theo walked to the rear of the room and toyed with an old bonnet that hung on the tree.

8

Before his father's death Vincent had visited the parsonage only occasionally for supper or an hour of company. After the funeral his sister Elizabeth made it plain that he was entirely *persona non grata*; the family wished to keep up a certain position. His mother felt that he was responsible for his own life, and that it was her duty to stand by her daughters.

He was utterly alone in Nuenen now; in place of people, he put his study of nature. He began with a hopeless struggle to follow nature, and everything went wrong; he ended by calmly creating from his own palette and nature agreed with it

250

and followed. When he was miserable in his aloneness, he thought of the scene in Weissenbruch's studio and the sharp-tongued painter's approval of pain. In his faithful Millet he found Weissenbruch's philosophy expressed more cogently: "I do not ever wish to suppress suffering, because often it is that which makes the artists express themselves most forcibly."

He became friends with a family of peasants by the name of De Groot. There were the mother, father, son, and two daughters, all of whom worked in the fields. The De Groots, like most of the peasants of the Brabant, had as much right to be called *gueules noires* as the miners of the Borinage. Their faces were negroid, with wide, dilated nostrils, humped noses, huge distended lips and long angular ears. The features thrust far forward from the forehead, the head was small and pointed. They lived in a hut of one room with holes in the walls for beds. There was a table in the centre of the room, two chairs, a number of boxes, and a suspension lamp that hung down from the rough, beamed ceiling.

The De Groots were potato eaters. With their supper they had a cup of black coffee and, perhaps once a week, a strip of bacon. They planted potatoes, dug up potatoes and ate potatoes; that was their life.

Stien de Groot was a sweet child of about seventeen. She wore a wide white bonnet to work, and a black jacket with a white collar. Vincent fell into the habit of going to visit them every evening. He and Stien laughed together a great deal.

"Look!" she would cry. "I'm a fine lady. I'm being drawed. Shall I put on my new bonnet for you, Mijnheer?"

"No, Stien, you're beautiful just as you are."

"Me, beautiful!"

She went off into gales of laughter. She had large cheerful eyes and a pretty expression. Her face was indigenous to the life. When she leaned over to dig potatoes in the field, he saw in the lines of her body a more authentic grace than even Kay had possessed. He had learned that the essential note in figure drawing was action, and that the great fault with the figures in the pictures of the old masters was that they did not work. He sketched the De Groots digging in the field, setting their table at home, eating steamed potatoes, and always Stien would peer over his shoulder and joke with him. Sometimes of a Sunday she would put on a clean bonnet and collar, and walk with him on the heath. It was the only amusement the peasants had.

"Did Margot Begeman like you?" she asked once.

"Yes."

"Then why did she try to kill herself?"

"Because her family wouldn't let her marry me."

"She was foolish. Do you know what I would have done instead of killing myself? I would have loved you!"

She laughed up into his face and ran to a clump of pine woods. All day long they laughed and played among the pines. Other strolling couples saw them. Stien had a natural gift for laughter; the smallest things Vincent said or did brought unrestrained shouts from her lips. She wrestled with him and tried to throw him on the ground. When she did not like the things he drew at her house, she would pour coffee over them or toss them into the fire. She came often to his studio to pose, and when she left, the place would be in chaos.

And so the summer and fall passed and winter came again. Vincent was forced by the snow to work in his studio all the time. The people of Nuenen did not like to pose and if it were not for the money, nobody would have come to him. In The Hague he had drawn almost ninety seamstresses in order to do a group picture of three. He wanted to paint the De Groot family at its supper of potatoes and coffee, but in order to get them right, he felt he first had to draw every peasant in the vicinity.

The Catholic priest had never favoured renting room in the caretaker's house to the man who was both heathen and artist, but since Vincent was quiet and courteous, he could find no reason to put him out. One day Adriana Schafrath came into the studio, all excited. "Father Pauwels wishes to see you immediately!"

Father Andreas Pauwels was a large man, red of face. He took a hurried look about the studio and decided he had never seen such mad confusion.

"What can I do for you, Father?" Vincent asked politely.

"You can't do anything for me! But I can do something for you! I shall see you through this affair, providing you do as you are told."

"What affair do you refer to, Father?"

"She is a Catholic and you are a Protestant, but I shall get a special dispensation from the Bishop. Be prepared to marry within a few days!"

Vincent came forward to look at Father Pauwels in the full light of the window. "I'm afraid I don't understand, Father," he said.

"Oh, yes you do. And all this pretence is of no use. Stien de Groot is with child! The honour of that family must be upheld."

"The devil she is!"

"You may well call on the devil. This is indeed the devil's work."

"Are you certain of this, Father? You're not mistaken?"

"I don't go about accusing people until I have positive proof."

"And did Stien tell you . . . did she say . . . I was the man?"

"No. She refused to tell us his name."

"Then why do you confer this honour on me?"

"You've been seen together many times. Doesn't she come often to this studio?"

"Yes."

"Haven't you gone walking with her in the fields on Sunday?"

"Yes, I have."

"Well, what further proof do I need?"

Vincent was silent for a moment. Then he said quietly, "I'm sorry to hear about this, Father, particularly if it is going to mean trouble for my friend Stien. But I assure you that my relations with her have been above reproach."

"Do you expect me to believe that?"

"No," replied Vincent, "I don't."

That evening, when Stien returned from the fields, he was waiting for her on the step of their hut. The rest of the family went in to eat supper. Stien sank down beside him.

"I'll soon have somebody else for you to draw," she said.

"Then it's true, Stien?"

"Sure. Want to feel?"

She took his hand and put it on her abdomen. He was conscious of the growing protuberance.

"Father Pauwels just informed me that I was the father."

Stien laughed. "I wish it had been you. But you never wanted to, did you?"

He looked at the sweat of the fields caked in her dark skin, the heavy, crooked, coarse features, the thick nose and lips. She smiled at him.

"I wish it had been too, Stien."

253

"So Father Pauwels said it was you. That's funny."

"What's funny about it?"

"Will you keep my secret?"

"I promise."

"It was the *kerkmeester* of his church!"

Vincent whistled. "Does your family know?"

"Of course not. And I'll never tell them. But they know it wasn't you."

Vincent went inside the hut. There was no change in the atmosphere. The De Groots accepted Stien's pregnancy in the same spirit that they would have the cow's in the field. They treated him as they had before, and he knew they believed in his innocence.

Not so the village. Adriana Schafrath had been listening at the door. She quickly communicated the news to her neighbours. Within the hour, twenty-six hundred inhabitants of Nuenen knew that Stien de Groot was to be brought to bed with Vincent's child, and that Father Pauwels was going to force them to marry.

November and winter had come. It was time to be moving. There was no use in his remaining in Nuenen any longer. He had painted everything there was to paint, learned everything there was to learn about peasant life. He did not think he could go on living in the recrudescence of village hatred. Clearly the time had come for him to leave. But where was he to go?

"Mijnheer Van Gogh," said Adriana sadly, after knocking on the door, "Father Pauwels says you must leave this house at once and take lodging elsewhere."

"Very well; as he wishes."

He walked about his studio, looking at his work. Two solid years of slaving. Hundreds of studies of weavers and their wives, of looms, and peasants in the field, of the pollards at the bottom of the vicarage garden, and the old church tower, the heath and hedges in the heat of the sun and the cool of a winter dusk.

A great heaviness fell upon him. His work was all so fragmentary. There were bits of every phase of peasant life in the Brabant, but no one piece of work that summed up the peasant, that caught the spirit of his hut and his steaming potatoes. Where was his *Angelus* of the Brabantine peasant? And how could he leave before he had painted it?

He glanced at the calendar. There were still twelve days until the first of the month. He called Adriana.

"Tell Father Pauwels that I have paid until the first and will not leave before then."

He gathered up his easel, paints, canvas, and brushes and trudged off to the De Groot hut. No one was at home. He set to work on a pencil sketch of the inside of the room. When the family returned from the fields, he tore up the paper. The De Groots sat down to their steamed potatoes, black coffee, and bacon. Vincent set up his canvas and plugged on until the family went to bed. All that night he worked on the picture in his studio. He slept during the day. When he awakened he burned his canvas with savage disgust and set out again for the De Groots'.

The old Dutch masters had taught him that drawing and colour were one. The De Groots sat down to the table in the same positions as they had all their lives. Vincent wanted to make it clear how these people, eating their potatoes under the lamplight, had dug the earth with those very hands they put in the dish; he wanted it to speak of *manual* labour, and how they had honestly earned their food.

His old habit of throwing himself violently at a canvas came in handy now; he worked with tremendous speed and vitality. He did not have to think about what he was doing; he had drawn hundreds of peasants, and huts, and families sitting before their steamed potatoes.

"Father Pauwels was here today," said the mother.

"What did he want?" asked Vincent.

"He offered us money if we would not pose for you."

"What did you tell him?"

"We said you were our friend."

"He has visited every house around here," put in Stien. "But they told him they would rather earn a sou posing for you than take his charity."

The following morning he destroyed his canvas again. A feeling, half of rage and half of impotence, seized him. He had only ten days left. He had to get out of Nuenen; it was becoming insufferable. But he could not leave until he had fulfilled his promise to Millet.

Every night he went back to the De Groots. He worked until they were too sleepy to sit up any longer. Each night he tried new combinations of colours, different values and proportions; and each day he saw that he had missed, that his work was incomplete.

The last day of the month came. Vincent had worked himself into a frenzy. He had gone without sleep and largely without food. He was living on nervous energy. The more he failed, the higher his excitement rose. He was waiting at the De Groots' when they came in from the fields. His easel was set up, his pigments mixed, his canvas stretched on the frame. This was his very last chance. In the morning he was leaving the Brabant, for ever.

He worked for hours. The De Groots understood. When they finished their supper, they remained at the table, talking softly in the patois of the fields. Vincent did not know what he was painting. He dashed off the thing without any thought or consciousness coming between his hand and the easel. By ten o'clock, the De Groots were falling asleep and Vincent was exhausted. He had done all he could with the canvas. He gathered his things, kissed Stien, and bade them all good-bye. He trudged home through the night, unaware that he was walking.

In the studio he set the canvas on a chair, lit his pipe, and stood regarding his work. The whole thing was wrong. It missed. The spirit wasn't there. He had failed again. His two years of labour in the Brabant had been wasted.

He smoked his pipe down to the hot dregs. He packed his bag. He gathered all his studies off the wall and from the bureau, and placed them in a large box. He threw himself on the divan.

He did not know how much time passed. He got up, ripped the canvas off the frame, threw it into a corner, and put on a new one. He mixed some paints, sat down, and began work.

One starts with a hopeless struggle to follow nature, and everything goes wrong; one ends by calmly creating from one's palette, and nature agrees with it and follows.

On croit que j'imagine—ce n'est pas vrai—je me souviens.

It was just as Pietersen had told him in Brussels; he had been too close to his models. He had not been able to get a perspective. He had been pouring himself into the mould of nature; now he poured nature into the mould of himself.

He painted the whole thing in the colour of a good, dusty, unpeeled potato. There was the dirty, linen table cloth, the smoky wall, the lamp hanging down from the rough rafters, Stien serving her father with steamed potatoes, the mother pouring the black coffee, the brother lifting a cup to his lips, and on all their faces the calm, patient acceptance of the eternal order of things.

The sun rose and a bit of light peered into the storeroom window. Vincent got up from his stool. He felt perfectly calm and peaceful. The twelve days' excitement was gone. He looked at his work. It reeked of bacon, smoke, and potato steam. He smiled. He had painted his *Angelus*. He had captured that which does not pass in that which passes. The Brabant peasant would never die.

He washed the picture with the white of an egg. He carried his box of drawings and paintings to the vicarage, left them with his mother, and bade her good-bye. He returned to his studio, wrote *The Potato Eaters* on his canvas, put a few of his best studies with it, and set out for Paris.

BOOK FIVE

PARIS

1

"Then you didn't get my last letter?" asked Theo the next morning, as they sat over their rolls and coffee.

"I don't think so," replied Vincent. "What was in it?"

"The news of my promotion at Goupils."

"Why, Theo, and you didn't tell me a word about it yesterday!"

"You were too excited to listen. I have charge of the gallery on the Boulevard Montmartre."

"Theo, that's splendid! An art gallery of your own!"

"It really isn't my own, Vincent. I have to follow the Goupil policy pretty closely. But they let me hang the Impressionists on the *entresol*, so . . ."

"Who are you exhibiting?"

"Monet, Degas, Pissarro and Manet."

"Never heard of them."

"Then you'd better come along to the gallery and have a good, long look!"

"What does that sly grin on your face mean, Theo?"

"Oh, nothing. Will you have more coffee? We must go in a few minutes. I walk to the shop every morning."

"Thanks. No, no, only half a cup. Deuce take it, Theo, boy, but it's good to eat breakfast across the table from you once again!"

"I've been waiting for you to come to Paris for a long time. You had to come eventually, of course. But I do think it would have been better if you had waited until June, when I move to the Rue Lepic. We'll have three large rooms there. You can't do much work here, you see."

Vincent turned in his chair and glanced about him. Theo's apartment consisted of one room, a tiny kitchen, and a cabinet. The room was cheerfully furnished with authentic Louis Philippes, but there was hardly space enough to move around.

"If I set up an easel," said Vincent, "we'd have to move some of your lovely furniture out into the courtyard."

"I know the place is crowded, but I had a chance to pick these pieces up at a bargain and they're exactly what I want for the new apartment. Come along, Vincent, I'll take you down the hill on my favourite walk to the Boulevard. You don't know Paris until you smell it in the early morning."

Theo put on the heavy black coat that crossed up high under his immaculate, white bow tie, gave a final pat of the brush to the little curl that stood up on each side of the parting in his hair, and then smoothed down his moustache and soft chin beard. He put on his black bowler hat, took his gloves and walking stick, and went to the front door.

"Well, Vincent, are you ready? Good Lord, but you are a sight! If you wore that outfit anywhere but in Paris, you'd be arrested!"

"What's the matter with it?" Vincent looked down at himself. "I've been wearing it for almost two years and nobody's said anything."

Theo laughed. "Never mind, Parisians are used to people like you. I'll get you some clothes tonight when the gallery closes."

They walked down a flight of winding stairs, passed the *concierge's* apartment and stepped through the door to the Rue Laval. It was a fairly broad street, prosperous and respectable looking, with large stores selling drugs, picture frames and antiques.

"Notice the three beautiful ladies on the third floor of our building," said Theo.

Vincent looked up and saw three plaster of Paris heads and

258

busts. Under the first was written, Sculpture, under the middle one, Architecture, and under the last, Painting.

"What makes them think Painting is such an ugly wench?"

"I don't know," replied Theo, "but anyway, you got into the right house."

The two men passed Le Vieux Rouen, Antiquities, where Theo had bought his Louis Philippe furniture. In a moment they were in the Rue Montmartre, which wound gracefully up the hill to the Avenue Clichy and the Butte Montmartre, and down the hill to the heart of the city. The street was full of morning sunlight, of the smell of Paris arising, of people eating croissants and coffee in the cafés, of the vegetable, meat, and cheese shops opening to the day's trade.

It was a teeming bourgeois section, crowded with small stores. Workingmen walked out in the middle of the street. Housewives fingered the merchandise in the bins in front of the shops and bargained querulously with the merchants.

Vincent breathed deeply. "It's Paris," he said. "After all these years."

"Yes, Paris. The capital of Europe. Particularly for an artist."

Vincent drank in the busy flow of life winding up and down the hill; the *garçons* in alternately striped red and black jackets; the housewives carrying long loaves of unwrapped bread under their arms; the pushcarts at the curb; the *femmes de chambre* in soft slippers; the prosperous business men on their way to work. After passing innumerable *Charcuteries, pâtisseries, boulangeries, blanchisseries* and small cafés, the Rue Montmartre curved to the bottom of the hill and swung into the Place Chateaudun, a rough circle formed by the meeting of six streets. They crossed the circle and passed Notre Dame de Lorette, a square, dirty, black stone church with three angels on the roof, floating off idyllically into the blue empyrean. Vincent looked closely at the writing over the door.

"Do they mean this *Liberté-Egalité-Fraternité* business, Theo?"

"I believe they do. The Third Republic will probably be permanent. The royalists are quite dead, and the socialists are coming into power. Emile Zola was telling me the other night that the next revolution will be against capitalism instead of royalty."

"Zola! How nice for you to know him, Theo."

"Paul Cezanne introduced me to him. We all meet once a week at the Cafe Batignolles. I'll take you there next time I go."

After leaving the Place Chateaudun, the Rue Montmartre lost its bourgeois character and assumed a more stately air. The shops became larger, the cafés more imposing, the people better dressed, the buildings more prosperous looking. Music halls and restaurants lined the sidewalks, hotels made an appearance, and carriages took the place of trade wagons.

The brothers stepped along at a brisk pace. The cold sunlight was invigorating, the flavour of the air suggestive of the rich and complex life of the city.

"Since you can't work at home," said Theo, "I suggest you go to Corman's Studio."

"What's it like?"

"Well, Corman is just as academic as most masters, but if you don't want his criticism, he'll let you alone."

"Is it expensive?"

Theo tapped Vincent's thigh with his walking stick. "Didn't I tell you I was promoted? I'm getting to be one of those plutocrats that Zola is going to wipe out with his next revolution!"

At length the Rue Montmartre flowed into the wide, imposing Boulevard Montmartre, with its large department stores, arcades, and expensive shops. The Boulevard, which became the Boulevard des Italiens a few blocks farther on and led to the Place de l'Opéra, was the most important thorough-fare in the city. Although the street was empty at this hour of the morning, the clerks within the stores were preparing for a busy day.

Theo's branch of the Goupil Gallery was located at number 19, just one short block to the right of the Rue Montmartre. Vincent and Theo crossed the wide boulevard, stopped along-side of a gas lamp in the centre to let a carriage go by, and then continued on to the gallery.

The well groomed clerks bowed respectfully as Theo walked through the salon of his gallery. Vincent remembered how he used to bow to Tersteeg and Obach when he was a clerk. In the air was the same aroma of culture and refinement, a smell he thought his nostrils had forgotten. On the walls of the salon were paintings by Bouguereau, Henner, and Delaroche. Above the main salon was a small balcony, with a flight of stairs at the rear leading to it.

"The pictures you'll want to see are up on the *entresol*," said Theo. "Come down when you're through and tell me what you think of them."

"Theo, what are you licking your chops about?"

Theo's grin became all the broader. "*A toute à l'heure*," he said and disappeared into his office.

2

"Am I in a madhouse?"

Vincent stumbled blindly to the lone chair on the *entresol*, sat down and rubbed his eyes. From the age of twelve he had been used to seeing dark and sombre paintings; paintings in which the brushwork was invisible, every detail of the canvas correct and complete, and flat colours shaded slowly into each other.

The paintings that laughed at him merrily from the walls were like nothing he had ever seen or dreamed of. Gone were the flat, thin surfaces. Gone was the sentimental sobriety. Gone was the brown gravy in which Europe had been bathing its pictures for centuries. Here were pictures riotously mad with the sun. With light and air and throbbing vivacity. Paintings of ballet girls backstage, done in primitive reds, greens, and blues thrown next to each other irreverently. He looked at the signature. Degas.

There were a group of outdoor scenes along a river bank, caught with all the ripe, lush colour of midsummer and a hot overhead sun. The name was Monet. In all the hundreds of canvases that Vincent had seen, there was not as much luminosity, breath, and fragrance as in one of these glowing pictures. The darkest colour Monet used was a dozen times lighter than the lightest colour to be found in all the museums of Holland. The brushwork stood out, unashamed, every stroke apparent, every stroke entering into the rhythm of nature. The surface was thick, deep, palpitant with heavy globs of ripe, rich paint.

Vincent stood before a picture of a man in his woollen undershirt, holding the rudder of a little boat with the intense Gallic concentration characteristic of the Frenchman enjoying himself on a Sunday afternoon. The wife sat by, passively. Vincent looked for the name of the artist.

"Monet again?" he said aloud. "That's funny. There's not the slightest resemblance to his outdoor scene."

261

He looked again and saw that he was mistaken. The name was Manet, not Monet. Then he remembered the story of Manet's *Picnic on the Grass*, and *Olympia*, and how the police had had to rope off the pictures to keep them from being slashed by knives and spat upon.

He did not know why, but the Manet painting reminded him of the books of Emile Zola. There seemed to be that same fierce quest after truth, the same unafraid penetration, the same feeling that character is beauty, no matter how sordid it may appear. He studied the technique closely, and saw that Manet put elemental colours next to each other without gradation, that many details were barely suggested, that colours, lines, lights and shades did not end with definite precision, but wavered into each other.

"Just as the eye sees them waver in nature,"said Vincent.

He heard Mauve's voice in his ears. "Is it impossible for you to make a definite statement about a line, Vincent?"

He sat down again and let the pictures sink in. After a time he caught one of the simple expedients by which painting had been so completely revolutionized. These painters filled the air of their pictures solid! And that living, moving, replete air did something to the objects that were to be seen in them! Vincent knew that, for the academicians, air did not exist; it was just a blank space in which they placed rigid, set objects.

But these new men! They had discovered the air! They had discovered light and breath, atmosphere and sun; they saw things filtered through all the innumerable forces that live in that vibrant fluid. Vincent realized that painting could never be the same again. Photographic machines and academicians would make exact duplicates; painters would see everything filtered through their own natures and the sun-swept air in which they worked. It was almost as though these men had created a new art.

He stumbled down the stairs. Theo was in the main salon. He turned with a smile on his lips, searching his brother's face eagerly.

"Well, Vincent?" he said.

"Oh, Theo!" breathed Vincent.

He tried to speak, but could not. His eyes darted up to the *entresol*. He turned and ran out of the gallery.

He walked up the broad boulevard until he came to an octagonal building which he recognized as the Opera. Through the canyon of stone buildings he caught sight of a bridge, and made for the river. He slid down to the water's edge and dribbled his fingers in the Seine. He crossed the bridge without looking at the bronze horsemen, and made his way through the labyrinth of streets on the Left Bank. He climbed steadily upward. He passed a cemetery, turned to his right and came to a huge railway station. Forgetting that he had crossed the Seine, he asked a gendarme to direct him to Rue Laval.

"The Rue Laval?" said the gendarme. "You are on the wrong side of the city, Monsieur. This is Montparnasse. You must go down the hill, cross the Seine, and go up again to Montmartre."

For many hours Vincent stumbled through Paris, not caring much where he went. There were broad, clean boulevards with imposing shops, then wretched, dirty alleys, then bourgeois streets with endless rows of wine shops. Once again he found himself on the crest of a hill on which there was a triumphal arch. To the east he looked down over a tree-lined boulevard enclosed on both sides by narrow strips of park, and ending in a large square with an Egyptian obelisk. To the west he overlooked an extensive wood.

It was late afternoon before he found the Rue Laval. The dull ache within him had been numbed by sheer fatigue. He went directly to where his pictures and studies were tied in bundles. He spread them all out on the floor.

He gazed at his canvases. God! but they were dark and dreary. God! but they were heavy, lifeless, dead. He had been painting in a long past century, and he had not known it.

Theo came home in the gloaming and found Vincent sitting dully on the floor. He knelt beside his brother. The last vestiges of daylight were blotted out of the room. Theo was silent for some time.

"Vincent," he said, "I know how you feel. Stunned. It's tremendous, isn't it? We're throwing overboard nearly everything that painting has held sacred."

Vincent's small, hurt eyes caught Theo's and held them.

"Theo, why didn't you tell me? Why didn't I know? Why didn't you bring me here sooner? You've let me waste six long years."

"Waste them? Nonsense. You've worked out your craft for yourself. You paint like Vincent Van Gogh, and nobody else in the world. If you had come here before you crystallized your own particular expression, Paris would have moulded you to suit itself."

"But what am I to do? Look at this junk!" He kicked his foot through a large, dark canvas. "It's all dead, Theo. And worthless."

"You ask me what you are to do? I'll tell you. You are to learn about light and colour from the Impressionists. That much you must borrow from them. But nothing more. You must not imitate. You must not get swamped. Don't let Paris submerge you."

"But, Theo, I must learn everything all over. Everything I do is wrong."

"Everything you do is right ... except your light and colour. You were an Impressionist from the day you picked up a pencil in the Borinage. Look at your drawing! Look at your brushwork! No one ever painted like that before Manet. Look at your lines! You almost never make a definite statement. Look at your faces, your trees, your figures in the fields! They are your impressions. They are rough, imperfect, filtered through your own personality. That's what it means, to be an Impressionist; not to paint like everyone else, not to be a slave to rules and regulations. You belong to your age, Vincent, and you're an Impressionist whether you like it or not."

"Oh, Theo, do I like it!"

"Your work is known in Paris among the young painters who count. Oh, I don't mean those who sell, but those who are making the important experiments. They want to know you. You'll learn some marvellous things from them."

"They know my work? The young Impressionists know my work?"

Vincent got on his knees so that he could see Theo more clearly. Theo thought of the days in Zundert, when they used to play together on the floor of the nursery.

"Of course. What do you think I've been doing in Paris all these years? They think you have a penetrating eye and a draftsman's fist. Now all you need to do is lighten your palette and learn how to paint living, luminous air. Vincent, isn't it wonderful to be living in a time when such important things are happening?"

"Theo, you old devil, you grand old devil!"

"Come on, get off your knees. Make a light. let's get all dressed up and go out for dinner. I'll take you to the Brasserie Universelle. They serve the most delicious *Chateaubriand* in

Paris. I'm going to treat you to a real banquet. With a bottle of champagne, old boy, to celebrate the great day when Paris and Vincent Van Gogh were joined together!"

3

The following morning Vincent took his drawing materials and went to Corman's. The studio was a large room on the third floor, with a strong north light coming in from the street. There was a nude male model posed at one end, facing the door. About thirty chairs and easels were scattered about for the students. Vincent registered with Corman and was assigned an easel.

After he had been sketching about an hour, the door to the hall opened and a woman stepped in. There was a bandage wrapped around her head and she was holding one hand to her jaw. She took one horrified look at the naked model, exclaimed "*Mon Dieu!*" and ran.

Vincent turned to the man sitting beside him.

"What do you suppose was the matter with her?"

"Oh, that happens every day. She was looking for the dentist next door. The shock of seeing a naked man usually cures their toothache. If the dentist doesn't move he'll probably go bankrupt. You're a newcomer, aren't you?"

"Yes. This is only my third day in Paris."

"What's your name?"

"Van Gogh. What's yours?"

"Henri Toulouse-Lautrec. Are you any relation to Theo Van Gogh?"

"He's my brother."

"Then you must be Vincent! Well, I'm glad to know you. Your brother is the best art dealer in Paris. He's the only one who will give the young men a chance. Not only that, he fights for us. If we are ever accepted by the Parisian public, it will be due to Theo Van Gogh. We all think he's mighty fine."

"So do I."

Vincent looked closely at the man. Lautrec had a squashed down head; his features, the nose, lips, and chin, stuck far out from the flat head. He wore a full black beard, which grew outward from his chin instead of downward.

"What makes you come to a beastly place like Corman's?" asked Lautrec.

"I must have some place to sketch. What about you?"

265

"Damned if I know. I lived in a brothel all last month up in Montmartre. Did portraits of the girls. That was real work. Sketching in a studio is child's play."

"I'd like to see your studies of those women."

"Would you really?"

"Certainly. Why not?"

"Most people think I'm crazy because I paint dance hall girls and clowns and whores. But that's where you find real character."

"I know. I married one in The Hague."

"*Bien!* This Van Gogh family is all right! Let me see the sketch you've done of the model, will you?"

"Take them all, I've done four."

Lautrec looked at the sketches for some moments and then said, "You and I will get along together, my friend. We think alike. Has Corman seen these yet?"

"No."

"When he does, you'll be through here. That is, as far as his criticism is concerned. He said to me the other day, 'Lautrec, you exaggerate, always you exaggerate. One line in each of your studies is caricature.' "

"And you replied, 'That, my dear Corman, is character, not caricature.' "

A curious light came into Lautrec's black, needle-point eyes. "Do you still want to see those portraits of my girls?"

"I certainly do."

"Then come along. This place is a morgue, anyway."

Lautrec had a thick, squat neck, and powerful shoulders and arms. When he rose to his feet, Vincent saw that his new friend was a cripple. Lautrec, on his feet, stood no higher than when he was seated. His thick torso came forward almost to the apex of a triangle at the waist, then fell in sharply to the tiny shrivelled legs.

They walked down the Boulevard Clichy, Lautrec leaning heavily on his stick. Every few moments he would stop to rest, pointing out some lovely line in the juxtaposition of two buildings. Just one block this side of the Moulin Rouge they turned up the hill toward the Butte Montmartre. Lautrec had to rest more frequently.

"You're probably wondering what's wrong with my legs, Van Gogh. Everyone does. Well, I'll tell you."

"Oh, please! You don't need to speak of it."

"You might as well know." He doubled over his stick,

leaning on it with his shoulders. "I was born with brittle bones. When I was twelve, I slipped on a dance floor and broke my right thigh bone. The next year I fell into a ditch and broke the left one. My legs have never grown an inch since."

"Does it make you unhappy?"

"No. If I had been normal I should never have been a painter. My father is a count of Toulouse. I was next in line for the title. If I had wanted to, I could have had a marshal's baton and ridden alongside of the King of France. That is, providing there was a King of France ... *Mais, sacrebleu,* why should anyone be a count when he can be a painter?"

"Yes, I'm afraid the days of the counts are over."

"Shall we go on? Degas's studio is just down this alley. They say I'm copying his work because he does ballet dancers and I do the girls from the Moulin Rouge. Let them say what they like. This is my place, 19 *bis,* Rue Fontaine. I'm on the ground floor, as you might have guessed."

He threw open the door and bowed Vincent in.

"I live alone," he said. "Sit down, if you can find a place to sit."

Vincent looked about. In addition to the canvases, frames, easels, stools, steps, and rolls of drapery, two large tables encumbered the studio. One was laden with bottles of rare wines and decanters of multi-coloured liqueurs. On the other were piled up dancers' slippers, periwigs, old books, women's dresses, gloves, stockings, vulgar photographs, and precious Japanese prints. There was just one little space among all this litter where Lautrec could sit and paint.

"What's the matter, Van Gogh?" he asked. "Can't you find a place to sit? Just shove that junk on the floor and bring the chair over to the window. There were twenty-seven girls in the house. I slept with every one of them. Don't you agree that it's necessary to sleep with a woman before you can fully understand her?"

"Yes."

"Here are the sketches. I took them down to a dealer on the Capucines. He said, 'Lautrec, why have you a fixation on ugliness? Why do you always paint the most sordid and immoral people you can find? These women are repulsive, utterly repulsive. They have debauch and sinister evil written all over their faces. Is that what modern art means, to create ugliness? Have you painters become so blind to beauty that you can paint only the scum of the earth?' I said 'Pardon me,

267

but I think I'm going to be sick, and I shouldn't like to do it all over your lovely carpet.' Is that light all right, Van Gogh? Will you have a drink? Speak up, what do you prefer? I have everything you could possibly want."

He hobbled about the chairs, tables, and rolls of drapery with agile movements, poured a drink and passed it to Vincent.

"Here's to ugliness, Van Gogh," he cried. "May it never infect the Academy!"

Vincent sipped his drink and studied Lautrec's twenty-seven sketches of the girls of a Montmartre sporting house. He realized that the artist had set them down as he saw them. They were objective portraits, without moral attitude or ethical comment. On the faces of the girls he had caught the misery and suffering, the callous carnality, the bestial debauch and spiritual aloofness.

"Do you like portraits of peasants, Lautrec?" he asked.

"Yes, if they're not sentimentalized."

"Well, I paint peasants. And it strikes me that these women are peasants too. Gardeners of the flesh, so to speak. Earth and flesh, they're just two different forms of the same matter, aren't they? And these women till the flesh, human flesh that must be tilled to make it produce life. This is good work, Lautrec; you've said something worth saying."

"And you don't think them ugly?"

"They are authentic and penetrating commentaries on life. That is the very highest kind of beauty, don't you think? If you had idealized or sentimentalized the women, you would have made them ugly because your portraits would have been cowardly and false. But you stated the full truth as you saw it, and that's what beauty means, isn't it?"

"Jesus Christ! Why aren't there more men in the world like you? Have another drink! And help yourself to those sketches! Take as many as you like!"

Vincent held a canvas up to the light, cast about in his mind for a moment, and then exclaimed, "Daumier! That's who it reminds me of."

Lautrec's face lit up.

"Yes, Daumier. The greatest of them all. And the only person I ever learned anything from. God! how magnificently that man could hate!"

"But why paint things if you hate them? I paint only things I love."

"All great art springs from hatred, Van Gogh. Oh, I see you're admiring my Gauguin."

"Whose painting did you say that was?"

"Paul Gauguin. Did you know Him?"

"No."

"Then you should. That's a native Martinique woman. Gauguin was out there for a while. He's completely *fou* on the subject of going primitive, but he's a superb painter. He had a wife, three children, and a position on the stock exchange that brought him thirty thousand francs a year. He bought fifteen thousand francs worth of paintings from Pissarro, Manet, and Sisley. He painted his wife's portrait on their wedding day. She thought it a delightful *beau geste*. Gauguin used to paint on Sundays; you know, the Stock Exchange Art Club? Once he showed a picture to Manet, who told him it was very good. 'Oh,' replied Gauguin, 'I am only an amateur!' 'Oh, no,' said Manet, 'There are no amateurs but those who make bad pictures.' That remark went to Gauguin's head like neat spirits and he's never drawn a sober breath since. Gave up his job on the Exchange, lived with his family in Rouen for a year on his savings, then sent his wife and children to her parents' home in Stockholm. He's been living off his wits ever since."

"He sounds interesting."

"Be careful when you meet him; he loves to torment his friends. Say, Van Gogh, what about letting me show you the Moulin Rouge and the Elysée-Montmartre? I know all the girls there. Do you like women, Van Gogh? I mean to sleep with? I love them. What do you say, shall we make a night of it sometime?"

"By all means."

"Splendid. I suppose we must go back to Corman's. Have another drink before you go? That's it. Now just one more and you'll empty the bottle. Look out, you'll knock that table over. Never mind, the charwoman will pick all that stuff up. Guess I'll have to move out of here pretty soon. I'm rich, Van Gogh. My father is afraid I'll curse him for bringing me into the world a cripple, so he gives me everything I want. When I move out of a place I never take anything but my work. I rent an empty studio and buy things one by one. When I'm just about to be suffocated, I move again. By the way, what kind of women do you prefer? Blondes? Redheads?

"Don't bother to lock it. Notice the way the metal roofs flow down to the Boulevard Clichy in a sort of black ocean.

Oh, hell! I don't have to pretend to you. I lean on this stick and point out beautiful scenes because I'm a God damned cripple and can't walk more than a few steps at a time! Well, we're all cripples in one way or another. Let's get along."

4

It looked so easy. All he had to do was throw away the old palette, buy some light pigments, and paint as an Impressionist. At the end of the first day's trial, Vincent was surprised and a bit nettled. At the end of the second day he was bewildered. Bewilderment was succeeded in turn by chagrin, anger, and fear. By the end of the week he was in a towering rage. After all his laborious months of experimentation with colour, he was still a novice. His canvases came out dark, dull, and sticky. Lautrec, sitting by Vincent's side at Corman's, watched the paint and curses fly, but refrained from offering any advice.

If it was a hard week for Vincent, it was a thousand times worse for Theo. Theo was a gentle soul, mild in his manners and delicate in his habits of life. He was an extremely fastidious person, in his dress, in his decorum, in his home and place of business. He had only a small fraction of Vincent's bruising vitality and power.

The little apartment on the Rue Laval was just large enough for Theo and his fragile Louis Philippes. By the end of the first week Vincent had turned the place into a junk shop. He paced up and down the living room, kicked furniture out of the way, threw canvases, brushes, and empty colour tubes all over the floor, adorned the divans and tables with his soiled clothing, broke dishes, splashed paint, and upset every last punctilious habit of Theo's life.

"Vincent, Vincent," cried Theo, "don't be such a Tartar!"

Vincent had been pacing about the tiny apartment, biting his knuckles and muttering to himself. He threw himself heavily into a fragile chair.

"It's no use," he groaned. "I began too late. I'm too old to change. God, Theo, I've tried! I've started twenty canvases this week. But I'm set in my technique, and I can't begin all over again I tell you, I'm done for! I can't go back to Holland and paint sheep after what I've seen here. And I came too late to get in the main swing of my craft. God, what will I do?"

He jumped up, lurched to the door for some fresh air,

slammed it shut, pried open a window, stared at the Restaurant Bataille for a moment, shut the window so hard he almost smashed the glass, strode to the kitchen for a drink, spilled half the water on the floor, and came back into the living room with a trickle of water running down each side of his chin.

"Well, what do you say, Theo? Must I give it up? Am I through? It looks that way, doesn't it?"

"Vincent, you're behaving like a child. Do quiet down for a moment and listen to me. No, no, don't pace the floor! I can't talk to you that way. And for goodness sake take off those heavy boots if you're going to kick that gilt chair every time you pass it!"

"But, Theo, I've let you support me for six long years. And what do you get out of it? A lot of brown-gravy pictures, and a hopeless failure on your hands."

"Listen, old boy, when you wanted to draw the peasants, did you catch the entire trick in a week? Or did it take you five years?"

"Yes, but I was just beginning then."

"You're just beginning with colour today! And it will probably take you another five years."

"Is there no end to this, Theo? Must I go to school all my life? I'm thirty-three; when in God's name do I reach maturity?"

"This is your last job, Vincent. I've seen everything that is being painted in Europe; the men on my *entresol* are the last word. Once you lighten your palette . . ."

"Oh, Theo, do you really think I can? You don't think I'm a failure?"

"I'm more inclined to think you're a jackass. The greatest revolution in the history of art, and you want to master it in a week! Let's go take a walk on the Butte and cool our heads. If I stay in this room with you another five minutes I shall probably explode."

The following afternoon Vincent sketched at Corman's until late, and then called for Theo at Goupils. An early April dusk had fallen, the long rows of six-storey stone buildings were bathed in a coral-pink glow of dying colour. All of Paris was having its *apéritif*. The sidewalk cafés on the Rue Montmartre were crowded with men chatting with their friends. From inside the cafés came the sound of soft music, playing to refresh the Parisians after their day of toil. The gas lamps were being lit, the *garçons* were laying table cloths in

271

the restaurants, the clerks in the department stores were pulling down the corrugated iron shutters and emptying the sidewalk bins of merchandise.

Theo and Vincent strolled along leisurely. They crossed the Place Chateaudun, with its flurry of carriages from the six converging streets, passed Notre Dame de Lorette, and wound up the hill to the Rue Laval.

"Shall we have an *apéritif*, Vincent?"

"Yes. Let's sit where we can watch the crowd."

"We'll go up to Bataille's, on the Rue des Abbesses. Some of my friends will probably drop by."

The Restaurant Bataille was frequented largely by painters. There were only four or five tables out in front, but the two rooms inside were comfortably large. Madame Bataille always led the artists to one room and the bourgeois to the other; she could tell at first glance to which class a man belonged.

"*Garçon!*" called Theo. "Bring me a Kummel Eckau OO."

"What do you suggest for me, Theo?"

"Try a cointreau. You'll have to experiment for a while to find your permanent drink."

The waiter put their drinks before them on saucers with the price marked in black letters. Theo lit a cigar, Vincent his pipe. Laundry women in black aprons passed, baskets of ironed clothes under their arms; a labourer went by, dangling an unwrapped herring by the tail; there were painters in smocks, with wet canvases strapped to the easel; business men in black derbies and grey checked coats; housewives in cloth slippers, carrying a bottle of wine or a paper of meat; beautiful women with long, flowing skirts, narrow waists, and tiny plumed hats perched forward on their heads.

"It's a gorgeous parade, isn't it, Theo?"

"Yes. Paris doesn't really awaken until the *apéritif* hour."

"I've been trying to think ... what is it that makes Paris so marvellous?"

"Frankly, I don't know. It's an eternal mystery. It has something to do with French character, I suppose. There's a pattern of freedom and tolerance here, an easygoing acceptance of life that ... Hello, here's a friend of mine I want you to meet. Good evening, Paul; how are you?"

"Very well, thanks, Theo."

"May I present my brother, Vincent Van Gogh? Vincent, this is Paul Gauguin. Sit down, Paul, and have one of your inevitable absinthes."

Gauguin raised his absinthe, touched the tip of his tongue to the liqueur and then coated the inside of his mouth with it. He turned to Vincent.

"How do you like Paris, Monsieur Van Gogh?"

"I like it very much."

"*Tiens! C'est curieux*. Still, some people do. As for myself, I find it one huge garbage can. With civilization as the garbage."

"I don't care much for this cointreau, Theo. Can you suggest something else?"

"Try an absinthe, Monsieur Van Gogh," put in Gauguin. "That is the only drink worthy of an artist."

"What do you say, Theo?"

"Why ask me? Suit yourself. *Garçon*. An absinthe for Monsieur. You seem rather pleased with yourself today, Paul. What's happened? Sell a canvas?"

"Nothing as sordid as all that, Theo. But I had a charming experience this morning."

Theo tipped Vincent a wink. "Tell us about it, Paul. *Garçon!* another absinthe for Monsieur Gauguin."

Gauguin touched the tip of his tongue to the new absinthe, wetted the inside of his mouth with it, and then began.

"Do you know that blind alley, the Impasse Frenier, which opens on the Rue des Forneaux? Well, five o'clock this morning I heard Mother Fourel, the carter's wife, scream, 'Help! My husband has hung himself!' I leaped out of bed, pulled on a pair of trousers (the proprieties!) grabbed a knife downstairs and cut the rope. The man was dead, but still warm, still burning. I wanted to carry him to his bed. 'Stop!' cried Mother Fourel, 'we must wait for the police!'

"On the other side my house overhangs fifteen yards of market gardener's bed. 'Have you a cantaloupe?' I called to the gardener. 'Certainly, Monsieur, a ripe one.' At breakfast I ate my melon without a thought of the man who had hung himself. There is good in life as you see. Beside the poison there is the antidote. I was invited out to luncheon, so I put on my best shirt, expecting to thrill the company. I related the story. Smiling, quite unconcerned, they all asked me for a piece of the rope with which he had hung himself."

Vincent looked closely at Paul Gauguin. He had the great, black head of a barbarian, with a massive nose that shot down from the corner of his left eye to the right corner of his mouth. His eyes were huge, almond shaped, protruding, invested with a fierce melancholy. Ridges of bone bulged over the eyes, under the eyes, ran down the long cheeks and across the wide chin. He was a giant of a man, with overwhelming brutal vitality.

Theo smiled faintly.

"Paul, I'm afraid you enjoy your sadism a little too much for it to be entirely natural. I'll have to be going now; I have a dinner engagement. Vincent, will you join me?"

"Let him stay with me, Theo," said Gauguin. "I want to get acquainted with this brother of yours."

"Very well. But don't pour too many absinthes into him. He's not used them. *Garçon. Combien!*"

"That brother of yours is all right, Vincent," said Gauguin. "He's still afraid to exhibit the younger men, but I suppose Valadon holds him down."

"He has Monet, Sisley, Pissarro, and Manet on the balcony."

"True, but where are the Seurats? And the Gauguins? And the Cezannes and Toulouse-Lautrecs? The other men are getting old now and their time is passing."

"Oh, then you know Toulouse-Lautrec?"

"Henri? Of course! Who doesn't know him? He's a damn fine painter, but he's crazy. He thinks that if he sleeps with five thousand women, he'll vindicate himself for not being a whole man. Every morning he wakes up with a gnawing inferiority because he has no legs; every night he drowns that inferiority in liquor and a woman's body. But it's back with him again the next morning. If he weren't crazy he'd be one of our best painters. Here's where we turn in. My studio is on the fourth floor. Look out for that step. The board is broken."

Gauguin went ahead and lighted a lamp. It was a shabby garret, with an easel, a brass bed, a table, and chair. In an alcove near the door Vincent saw some crude and obscene photographs.

"From these pictures I would say you don't think very highly of love?"

"Where will you sit, on the bed or the chair? There's some tobacco for your pipe on the table. Well, I like women, providing they are fat and vicious. Their intelligence annoys me. I have always wanted a mistress who was fat and I have never found one. To make a fool of me, they are always pregnant. Did you read a short story published last month by a young chap by the name of Maupassant? He's Zola's

274

protégé. A man who loves fat women has Christmas dinner served in his home for two and goes out to find company. He comes across a woman who suits him perfectly, but when they get to the roast, she is delivered of a bouncing baby boy!"

"But all this has very little to do with love, Gauguin."

Gauguin stretched out on the bed, put one muscular arm under his head and blew clouds of smoke at the unpainted rafters.

"I don't mean to say that I am not susceptible to beauty, Vincent, but simply that my senses will have none of it. As you perceive, I do not know love. To say, 'I love you' would break all my teeth. But I have no complaints to make. Like Jesus I say, 'The flesh is the flesh and the spirit is the spirit.' Thanks to this, a small sum of money satisfies my flesh, and my spirit is left in peace."

"You certainly dismiss the matter very lightly!"

"No, whom one gets in bed with is no light matter. With a woman who feels pleasure, I feel twice as much pleasure. But I'd rather take the empty external gesture, and not get my emotions involved. I save them for my painting."

"I've been coming to that point of view myself of late. No, thanks, I don't think I could stand any more absinthe. Not at all, go right ahead. My brother Theo thinks highly of your work. May I see some of your studies?"

Gauguin jumped up.

"You may not. My studies are personal and private, like my letters. But I'll show you my paintings. You won't be able to see much in this light. Well, all right if you insist."

Gauguin went on his knees, pulled a stack of canvases from under the bed, and stood them one by one against the absinthe bottle on the table. Vincent had been prepared to see something unusual, but he could feel nothing but stunned amazement at Gauguin's work. He saw a confused mass of sun-drenched pictures; trees such as no botanist could discover; animals the existence of which had never been suspected by Cuvier; men whom Gauguin alone could have created; a sea that might have flowed out of a volcano; a sky which no God could inhabit. There were awkward and angular natives, with the mystery of the infinite behind their naïve, primitive eyes; dream canvases done in blazes of pink and violet and quivering red; sheer decorative scenes in which wild flora and fauna burst with the heat and light of the sun.

"You're like Lautrec," murmured Vincent. "You hate. You hate with all your might."

Gauguin laughed. "What do you think of my painting, Vincent?"

"Frankly, I don't know. Give me time to think about it. Let me come back and see your work again."

"Come as often as you like. There is only one young man in Paris today whose painting is as good as mine; Georges Seurat. He, too, is a primitive. All the rest of the fools around Paris are civilized."

"Georges Seurat?" asked Vincent. "I don't believe I've heard of him."

"No, you wouldn't have. There's not a dealer in town will exhibit his canvases. And yet he's a great painter."

"I'd like to meet him, Gauguin."

"I'll take you up there later. What do you say we have dinner and go up to Bruant's? Have you any money? I've only about two francs. We'd better take this bottle with us. You go first. I'll hold the lamp until you're half way down, so you won't break your neck."

5

It was almost two in the morning before they got around to Seurat's house.

"Aren't you afraid we'll wake him up?" asked Vincent.

"Lord, no! He works all night. And most of the day. I don't think he ever sleeps. Here's the house. It belongs to Georges's mother. She once said to me, 'My boy, Georges, he wants to paint. Very well then, let him paint. I have enough money for the two of us. Just so long as he is happy.' He's a model son to her. Doesn't drink, smoke, swear, go out nights, pursue the ladies, or spend money on anything but materials. He has only one vice: painting. I've heard he has a mistress and a son living close by, but he never mentions them."

"The house looks black," said Vincent. "How are we going to get in without waking the whole family?"

"Georges has the attic. We will probably see a light from the other side. We'll throw some gravel at his window. Here, you'd better let me. If you don't throw it just right it'll hit the third floor window and wake his mother."

Georges Seurat came down to open the door, put a finger to

276

his lips, and led them up three flights of stairs. He closed the door of his attic behind him.

"Georges," said Gauguin, "I want you to meet Vincent Van Gogh, Theo's brother. He paints like a Dutchman, but aside from that he's a damn fine fellow."

Seurat's attic was of tremendous size, running almost the full length of the house. There were huge, unfinished canvases on the walls, with scaffolding before them. A high square table had been placed under the gas lamp; lying flat on this table was a wet canvas.

"I'm happy to know you, Monsieur Van Gogh. You'll pardon me for just a few moments, won't you? I have another little square of colour to fill in before my paint dries."

He climbed on top of a high stool and crouched over his canvas. The gas lamp burned with a steady, yellowish flare. About twenty tiny pots of colour formed a neat line across the table. Seurat touched the tip of the smallest painting brush Vincent had ever seen into one of the pots and began putting little points of colour on the canvas with mathematical precision. He worked quietly and without emotion. His manner was aloof and detached, like that of a mechanic. Dot dot dot dot. He held his brush straight up in his hand, barely touched it to the pot of paint, and then dot dot dot dot on the canvas, hundreds upon hundreds of minute dots.

Vincent watched him, agape. At length Seurat turned on his stool.

"There," he said, "I've got that space hollowed out."

"Would you mind showing it to Vincent, Georges?" asked Gauguin. "Where he comes from they paint cows and sheep. He didn't know there was a modern art until a week ago."

"If you'll sit on this stool, Monsieur Van Gogh."

Vincent climbed up on the stool and looked at the canvas spread out before him. It was like nothing he had ever seen before, either in art or life. The scene represented the Island of the Grande Jatte. Architectural human beings, made out of infinitely graduated points of colour, stood up like poles in a Gothic cathedral. The grass, the river, the boats, the trees, all were vague and abstract masses of dotted light. The canvas was done in all the brightest shades of the palette, lighter than those Manet or Degas or even Gauguin dared to use. The picture was a withdrawal into a region of almost abstract harmony. If it was alive, it was not with the life of nature. The air was filled with glittering luminosity, but there was not a

277

breath to be found anywhere. It was a still life of vibrant life, from which movement had been forever banished.

Gauguin stood at Vincent's side and laughed at the expression on his face.

"It's all right, Vincent, Georges's canvases strike everyone that way the first time they look at them. Out with it! What do you think?"

Vincent turned apologetically to Seurat.

"You will forgive me, Monsieur, but so many strange things have happened to me in the last few days that I cannot find my balance. I trained myself in the Dutch tradition. I had no idea what the Impressionists stood for. And now I suddenly find everything I believed in discarded."

"I understand," said Seurat quietly. "My method is revolutionizing the whole art of painting, so you could not be expected to take it all in with one glance. You see, Monsieur, up to the present, painting has been a matter of personal experience. It is my aim to make it an abstract science. We must learn to pigeonhole our sensations and arrive at a mathematical precision of mind. Every human sensation can be, and must be reduced to an abstract statement of colour, line, and tone. You see these little pots of colour on my table?"

"Yes, I've been noticing them."

"Each of those pots, Monsieur Van Gogh, contains a specific human emotion. With my formula they can be made in the factories and sold in the chemists' shops. No more haphazard mixing of colours on the palette; that method belongs to a past age. From now on the painter will go to the chemist's shop and simply pry the lids off his little pots of colour. This is an age of science, and I am going to make a science out of painting. Personality must disappear, and painting must become precise, like architecture. Do you follow me, Monsieur?"

"No," said Vincent, "I'm afraid I don't."

Gauguin nudged Vincent.

"See here, Georges, why do you insist upon calling this your method. Pissarro worked it out before you were born."

"It's a lie!"

A flush spread over Seurat's face. He sprang off his stool, walked quickly to the window, rapped on the sill with the ends of his fingers, then stormed back.

"Who said Pissarro worked it out before me? I tell you it's

my method. I was the first to think of it. Pissarro learned his pointillism from me. I've been through the history of art since the Italian primitives, and I tell you, no one thought of it before me. How dare you ...!"

He bit his lip savagely, walked to one of his scaffolds, and turned a hunched back on Vincent and Gauguin.

Vincent was utterly amazed at the transition. The man leaning over his canvas on the table had had architectural features, perfect and cold. He had had dispassionate eyes, the impersonal manner of a scientist in a laboratory. His voice had been cool, almost pedagogic. The same veil of abstraction had been over his eyes that he threw over his paintings. But the man at the end of the attic was biting the thick, red under lip that stuck out from the full beard, and was angrily rumpling the mass of curly brown hair that had been so neat before.

"Oh, come, Georges," said Gauguin, winking at Vincent. "Everyone knows that it's your method. Without you there would have been no pointillism."

Mollified, Seurat came back to the table. The glow of anger died slowly out of his eyes.

"Monsieur Seurat," said Vincent, "how can we make painting an impersonal science when it is essentially the expression of the individual that counts?"

"Look! I will show you."

Seurat grabbed a box of crayons from the table and crouched down on the bare plank floor. The gaslight burned dimly above them. The night was completely still. Vincent knelt on one side of him, and Gauguin squatted on the other. Seurat was still excited, and spoke with animation.

"In my opinion," he said, "all effects in painting can be reduced to formulae. Suppose I want to draw a circus scene. here's a bareback rider, here the trainer, here the gallery and spectators. I want to suggest gaiety. What are the three elements of painting? Line, tone and colour. Very well, to suggest gaiety, I bring all my lines above the horizontal, so. I make my luminous colours dominant, so, and my warm tone dominant, so. There! Doesn't that suggest the abstraction of gaiety?'

"Well," replied Vincent, "it may suggest the abstraction of gaiety, but it doesn't catch gaiety itself."

Seurat looked up from his crouching position. His face was in the shadow. Vincent observed what a beautiful man he was.

279

"I'm not after gaiety itself. I'm after the essence of gaiety. Are you acquainted with Plato. my friend?"

"Yes."

"Very well, what painters must learn to portray is not a thing, but the essence of a thing. When the artist paints a horse, it should not be one particular horse that you can recognize in the street. The camera can take photographs; we must go beyond that. What we must capture when we paint a horse, Monsieur Van Gogh, is Plato's *horsiness*, the external spirit of a horse. And when we paint a man, it should not be the *concierge*, with a wart on the end of his nose, but manness, the spirit and essence of all men. Do you follow me, my friend?"

"I follow," said Vincent, "but I don't agree."

"We'll come to the agreement later."

Seurat got off his haunches, slipped out of his smock, and wiped the circus picture off the floor with it.

"Now we go on to calmness," he continued. "I am doing a scene on the Island of the Grande Jatte. I make all my lines horizontal, so. For tone I use perfect equality between warm and cold, so; for colour, equality between dark and light, so. Do you see it?"

"Go on, Georges," said Gauguin, "and don't ask foolish questions."

"Now we come to sadness. We make all our lines run in a descending direction, like this. We make the cold tones dominant, so; and the dark colours dominant, so. There! The essence of sadness! A child could draw it. The mathematical formulae for apportioning space on a canvas will be set down in a little book. I have already worked them out. The painter need only read the book, go to the chemist's shop, buy the specified pots of colour, and obey the rules. He will be a scientific and perfect painter. He can work in sunlight or gaslight, be a monk or a libertine, seven years old or seventy, and all the paintings will achieve the same architectural, impersonal perfection."

Vincent blinked. Gauguin laughed.

"He thinks you're crazy, Georges."

Seurat mopped up the last drawing with his smock, then flung it into a dark corner.

"Do you, Monsieur Van Gogh?" he asked.

"No, no," protested Vincent, "I've been called crazy too

280

many times myself to like the sound of the word. But I must admit this; your ideas are very queer!"

"He means yes, Georges," said Gauguin.

There was a sharp knock on the door.

"Mon Dieu!" groaned Gauguin, "we've awakened your mother again! She told me if I didn't stay away from here nights, she'd take the hairbrush to me!"

Seurat's mother came in. She had on a heavy robe and nightcap.

"Georges, you promised me you wouldn't work all night any more. Oh, it's you, is it, Paul? Why don't you pay your rent? Then you'd have a place to sleep at nights."

"If you'd only take me in here, Mother Seurat, I wouldn't have to pay any rent at all."

"No, thanks, one artist in the family is enough. Here, I've brought you coffee and brioches. If you must work, you have to eat, I suppose. I'll have to go down and get your bottle of absinthe, Paul."

"You haven't drunk it all up, have you, Mother Seurat?"

"Paul, remember what I told you about the hairbrush."

Vincent came out of the shadows.

"Mother," said Seurat, "this is a new friend of mine, Vincent Van Gogh."

Mother Seurat took his hand.

"Any friend of my son's is welcome here, even if it is four in the morning. What will you have to drink, Monsieur?"

"If you don't mind, I'll have a glass of Gauguin's absinthe."

"You will not!" exclaimed Gauguin. "Mother Seurat keeps me on rations. Only one bottle a month. Take something else. Your heathen palate doesn't know the difference between absinthe and *chartreuse jaune.*"

The three men and Mother Seurat sat chatting over their coffee and brioches until the dawning sun struck a tiny triangle of yellow light on the north window.

"I may as well dress for the day," said Mother Seurat. "Come to dinner with Georges and me some evening, Monsieur Van Gogh. We shall be happy to have you."

At the front door Seurat said to Vincent, "I have explained my method rather crudely, I'm afraid. Come back often as you like, and we will work together. When you come to understand my method you will see that painting can never be the same again. Well, I must return to my canvas. I have another small space to hollow out before I go to sleep. Please present my compliments to your brother."

Vincent and Gauguin walked down the deserted stone canyons and climbed the hill to Montmartre. Paris had not yet awakened. The green shutters were closed tight, the blinds were drawn in the shops, and the little country carts were on their way home again after having dropped their vegetables, fruits, and flowers at the Halles.

"Let's go up to the top of the Butte and watch the sun awaken Paris," said Gauguin.

"I'd like that."

After gaining the Boulevard Clichy, they took the Rue Lepic which wound by the Moulin de la Galette and made its tortuous way up the Montmartre hill. The houses became fewer and fewer; open plains of flowers and trees appeared. The Rue Lepic stopped short. The two men took a winding path through the brush.

"Tell me frankly, Gauguin," said Vincent, "what do you think of Seurat?"

"Georges? I thought you'd ask that. He knows more about colour than any man since Delacroix. He has intellectual theories about art. That's wrong. Painters should not think about what they are doing. Leave the theories to the critics. Georges will make a definite contribution to colour, and his Gothic architecture will probably hasten the primitive reaction in art. But he's *fou*, completely *fou*, as you saw for yourself."

It was a stiff climb, but when they reached the summit, all of Paris spread out before them, the lake of black roofs and the frequent church spires emerging from the mist of night. The Seine cut the city in half like a winding stream of light. The houses flowed down the hill of Montmartre to the valley of the Seine, then struggled up again on Montparnasse. The sun broke clear and lit up the Bois de Vincennes beneath it. At the other end of the city the green verdure of the Bois de Boulogne was still dark and somnolent. The three landmarks of the city, the Opera in the centre, Notre Dame in the east and the Arc de Triomphe in the west, stood up in the air like mounds of variegated stone.

Peace descended upon the tiny apartment in the Rue Laval. Theo thanked his lucky stars for the moment of calm. But it did not last long. Instead of working his way slowly and minutely through his antiquated palette, Vincent began to imitate his friends. He forgot everything he had ever learned about painting in his wild desire to be an Impressionist. His canvases looked like atrocious copies of Seurats, Toulouse-Lautrecs, and Gauguins. He thought he was making splendid progress.

"Listen, old boy," said Theo one night, "what's your name?"

"Vincent Van Gogh."

"You're quite certain it's not Georges Seurat, or Paul Gauguin?"

"What the devil are you driving at, Theo?"

"Do you really think you can become a Georges Seurat? Don't you realize that there has only been one Lautrec since the beginning of time? And only one Gauguin ... thank God! It's silly for you to try to imitate them."

"I'm not imitating them. I'm learning from them."

"You're imitating. Show me any one of your new canvases, and I'll tell you who you were with the night before."

"But I'm improving all the time, Theo. Look how much lighter these pictures are."

"You're going downhill every day. You paint less like Vincent Van Gogh with each picture. There's no royal road for you, old boy. It's going to take years of hard labour. Are you such a weakling that you have to imitate others? Can't you just assimilate what they have to offer?"

"Theo, I tell you these canvases are good!"

"And I tell you they're awful."

The battle was on.

Each night that he came home from the gallery, exhausted and nervously on edge, Theo found Vincent waiting for him impatiently with a new canvas. He would leap savagely upon Theo before his brother had a chance to take off his hat and coat.

"There! Now tell me this one isn't good! Tell me that my palette isn't improving! Look at that sunlight effect! Look at this ..."

Theo had to choose between telling a lie and spending a

pleasant evening with an affable brother, or telling the truth and being pursued violently about the house until dawn. Theo was frightfully tired. He could not afford to tell the truth. But he did.

"When were you at Durand-Ruel's last?" he demanded, wearily.

"What does that matter?"

"Answer my question."

"Well," said Vincent sheepishly, "yesterday afternoon."

"Do you know, Vincent, there are almost five thousand painters in Paris trying to imitate Edouard Manet? And most of them do it better than you."

The battleground was too small for either of them to survive.

Vincent tried a new trick. He threw all the Impressionists into one lone canvas.

"Delightful," murmured Theo that night. "We'll name this one, *Recapitulation*. We'll label everything on the canvas. That tree is a genuine Gauguin. The girl in the corner is undoubtedly a Toulouse-Lautrec. I would say that your sunlight on the stream is Sisley, the colour, Monet, the leaves, Pissarro, the air, Seurat, and the central figure, Manet."

Vincent fought bitterly. He worked hard all day, and when Theo came home at night, he was chastised like a little child. Theo had to sleep in the living room, so Vincent could not paint there at night. His quarrels with Theo left him too excited and wrought up to sleep. He spent the long hours haranguing his brother. Theo battled with him until he fell asleep from sheer exhaustion, the light still burning, and Vincent gesticulating excitedly. The only thing that kept Theo going was the thought that soon they would be in the Rue Lepic, where he would have a bedroom to himself and a good strong lock on the door.

When Vincent tired of arguing about his own canvases, he filled Theo's nights, with turbulent discussions of art, the art business, and the wretched business of being an artist.

"Theo, I can't understand it," he complained. "Here you are the manager of one of the most important art galleries in Paris, and you won't even exhibit one of your own brother's canvases."

"Valadon won't let me."

"Have you tried?"

284

"A thousand times."

"All right, we'll admit that my paintings are not good enough. But what about Seurat? And Gauguin? And Lautrec?"

"Every time they bring me new canvases, I beg Valadon to let me hang them on the *entresol*."

"Are you master in that gallery, or is someone else?"

"Alas, I only work there."

"Then you ought to get out. It's degrading, simply degrading. Theo, I wouldn't stand for it. I'd leave them."

"Let's talk it over at breakfast, Vincent. I've had a hard day and I want to go to sleep."

"I don't want to wait until breakfast. I want to talk about it right now. Theo, what good does it do to exhibit Manet and Degas? They're already being accepted. They're beginning to sell. It's the younger men you have to fight for now."

"Give me time! Perhaps in another three years . . ."

"No! We can't wait three years. We've got to have action now. Oh, Theo, why don't you throw up your job and open an art gallery of your own? Just think, no more Valadon, no more Bouguereau, no more Henner!"

"That would take money, Vincent. I haven't saved anything."

"We'd get the money somehow."

"The art business is slow to develop, you know."

"Let it be slow. We'll work night and day until we've established you."

"And what would we do in the meanwhile? We have to eat."

"Are you reproaching me for not earning my own living?"

"For goodness' sake, Vincent, go to bed. I'm exhausted."

"I won't go to bed. I want to know the truth. Is that the only reason you don't leave Goupils? Because you have to support me? Come on, tell the truth. I'm a millstone around your neck. I hold you down. I make you keep your job. If it wasn't for me, you'd be free."

"If only I were a little bit bigger, or a little bit stronger, I'd hand you a sound thrashing. As it is, I think I'll hire Gauguin to come in and do it. My job is with Goupils, Vincent, now and always. Your job is painting, now and always. Half of my work at Goupils belongs to you ; half of your painting belongs to me. Now get off my bed and let me go to sleep, or I'll call a *gendarme!*"

The following evening Theo handed Vincent an envelope and said, "If you're not doing anything tonight, we might go to this party."

"Who's giving it?"

"Henri Rousseau. Take a look at the invitation."

There were two verses of a simple poem and some hand-painted flowers on the card.

"Who is he?" asked Vincent.

"We call him *le Douanier*. He was a customs collector in the provinces until he was forty. Used to paint on Sundays, just as Gauguin did. He came to Paris a few years ago and settled in the labourers' section around the Bastille. He's never had a day of education or instruction in his life, yet he paints, writes poetry, composes music, gives lessons on the violin to the workers' children, plays on the piano, and teaches drawing to a couple of old men."

"What sort of things does he paint?"

"Fantastic animals, largely, peering out of even more fantastic jungles. The closest he ever got to a jungle is the Jardin d'Acclimation in the Bois de Boulogne. He's a peasant and a natural primitive, even if Paul Gauguin does laugh at him."

"What do you think of his work, Theo?"

"Well, I don't know. Everyone calls him an imbecile and a madman."

"Is he?"

"He's something of a child, a primitive child. We'll go to the party tonight and you'll have a chance to judge for yourself. He has all his canvases up on the walls."

"He must have money if he can give parties."

"He's probably the poorest painter in Paris today. He even has to rent the violin he gives lessons on, because he can't afford to buy it. But he has a purpose in giving these parties. You'll discover it for yourself."

The house in which Rousseau lived was occupied by the families of manual labourers. Rousseau had a room on the fourth floor. The street was full of squalling children; the combined stench of cooking, washing, and latrines in the hallway was thick enough to strangle one.

Henri Rousseau answered Theo's knock. He was a short, thickset man, built a good deal on Vincent's lines. His fingers were short and stumpy, his head almost square. He had a stubby nose and chin, and wide, innocent eyes.

"You honour me by coming, Monsieur Van Gogh," he said in a soft, affable tone.

Theo introduced Vincent. Rousseau offered them chairs. The room was colourful, almost gay. Rousseau had put up his peasant curtains of red and white checked cloth at the windows. The walls were filled solid with pictures of wild animals and jungles and incredible landscapes.

Four young boys were standing by the battered old piano in the corner, holding violins in their hands nervously. On the mantel over the fireplace were the homely little cookies that Rousseau had baked and sprinkled with caraway seed. A number of benches and chairs were scattered about the room.

"You are the first to arrive, Monsieur Van Gogh," said Rousseau. "The critic, Guillaume Pille, is doing me the honour of bringing a party."

A noise came up from the street; the cries of children's voices and the rumble of carriage wheels over the cobblestones. Rousseau flung open his door. Pretty feminine voices floated up from the hall.

"Keep going. Keep going," boomed a voice. "One hand on the banister and the other on your nose!"

A shout of laughter followed this witticism. Rousseau, who had heard it clearly, turned to Vincent and smiled. Vincent thought he had never seen such clear, innocent eyes in a man, eyes so free from malice and resentment.

A party of some ten or twelve people burst into the room. The men were dressed in evening clothes, the women in sumptuous gowns, dainty slippers, and long white gloves. They brought into the room the fragrance of costly perfume, of delicate powders, of silk and old lace.

"Well, Henri," cried Guillaume Pille in his deep, pompous voice, "you see we have come. But we cannot stay long. We are going to a ball at the Princess de Broglie's. Meanwhile you must entertain my guests."

"Oh, I want to meet him," gushed a slim, auburn-haired girl in an Empire gown cut low across the breasts. "Just think, this is the great painter of whom all Paris is talking. Will you kiss my hand, Monsieur Rousseau?"

"Take care, Blanche," someone said. "You know ... these artists ..."

Rousseau smiled and kissed her hand. Vincent shrank into a corner. Pille and Theo chatted for a moment. The rest of the

287

party walked about the room in pairs, commenting on the different canvases with gales of laughter, fingering Rousseau's curtains, his ornaments, ransacking every corner of the room for a new joke.

"If you will sit down, ladies and gentlemen," said Rousseau, "my orchestra will play one of my own compositions. I have dedicated it to Monsieur Pille. It is called *Chanson Raval.*"

"Come, come everybody!" shouted Pille. "Rousseau is going to entertain us. Jeanie! Blanche! Jacques! Come sit down. This will be precious."

The four trembling boys stood before a lone music rack and tuned their violins. Rousseau sat at his piano and closed his eyes. After a moment he said, "Ready," and began to play. The composition was simple pastoral. Vincent tried to listen, but the snickers of the crowd drowned out the music. At the end they all applauded vociferously. Blanche went to the piano, put her hands on Rousseau's shoulders and said, "That was beautiful, Monsieur, beautiful. I have never been so deeply stirred."

"You flatter me, Madame."

Blanche screamed with laughter.

"Guillaume, did you hear that? He thinks I'm flattering him!"

"I will play you another composition now," said Rousseau.

"Sing us one of your poems to it, Henri. You know you have so many poems."

Rousseau grinned childishly.

"Very well, Monsieur Pille, I will chant a poem to it, if you wish."

He went to a table, took out a sheaf of poems, thumbed through them and selected one. He sat down at the piano and began to play. Vincent thought the music good. The few lines he could catch of the poem he also thought charming. But the effect of the two together was quite ludicrous. The crowd howled. They slapped Pille on the back.

"Oh, Guillaume, you are a dog. What a sly one you are."

Finished with his music, Rousseau went out to the kitchen and returned with a number of thick, rough cups of coffee, which he passed about to the guests. They picked the caraway seeds off the cookies and threw them into each other's coffee. Vincent smoked his pipe in the corner.

"Come, Henri, show us your latest paintings. That is what we

288

have come for. We must see them here, in your atelier, before they are bought for the Louvre."

"I have some lovely new ones," said Rousseau. "I will take them off the wall for you."

The crowd gathered about the table, trying to outdo each other in the extravagance of their compliments.

"This is divine, simply divine," breathed Blanche. "I must have it for my boudoir. I just can't live another day without it! *Cher Maître*, how much is this immortal masterpiece?"

"Twenty-five francs."

"Twenty-five francs! Only imagine, twenty-five francs for a great work of art! Will you dedicate it to me?"

"I will be honoured."

"I promised Françoise I would bring her one," said Pille. "Henri, this is for my fiancée. It must be the very finest thing you have ever done."

"I know just the one for you, Monsieur Pille."

He took down a painting of some sort of weird animal peering through a fairy tale jungle. Everyone howled at Pille.

"What is it?"

"It's a lion."

"It is not, it's a tiger."

"I tell you, it's my washerwoman ; I recognize her."

"This one is a little larger, Monsieur," said Rousseau sweetly. "It will cost you thirty francs."

"It's worth it, Henri, it's worth it. Some day my grand-children will sell this exquisite canvas for thirty thousand francs!"

"I want one. I want one," several of the others exclaimed. "I've got to take one to my friends. This is the best show of the season."

"Come along, everyone," shouted Pille. "We'll be late for the ball. And bring your paintings. We'll cause a riot at the Princess de Broglie's with these things. Au revoir, Henri. We had a perfectly marvellous time. Give another party soon.'

"Good-bye, *cher Maître*," said Blanche, flickering her perfumed handkerchief under his nose. "I will never forget you. You will live in my memory forever."

"Leave him alone, Blanche," cried one of the men. "The poor fellow won't be able to sleep all night."

They trouped down the stairs noisily, shouting their jokes at each other, leaving a cloud of expensive perfume behind them to mingle with the stench of the building.

Theo and Vincent walked to the door. Rousseau was standing at the table, looking down at the pile of coins.

"Do you mind going home alone, Theo?" Vincent asked quietly. "I want to stay and get acquainted."

Theo left. Rousseau did not notice Vincent close the door and then lean against it. He went on counting the money on the table.

"Eighty francs, ninety francs, one hundred, a hundred and five."

He looked up and saw Vincent watching him. The simple, childlike expression returned to his eyes. He pushed the money aside and stood there, grinning foolishly.

"Take off the mask, Rousseau," said Vincent. "I, too, am a peasant and a painter."

Rousseau left the table, crossed to Vincent and gripped his hand warmly.

"Your brother has shown me your pictures of the Dutch peasants. They are good. They are better than Millet's. I have looked at them many, many times. I admire you, Monsieur."

"And I have looked at your pictures, Rousseau, while those . . . were making fools of themselves. I admire you, too."

"Thank you. Will you sit down? Will you fill your pipe with my tobacco? It is a hundred and five francs, Monsieur. I will be able to buy tobacco, and food, and canvas to paint on."

They sat on opposite sides of the table and smoked in friendly, ruminative silence.

"I suppose you know they call you a crazy man, Rousseau?"

"Yes, I know. And I have heard that in The Hague they think you are crazy, too."

"Yes, that's so."

"Let them think what they like. Some day my paintings will hang in the Luxembourg."

"And mine," said Vincent, "will hang in the Louvre."

They read the thought in each other's eyes and broke into spontaneous, whole-hearted laughter.

"They're right, Henri," said Vincent, "We are crazy!"

"Shall we go have a drink on it?" asked Rousseau.

7

Gauguin knocked on the door of the apartment the following Wednesday toward dinner time.

"Your brother asked me to take you over to the Café Batignolles this evening. He has to work late at the gallery. These are interesting canvases. May I look?"

"Of course. I did some of them in the Brabant, others in The Hague."

Gauguin gazed at the pictures for a long while. Several times he raised his hand, opened his mouth, and made as if to speak. He did not seem able to formulate his thoughts.

"Forgive me for asking, Vincent," he said, finally, "but are you by any chance an epileptic?"

Vincent was just slipping into a sheepskin coat which, to Theo's dismay, he had found in a second-hand store and insisted upon wearing. He turned about and stared at Gauguin.

"Am I a what?" he demanded.

"An epileptic. One of those fellows who has nervous fits?"

"Not that I know of, Gauguin. Why do you ask?"

"Well ... these pictures of yours ... they look as though they were going to burst right out of the canvas. When I look at your work ... and this isn't the first time it's happened to me ... I begin feeling a nervous excitement that I can hardly contain. I feel that if the picture doesn't explode, I most certainly will! Do you know where your paintings affect me most?"

"No. Where?"

"In the bowels. My whole insides begin to tremble. I get feeling so excited and perturbed, I can hardly restrain myself."

"Perhaps I could sell them as laxatives. You know, hang one in the lavatory and look at it at a certain hour every day?"

"Seriously speaking, Vincent, I don't think I could live with your pictures. They'd drive me mad inside of a week."

"Shall we go?"

They walked up the Rue Montmartre to the Boulevard Clichy.

"Have you had dinner?" asked Gauguin.

"No. Have you?"

"No. Shall we go up to Bataille's?"

"Good idea. Got any money?"

"Not a centime. How about you?"

"I'm flat, as usual. I was waiting for Theo to take me out."

"Zut! I guess we don't eat."

"Let's go up and see what the *plat du jour* is, anyway."

They took the Rue Lepic up the hill, then turned right on

the Rue des Abbesses. Madame Bataille had an ink-scrawled menu tacked to one of her imitation potted trees in front.

"Uummm," said Vincent, *"côté de veau aux petits pois.* My favourite dish."

"I hate veal," said Gauguin. "I'm glad we don't have to eat."

"Quelle blague!"

They wandered down the street and into the little triangular park at the foot of the Butte.

"Hello," said Gauguin, "there's Paul Cezanne, asleep on a bench. Why that idiot uses his shoes for a pillow is beyond me. Let's wake him up."

He pulled the belt out of his trousers, doubled it up, and gave the sleeping man a whack across the stockinged feet. Cezanne sprang off the bench with a yowl of pain.

"Gauguin, you infernal sadist! Is that your idea of a joke? I shall be forced to crack your skull one of these days."

"Serves you right for leaving your feet exposed. Why do you put those filthy Provence boots under your head? I should think they'd be worse than no pillow at all."

Cezanne rubbed the bottom of each foot in turn, then slipped on his boots, grumbling.

"I don't use them for a pillow. I put them under my head so no one will steal them while I'm asleep."

Gauguin turned to Vincent. "You'd think he was a starving artist the way he talks. His father owns a bank, and half of Aix-en-Provence. Paul, this is Vincent Van Gogh, Theo's brother."

Cezanne and Vincent shook hands.

"It's too bad we didn't find you a half hour ago, Cezanne," said Gauguin. "You could have joined us for dinner. Bataille has the best *côté de veau aux petits pois* I've ever tasted."

"It was really good, was it?" asked Cezanne.

"Good? It was delicious! Wasn't it, Vincent?"

"Certainly was."

"Then I think I'll go have some. Come and keep me company, will you?"

"I don't know whether I could eat another portion. Could you, Vincent?"

"I hardly think so. Still, if Monsieur Cezanne insists . . ."

"Be a good fellow, Gauguin. You know I hate to eat alone. Take something else if you've had enough veal."

"Well, just to oblige you. Come along, Vincent."

They went back up the Rue des Abbesses to Bataille's.

"Good evening, gentlemen," said the waiter. "Have you chosen?"

"Yes," replied Gauguin, "bring us three *plats du jour.*"

"*Bien.* And what wine?"

"You choose the wine, Cezanne. You know more about those things than I do."

"Let's see, there's Sainte-Estephe, Bordeaux, Sauterne, Beaune . . ."

"Have you ever tried the Pommard?" interrupted Gauguin, guilelessly. "I often think it's the best wine they have."

"Bring us a bottle of Pommard," said Cezanne to the waiter.

Gauguin bolted his veal and green peas in no time, then turned to Cezanne while the latter was still in the middle of his dinner.

"By the way, Paul," he remarked. "I hear that Zola's 'L'Oeuvre' is selling by the thousands."

Cezanne shot him a black, bitter look, and shoved his dinner away with distaste. He turned to Vincent.

"Have you read that book, Monsieur?"

"Not yet. I just finished 'Germinal' "

" 'L'Oeuvre' is a bad book," said Cezanne, "and a false one. Besides, it is the worst piece of treachery that has ever been committed in the name of friendship. The book is about a painter, Monsieur Van Gogh. About me! Emile Zola is my oldest friend. We were raised together in Aix. We went to school together. I came to Paris only because he was here. We were closer than brothers, Emile and I. All during our youth we planned how, side by side, we would become great artists. And now he does this to me."

"What has he done to you?" asked Vincent.

"Ridiculed me. Mocked me. Made me a laughing stock to all Paris. Day after day I told him about my theories of light, my theories of representing solids under surface appearances, my ideas of a revolutionary palette. He listened to me, he encouraged me, he drew me out. And all the time he was only gathering material for his book, to show what a fool I was. "

He drained his wine glass, turned back to Vincent and continued, his small, sour eyes smouldering with passionate hatred.

"Zola has combined three of us in that book, Monsieur Van Gogh ; myself, Bazille, and a poor, wretched lad who used to sweep out Manet's studio. The boy had artistic ambitions, but finally hanged himself in despair. Zola paints me as a visionary, another misguided wretch who thinks he is revolutionizing art, but who doesn't paint in the conventional manner simply because he hasn't enough talent to paint at all. He makes me hang myself from the scaffolding of my masterpiece, because in the end I realize that what I mistook for genius was only insane daubing. Up against me he puts another artist from Aix, a sentimental sculptor who turns out the most hackneyed, academic trash, and makes him a great artist."

"That's really amusing," said Gauguin, "when you remember that Zola was the first to champion Edouard Manet's revolution in painting. Emile has done more for Impressionist painting than any man alive."

"Yes, he worshipped Manet because Edouard overthrew the academicians. But when I try to go beyond the Impressionists, he calls me a fool and an idiot. As for Emile, he is a mediocre intelligence and a detestable friend. I had to stop going to his house long ago. He lives like a damned bourgeois. Rich rugs on the floor, vases on the mantelpiece, servants, a desk of carved and sculptured wood for him to write his masterpieces. Phew! He's more middle class than Manet ever dared to be. They were brother bourgeois under the skin, those two; that's why they got along so well together. Just because I come from the same town as Emile, and he knew me as a child, he thinks I can't possibly do any important work."

"I heard that he wrote a *brochure* for your pictures at the Salon des Refusées a few years back. What happened to it?"

"Emile tore it up, Gauguin, just before it was to have gone to the printers."

"But why?" asked Vincent.

"He was afraid the critics would think he was sponsoring me only because I was an old friend. If he had published that *brochure,* I would have been established. Instead he published 'L'Oeuvre.' So much for friendship. My pictures in the Salon des Refusées are laughed at by ninety-nine people out of a hundred. Durand-Ruel exhibits Degas, Monet, and my friend Guillaumin, but they refuse to give me two inches of space. Even your brother, Monsieur Van Gogh, is afraid to put me on his *entresol*. The only dealer in Paris who will put my pictures in his window is Pere Tanguy, and he, poor soul, couldn't sell a crust of bread to a starving millionaire."

"Is there any Pommard left in that bottle, Cezanne?" asked Gauguin. "Thanks. What I have against Zola is that he makes his washerwomen talk like real washerwomen, and when he leaves them he forgets to change his style."

"Well, I've had enough of Paris. I'm going back to Aix and spend the rest of my life there. There's a hill rising up from the valley that overlooks the whole country-side. There's clear, bright sunlight in Provence, and colour. What colour! I know a plot of ground near the top of the hill that's for sale. It's covered with pine trees. I'll build a studio there, and plant an apple orchard. And I'll build a big stone wall around my ground. I'll mix broken bottles into the cement at the top of the wall to keep the world out. And I'll never leave Provence again, never, never!"

"A hermit, eh?" murmured Gauguin into his glass of Pommard.

"Yes, a hermit."

"The hermit of Aix. What a charming title. We'd better be getting on to the Cafe Batignolles. Everyone will be there by now."

8

Nearly everyone was there. Lautrec had a pile of saucers in front of him high enough to rest his chin on. Georges Seurat was chatting quietly with Anquetin, a lean, lanky painter who was trying to combine the method of the Impressionists with that of the Japanese prints. Henri Rousseau was taking cookies out of his pocket and dipping them into a *cafe au lait*, while Theo carried on an animated discussion with two of the more modern Parisian critics.

Batignolles had formerly been a suburb at the entrance of the Boulevard Clichy, and it was here that Edouard Manet had gathered the kindred spirits of Paris about him. Before Manet's death, the Ecole des Batignolles was in the habit of meeting twice a week at the café. Legros, Fantin-Latour, Courbet, Renoir, all had met there and worked out their theories of art, but now the Ecole had been taken over by the younger men.

Cezanne saw Emile Zola. He walked to a far table, ordered a coffee, and sat aloof from the crowd. Gauguin introduced Vincent to Zola and then dropped into a chair alongside of Toulouse-Lautrec. Zola and Vincent were left alone at their table.

"I saw you come in with Paul Cezanne, Monsieur Van

295

Gogh. No doubt he said something to you about me?"

"Yes."

"What was it?"

"I'm afraid your book has wounded him very deeply."

Zola sighed and pushed the table out from the leather cushioned bench to give his huge paunch more room.

"Have you ever heard of the Schewininger cure?" he asked. "They say if a man doesn't drink anything with his meals, he can lose thirty pounds in three months."

"I haven't heard of it."

"It hurt me very deeply to write that book about Paul Cezanne, but every word of it is true. You are a painter. Would you falsify a portrait of a friend simply because it made him unhappy? Of course you wouldn't. Paul is a splendid chap. For years he was my dearest friend. But his work is simply ludicrous. You know we are very tolerant at my house, Monsieur, but when my friends come, I must lock Paul's canvases in a cupboard so he will not be laughed at."

"But surely his work can't be as bad as all that."

"Worse, my dear Van Gogh, worse. You haven't seen any of it? That explains your incredulity. He draws like a child of five. I give you my word, I think he has gone completely crazy."

"Gauguin respects him."

"It breaks my heart," continued Zola, "to see Cezanne waste his life in this fantastic fashion. He should go back to Aix and take over his father's position in the bank. He could make something of his life that way. As things are now ... some day he will hang himself ... just as I predicted in 'L'Oeuvre.' Have you read that book, Monsieur?"

"Not yet. I just finished 'Germinal.' "

"So? And what do you think of it?"

"I think it is the finest thing since Balzac."

"Yes, it is my masterpiece. It appeared *en feuilleton* in 'Gil Blas' last year. I got a good piece of money for that. And now the book has sold over sixty thousand copies. My income has never been as large as it is today. I'm going to add a new wing onto my house at Medan. The book has already caused four strikes and revolts in the mining regions of France. 'Germinal' will cause a gigantic revolution, and when it does, good-bye to capitalism! What sort of thing do you paint, Monsieur ... What did Gauguin say your first name was?"

296

"Vincent. Vincent Van Gogh. Theo Van Gogh is my brother."

Zola laid down the pencil with which he had been scribbling on the stone topped table, and stared at Vincent.

"That's curious," he said.

"What is?"

"Your name. I've heard it somewhere before."

"Perhaps Theo mentioned it to you."

"He did, but that wasn't it. Wait a minute! It was ... it was ... 'Germinal!' Have you ever been in the coal mining regions?"

"Yes. I lived in the Belgian Borinage for two years."

"The Borinage! Petit Wasmes! Marcasse!"

Zola's large eyes almost popped out of his rotund, bearded face.

"So you're the second coming of Christ!"

Vincent flushed. "What do you mean by that?"

"I spent five weeks in the Borinage, gathering material for 'Germinal'. The *gueules noires* speak of a Christ-man who worked among them as an evangelist."

"Lower your voice, I beg you!"

Zola folded his hands over his fat paunch and pushed it inward.

"Don't be ashamed, Vincent," he said. "What you tried to accomplish there was worth while. You simply chose the wrong medium. Religion will never get people anywhere. Only the base in spirit will accept misery in this world for the promise of bliss in the next."

"I found that out too late."

"You spent two years in the Borinage, Vincent. You gave away your food, your money, your clothes. You worked yourself to the point of death. And what did you get for it? Nothing. They called you a crazy man and expelled you from the Church. When you left, conditions were no better than when you came."

"They were worse."

"But my medium will do it. The written word will cause the revolution. Every literate miner in Belgium and France has read my book. There is not a café, not a miserable shack in the whole region, that hasn't a well-thumbed copy of 'Germinal'. Those who can't read have it read to them over and over again. Four strikes already. And dozens more coming. The whole country is rising. 'Germinal' will create a new society, where your religion couldn't. And what do I get as my reward?"

"What?"

"Francs. Thousands upon thousands of them. Will you join me in a drink?"

The discussion around the Lautrec table became animated. Everyone turned his attention that way.

"How is '*ma methode*,' Seurat?" asked Lautrec, cracking his knuckles one by one.

Seurat ignored the gibe. His exquisitely perfect features and calm, mask-like expression suggested, not the face of one man, but the essence of masculine beauty.

"There is a new book on colour refraction by an American, Ogden Rood. I think it is an advance on Helmholtz and Chevral, though not quite so stimulating as de Superville's work. You could all read it with profit."

"I don't read books about painting," said Lautrec. "I leave that to the layman."

Seurat unbuttoned the black and white checked coat and straightened out the large blue tie sprinkled with polka dots.

"You yourself are a layman," he said, "so long as you guess at the colours you use."

"I don't guess. I know by instinct."

"Science is a method, Georges," put in Gauguin. "We have become scientific in our application of colour by years of hard work and experimentation."

"That's not enough, my friend. The trend of our age is toward objective production. The days of inspiration, of trial and error, are gone forever."

"I can't read those books," said Rousseau. "They give me a headache. Then I have to go paint all day to get rid of it."

Everyone laughed. Anquetin turned to Zola and said, "Did you see the attack on 'Germinal' in this evening's paper?"

"No. What did it say?"

"The critic called you the most immoral writer of the nineteenth century."

"Their old cry. Can't they find anything else to say against me?"

"They're right, Zola," said Lautrec. "I find your books carnal and obscene."

"You certainly ought to recognize obscenity when you see it!"

"Had you that time, Lautrec!"

"Garçon," called Zola. "A round of drinks."

"We're in for it now," murmured Cezanne to Anquetin. "When Emile buys the drinks, it means you have to listen to an hour's lecture."

The waiter served the drinks. The painters lit their pipes and gathered into a close, intimate circle. The gas lamps illuminated the room in spirals of light. The hum of conversation from the other tables was low and chordal.

"They call my books immoral," said Zola, "for the same reason that they attribute immorality to your paintings, Henri. The public cannot understand that there is no room for moral judgements in art. Art is amoral; so is life. For me there are no obscene pictures or books; there are only poorly conceived and poorly executed ones. A whore by Toulouse-Lautrec is moral because he brings out the beauty that lies beneath her external appearance; a pure country girl by Bouguereau is immoral because she is sentimentalized and so cloyingly sweet that just to look at her is enough to make you vomit!"

"Yes, that's so," nodded Theo.

Vincent saw that the painters respected Zola, not because he was successful—they despised the ordinary connotations of success—but because he worked in a medium which seemed mysterious and difficult to them. They listened closely to his words.

"The ordinary human brain thinks in terms of duality; light and shade, sweet and sour, good and evil. That duality does not exist in nature. There is neither good nor evil in the world, but only being and doing. When we describe an action, we describe life; when we call that action names—like depravity or obscenity—we go into the realm of subjective prejudice."

"But, Emile," said Theo. "What would the mass of people do without its standard of morality?"

"Morality is like religion," continued Toulouse-Lautrec; "a soporific to close people's eyes to the tawdriness of their life."

"Your amorality is nothing but anarchism, Zola," said Seurat, "and nihilistic anarchism, at that. It's been tried before, and it doesn't work."

"Of course we have to have certain codes," agreed Zola. "The public weal demands sacrifices from the individual. I don't object to morality, but only to the pudency that spits upon *Olympia,* and wants Maupassant suppressed. I tell you, morality in France today is entirely confined to the erogenous zone. Let people sleep with whom they like; I know a higher morality than that."

"That reminds me of a dinner I gave a few years ago," said Gauguin. "One of the men I invited said, 'You understand, my friend, that I can't take my wife to these dinners of yours when your mistress is present.' 'Very well,' I replied, 'I'll send her out for the evening.' When the dinner was over and they all went home, our honest Madame, who had yawned the whole evening, stopped yawning and said to her husband, 'Let's have some nice piggy talk before we do it.' And her husband said, 'Let's not do anything but talk. I have eaten too much this evening.' "

"That tells the whole story!" shouted Zola, above the laughter.

"Put aside the ethics for a moment and get back to immorality in art," said Vincent. "No one ever calls my pictures obscene, But I am invariably accused of an even greater immorality, ugliness."

"You hit it that time, Vincent," said Toulouse-Lautrec.

"Yes, that's the essence of the new immorality for the public," agreed Gauguin. "Did you see what the *Mercure de France* called us this month? The cult of ugliness."

"The same criticism is levied against me," said Zola. "A countess said to me the other day, 'My dear Monsieur Zola, why does a man of your extraordinary talent go about turning up stones just to see what sort of filthy insects are crawling underneath them?' "

Lautrec took an old newspaper clipping out of his pocket.

"Listen to what the critic said about my canvases at the last Salon des Independents. 'Toulouse-Lautrec may be reproached for taking delight in representing trivial gaiety, coarse amusements and "low subjects". He appears to be insensible to beauty of feature, elegance of form and grace of movement. It is true that he paints with a loving brush beings ill-formed, stumpy and repulsive in their ugliness, but of what good is such perversion?' "

"Shades of Frans Hals," murmured Vincent.

"Well, he's right," said Seurat. "If you men are not per-verted, you're at least misguided. Art has to do with abstract things, like colour, design, and tone. It should not be used to improve social conditions or search for ugliness. Painting should be like music, divorced from the everyday world."

"Victor Hugo died last year," said Zola, "and with him a whole civilization died. A civilization of pretty gestures, romance, artful lies and subtle evasions. my books stand for the new civilization; the unmoral civilization of the twentieth century. So do your paintings. Bouguereau is still dragging his carcass around Paris, but he took ill the day that Edouard Manet exhibited *Picnic on the Grass*, and he died the day Mane finished *Olympia*. Well, Manet is gone now, and so is Daumier, but we still have Degas, Lautrec and Gauguin to carry on their work."

"Put the name of Vincent Van Gogh on that list," said Toulouse-Lautrec.

"Put it at the head of the list," said Rousseau.

"Very well, Vincent," said Zola with a smile, "you have been nominated for the cult of ugliness. Do you accept the nomination?"

"Alas," said Vincent, "I'm afraid I was born into it."

"Let's formulate our manifesto, gentlemen," said Zola. "First, we think all truth beautiful, no matter how hideous its face may seem. We accept all of nature, without any repudiation. We believe there is more beauty in a harsh truth than in a pretty lie, more poetry in earthiness than in all the salons of Paris. We think pain good, because it is the most profound of all human feelings. We think sex beautiful, even when portrayed by a harlot and a pimp. We put character above ugliness, pain above prettiness, and hard, crude reality above all the wealth in France. We accept life in its entirety, without making moral judgements. We think the prostitute as good as the countess, the *concierge* as good as the general, the peasant as good as the cabinet minister, for they all fit into the pattern of nature, and are woven into the design of life!"

"Glasses up, gentlemen," cried Toulouse-Lautrec. "We drink to amorality and the cult of ugliness. May it beautify and recreate the world."

"Tosh!" said Cezanne.

"And 'Tosh!' again," said Georges Seurat.

9

At the beginning of June, Theo and Vincent moved to their new apartment at 54, Rue Lepic, Montmartre. The house was just a short way from the Rue Laval; they had only to go up the Rue Montmartre a few blocks to the Boulevard Clichy, and then take the winding Rue Lepic up past the Moulin de la Galette, almost into the countrified part of the Butte.

Their apartment was on the third floor. It had three rooms, a cabinet and a kitchen. The living room was comfortable with Theo's beautiful old cabinet, Louis Philippes, and a big stove to protect them against the Paris cold. Theo had a talent for home-making. He loved to have everything just right. His bedroom was next to the living room. Vincent slept in the cabinet, behind which was his studio, an ordinary sized room with one window.

"You won't have to work at Corman's any longer, Vincent," said Theo. They were arranging and rearranging the furniture in the living room.

"No, thank heavens. Still, I needed to do a few female nudes."

Theo placed the sofa across the room from the cabinet and surveyed the room critically. "You haven't done a complete canvas in colour for some time, have you?" he asked.

"No."

"Why not?"

"What would be the use? Until I can mix the right colours . . . where do you want this armchair, Theo? Under the lamp or next to the window? But now that I've got a studio of my own . . ."

The following morning Vincent got up with the sun, arranged the easel in his new studio, put a piece of canvas on a frame, laid out the shining new palette that Theo had bought him, and softened up his brushes. When it was time for Theo to rise, he put on the coffee and went down to the *pâtisserie* for crisp, fresh croissants.

Theo could feel Vincent's turbulent excitement across the breakfast table.

"Well, Vincent," he said, "you've been to school for three months. Oh, I don't mean Corman's, I mean the school of Paris! You've seen the most important painting that has been done in Europe in three hundred years. And now you're ready to . . ."

Vincent pushed aside his half-eaten breakfast and jumped to his feet. "I think I'll begin . . ."

"Sit down. Finish your breakfast. You have plenty of time. There's nothing for you to worry about. I'll buy your paints and canvas wholesale, so you'll always have plenty on hand. You'd better have your teeth operated on, too; I want to get you into perfect health. But for goodness sake, go about your work slowly and carefully!"

"Don't talk nonsense, Theo. Have I ever gone about anything slowly and carefully?"

When Theo came home that night he found that Vincent had lashed himself into a fury. He had been working progressively at his craft for six years under the most heartbreaking conditions; now that everything was made easy for him, he was faced with a humiliating impotence.

It was ten o'clock before Theo could get him quieted down. When they went out to dinner, some of Vincent's confidence had returned. Theo looked pale and worn.

The weeks that followed were torture for both of them. When Theo returned from the gallery he would find Vincent in any one of his hundred different kinds of tempests. The strong lock on his door did him absolutely no good. Vincent sat on his bed until the early hours of the morning, arguing with him. When Theo fell asleep, Vincent shook him by the shoulder and woke him up.

"Stop pacing the floor and sit still for a moment," begged Theo one night. "And stop drinking that damned absinthe. That's not how Gauguin developed his palette. Now listen to me, you infernal idiot, you must give yourself at least a year before you even begin to look at your work with a critical eye. What good is it going to do to make yourself sick? You're getting thin and nervous. You know you can't do your best work in that condition."

The hotness of a Parisian summer came on. The sun burned up the streets. Paris sat in front of its favourite cafe until one and two in the morning, sipping cold drinks. The flowers on the Butte Montmartre burst into a riot of colour. The Seine wound its glistening way through the city, through banks of trees and cool patches of green grass.

Every morning Vincent strapped his easel to his back and went looking for a picture. He had never known such hot, constant sun in Holland, nor had he ever seen such deep, elemental colour. Nearly every evening he returned from his painting in time to join the heated discussions on the *entresol* of Goupils.

One day Gauguin came in to help him mix some pigments.

"From whom do you buy these colours?" he asked.

"Theo gets them wholesale."

"You should patronize Pére Tanguy. His prices are

the lowest in Paris, and he trusts a man when he's broke."

"Who is this Père Tanguy? I've heard you mention him before."

"Haven't you met him yet? Good Lord, you mustn't hesitate another moment. You and Père are the only two men I've ever met whose communism really comes from the heart. Put on that beautiful rabbit-fur bonnet of yours. We're going down to the Rue Clauzel."

As they wound down the Rue Lepic, Gauguin told Père Tanguy's story. "He used to be a plasterer before he came to Paris. He worked as a colour-grinder in the house of Edouard, then took the job of *concierge* somewhere on the Butte. His wife looked after the house and Père began peddling colours through the quarter. He met Pissarro, Monet, and Cezanne, and since they liked him, we all started buying our colours from him. He joined the communists during the last uprising; one day while he was dreaming on sentry duty, a band from Versailles descended on his post. The poor fellow just couldn't fire on another human being. He threw away his musket. He was sentenced to serve two years in the galleys at Brest for this treachery, but we got him out.

"He saved a few francs and opened this little shop in the Rue Clauzel. Lautrec painted the front of it blue for him. He was the first man in Paris to exhibit a Cezanne canvas. Since then we've all had our stuff there. Not that he ever sells a canvas. Ah, no! You see, Père is a great lover of art, but since he is poor, he can't afford to buy pictures. So he exhibits them in his little shop, where he can live among them all day."

"You mean he wouldn't sell a painting even if he got a good offer?"

"Decidedly not. He takes only pictures that he loves, and once he gets attached to a canvas, you can't get it out of the shop. I was there one day when a well-dressed man came in, admired a Cezanne and asked how much it was. Any other dealer in Paris would have been delighted to sell it for sixty francs. Père Tanguy looked at the canvas for a long time and then said, 'Ah, yes, this one. It is a particularly good Cezanne. I cannot let it go under six hundred francs.' When the man ran out, Père took the painting off the wall and held it before him with tears in his eyes."

"Then what good does it do to have him exhibit your work?"

"Well, Pére Tanguy is a strange fellow. All he knows about art is how to grind colours. And yet he has an infallible sense of the authentic. If he asks for one of your canvases, give it to him. It will be your formal initiation into Parisian art. Here's the Rue Clauzel ; let's turn in."

The Rue Clauzel was a one block street connecting the Rue des Martyres and the Rue Henri Monnier. It was filled with small shops, on top of which were two of three storeys of white-shuttered dwellings. Pére Tanguy's shop was just across the street from an *école primaire de filles*.

Pére Tanguy was looking over some Japanese prints that were just becoming fashionable in Paris.

"Pére, I've brought a friend, Vincent Van Gogh. He's an ardent communist."

"I am happy to welcome you to my shop," said Pére Tanguy in a soft, almost feminine voice.

Tanguy was a little man with a pudgy face and the wistful eyes of a friendly dog. He wore a wide brimmed straw hat which he pulled down to the level of his brows. He had short arms, stumpy hands, and a rough beard. His right eye opened half again as far as the left one.

"You are really a communist, Monsieur Van Gogh?" he asked shyly.

"I don't know what you mean by communism, Pére Tanguy. I think everyone should work as much as he can, at the job he likes best, and in return get everything he needs."

"Just as simply as that," laughed Gauguin.

"Ah, Paul," said Pére Tanguy, "you worked on the Stock Exchange. It is money that makes men animals, is it not?" ·

"Yes, that, and lack of money."

"No, never lack of money, only lack of food and the necessities of life."

"Quite so, Pére Tanguy," said Vincent.

"Our friend, Paul," said Tanguy, "despises the men who make money, and he despises us because we can't make any. But I would rather belong to the latter class. Any man who lives on more than fifty centimes a day is a scoundrel."

"Then virtue," said Gauguin, "has descended upon me by force of necessity. Pére Tanguy, will you trust me for a little more colour? I know I owe you a large bill, but I am unable to work unless . . ."

"Yes, Paul, I will give you credit. If I had a little less trust in people, and you had a little more, we would both be better off.

305

Where is the new picture you promised me? Perhaps I can sell it and get back the money for my colours."

Gauguin winked at Vincent. "I'll bring you two of them, Père, to hang side by side. Now if you will let me have one tube of black, one of yellow . . ."

"Pay your bill and you'll get more colour!"

The three men turned simultaneously. Madame Tanguy slammed the door to their living quarters and stepped into the shop. She was a wiry little woman with a hard, thin face and bitter eyes. She stormed up to Gauguin.

"Do you think we are in business for charity? Do you think we can eat Tanguy's communism? Settle up that bill, you rascal, or I shall put the police on you!"

Gauguin smiled in his most winning manner, took Madame Tanguy's hand and kissed it gallantly.

"Ah, Xantippe, how charming you look this morning."

Madame Tanguy did not understand why this handsome brute was always calling her Xantippe, but she liked the sound of it and was flattered.

"Don't think you can get around me, you loafer. I slave my life away to grind those filthy colours, and then you come and steal them."

"My precious Xantippe, don't be so hard on me. You have the soul of an artist. I can see it spread all over your lovely face."

Madame Tanguy lifted her apron as though to wipe the soul of the artist off her face. "Phaw!" she cried. "One artist in the family is enough. I suppose he told you he wants to live on only fifty centimes a day. Where do you think he would get that fifty centimes if I didn't earn it for him?"

"All Paris speaks of your charm and ability, dear Madame."

He leaned over and once again brushed his lips across her gnarled hand. She softened.

"Well, you are a scoundrel and a flatterer, but you can have a little colour this time. Only see that you pay your bill."

"For this kindness, my lovely Xantippe, I shall paint your portrait. One day it will hang in the Louvre and immortalize us both."

The little bell on the front door jingled. A stranger walked in. "That picture you have in the window," he said. "That still life. Who is it by?"

"Paul Cezanne."

"Cezanne? Never heard of him. Is it for sale?"

"Ah, no, alas, it is already . . ."

Madame Tanguy threw off her apron, pushed Tanguy out of the way, and ran up to the man eagerly.

"But of course it is for sale. It is a beautiful still life, is it not, Monsieur? Have you ever seen such apples before? We will sell it to you cheap, Monsieur, since you admire it."

"How much?"

"How much, Tanguy?" demanded Madame, with a threat in her voice.

Tanguy swallowed hard. "Three hun . . ."

"Tanguy!"

"Two hun . . ."

"TANGUY!"

"Well, one hundred francs."

"A hundred francs?" said the stranger. "For an unknown painter? I'm afraid that's too much. I was only prepared to spend about twenty-five."

Madame Tanguy took the canvas out of the window.

"See, Monsieur, it is a big picture. There are four apples. Four apples are a hundred francs. You only want to spend twenty-five. Then why not take one apple?"

The man studied the canvas for a moment and said, "Yes, I could do that. Just cut this apple the full length of the canvas and I'll take it."

Madame ran back to her apartment, got a pair of scissors, and cut off the end apple. She wrapped it in a piece of paper, handed it to the man, and took the twenty-five francs. He walked out with the bundle under his arm.

"My favourite Cezanne," moaned Tanguy. "I put it in the window so people could see it for a moment and go away happy."

Madame put the mutilated canvas on the counter.

"Next time someone wants a Cezanne, and hasn't much money, sell him an apple. Take anything you can get for it. They're worthless anyway, he paints so many of them. And you needn't laugh, Paul Gauguin, the same goes for you. I'm going to take those canvases of yours off the wall and sell every one of your naked heathen females for five francs apiece."

"My darling Xantippe," said Gauguin, "we met too late in life. If only you had been my partner on the Stock Exchange, we would have owned the Bank of France by now."

When Madame retired to her quarters at the rear Père Tanguy said to Vincent, "You are a painter, Monsieur? I hope

307

you will buy your colours here. And perhaps you will let me see some of your pictures?"

"I shall be happy to. These are lovely Japanese prints. Are they for sale?"

"Yes. They have become very fashionable in Paris since the Goncourt brothers have taken to collecting them. They are influencing our young painters a great deal."

"I like these two. I want to study them. How much are they?"

"Three francs apiece."

"I'll take them. Oh, Lord, I forgot. I spent my last franc this morning. Gauguin, have you six francs?"

"Don't be ridiculous."

Vincent laid the Japanese prints down on the counter with regret.

"I'm afraid I'll have to leave them, Pére Tanguy."

Pére pressed the prints into Vincent's hand and looked up at him with a shy, wistful smile on his homely face.

"You need this for your work. Please take them. You will pay me another time."

10

Theo decided to give a party for Vincent's friends. They made four dozen hard-boiled eggs, brought in a keg of beer, and filled innumerable trays with brioches and pastries. The tobacco smoke was so thick in the living room that when Gauguin moved his huge bulk from one end to the other, he looked like an ocean liner coming through the fog. Lautrec perched himself in one corner, cracked eggs on the arm of Theo's favourite armchair, and scattered the shells over the rug. Rousseau was all excited about a perfumed note he had received that day from a lady admirer who wanted to meet him. He told the story with wide eyed amazement over and over again. Seurat was working out a new theory, and had Cezanne pinned against the window, explaining to him. Vincent poured beer from the keg, laughed at Gauguin's obscene stories, wondered with Rousseau who his lady friend could be, argued with Lautrec whether lines or points of colour were most effective in capturing an impression, and finally rescued Cezanne from the clutches of Seurat.

The room fairly burst with excitement. The men in it were all powerful personalities, fierce egoists, and vibrant iconoclasts. Theo called them monomaniacs. They loved to argue, fight, curse, defend their own theories and damn everything else. Their voices were strong and rough; the number of things they loathed in the world was legion. A hall twenty times the size of Theo's living room would have been too small to contain the dynamic force of the fighting, strident painters.

The turbulence of the room, which fired Vincent to gesticulatory enthusiasm and eloquence, gave Theo a splitting headache. All this stridency was foreign to his nature. He was tremendously fond of the men in the room. Was it not for them he carried on his quiet, endless battle with Goupils? But he found the rough, uncouth clamour of their personalities alien to his nature. There was a good bit of the feminine in Theo. Toulouse-Lautrec, with his usual vitriolic humour, once remarked,

"Too bad Theo is Vincent's brother. He would have made him such a splendid wife."

Theo found it just as distasteful to sell Bouguereaus as it would have been for Vincent to paint them. And yet, if he sold Bouguereau, Valadon would let him exhibit Degas. One day he would persuade Valadon to let him hang a Cezanne, then a Gauguin or a Lautrec, and finally, some distant day, a Vincent Van Gogh . . .

He took one last look at the noisy, quarrelsome, smoke laden room, slipped out of the front door unnoticed, and walked up the Butte where, alone, he gazed at the lights of Paris spread out before him.

Gauguin was arguing with Cezanne. He waved a hard-boiled egg and a brioche in one hand, a glass of beer in the other. It was his boast that he was the only man in Paris who could drink beer with a pipe in his mouth.

"Your canvases are cold, Cezanne," he shouted. "Ice cold. It freezes me just to look at them. There's not an ounce of emotion in all the miles of canvas you've flung paint at."

"I don't try to paint emotion," retorted Cezanne. "I leave that to the novelists. I paint apples and landscapes."

"You don't paint emotion because you can't. You paint with your eyes, that's what you paint with."

"What does anyone else paint with?"

"With all sorts of things." Gauguin took a quick look about the room. "Lautrec, there, paints with his spleen. Vincent paints with his heart. Seurat paints with his mind, which is almost as bad as painting with your eyes. And Rousseau paints with his imagination."

"What do you paint with, Gauguin?"

"Who me? I don't know. Never thought about it."

"I'll tell you," said Lautrec. "You paint with your genital!"

When the laugh on Gauguin died down, Seurat perched himself on the arm of a divan and cried, "You can sneer at a man painting with his mind, but it's just helped me discover how we can make our canvases doubly effective."

"Do I have to listen to the *blague* all over again?" moaned Cezanne.

"Shut up, Cezanne! Gauguin, sit down somewhere and don't clutter up the whole room. Rousseau, stop telling that infernal story about your admirer. Lautrec, throw me an egg. Vincent, can I have a brioche? Now listen, everybody!"

"What's up, Seurat? I haven't seen you so excited since that fellow spat on your canvas at the Salon des Refusées!"

"Listen! What is painting today? Light. What kind of light? Gradated light. Points of colour flowing into each other . . ."

"That's not painting, that's pointillism!"

"For God's sake, Georges, are you going intellectual on us again?"

"Shut up! We get through with a canvas. Then what do we do? We turn it over to some fool who puts it into a hideous gold frame and kills our every last effect. Now I propose that we should never let a picture out of our hands until we've put it into a frame and painted the frame so that it becomes an integral part of the picture."

"But, Seurat, you're stopping too soon. Every picture must be hung in a room. And if the room is the wrong colour, it will kill the picture and frame both."

"That's right, why not paint the room to match the frame?"

"A good idea," said Seurat.

"What about the house the room is in?"

"And the city that the house is in."

"Oh, Georges, Georges, you do get the damndest ideas!"

"That's what comes from painting with your brain."

"The reason you imbeciles don't paint with your brains is that you haven't any!"

"Look at Georges's face, everybody. Quick! We got the scientist riled up that time, all right."

"Why do you men always fight among yourselves?" demanded Vincent. "Why don't you try working together?"

"You're the communist of this group," said Gauguin. "Suppose you tell us what we'd get if we worked together?"

310

"Very well," said Vincent, shooting the hard, round yolk of an egg into his mouth, "I will tell you. I've been working out a plan. We're a lot of nobodies. Manet, Degas, Sisley, and Pissarro paved the way for us. They've been accepted and their work is exhibited in the big galleries. All right, they're the painters of the Grande Boulevard. But we have to go into the side streets. We're the painters of the Petit Boulevard. Why couldn't we exhibit our painting in the little restaurants of the side streets, the workingman's restaurants? Each of us would contribute, say, five canvases. Every afternoon we would put them up in a new place. We'd sell the pictures for whatever the workers could afford. In addition to having our work constantly before the public, we would be making it possible for the poor people of Paris to see good art, and buy beautiful pictures for almost nothing."

"*Tiens,*" breathed Rousseau, his eyes wide with excitement, "that's wonderful."

"It takes me a year to finish a canvas," grumbled Seurat. "Do you think I'm going to sell it to some filthy carpenter for five sous?"

"You could contribute your little studies."

"Yes, but suppose the restaurants won't take our pictures?"

"Of course they will."

"Why not? It costs them nothing, and makes their places beautiful."

"How would we handle it. Who would find the restaurants?"

"I have that all figured out," cried Vincent. "We'll make Pére Tanguy our manager. He'll find the restaurants, hang the pictures, and take in the money."

"Of course. He's just the man."

"Rousseau, be a good fellow and run down to Pére Tanguy's. Tell him he's wanted on important business."

"You can count me out of this scheme," said Cezanne.

"What's the matter?" asked Gauguin. "Afraid your lovely pictures will be soiled by the eyes of workingmen?"

"It isn't that. I'm going back to Aix at the end of the month."

"Try it just once, Cezanne," urged Vincent. "If it doesn't work, you're nothing out."

"Oh, very well."

"When we get through with the restaurants," said Lautrec, "we might start on the bordellos. I know most of the Madames on Montmartre. They have a better clientele, and I think we could get higher prices."

Père Tanguy came running in, all excited. Rousseau had been able to give him only a garbled account of what was up. His round straw hat was sitting at an angle, and his pudgy little face was lit up with eager enthusiasm.

When he heard the plan he exclaimed, "Yes, yes, I know the very place. The Restaurant Norvins. The owner is a friend of mine. His walls are bare, and he'll be pleased. When we are through there, I know another one on the Rue Pierre. Oh, there are thousands of restaurants in Paris."

"When is the first exhibition of the club of the Petit Boulevard to take place?" asked Gauguin.

"Why put it off?" demanded Vincent. "Why not begin tomorrow?"

Tanguy hopped about on one foot, took off his hat, then crammed it on his head again.

"Yes, yes, tomorrow! Bring me your canvases in the morning. I will hang them in the Restaurant Norvins in the afternoon. And when the people come for their dinner, we will cause a sensation. We will sell the pictures like holy candles on Easter. What's this you're giving me? A glass of beer? Good! Gentlemen, we drink to the Communist Art Club of the Petit Boulevard. May its first exhibition be a success."

11

Père Tanguy knocked on the door of Vincent's apartment the following noon.

"I've been around to tell all the others," he said. "We can only exhibit at Norvins providing we eat our dinner there."

"That's all right."

"Good. The others have agreed. We can't hang the pictures until four-thirty. Can you be at my shop at four? We are all going over together."

"I'll be there.

When they reached the blue shop on the Rue Clauzel, Père Tanguy was already loading the canvases into a handcart. The others were inside, smoking and discussing Japanese prints.

"Alors," cried Père, "we are ready."

"May I help you with the cart, Père?" asked Vincent.

"No, no, I am the manager."

He pushed the cart to the centre of the street and began the

312

long climb upward. The painters walked behind, two by two. First came Gauguin and Lautrec; they loved to be together because of the ludicrous picture they made. Seurat was listening to Rousseau, who was all excited over a second perfumed letter he had received that afternoon. Vincent and Cezanne, who sulked and kept uttering words like dignity and decorum, brought up the rear.

"Here, Père Tanguy," said Gauguin, after they wound up the hill a way, "that cart is heavy, loaded down with immortal masterpieces. Let me push it for a while."

"No, no," cried Père, running ahead. "I am the colour bearer of this revolution. When the first shot is fired, I shall fall."

They made a droll picture, the ill-assorted, fantastically dressed men, walking in the middle of the street behind a common pushcart. They did not mind the stares of the amused passers-by. They laughed and talked in high spirits.

"Vincent," cried Rousseau, "have I told you about the letter I got this afternoon? Perfumed, too. From the same lady."

He ran along at Vincent's side, waving his arms, telling the whole interminable story over again. When he finally finished and dropped back with Seurat, Lautrec called Vincent.

"Do you know who Rousseau's lady is?" he asked.

"No. How should I?"

Lautrec snickered. "It's Gauguin. He's giving Rousseau a love affair. The poor fellow has never had a woman. Gauguin is going to feed him with perfumed letters for a couple of months and then make an assignation. He'll dress up in women's clothes and meet Rousseau in one of the Montmartre rooms with peepholes. We're all going to be at the holes watching Rousseau make love for the first time. It should be priceless."

"Gauguin, you're a fiend."

"Oh, come, Vincent," said Gauguin. "I think it's an excellent joke."

At length they arrived at the Restaurant Norvins. It was a modest place, tucked away between a wine shop and a supply store for horses. The outside was painted a varnish-yellow, the walls of the inside a light blue. There were perhaps twenty square tables with red and white checked tablecloths. At the back, near the kitchen door, was a high booth for the proprietor.

For a solid hour the painters quarrelled about which pictures should be hung next to which. Pére Tanguy was almost distraught. The proprietor was getting angry, for the dinner hour was near and the restaurant was in chaos. Seurat refused to let his pictures go up at all because the blue of the walls killed his skies. Cezanne would not allow his still lifes to hang next to Lautrec's "miserable posters," and Rousseau was offended because they wanted to stick his things on the back wall near the kitchen. Lautrec insisted that one of his large canvases be hung in the *lavabo*.

"That is the most contemplative moment in a man's day," he said.

Pére Tanguy came to Vincent almost in despair. "Here," he said, "take these two francs, add to it whatever you can, and hustle everyone across the street to a bar. If only I had fifteen minutes to myself, I could finish."

The ruse worked. When they all trooped back to the restaurant, the exhibition was in order. They stopped quarrelling and sat down at a large table by the street door. Pére Tanguy had put signs up all over the walls: THESE PAINTINGS FOR SALE, CHEAP. SEE THE PROPRIETOR.

It was five-thirty. Dinner was not served until six. The men fidgeted like schoolgirls. Every time the front door opened, all eyes turned to it hopefully. The customers of Norvins never came until the dot of six.

"Look at Vincent," whispered Gauguin to Seurat. "He's as nervous as a prima donna."

"Tell you what I'll do, Gauguin," said Lautrec, "I'll wager you the price of dinner that I sell a canvas before you do."

"You're on."

"Cezanne, I'll give you three to one odds." It was Lautrec.

Cezanne grew crimson at the insult, and everyone laughed at him.

"Remember," said Vincent, "Pére Tanguy is to do all the selling. Don't anyone try to bargain with the buyers."

"Why don't they come?" asked Rousseau. "It's late."

As the clock on the wall drew nearer six, the group became more and more jumpy. At length all bantering stopped. The men did not move their eyes from the door. A feeling of tension settled over them.

"I didn't feel this way when I exhibited with the Independents, before all the critics of Paris," murmured Seurat.

"Look, look!" whispered Rousseau, "that man, crossing the street. He's coming this way. He's a customer."

314

The man walked past Norvins and disappeared. The clock on the wall chimed six times. On the last chime the door was opened and a labourer came in. He was shabbily dressed. Lines of fatigue were written inward and downward on his shoulders and back.

"Now," said Vincent, "we shall see."

The labourer slouched to a table at the other side of the room, threw his hat on a rack, and sat down. The six painters strained forward, watching him. The man scanned the menu, ordered a *plat du jour,* and within a moment was scooping up his soup with a large spoon. He did not raise his eyes from his plate.

"*Tiens,*" said Vincent, "*c'est curieux.*"

Two sheet-metal workers walked in. The proprietor bade them good evening. They grunted, dropped into the nearest chairs, and immediately plunged into a fierce quarrel about something that had happened during the day.

Slowly the restaurant filled. A few women came in with the men. It seemed as though everyone had his regular table. The first thing they looked at was the menu ; when they were served, they were so intent upon their food that they never once glanced up. After dinner they lighted their pipes, chatted, unfolded their copies of the evening paper, and read.

"Would the gentlemen like to be served with their dinner now?" asked the waiter, about seven o'clock.

No one answered. The waiter walked away. A man and a woman entered.

As he was throwing his hat on the rack, the man noticed a Rousseau tiger peering through a jungle. He pointed it out to his comrade. Everyone at the painters' table stiffened. Rousseau half rose. The woman said something in a low tone and laughed. They sat down, and holding their heads close together, devoured the menu voraciously.

At a quarter to eight the waiter served the soup without asking. Nobody touched it. When it had grown cold, the waiter took it away. He brought the *plat du jour.* Lautrec drew pictures in the gravy with his fork. Only Rousseau could eat. Everyone, even Seurat, emptied his carafe of sour red wine. The restaurant was hot with the smell of food, with the odours of people who had laboured and perspired in the heat of the sun.

One by one the customers paid their checks, returned the cursory *bonsoir* of the proprietor and filed out.

"I'm sorry, gentlemen," said the waiter, "but it's eight-thirty, and we are closing."

Pére Tanguy took the pictures off the walls and carried them out into the street. He pushed the cart home through the slowly falling dusk.

12

The spirit of old Goupil and Uncle Vincent Van Gogh had vanished forever from the galleries. In their place had come a policy of selling pictures as though they were any other commodity, such as shoes or herrings. Theo was constantly being harassed to make more money and sell poorer pictures.

"See here, Theo," said Vincent, "why don't you leave Goupils?"

"The other art dealers are just as bad," replied Theo wearily. "Besides, I've been with them so long. I'd better not change."

"You must change. I insist that you must. You're becoming unhappier every day down there. Let go of me! I can walk around if I like. Theo, you're the best known and best liked young art dealer in Paris. Why don't you open a shop for yourself?"

"Oh, Lord, do we have to go over all that again?"

"Look, Theo, I've got a marvellous idea. We'll open a communist art shop. We will all give you our canvases, and whatever money you take in, we'll live on equally. We can scrape together enough francs to open a little shop in Paris, and we'll take a house out in the country where we'll all live and work. Portier sold a Lautrec the other day, and Pére Tanguy has sold several Cezannes. I'm sure we could attract the young art buyers of Paris. And we wouldn't need much money to run that house in the country. We'd live together simply, instead of keeping up a dozen establishments in Paris."

"Vincent, I have a frightful headache. Let me go to sleep now, will you?"

"No, you can sleep on Sunday. Listen, Theo ... where are you going? All right, undress if you like, but I'm going to talk to you anyway. Here, I'll sit by the head of your bed. Now if you're unhappy at Goupils, and all the young painters of Paris are willing, and we can get a little money together ..."

Pére Tanguy and Lautrec came in with Vincent the following night. Theo had hoped Vincent would be out for the evening. Père Tanguy's little eyes were dancing with excitement.

"Monsieur Van Gogh, Monsieur Van Gogh, it is a wonderful idea. You must do it. I will give up my shop and move to the country with you. I will grind the colours, stretch the canvas, and build the frames. I ask only for my food and shelter."

Theo put down his book with a sigh.

"Where are we going to get the money to begin this enterprise? The money to open a shop, and rent a house, and feed the men?"

"Here, I brought it with me," cried Père Tanguy. "Two hundred and twenty francs. All I have saved up. Take it, Monsieur Van Gogh. It will help begin our colony."

"Lautrec, you're a sensible man. What do you say to all this nonsense?"

"I think it a damned good idea. As things go now, we are not only fighting all of Paris, but fighting among ourselves. If we could present a united front . . ."

"Very well, you are wealthy. Will you help us?"

"Ah, no. If it is to be a subsidized colony, it will lose its purpose. I will contribute two hundred and twenty francs, the same as Père Tanguy."

"It's such a crazy idea! If you men knew anything about the business world . . ."

Père Tanguy ran up to Theo and wrung his hand.

"My dear Monsieur Van Gogh, I beseech you, do not call it a crazy idea. It is a glorious idea. You must, you simply must . . ."

"There's no crawling out now, Theo," said Vincent. "We've got you! We're going to raise some money and make you our master. You've said good-bye to Goupils. You're through there. You're now manager of the Communist Art Colony."

Theo ran a hand over his eyes.

"I can just see myself managing you bunch of wild animals."

When Theo got home the next night he found his house crammed to the doors with excited painters. The air was blue with foul tobacco smoke, and churned by loud, turbulent voices. Vincent was seated on a fragile table in the middle of the living room, master of ceremonies.

"No, no," he cried, "there will be no pay. Absolutely no money. We will never see money from one year to the next. Theo will sell the pictures and we will receive our food, shelter, and materials."

317

"What about the men whose work never sells?" demanded Seurat. "How long are we going to support them?"

"As long as they want to stay with us and work."

"Wonderful," grunted Gauguin. "We'll have all the amateur painters in Europe on our doorstep."

"Here's Monsieur Van Gogh!" shouted Pére Tanguy, catching a sight of Theo as he stood leaning against the door. "Three cheers for our manager."

"Hurrah for Theo! Hurrah for Theo! Hurrah for Theo!"

Everyone was enormously excited. Rousseau wanted to know if he could still give violin lessons at the colony. Anquetin said he owed three months rent, and that they'd better find the country house very soon. Cezanne insisted that a man be allowed to spend his own money, if he had any. Vincent cried, "No, that would kill our communism. We must all share and share alike." Lautrec wanted to know if they could have women at the house. Gauguin insisted that everyone be forced to contribute at least two canvases a month.

"Then I won't come in!" shouted Seurat. "I finish only one big canvas a year."

"What about materials?" demanded Pére Tanguy. "Do I give everyone the same amount of colour and canvas each week?"

"No, no, of course not," cried Vincent. "We all get as much material as we need, no more and no less. Just like food."

"Yes, but what happens to the surplus money? After we begin selling our pictures? Who gets the profits?"

"Nobody gets the profits," said Vincent. "As soon as we have a little money over, we'll open a house in Brittany. Then we'll open another in Provence. Soon we'll have houses all over the country, and we'll be travelling from one place to another."

"What about the railroad fare? Do we get that out of the profits?"

"Yes, and how much can we travel? Who's to decide that?"

"Suppose there are too many painters for one house during the best season? Who gets left out in the cold, will you tell me?"

"Theo, Theo, you're the manager of this business. Tell us all about it. Can anyone join? Is there a limit to the membership? Will we have to paint according to any system? Will we have models out there at the house?"

At dawn the meeting broke up. The people downstairs had

318

exhausted themselves rapping on the ceiling with broomsticks. Theo went to bed about four, but Vincent, Pére Tanguy, and some of the more enthusiastic ones surrounded his bed and urged him to give Goupils notice on the first of the month.

The excitement grew in intensity with the passing of the weeks. The art world of Paris was divided into two camps. The established painters spoke of those crazy men, the Van Gogh brothers. All the others spoke endlessly about the new experiment.

Vincent talked and worked like mad all night and day. There were so many thousands of details to be settled; how they were to get the money, where the shop was to be located, how prices were to be charged, what men could belong, who would manage the house in the country and how. Theo, almost against his will, was drawn into the febrile excitement. The apartment on the Rue Lepic was crowded every night of the week. Newspaper men came to get stories. Art critics came to discuss the new movement. Painters from all over France returned to Paris to get into the organization.

If Theo was king, Vincent was the royal organizer. He drew up countless plans, constitutions, budgets, pleas for money, codes of rules and regulations, manifestos for the papers, pamphlets to acquaint Europe with the purpose of the Communist Art Colony.

He was so busy he forgot to paint.

Almost three thousand francs rolled into the coffers of the organization. The painters contributed every last franc they could spare. A street fair was held on the Boulevard Clichy, and each man hawked his own canvases. Letters came in from all over Europe, sometimes containing soiled and crumpled franc notes. Art loving Paris came to the apartment, caught the enthusiasm of the new movement, and threw a bill into the open box before they left. Vincent was secretary and treasurer.

Theo insisted that they must have five thousand francs before they could begin. He had located a shop on the Rue Tronchet which he thought well situated, and Vincent had discovered a superb old mansion in the forest of St. Germain-en-Laye that could be had for almost nothing. The canvases of the painters who wanted to join kept pouring into the Rue Lepic apartment, until there was no space left to move about. Hundreds and hundreds of people went in and out of the little apartment. They argued, fought, cursed, ate, drank, and gesticulated wildly. Theo was given notice to move.

At the end of the month the Louis Philippe furniture was in shreds.

Vincent had no time even to think about his palette now. There were letters to be written, people to be interviewed, houses to be looked at, enthusiasm to be kindled in every new painter and amateur he met. He talked until he went hoarse. A feverish energy came into his eyes. He took his food fitfully, and almost never found a chance to sleep. He was forever going, going, going.

By the beginning of spring, the five thousand francs were collected. Theo was giving notice to Goupils on the first of the month. He had decided to take the shop on the Rue Tronchet. Vincent put down a small deposit on the house in St. Germain. The list of members with which the colony would be opened was drawn up by Theo, Vincent, Pére Tanguy, Gauguin and Lautrec. From the piles of canvases amassed at the apartment, Theo picked those he was going to show in his first exhibit. Rousseau and Anquetin had a bitter quarrel as to who was going to decorate the inside of the shop, and who the outside. Theo no longer minded being kept awake. He was now as enthusiastic as Vincent had been in the beginning. He worked feverishly to get everything organized so that the colony might open by summer. He debated endlessly with Vincent whether the second house should be located on the Atlantic or the Mediterranean.

One morning Vincent went to sleep about four o'clock, utterly exhausted. Theo did not awaken him. He slept until noon, and awoke refreshed. He wandered into his studio. The canvas on the easel was many weeks old. The paint on the palette was dry, cracked, and covered with dust. The tubes of pigment had been kicked into the corners. His brushes lay about, caked solid with old paint.

A voice within him asked, softly, "One moment, Vincent. Are you a painter? Or are you a communist organizer?"

He took the stacks of ill-assorted canvases into Theo's room and piled them on the bed. In the studio he left only his own pictures. He stood them on the easel, one by one, gnawing his hangnails as he gazed at them.

Yes, he had made progress. Slowly, slowly, his colour had lightened, struggled toward a crystal luminosity. No longer were they imitative. No longer could the traces of his friends

320

be detected on the canvas. He realized for the first time that he had been developing a very individual sort of technique. It was like nothing else he had ever seen. He did not even know how it had got there.

He had strained Impressionism through his own nature, and had been on the verge of achieving a very curious means of expression. Then, suddenly, he had stopped.

He put his more recent canvases on the easel. Once he nearly cried out. He had almost, almost caught something! His pictures were beginning to show a definite method, a new attack with the weapons he had forged through the winter.

His many weeks of rest had given him a clear perspective on his work. He saw that he was developing an Impressionist technique all his own.

He took a careful look at himself in the mirror. His beard needed trimming, his hair needed cutting, his shirt was soiled, and his trousers hung like a limp rag. He pressed his suit with a hot iron, put on one of Theo's shirts, took a five franc note out of the treasury box, and went to the barber. When he was all cleaned up, he walked meditatively to Goupils on the Boulevard Montmartre.

"Theo," he said, "can you come out with me for a short time?"

"What's up?"

"Get your hat. Is there a café about where no one could possibly find us?"

Seated at the very rear of a café, in a secluded corner, Theo said, "You know, Vincent, this is the first time I've had a word alone with you for a month?"

"I know, Theo. I'm afraid I've been something of a fool."

"How so?"

"Theo, tell me frankly, am I a painter? Or am I a communist organizer?"

"What do you mean?"

"I've been so busy organizing this colony, I've had no time to paint. And once the house is started, I'll never catch a moment."

"I see."

"Theo, I want to paint. I haven't put in this seven years of labour just to be a house manager for other painters. I tell you, I'm hungry for my brushes, Theo, so hungry I could almost run away from Paris on the next train."

"But, Vincent, now, after all we've . . ."

"I told you I'd been a fool. Theo, can you stand to hear a confession?"

"Yes?"

"I'm heartily sick of the sight of other painters. I'm tired of their talk, of their theories, of their interminable quarrels. Oh, you needn't smile, I know I've done my share of the fighting. That's just the point. What was it Mauve used to say? 'A man can either paint, or talk about painting, but he can't do both at the same time.' Well, Theo, have you been supporting me for seven years just to hear me spout ideas?"

"You've done a lot of good work for the colony, Vincent."

"Yes, but now that we're ready to move out there, I realize that I don't want to go. I couldn't possibly live there and do any work. Theo, I wonder if I can make you understand ... But of course I can. When I was alone in the Brabant and The Hague, I thought of myself as an important person. I was one lone man, battling the whole world. I was an artist, the only artist living. Everything I painted was valuable. I knew that I had great ability, and that eventually the world would say, 'He is a splendid painter.' "

"And now?"

"Alas, now I am just one of many. There are hundreds of painters all about me. I see myself caricatured on every side. Think of all the wretched canvases in our apartment, sent by painters who want to join the colony. They, too, think they are going to be great painters. Well, maybe I'm just like them. How do I know? What have I to bolster up my courage now? Before I came to Paris I didn't know there were hopeless fools who deluded themselves all their lives. Now I know. That hurts."

"It has nothing to do with you."

"Perhaps not. But I'll never be able to stamp out that little germ of doubt. When I am alone, in the country, I forget that there are thousands of canvases being painted every day. I imagine that mine is the only one, and that it is a beautiful gift to the world. I would still go on painting even if I knew my work to be atrocious, but this ... this artist's illusion ... helps. Do you understand?"

"Yes."

"Besides, I am not a city painter. I don't belong here. I am a peasant painter. I want to go back to my fields. I want to find a sun so hot that it will burn everything out of me but the desire to paint!"

"So ... you want to ... leave ... Paris?"

"Yes. I must."

"And what about the colony?"

"I am going to withdraw. But you must carry on."

Theo shook his head. "No, not without you."

"Why not?"

"I don't know. I was only doing it for you ... because you wanted it."

They were silent for some moments.

"You haven't given notice yet, Theo?"

"No. I was going to on the first."

"I suppose we can return the money to the people it belongs to?"

"Yes ... When do you think you'll be going?"

"Not until my palette is clear."

"I see."

"Then I'll go away. To the South, probably. I don't know where. So that I can be alone. And paint and paint and paint. By myself."

He threw his arm about Theo's shoulder with rough affection.

"Theo, tell me you don't despise me. To throw everything up this way when I've put you through so much."

"Despise you?"

Theo smiled with infinite sadness. He reached up and patted the hand that lay on his shoulder.

"... No ... no, of course not. I understand. I think you are right. Well ... old boy ... you'd better finish your drink. I must be getting back to Goupils."

13

Vincent laboured on for another month, but although his palette was now almost as clear and light as that of his friends, he could not seem to reach a form of expression that satisfied him. At first he thought it was the crudity of his drawing, so he tried working slowly, and in cold blood. The meticulous process of putting on the paint was torture to him, but looking at the canvas afterwards was even worse. He tried hiding his brush work in flat surfaces; he tried working with thin colour instead of rich spurts of pigment. Nothing seemed to help. Again and again he felt that he was fumbling toward a medium that would not only be unique, but which would enable him to say everything he wanted to say. And yet he could not quite grasp it.

"I almost got it that time," he murmured one evening in the apartment. "Almost, but not quite. If I could only find out what was standing in my way."

"I think I can tell you that," said Theo, taking the canvas from his brother.

"You can? What is it?"

"It's Paris."

"Paris?"

"Yes. Paris has been your training ground. As long as you remain here, you'll be nothing but a schoolboy. Remember our school in Holland, Vincent? We learned how other people did things, and how they should be done, but we never actually did anything for ourselves."

"You mean I don't find the subjects here sympathetic?"

"No, I mean that you're unable to make a clean break from your teachers. I'll be awfully lonely without you, Vincent, but I know that you have to go. Somewhere in this world there must be a spot that you can make all your own. I don't know where it is; it's up to you to find it. But you must cut away from your schoolhouse before you can reach maturity."

"Do you know, old boy, what country I've been thinking a lot about of late?"

"No."

"Africa."

"Africa! Not really?"

"Yes. I've been thinking of the blistering sun all during this damnably long and cold winter. That's where Delacroix found his colour, and maybe I could find myself there."

"Africa is a long ways off, Vincent," said Theo, meditatively.

"Theo, I want the sun. I want it in its most terrific heat and power. I've been feeling it pull me southward all winter, like a huge magnet. Until I left Holland I never knew there was such a thing as a sun. Now I know there's no such thing as painting without it. Perhaps that something I need to bring me to maturity is a hot sun. I'm chilled to the bone from the Parisian winter, Theo, and I think some of that cold has gotten into my palette and brushes. I never was one to go at a thing half-heartedly; once I could get the African sun to burn the cold out of me, and set my palette on fire . . ."

"Hummmm," said Theo, "we'll have to think that over. Maybe you're right."

Paul Cezanne gave a farewell party for all his friends. He had arranged through his father to buy the plot of land on the hill overlooking Aix, and he was returning home to build a studio.

"Get out of Paris, Vincent," he said, "and come down to Provence. Not to Aix, that's my territory, but to some place near by. The sun is hotter and purer there than anywhere else in the world. You'll find light and clean colour in Provence such as you've never seen before. I'm staying there for the rest of my life."

"I'll be the next one out of Paris," said Gauguin. "I'm going back to the tropics. If you think you have real sun in Provence, Cezanne, you ought to come to the Marquesas. There the sunlight and colour are just as primitive as the people."

"You men ought to join the sun worshippers," said Seurat.

"As for myself," announced Vincent, "I think I'm going to Africa."

"Well, well," murmured Lautrec, "we have another little Delacroix on our hands."

"Do you mean that, Vincent?" asked Gauguin.

"Yes. Oh, not right away, perhaps. I think I ought to stop off somewhere in Provence and get used to the sun."

"You can't stop at Marseilles," said Seurat. "That town belongs to Monticelli."

"I can't go to Aix," said Vincent, "because it belongs to Cezanne. Monet had already done Antibes, and I agree that Marseilles is sacred to 'Fada.' Has anyone a suggestion as to where I might go?"

"Wait!" exclaimed Lautrec, "I know the very place. Have you ever thought of Arles?"

"Arles? That's an old Roman settlement, isn't it?"

"Yes. It's on the Rhône, a couple of hours from Marseilles. I was there once. The colouring of the surrounding country makes Delacroix's African scenes look anaemic."

"You don't tell me? Is there good sun?"

"Sun? Enough to drive you crazy. And you should see the Arlesiennes; the most gorgeous women in the world. They still retain the pure, delicate features of their Greek ancestors, combined with the robust, sturdy stature of their Roman conquerors. Yet curiously enough, their aroma is distinctly

Oriental; I suppose that's a result of the Saracen invasion back in the eighth century. It was at Arles that the true Venus was found, Vincent. The model was an Arlesienne!"

"They sound fascinating," said Vincent.

"They are. And just wait until you feel the mistral."

"What's the mistral?" asked Vincent.

"You'll find out when you get there," replied Lautrec with a twisted grin.

"How about the living? Is it cheap?"

"There's nothing to spend your money on, except food and shelter, and they don't cost much. If you're keen to get away from Paris, why don't you try it?"

"Arles," murmured Vincent to himself. "Arles and the Arlesiennes. I'd like to paint one of those women!"

Paris had excited Vincent. He had drunk too many absinthes, smoked too many pipefuls of tobacco, engaged too much in external activities. His gorge was high. He felt a tremendous urge to get away somewhere by himself where it would be quiet, and he could pour his surging, nervous energy into his craft. He needed only a hot sun to bring him to fruition. He had the feeling that the climax of his life, the full creative power toward which he had been struggling these eight long years, was not so very far off. He knew that nothing he had painted as yet was of any value; perhaps there was a short stretch just ahead in which he could create those few pictures which would justify his life.

What was it Monticelli had said? "We must put in ten years of hard labour, so that in the end we will be able to paint two or three authentic portraits."

In Paris he had security, friendship, and love. There was always a good home for him with Theo. His brother would never let him go hungry, would never make him ask twice for painting supplies, or deny him anything that was in his power to give, least of all full sympathy.

He knew that the moment he left Paris his troubles would begin. He could not manage his allowance away from Theo. Half the time he would be forced to go without food. He would have to live in wretched little cafés, lacerate himself because he could not buy pigments, find his words choking in his throat because there was no friendly soul with whom he could talk.

"You'll like Arles," said Toulouse-Lautrec the next day. "It's quiet, and no one will bother you. The heat is dry, the

326

colour magnificent, and it is the only spot in Europe where you can find sheer Japanese clarity. It's a painter's paradise. If I weren't so attached to Paris, I'd go myself."

That evening Theo and Vincent went to a Wagnerian concert. They came home early and spent a quiet hour conjuring up memories of their childhood in Zundert. The next morning Vincent prepared the coffee for Theo, and when his brother had left for Goupils, gave the little apartment the most thorough cleaning it had had since they moved in. On the walls he put a painting of pink shrimps, a portrait of Père Tanguy in his round straw hat, the Moulin de la Galette, a female nude seen from the back, and a study of the Champs Elysèes.

When Theo came home that evening he found a note on the living room table.

Dear Theo:

I have gone to Arles, and will write you as soon as I get there.

I have put some of my paintings on the wall so that you won't forget me.

With a handshake in thought,
                                                   Vincent

BOOK SIX

ARLES

1

The Arlesian sun smote Vincent between the eyes, and broke him wide open. It was a whorling liquid ball of lemon-yellow fire, shooting across a hard blue sky and filling the air with blinding light. The terrific heat and intense clarity of the air created a new and unfamiliar world.

He dropped out of the third-class carriage early in the morning and walked down the winding road that led from the station to the Place Lamartine, a market square bounded on one side by the embankment of the Rhône, on the other by cafés and wretched hotels. Arles lay straight ahead, pasted against the side of a hill with a neat mason's trowel, drowsing in the hot, tropical sun.

327

When it came to looking for a place to live, Vincent was indifferent. He walked into the first hotel he passed in the Place, the Hotel de la Gare, and rented a room. It contained a blatant brass bed, a cracked pitcher in a washbowl, and an odd chair. The proprietor brought in an unpainted table. There was no room to set up an easel, but Vincent meant to paint out of doors all day.

He threw his valise on the bed and dashed out to see the town. There were two approaches to the heart of Arles from the Place Lamartine. The circular road on the left was for wagons; it skirted the edge of the town and wound slowly to the top of the hill, passing the old Roman forum and amphitheatre on the way. Vincent took the more direct approach which led through a labyrinth of narrow cobblestone streets. After a long climb he reached the sun-scorched Place de la Mairie. On the way up he passed cold stone courts and quadrangles which looked as though they had come down untouched from the early Roman days. In order to keep out the maddening sun, the alleys had been made so narrow that Vincent could touch both rows of houses with outstretched fingertips. To avoid the torturing mistral, the streets wound about in a hopeless maze on the side of the hill, never going straight for more than ten yards. There was refuse in the streets, dirty children in the doorways, and over everything a sinister, hunted aspect.

Vincent left the Place de la Mairie, walked through a short alley to the main marketing road at the back of the town, strolled through the little park and then stumbled down the hill to the Roman arena. He leaped from tier to tier like a goat, finally reaching the top. He sat on a block of stone, dangled his legs over a sheer drop of hundreds of feet, lit his pipe, and surveyed the domain of which he had appointed himself lord and master.

The town below him flowed down abruptly to the Rhône like a kaleidoscopic waterfall. The roofs of the houses were fitted into each other in an intricate design. They had all been tiled in what was originally red clay, but the burning, incessant sun had baked them to a maze of every colour, from the lightest lemon and delicate shell pink to a biting lavender and earthy loam-brown.

The wide, rapidly flowing Rhône made a sharp curve at the bottom of the hill on which Arles was plastered, and shot downward to the Mediterranean. There were stone embankments on either side of the river. Trinquetaille glistened like a painted city on the other bank. Behind Vincent were the mountains, huge ranges sticking upward into the clear white light. Spread out before him was a panorama of tilled fields, of orchards in blossom, the rising mound of Montmajour, fertile valleys ploughed into thousands of deep furrows, all converging at some distant point in infinity.

But it was the colour of the countryside that made him run a hand over his bewildered eyes. The sky was so intensely blue, such a hard, relentless, profound blue that it was not blue at all ; it was utterly colourless. The green of the fields that stretched below him was the essence of the colour green, gone mad. The burning lemon-yellow of the sun, the blood-red of the soil, the crying whiteness of the lone cloud over Montmajour, the ever reborn rose of the orchards ... such colourings were incredible. How could he paint them? How could he ever make anyone believe that they existed, even if he could transfer them to his palette? Lemon, blue, green, red, rose; nature run rampant in five torturing shades of expression.

Vincent took the wagon road to the Place Lamartine, grabbed up his easel, paints, and canvas and struck out along the Rhône. Almond trees were beginning to flower everywhere. The glistening white glare of the sun on the water sent stabs of pain into his eyes. He had left his hat in the hotel. The sun burned through the red of his hair, sucked out all the cold of Paris, all the fatigue, discouragement, and satiety with which city life had glutted his soul.

A kilometre down the river he found a drawbridge with a little cart going over it, outlined against a blue sky. The river was as blue as a well, the banks orange, coloured with green grass. A group of washerwomen in smocks and many-coloured caps were pounding dirty clothes in the shade of a lone tree.

Vincent set up his easel, drew a long breath, and shut his eyes. No man could catch such colourings with his eyes open. There fell away from him Seurat's talk about scientific pointillism, Gauguin's harangues about primitive decorativeness, Cezanne's appearances beneath solid surfaces, Lautrec's lines of colour and lines of splenetic hatred.

There remained only Vincent.

He returned to his hotel about dinner time. He sat down at a little table in the bar and ordered an absinthe. He was too excited, too utterly replete to think of food. A man sitting at a nearby table observed the paint splashed all over Vincent's hands, face, and clothing, and fell into conversation with him.

"I'm a Parisian journalist," he said. "I've been down here for three months gathering material for a book on the Provençal language."

"I just arrived from Paris this morning," said Vincent.

"So I noticed. Intend to stay long?"

"Yes. I imagine so."

"Well, take my advice and don't. Arles is the most violently insane spot on the globe."

"What makes you think that?"

"I don't think it. I know it. I've been watching these people for three months, and I tell you, they're all cracked. Just look at them. Watch their eyes. There's not a normal, rational person in this whole Tarascon vicinity!"

"That's a curious thing to say," observed Vincent.

"Within a week you'll be agreeing with me. The country around Arles is the most torn, desperately lashed section in Provence. You've been out in that sun. Can't you imagine what it must do to these people who are subject to its blinding light day after day? I tell you, it burns the brains right out of their heads. And the mistral. You haven't felt the mistral yet? Oh, dear, wait until you do. It whips this town into a frenzy two hundred days out of every year. If you try to walk the streets, it smashes you against the buildings. If you are out in the fields, it knocks you down and grinds you into the dirt. It twists your insides until you think you can't bear it another minute. I've seen that infernal wind tear out windows, pull up trees, knock down fences, lash the men and animals in the fields until I thought they would surely fly in pieces. I've been here only three months, and I'm going a little *fou* myself. I'm getting out tomorrow morning!"

"Surely you must be exaggerating?" asked Vincent. "The Arlesians looked all right to me, what little I saw of them today."

"What little you saw of them is right. Wait until you get to know them. Listen, do you know what my private opinion is?"

"No, what? Will you join me in an absinthe?"

"Thanks. In my private opinion, Arles is epileptic. It whips itself up to such an intense pitch of nervous excitement that you are positive it will burst into a violent fit and foam at the mouth."

"And does it?"

330

"No. That's the curious part. This country is forever reaching a climax, and never having one. I've been waiting for three months to see a revolution, or a volcano erupt from the Place de la Mairie. A dozen times I thought the inhabitants would all suddenly go mad and cut each other's throats! But just when they get to a point where an explosion is imminent, the mistral dies down for a couple of days and the sun goes behind the clouds."

"Well," laughed Vincent, "if Arles never reached a climax, you can't very well call it epileptic, now can you?"

"No," replied the journalist, "but I can call it epileptoidal."

"What the devil is that?"

"I'm doing an article on the subject for my paper in Paris. It was this German article that gave me the idea."

He pulled a magazine out of his pocket and shoved it across the table to Vincent.

"These doctors have made a study of the cases of several hundred men who suffered from nervous maladies which looked like epilepsy, but which never resulted in fits. You'll see by these charts how they have mapped the rising curve of nervousness and excitement; what the doctors call volatile tension. Well, in every last one of these cases the subjects have gone along with increasing fever until they reached the age of thirty-five to thirty-eight. At the average age of thirty-six they burst into a violent epileptic fit. After that it's a case of a half dozen more spasms and, within a year or two, good-bye."

"That's much too young to die," said Vincent. "A man is only beginning to get command of himself by that time."

The journalist put the magazine back in his pocket.

"Are you going to stop at this hotel for some time?" he asked. "My article is almost finished; I'll mail you a copy as soon as it's published. My point is this: Arles is an epileptoidal city. It's pulse has been mounting for centuries. It's approaching its first crisis. It's bound to happen. And soon. When it does, we're going to witness a frightful catastrophe. Murder, arson, rape, wholesale destruction! This country can't go on forever in a whipped, tortured state. Something must and will happen. I'm getting out before the people start foaming at the mouth! I advise you to come along!"

"Thanks," said Vincent, "I like it here. I think I'll turn in now. Will I see you in the morning? No? Then good luck to you. And don't forget to send me a copy of the article."

2

Every morning Vincent arose before dawn, dressed, and tramped several kilometres down the river or into the country to find a spot that stirred him. Every night he returned with a finished canvas, finished because there was nothing more he could do with it. Directly after supper he went to sleep.

He became a blind painting machine, dashing off one sizzling canvas after another without even knowing what he did. The orchards of the country were in bloom. He developed a wild passion to paint them all. He no longer thought about his painting. He just painted. All his eight years of intense labour were at last expressing themselves in a great burst of triumphal energy. Sometimes, when he began working at the first crack of dawn, the canvas would be completed by noon. He would tramp back to town, drink a cup of coffee and trudge out again in another direction with a new canvas.

He did not know whether his painting was good or bad. He did not care. He was drunk with colour.

No one spoke to him. He spoke to no one. What little strength he had left from his painting, he spent in fighting the mistral. Three days out of every week he had to fasten his easel to pegs driven into the ground. The easel waved back and forth in the wind like a sheet on a clothes line. By night he felt as buffeted and bruised as though he had been given a severe beating.

He never wore a hat. The fierce sun was slowly burning the hair off the top of his head. When he lay on his brass bed in the little hotel at night he felt as though his head were encased in a ball of fire. The sun struck him completely blind. He could not tell the green of the fields from the blue of the sky. But when he returned to his hotel he found that the canvas was somehow a glowing, brilliant transcription of nature.

One day he worked in an orchard of lilac ploughland with a red fence and two rose-coloured peach trees against a sky of glorious blue and white.

"It is probably the best landscape I have ever done," he murmured to himself.

When he reached his hotel he found a letter telling him that Anton Mauve had died in The Hague. Under his peach trees he wrote, "Souvenir de Mauve. Vincent and Theo," and sent it off immediately to the house on the Uileboomen.

The following morning he found an orchard of plum trees

in blossom. While he was at work, a vicious wind sprang up, returning at intervals like waves of the sea. In between, the sun shone, and all the white flowers sparkled on the trees. At the risk every minute of seeing the whole show on the ground, Vincent went on painting. It reminded him of the Scheveningen days when he used to paint in the rain, in sandstorms, and with the storm-spray of the ocean dashing over him and his easel. His canvas had a white effect with a good deal of yellow in it, and blue and lilac. When he finished he saw something in his picture that he had not meant to put there, the mistral.

"People will think I was drunk when I painted this," he laughed to himself.

A line from Theo's letter of the day before came back to him. Mijnheer Tersteeg, on a visit to Paris, had stood before a Sisley and murmured to Theo, "I cannot help thinking that the artist who painted this was a bit tipsy."

"If Tersteeg could see my Arlesian pictures," thought Vincent, "he would say it was delirium tremens in full career."

The people of Arles gave Vincent a wide berth. They saw him dashing out of town before sunrise, heavy easel loaded on his back, hatless, his chin stuck forward eagerly, a feverish excitement in his eyes. They saw him return with two fire holes in his face, the top of his head as red as raw meat, a wet canvas under his arm, gesticulating to himself. The town had a name for him. Everyone called him by it.

"Fou-rou!"

"Perhaps I am a red-headed crazy man," he said to himself, "but what can I do?"

The owner of the hotel swindled Vincent out of every franc he could. Vincent could not get anything to eat, for nearly everyone in Arles ate at home. The restaurants were expensive. Vincent tried them all to find some strong soup, but there was none to be had.

"Is it hard to cook potatoes, Madame?" he asked in one place.

"Impossible, Monsieur."

"Then have you some rice?"

"That is tomorrow's dish."

"What about macaroni?"

"There was no room on the range for macaroni."

At length he had to give up all serious thoughts of food, and live on whatever came his way. The hot sun built up his vitality, even though his stomach was getting little attention. In place of sane food he put absinthe, tobacco, and Daudet's tales of Tartarin. His innumerable hours of concentration before the easel rubbed his nerves raw. He needed stimulants. The absinthe made him all the more excited for the following day, an excitement whipped by the mistral and baked into him by the sun.

As the summer advanced, everything became burnt up. He saw about him nothing but old gold, bronze and copper, covered by a greenish azure sky of blanched heat. There was sulphur-yellow on everything the sunlight hit. His canvases were masses of bright burning yellow. He knew that yellow had not been used in European painting since the Renaissance, but that did not deter him. The yellow pigment oozed out of the tubes on to the canvas, and there it stayed. His pictures were sun steeped, sun burnt, tanned with the burning sun and swept with air.

He was convinced that it was no more easy to make a good picture than it was to find a diamond or a pearl. He was dissatisfied with himself and what he was doing, but he had just a glimmer of hope that it was going to be better in the end. Sometimes even that hope seemed a Fata Morgana. Yet the only time he felt alive was when he was slogging at his work. Of personal life, he had none. He was just a mechanism, a blind painting automaton that had food, liquid, and paint poured into it each morning, and by nightfall turned out a finished canvas.

And for what purpose? For sale? Certainly not! He knew that nobody wanted to buy his pictures. Then what was the hurry? Why did he drive and spur himself to paint dozens and dozens of canvases when the space under his miserable brass bed was already piled nearly solid with paintings?

The desire to succeed had left Vincent. He worked because he had to, because it kept him from suffering too much mentally, because it distracted his mind. He could do without a wife, a home, and children; he could do without love and friendship and health; he could do without security, comfort, and food; he could even do without God. But he could not do without something which was greater than himself, which was his life—the power and ability to create.

He tried to hire models, but the people of Arles would not sit for him. They thought they were being done badly. They were afraid their friends would laugh at the portraits. Vincent knew that if he painted prettily like Bouguereau, people would not be ashamed to let themselves be painted. He had to give up the idea of models, and work always on the soil.

As the summer ripened, a glorious strong heat came on and the wind died. The light in which he worked ranged from pale sulphur-yellow to pale golden-yellow. He thought often of Renoir and that pure clear line of his. That was the way everything looked in the clear air of Provence, just as it looked in the Japanese prints.

Early one morning he saw a girl with a coffee-tinted skin, ash-blond hair, grey eyes, and a print bodice of pale rose under which he could see the breasts, shapely, firm and small. She was a woman as simple as the fields, every line of her virgin. Her mother was an amazing figure in dirty yellow and faded blue, thrown up in strong sunlight against a square of brilliant flowers, snow-white and lemon-yellow. They posed for him for several hours in return for a small sum.

When he returned to his hotel that evening, Vincent found himself thinking of the girl with the coffee-tinted skin. Sleep would not come. He knew that there were houses in Arles, but they were mostly five-franc places patronized by the Zouaves, Negroes brought to Arles to be trained for the French army.

It was months since Vincent had spoken to a woman, except to ask for a cup of coffee or a bag of tobacco. He remembered Margot's loving words, the wandering fingers over his face that she followed with a trail of loving kisses.

He jumped up, hurried across the Place Lamartine and struck into the black maze of stone houses. After a few moments of climbing he heard a great hubbub ahead. He broke into a run and reached the front door of a brothel in the Rue des Ricolettes just as the gendarmes were carting away two Zouaves who had been killed by drunken Italians. The red fezzes of the soldiers were lying in pools of blood on the rough cobblestone street. A squad of gendarmes hustled the Italians to jail, while the infuriated mob stormed after them, shouting,

"Hang them! Hang them!"

Vincent took advantage of the excitement to slip into the Maison de Tolérance, Numero I, in the Rue des Ricolettes.

Louis, the proprietor, welcomed him and led him into a little room on the left of the hall, where a few couples sat drinking.

"I have a young girl by the name of Rachel who is very nice," said Louis. "Would Monsieur care to try her? If you do not like the looks of her, you can choose from all the others."

"May I see her?"

Vincent sat down at a table and lit his pipe. There was laughter from the outside hall, and a girl danced in. She slid into the chair opposite Vincent and smiled at him.

"I'm Rachel," she said.

"Why," exclaimed Vincent, "you're nothing but a baby!"

"I'm sixteen," said Rachel proudly.

"How long have you been here?"

"At Louis's? A year."

"Let me look at you."

The yellow gas lamp was at her back; her face had been in the shadows. She put her head against the wall and tilted her chin up towards the light so that Vincent could see her.

He saw a round, plump face, wide, vacant blue eyes, a fleshy chin and neck. Her black hair was coiled on top of her head, giving the face an even more ball-like appearance. She had on only a light printed dress and a pair of sandals. The nipples of her round breasts pointed straight out at him like accusing fingers.

"You're pretty, Rachel," he said.

A bright, childlike smile came into her empty eyes. She whirled about and took his hand in hers.

"I'm glad you like me," she said. "I like the men to like me. That makes it nicer, don't you think?"

"Yes. Do you like me?"

"I think you're a funny man, *fou-rou*."

"*Fou-rou!* Then you know me?"

"I've seen you in the Place Lamartine. Why are you always rushing places with that big bundle on your back? And why don't you wear a hat? Doesn't the sun burn you? Your eyes are all red. Don't they hurt?"

Vincent laughed at the naïveté of the child.

"You're very sweet, Rachel. Will you call me by my real name if I tell it to you?"

"What is it?"

"Vincent."

"No, I like *fou-rou* better. Do you mind if I call you

336

fou-rou? And can I have something to drink? Old Louis is watching me from the hall."

She ran her fingers across her throat; Vincent watched them sink into the soft flesh. She smiled with her empty blue eyes, and he saw that she was smiling to be happy, so that he might be happy, too. Her teeth were regular but dark; her large underlip drooped down almost to meet the sharp horizontal crevice just above her thick chin.

"Order a bottle of wine," said Vincent, "but not an expensive one, for I haven't much money."

When the wine came, Rachel said, "Would you like to drink it in my room? It's more homey there."

"I would like that very much."

They walked up a flight of stone steps and entered Rachel's cell. There was a narrow cot, a bureau, a chair, and several coloured Julien medallions on the white walls. Two torn and battered dolls sat on top of the bureau.

"I brought these from home with me," she said. "Here, *fou-rou*, take them. This is Jacques and this is Catherine. I used to play house with them. Oh, *fou-rou*, don't you look droll!"

Vincent stood there grinning foolishly with a doll in each arm until Rachel finished laughing. She took Catherine and Jacques from him, tossed them on the bureau, kicked her sandals into a corner and slipped out of her dress.

"Sit down, *fou-rou*," she said, "and we'll play house. You'll be papa and I'll be mama. Do you like to play house?"

She was a short, thickset girl with swelling, convex thighs, a deep declivity under the pointed breasts, and a plump, round belly which rolled down into the pelvic triangle.

"Rachel," said Vincent, "if you are going to call me *fou-rou*, I have a name for you, too."

Rachel clapped her hands and flung herself on to his lap.

"Oh, tell me, what is it? I like to be called new names!"

"I'm going to call you *Le Pigeon.*"

Rachel's blue eyes went hurt and perplexed.

"Why am I a pigeon, papa?"

Vincent ran his hand lightly over her rotund, cupid's belly.

"Because you look like a pigeon, with your gentle eyes and fat little tummy."

"Is it nice to be a pigeon?"

"Oh, yes. Pigeons are very pretty and lovable ... and so are you."

337

Rachel leaned over, kissed him on the ear, sprang up from the cot and brought two water tumblers for their wine.

"What funny little ears you have, *fou-rou*," she said, between sips of the red wine. She drank it as a baby drinks, with her nose in the glass.

"Do you like them?" asked Vincent.

"Yes. They're so soft and round, just like a puppy's."

"Then you can have them."

Rachel laughed loudly. She raised her glass to her lips. The joke struck her as funny again and she giggled. A trickle of red wine spilled down her left breast, wound its way over the pigeon belly and disappeared in the black triangle.

"You're nice, *fou-rou*," she said. "Everyone speaks as though you were crazy. But you're not, are you?"

Vincent grimaced.

"Only a little," he said.

"And will you be my sweetheart?" Rachel demanded. "I haven't had one for over a month. Will you come to see me every night?"

"I'm afraid I can't come every night, Pigeon."

Rachel pouted. "Why not?"

"Well, among other things, I haven't the money."

Rachel tweaked his right ear, playfully.

"If you haven't five francs. *fou-rou*, will you cut off your ear and give it to me? I'd like to have it. I'd put it on my bureau and play with it every night."

"Will you let me redeem it if I get the five francs later?"

"Oh, *fou-rou*, you're so funny and nice. I wish more of the men who came here were like you."

"Don't you enjoy it here?"

"Oh, yes, I have a very nice time, and I like it all ... except the Zouaves, that is."

Rachel put down her wine glass and threw her arms prettily about Vincent's neck. He felt her soft paunch against his waistcoat, and the points of her bud-like breasts burning into him. She buried her mouth on his. He found himself kissing the soft, velvety inner lining of her lower lip.

"You will come back to see me again, *fou-rou*? You won't forget me and go to see some other girl?"

"I'll come back, Pigeon."

"And shall we do it now? Shall we play house?"

When he left the place a half hour later, he was consumed

338

by a thirst which could be quenched only by innumerable glasses of clear cold water.

4

Vincent came to the conclusion that the more finely a colour was pounded, the more it became saturated with oil. Oil was only the carrying medium for colour; he did not care much for it, particularly since he did not object to his canvases having a rough look. Instead of buying colour that had been pounded on the stone for God knows how many hours in Paris, he decided to become his own colour man. Theo asked Pére Tanguy to send Vincent the three chromes, the malachite, the vermilion, the orange lead, the cobalt, and the ultramarine. Vincent crushed them in his little hotel room. After that his colours not only cost less, but they were fresher and more lasting.

He next became dissatisfied with the absorbent canvas on which he painted. The thin coat of plaster with which they were covered did not suck up his rich colours. Theo sent him rolls of unprepared canvas; at night he mixed the plaster in a little bowl and spread it over the canvas he planned to paint the following day.

Georges Seurat had made him sensitive to the sort of frame his work was to rest in. When he sent his first Arlesian canvases to Theo, he explained just what sort of wood had to be used, and what colour it had to be painted. But he could not be happy until he saw his paintings in frames that he made himself. He bought plain strips of wood from his grocer, cut them down to the size he wanted, and then painted them to match the composition of the picture.

He made his colours, built his stretchers, plastered his canvas, painted his pictures, carpentered his frames, and painted them.

"Too bad I can't buy my own pictures," he murmured aloud. "Then I'd be completely self-sufficient."

The mistral came up again. All nature seemed in a rage. The skies were cloudless. The brilliant sunshine was accompanied by intense dryness and piercing cold. Vincent did a still life in his room; a coffee pot in blue enamel, a cup of royal blue and gold, a milk jug in squares of pale blue and white, a jug in majolica, blue with a pattern in reds, greens and browns, and lastly, two oranges and three lemons.

When the wind died down he went out again and did a view on the Rhône, the iron bridge at Trinquetaille, in which the sky and river were the colour of absinthe, the quays a shade of lilac, the figures leaning on their elbows on the parapet blackish, the iron bridge an intense blue with a note of vivid orange in the black background and a touch of intense malachite green. He was trying to get at something utterly heartbroken and therefore utterly heartbreaking.

Instead of trying to reproduce exactly what he had before his eyes, he used colour arbitrarily to express himself with greater force. He realized that what Pissarro had told him in Paris was true. "You must boldly exaggerate the effects, either in harmony or discord, which colours produce." In Maupassant's preface to "Pierre et Jean" he found a similar sentiment. "The artist has the liberty to exaggerate, to create in his novel a world more beautiful, more simple, more consoling than ours."

He did a day's hard, close work among the cornfields in full sun. The result was a ploughed field, a big field with clods of violet earth, climbing toward the horizon; a sower in blue and white; on the horizon a field of short, ripe corn; over all a yellow sky with a yellow sun.

Vincent knew that the Parisian critics would think he worked too fast. He did not agree. Was it not emotion, the sincerity of his feeling for nature, that impelled him? And if the emotions were sometimes so strong that he worked without knowing he worked, if sometimes the strokes came with a sequence and coherence like words in a speech, then too the time would come when there would again be heavy days, empty of inspiration. He had to strike while the iron was hot, put the forged bars on one side.

He strapped his easel to his back and took the road home which led past Montmajour. He walked so rapidly that he soon overtook a man and a boy who were dallying ahead of him. He recognized the man as old Roulin the Arlesian *facteur des postes*. He had often sat near Roulin in the café, and had wanted to speak to him, but the occasion had never arisen.

"Good day, monsieur Roulin," he said.

"Ah, it is you, the painter," said Roulin. "Good day. I have been taking my boy for a Sunday afternoon stroll."

"It has been a glorious day, hasn't it?"

"Ah, yes, it is lovely when that devil mistral does not blow. You have painted a picture today, Monsieur?"

"Yes."

"I am an ignorant man, Monsieur, and know nothing about art. But I would be honoured if you would let me look."

"With pleasure."

The boy ran ahead, playing. Vincent and Roulin walked side by side. While Roulin looked at the canvas, Vincent studied him. Roulin was wearing his blue postman's cap. He had soft, inquiring eyes and a long, square, wavy beard which completely covered his neck and collar and came to rest on the dark blue postman's coat. Vincent felt the same soft, wistful quality about Roulin that had attracted him to Père Tanguy. He was homely in a pathetic sort of way, and his plain, peasant's face seemed out of place in the luxuriant Greek beard.

"I am an ignorant man, Monsieur," repeated Roulin, "and you will forgive me for speaking. But your cornfields are so very alive, as alive as the field we passed back there, for instance, where I saw you at work."

"Then you like it?"

"As for that, I cannot say. I only know that it makes me feel something, in here."

He ran his hand upward over his chest.

They paused for a moment at the base of Montmajour. The sun was setting red over the ancient abbey, its rays falling on the trunks and foliage of pines growing among a tumble of rocks, colouring the trunks and foliage with orange fire, while the other pines in the distance stood out in Prussian blue against a sky of tender, blue-green cerulean. The white sand and the layers of white rocks under the trees took on tints of blue.

"That is alive, too, is it not, Monsieur?" asked Roulin.

"It will still be alive when we are gone, Roulin."

They walked along, chatting in a quiet, friendly manner. There was nothing of the abrasive quality in Roulin's words. His mind was simple, his thoughts at once simple and profound. He supported himself, his wife, and four children on a hundred and thirty-five francs a month. He had been a postman twenty-five years without a promotion, and with only infinitesimal advances in salary.

"When I was young, Monsieur," he said, "I used to think a lot about God. But He seems to have grown thinner with the years. He is still in that cornfield you painted, and in the

341

sunset by Montmajour, but when I think about men ... and the world they have made ..."

"I know, Roulin, but I feel more and more that we must not judge God by this world. It's just a study that didn't come off. What can you do in a study that has gone wrong, if you are fond of the artist? You do not find much to criticize; you hold your tongue. But you have a right to ask for something better."

"Yes, that's it," exclaimed Roulin, "something just a tiny bit better."

"We should have to see some other work by the same hand before we judge him. This world was evidently botched up in a hurry on one of his bad days, when the artist did not have his wits about him."

Dusk had fallen over the winding country road. The first chips of stars poked through the heavy cobalt blanket of night. Roulin's sweet innocent eyes searched Vincent's face. "Then you think there are other worlds besides this, Monsieur?"

"I don't know, Roulin. I gave up thinking about that sort of thing when I became interested in my work. But this life seems so incomplete, doesn't it? Sometimes I think that just as trains and carriages are means of locomotion to get us from one place to another on this earth, so typhoid and consumption are means of locomotion to get us from one world to another."

"Ah, you think of things, you artists."

"Roulin, will you do me a favour? Let me paint your portrait. The people of Arles won't pose for me."

"I should be honoured, Monsieur. But why do you want to paint me. I am not an ugly man."

"If there were a God, Roulin, I think he would have a beard and eyes just like yours."

"You are making fun of me, Monsieur!"

"On the contrary, I am in earnest."

"Will you come and share supper with us tomorrow night? We have a very plain board, but we will be happy to have you."

Madame Roulin proved to be a peasant woman who reminded him a little of Madame Denis. There was a red and white checked cloth on the table, a little stew with potatoes, home-baked bread and a bottle of sour wine. After dinner Vincent sketched Madame Roulin, chatting with the postman as he worked.

342

"During the Revolution I was a republican," said Roulin, "but now I see that we have gained nothing. Whether our rulers be kings or ministers, we poor people have just as little as before. I thought when we were a republic everyone would share and share alike."

"Ah, no, Roulin."

"All my life I have tried to understand, Monsieur, why one man should have more than the next, why one man should work hard while his neighbour sits by in idleness. Perhaps I am too ignorant to understand. Do you think if I were educated, Monsieur, I would be able to understand that better?"

Vincent glanced up quickly to see if Roulin were being cynical. There was the same look of naïve innocence on his face.

"Yes, my friend," he said, "most educated people seem to understand that state of affairs very well. But I am ignorant like you, and I shall never be able to understand or accept it."

5

He rose at four in the morning, walked three and four hours to reach the spot he wanted, and then painted until dark. It was not pleasant, this trudging ten or twelve kilometres home on a lonely road, but he liked the reassuring touch of the wet canvas under his arm.

He did seven large pictures in seven days. By the end of the week he was nearly dead with work. It had been a glorious summer, but now he was painted out. A violent mistral arose and raised clouds of dust which whitened the trees. Vincent was forced to remain quiet. He slept for sixteen hours at a stretch.

He had a very thin time of it, for his money ran out on Thursday, and Theo's letter with the fifty francs was not expected until Monday noon. It was not Theo's fault. He still sent fifty francs every ten days in addition to all the painting supplies. Vincent had been wild to see his new pictures in frames, and had ordered too many of them for his budget. During those four days he lived on twenty-three cups of coffee and a loaf of bread for which the baker trusted him.

An intense reaction set in against his work. He did not think his pictures worthy of the goodness he had had from Theo. He wanted to win back the money he had already spent in order to return it to his brother. He looked at his paintings one by one and reproached himself that they were not worth what they had cost. Even if a tolerable study did come out of it from time to time, he knew that it would have been cheaper to buy it from somebody else.

All during the summer ideas for his work had come to him in swarms. Although he had been solitary, he had not had time to think or feel. He had gone on like a steam-engine. But now his brain felt like stale porridge, and he did not even have a franc to amuse himself by eating or going to visit Rachel. He decided that everything he had painted that summer was very, very bad.

"Anyway," he said to himself, "a canvas that I have covered is worth more than a blank canvas. My pretensions go no further; that is my right to paint, my reason for painting."

He had the conviction that simply by staying in Arles he would set his individuality free. Life was short. It went fast. Well, being a painter, he still had to paint.

"These painter's fingers of mine grow supple," he thought, "even though the carcass is going to pieces."

He drew up a long list of colours to send to Theo. Suddenly he realized that not one colour on his list would be found on the Dutch palette, in Mauve, Maris, or Weissenbruch. Arles had made his break with the Dutch tradition complete.

When his money arrived on Monday, he found a place where he could get a good meal for a franc. It was a queer restaurant, altogether grey; the floor was of grey bitumen like a street pavement, there was grey paper on the walls, green blinds always drawn, and a big green curtain over the door to keep the dust out. A very narrow, very fierce ray of sunlight stabbed through a blind.

After he had been resting for over a week, he decided to do some night painting. He did the grey restaurant while the patrons were at their meal and the waitresses were scurrying back and forth. He painted the thick, warm cobalt sky of night, studded with thousands of bright Provençal stars, as seen from the Place Lamartine. He went out on the roads and did cypresses under the moonlight. He painted the Café de Nuit, which remained open all night so that prowlers could take refuge there when they had no money to pay for a lodging, or when they were too drunk to be taken to one.

He did the exterior of the café one night, and the interior the next. He tried to express the terrible passions of humanity by means of red and green. He did the interior in blood red and dark yellow with a green billiard table in the middle. He put in four lemon-yellow lamps with a glow of orange and green. Everywhere there was the clash and contrast of the most alien red and greens in the figures of little sleeping hooligans. He was trying to express the idea that the café was a place where one could ruin oneself, run mad, or commit a crime.

The people of Arles were amused to find their *fou-rou* painting in the streets all night and sleeping in the daytime. Vincent's activities were always a treat for them.

When the first of the month came, the hotel owner not only raised the rent on the room, but decided to charge Vincent a daily storage fee for the closet in which he kept his canvases. Vincent loathed the hotel and was outraged by the voraciousness of the owner. The grey restaurant in which he ate was satisfactory, but he had sufficient money to eat there only two or three days out of every ten. Winter was coming, he had no studio in which to work, the hotel room was depressing and humiliating. The food he was forced to eat in the cheap restaurants was poisoning his stomach again.

He had to find a permanent home and studio of his own.

One evening, as he was crossing the Place Lamartine with old Roulin, he noticed a *For Rent* sign on a yellow house just a stone's throw from his hotel. The house had two wings with a court in the centre. It faced the Place and the town on the hill. Vincent stood looking at it wistfully.

"Too bad it's so large," he said to Roulin. "I'd like to have a house like that."

"It is not necessary to rent the whole house, Monsieur. You can rent just the right wing, for example."

"Really! How many rooms do you think it has? Would it be expensive?"

"I should say it had about three or four rooms. It will cost you very little, not half what the hotel costs. I will come and look at it with you tomorrow during my dinner time, if you like. Perhaps I can help you get a good price."

The following morning Vincent was so excited he could do nothing but pace up and down the Place Lamartine and survey the yellow house from all sides. It was built sturdily and got all the sun. On closer inspection Vincent found that there were two separate entrances to the house, and that the left wing was already occupied.

Roulin joined him after the midday meal. They entered the

345

right wing of the house together. There was a hallway inside which led to a large room, with a smaller room opening off it. The walls were whitewashed. The hall and stairway leading up to the second floor were paved with clean red brick. Upstairs there was another large room with a cabinet. The floors were of scrubbed red tile, and the whitewashed walls caught the clean, bright sun.

Roulin had written a note to the landlord, who was waiting for them in the upstairs room. He and Roulin conversed for some moments in a fast Provençal of which Vincent could understand very little. The postman turned to Vincent.

"He insists upon knowing how long you will keep the place."

"Tell him indefinitely."

"Will you agree to take it for at least six months?"

"Oh, yes! Yes!"

"Then he says he will give it to you for fifteen francs a month."

Fifteen francs! For a whole house! Only a third of what he paid at the hotel. Even less than he had paid for his studio in The Hague. A permanent home for fifteen francs a month. He drew the money out of his pocket, hurriedly.

"Here! Quick! Give it to him. The house is rented."

"He wants to know when you are going to move in," said Roulin.

"Today. Right now."

"But, Monsieur, you have no furniture. How can you move in?"

"I will buy a mattress and a chair. Roulin, you don't know what it means to spend your life in miserable hotel rooms. I must have this place immediately!"

"Just as you wish, Monsieur."

The landlord left. Roulin went back to work. Vincent walked from one room to another, up and down the stairs again, surveying over and over every inch of his domain. Theo's fifty francs had arrived just the day before; he still had some thirty francs in his pocket. He rushed out, bought a cheap mattress and a chair and carried them back to the yellow house. He decided that the room on the ground floor would be his bedroom, the top room his studio. He threw the mattress on the red tile floor, carried the chair up to his studio, and went back to his hotel for the last time.

The proprietor added forty francs to Vincent's bill on some

346

thin pretext. He refused to let Vincent have his canvases until the money was handed over. Vincent had to go to the police court to get his paintings back, and even then had to pay half the fictitious charge.

Late that afternoon he found a merchant who was willing to give him a small gas stove, two pots, and a kerosene lamp on credit. Vincent had three francs left. He bought coffee, bread, potatoes and a little meat for soup. He left himself without a centime. At home he set up a kitchen in the cabinet on the ground floor.

When night closed over the Place Lamartine and the yellow house, Vincent cooked his soup and coffee on the little stove. He had no table, so he spread a paper over the mattress, put out his supper, and ate it sitting cross-legged on the floor. He had forgotten to buy a knife and fork. He used the handle of his brush to pick the pieces of meat and potato out of the pot. They tasted slightly of paint.

When he finished eating, he took the kerosene lamp and mounted the red brick stairs to the second floor. The room was barren and lonely, with only the stark easel standing against the moonlit window. In the background was the dark garden of the Place Lamartine.

He went to sleep on the mattress. When he awakened in the morning he opened the windows and saw the green of the garden, the rising sun, and the road winding up into the town. He looked at the clean red bricks of the floor, the spotlessly whitewashed walls, the spaciousness of the rooms. He boiled himself a cup of coffee and walked about drinking from the pot, planning how he would furnish his house, what pictures he would hang on the walls, how he would pass the happy hours in a real home of his own.

The next day he received a letter from his friend Paul Gauguin, who was imprisoned, ill and poverty stricken, in a wretched café in Pont-Aven, in Brittany. "I can't get out of this hole," wrote Gauguin, "because I can't pay my bill, and the owner has all my canvases under lock and key. In all the variety of distresses that humanity, nothing maddens me more than the lack of money. Yet I feel myself doomed to perpetual beggary."

Vincent thought of the painters of the earth, harassed, ill, destitute, shunned and mocked by their fellow men, starved and tortured to their dying day. Why? What was their crime? What was their great offence that made them outcasts and pariahs? How could such persecuted souls do good work? The painter of the future—ah, he would be such a colourist and a man as had never yet existed. He would not live in miserable cafés, and go to the Zouave brothels.

And poor Gauguin. Rotting away in some filthy hole in Brittany, too sick to work, without a friend to help him or a franc in his pocket for wholesome food and a doctor. Vincent thought him a great painter and a great man. If Gauguin should die. If Gauguin should have to give up his work. What a tragedy for the painting world.

Vincent slipped the letter into his pocket, left the yellow house, and walked along the embankment of the Rhone. A barge loaded with coal was moored to the quay. Seen from above, it was all shining and wet from a shower. The water was of yellowish white, and clouded pearl grey. The sky was lilac, barred with orange to the west, the town violet. On the boat some labourers in dirty blue and white came and went, carrying the cargo on shore.

It was pure Hokusai. It carried Vincent back to Paris, to the Japanese prints in Père Tanguy's shop . . . and to Paul Gauguin who, of all his friends, he loved the most dearly.

He knew at once what he had to do. The yellow house was large enough for two men. Each of them could have his own bedroom and studio. If they cooked their meals, ground their colours, and guarded their money, they could live on his hundred and fifty francs a month. The rent would be no more, the food very little. How marvellous it would be to have a friend again, a painter friend who talked one's language and understood one's craft. And what wonderful things Gauguin could teach him about painting.

He had not realized before how utterly lonely he had been. Even if they couldn't live on Vincent's hundred and fifty francs, perhaps Theo would send an extra fifty in return for a monthly canvas from Gauguin.

Yes! Yes! He must have Gauguin with him here in Arles. The hot Provence sun would burn all the illness out of him, just as it had out of Vincent. Soon they would have a working studio going full blaze. Theirs would be the very first studio in the South. They would carry on the tradition of Delacroix and Monticelli. They would drench painting in sunlight and colour, awaken the world to riotous nature

Gauguin had to be saved!

Vincent turned, broke into a dog-trot and ran all the way back to the Place Lamartine. He let himself into the yellow house, dashed up the red brick stairs, and began excitedly planning the rooms.

"Paul and I will each have a bedroom up here. We'll use the rooms on the lower floor for studios. I'll buy beds and mattresses and bedclothes and chairs and tables, and we'll have a real home. I'll decorate the whole house with sunflowers and orchards in blossom.

"Oh, Paul, Paul, how good it will be to have you with me again!"

6

It was not so easy as he had expected. Theo was willing to add fifty francs a month to the allowance in return for a Gauguin canvas, but there was the matter of the railroad fare which neither Theo nor Gauguin could provide. Gauguin was too ill to move, too much in debt to get out of Pont-Aven, too sick at heart to enter into any schemes with enthusiasm. Letters flew thick and fast between Arles, Paris, and Pont-Aven.

Vincent was now desperately in love with his yellow house. He bought himself a table and a chest of drawers with Theo's allowance.

"At the end of the year," he wrote to Theo, "I shall be a different man. But don't think I'm going to leave here then. By no means. I'm going to spend the rest of my life in Arles. I'm going to become the painter of the South. And you must consider that you have a country house in Arles. I am keen to arrange it all so that you will come here always to spend your holidays."

He spent a minimum for the bare necessities of life, and sunk all the rest into the house. Each day he had to make a choice between himself and the yellow house. Should he have meat for dinner, or buy that majolica jug? Should he buy a new pair of shoes, or get that green quilt for Gauguin's bed? Should he order a pine frame for his new canvas, or buy those rush-bottom chairs?

Always the house came first.

The yellow house gave him a sense of tranquillity, because he was working to secure the future. He had drifted too much, knocked about without rhyme or reason. But now he was never going to move again. After he was gone, another painter would find a going concern. He was establishing a permanent studio which would be used by generation after generation of painters to interpret and portray the South. He became obsessed with the idea of painting such decorations for the house as would be worthy of the money spent on him during the years in which he had been unproductive.

He plunged into his work with renewed energy. He knew that looking at a thing a long time ripened him and gave him a deeper understanding. He went back fifty times to Montmajour to study the field at its base. The mistral made it hard for him to get his brush work connected and interwoven with feeling, with the easel waving violently before him in the wind. He worked from seven in the morning until six at night without stirring. A canvas a day!

"Tomorrow will be a scorcher," said Roulin one evening, very late in the fall. They were sitting over a bock in the Café Lamartine. "And after that, winter."

"What is winter like in Arles?" asked Vincent.

"It's mean. Lots of rain, a miserable wind, and a biting cold. But winter is very short here. Only a couple of months."

"So tomorrow will be our last nice day. Then I know the very spot I want to do. Imagine an autumn garden, Roulin, with two cypresses, bottle green, shaped like bottles, and three little chestnut trees with tobacco and orange coloured leaves. There is a little yew with pale lemon foliage and a violet trunk, and two little bushes, blood-red, and scarlet purple leaves. And some sand, some grass, and some blue sky."

"Ah, Monsieur, when you describe things, I see that all my life I have been blind."

The next morning Vincent arose with the sun. He was in high spirits. He trimmed his beard with a pair of scissors, combed down what little hair the Arlesian sun had not burned off his scalp, put on his only whole suit of clothes, and as a special fond gesture of farewell to the sun, wore his rabbit-fur bonnet from Paris.

Roulin's prediction had been right. The sun rose, a yellow ball of heat. The rabbit-fur bonnet had no peak, and the sun pried into his eyes. The autumn garden was a two hour walk from Arles, on the road to Tarascon. It nestled askew on the side of a hill. Vincent planted his easel in a furrowed cornfield, behind and to the side of the garden. He threw his bonnet to the ground, took off his good coat, and set the canvas to the easel. Although it was still early morning, the sun scorched the top of his head and threw before his eyes the veil of dancing fire to which he had become accustomed.

He studied the scene before him carefully, analysed the component colours, and etched the design on his mind. When he was confident that he understood the scene, he softened his brushes, took the caps off his tubes of pigments, and cleaned the knife with which he spread on his thick colour. He glanced once more at the garden, burnt the image on the blank canvas before him, mixed some colour on the palette, and raised his brush.

"Must you begin so soon, Vincent?" asked a voice behind him.

Vincent whirled about.

"It is early yet, my dear. And you have the whole long day to work."

Vincent gaped at the woman in utter bewilderment. She was young, but not a child. Her eyes were as blue as the cobalt sky of an Arlesian night, and her hair, which she wore in a great flowing mass down her back, was as lemon-yellow as the sun. Her features were even more delicate than those of Kay Vos, but they had about them the mellow maturity of the South-land. Her colouring was burnt gold, her teeth, between the smiling lips, as white as an oleander seen through a blood-red vine. She wore a long white gown which clung to the lines of her body and was fastened only by a square silver buckle at the side. She had a simple pair of sandals on her feet. Her figure was sturdy, robust, yet flowing downward with the eye in pure, voluptuous curves.

"I've stayed away so very long, Vincent," she said.

She placed herself between Vincent and the easel, leaning against the blank canvas and shutting out his view of the garden. The sun caught up the lemon-yellow hair and sent waves of flame down her back. She smiled at him so whole-heartedly, so fondly, that he ran a hand over his eyes to see if he had suddenly gone ill, or fallen asleep.

"You do not understand, my dear, dear boy," the woman said. "How could you, when I've stayed away so long?"

"Who are you?"

"I am your friend, Vincent. The best friend you have in the world."

"How do you know my name? I have never seen you before."

"Ah, no, but I have seen you, many, many times."

"What is your name?"

"Maya."

"Is that all? Just Maya?"

"For you, Vincent, that is all."

"Why have you followed me here to the fields?"

"For the same reason that I have followed you all over Europe . . . so that I might be near you."

"You mistake me for someone else. I can't possibly be the man you mean."

The woman put a cool white hand on the burnt red hair of his head and smoothed it back lightly. The coolness of her hand and the coolness of her soft, low voice was like the refreshing water from a deep green well.

"There is only one Vincent Van Gogh. I could never mistake him."

"How long do you think you have known me?"

"Eight years, Vincent."

"Why, eight years ago I was in . . ."

". . . Yes, dear, in the Borinage."

"You knew me then?"

"I saw you for the first time one late fall afternoon, when you were sitting on a rusty iron wheel in front of Marcasse . . ."

". . . Watching the miners go home!"

"Yes. When I first looked at you, you were sitting there, idly. I was about to pass by. Then you took an old envelope and a pencil from your pocket and began sketching. I looked over your shoulder to see what you had done. And when I saw . . . I fell in love."

"You fell in love? You fell in love with me?"

"Yes, Vincent, my dear, good Vincent, in love with you."

"Perhaps I was not so bad to look at then."

"Not half so good as you are to look at now."

"Your voice . . . Maya . . . it sounds so queer. Only once before has a woman spoken to me in that voice . . ."

". . . Margot's voice. She loved you, Vincent, as well as I do."

"You knew Margot?"

"I stayed in the Brabant for two years. I followed you to the fields each day. I watched you work in the wrangle room behind the kitchen. And I was happy because Margot loved you."

"Then you did not love me any more?"

She caressed his eyes with the cool tips of her fingers.

"Ah, yes. I loved you. I have never ceased to love you since that very first day."

"And you weren't jealous of Margot?"

The woman smiled. Across her face went a flash of infinite sadness and compassion. Vincent thought of Mendes da Costa.

"No, I was not jealous of Margot. Her love was good for you. But your love for Kay I did not like. It injured you."

"Did you know me when I was in love with Ursula?"

"That was before my time."

"You would not have liked me then."

"No."

"I was a fool."

"Sometimes one has to be a fool in the beginning, to become wise in the end."

"But if you loved me when we were in the Brabant, why didn't you come to me?"

"You were not ready for me, Vincent."

"And now ... I am ready?"

"Yes."

"You still love me? Even now ... today ... this moment?"

"Now ... today ... this moment ... and for eternity."

"How can you love me? Look, my gums are diseased. Every tooth in my mouth is false. All the hair has been burnt off my head. My eyes are as red as a syphilitic's. My face is nothing but jagged bone. I am ugly. The ugliest of men! My nerves are shattered, my body gone sterile, my insides poisoned from tip to toe. How can you love such a wreck of a man?"

"Will you sit down, Vincent?"

Vincent sat on his stool. The woman sank to her knees in the soft loam of the field.

"Don't," cried Vincent. "You'll get your white gown all dirty. Let me put my coat under you."

The woman restrained him with the faintest touch of her hand. "Many times I have soiled my gown in following you, Vincent, but always it has come clean again."

She cupped his chin in the palm of her strong white hand, and with her fingertips smoothed back the few charred hairs behind his ear.

"You are not ugly, Vincent. You are beautiful. You have tormented and tortured this poor body in which your soul is wrapped, but you cannot injure your soul. It is that I love.

353

And when you have destroyed yourself by your passionate labours, that soul will go on ... endlessly. And with it, my love for you."

The sun had risen another hour in the sky. It beat down in fierce heat upon Vincent and the woman.

"Let me take you where it is cool," said Vincent. "There are some cypress trees just below on the road. You will be more comfortable in the shade."

"I am happy here with you. I do not mind the sun. I have grown used to it."

"You have been in Arles long?"

"I came with you from Paris."

Vincent jumped up in anger and kicked over his stool.

"You are a fraud! You've been sent here on purpose to ridicule me. Someone told you of my past, and is paying you to make a fool of me. Go away. I'll not talk to you any more!"

The woman held his anger with the smile of her eyes.

"I am no fraud, my dear. I am the most real thing in your life. You can never kill my love for you."

"That's a lie! You don't love me. You're mocking me. I'll show your game up."

He seized her roughly in his arms. She swayed inward to him.

"I'm going to hurt you if you don't go away and stop torturing me!"

"Hurt me, Vincent. You've hurt me before. It's part of love to be hurt."

"Very well then, take your medicine!"

He pressed her body to him. He brought his mouth down on hers, hurting her with his teeth, crushing his kiss upon her.

She opened soft, warm lips to him and let him drink deeply of the sweetness of her mouth. Her whole body yearned upward to him, muscle to muscle, bone to bone, flesh to flesh, in complete and final surrender.

Vincent thrust her away from him and stumbled to his stool. The woman sank down on the ground beside him, put one arm on his leg, and rested her head against it. He stroked the long, rich mass of lemon-yellow hair.

"Are you convinced now?" she asked.

After many moments Vincent said. "You have been in Arles since I came. Did you know about *Le Pigeon*?"

"Rachel is a sweet child."

354

"And you don't object?"

"You are a man, Vincent, and need women. Since it was not yet time to come to you and give myself, you had to go where you could. But now ..."

"Now?"

"You need to no longer. Ever again."

"You mean that you ...?"

"Of course, Vincent dear. I love you."

"Why should you love me? Women have always despised me."

"You were not meant for love. You had other work to do."

"Work? Bah! I've been a fool. Of what good are all these hundreds of paintings? Who wants to own them? Who will buy them? Who will give me one grudging word of praise, say that I have understood nature or portrayed its beauty?"

"The whole world will say it one day, Vincent."

"One day. What a dream. Like the dream of thinking that I will one day be a healthy man, with a home and a family and enough money from my painting to live on. I have been painting for eight long years. Not once in all that time has anyone wanted to buy a picture I've painted. I've been a fool."

"I know, but what a glorious fool. After you are gone, Vincent, the world will understand what you have tried to say. The canvases that today you cannot sell for a hundred francs will one day sell for a million. Ah, you smile, but I tell you it is true. Your pictures will hang in the museums of Amsterdam and The Hague, in Paris and Dresden, Munich and Berlin, Moscow and New York, Your pictures will be priceless, because there will be none for sale. Books will be written about your art, Vincent, novels and plays built around your life. Wherever two men come together who love painting, there the name of Vincent Van Gogh will be sacred."

"If I could not still taste your mouth on mine, I would say I was dreaming or going mad."

"Come sit beside me, Vincent. Put your hand in mine."

The sun was directly overhead. The hillside and valley were bathed in a mist of sulphur-yellow. Vincent lay in the furrow of the field beside the woman. For six long months he had had no one to talk to but Rachel and Roulin. Within him there was a great flood of words. The woman looked deep into his eyes, and he began to speak. He told her of Ursula and the days when he had been a Goupil clerk. He told her of his struggles and disappointments, of his love for Kay, and the life he had

355

tried to build with Christine. He told her of his hopes in painting, of the names he had been called, and the blows he had received, of why he wanted his drawing to be crude, his work unfinished, his colour explosive; of all the things he wanted to accomplish for painting and painters, and how his body was wracked with exhaustion and disease.

The longer he talked, the more excited he became. Words flew out of his mouth like pigments from his tubes. His whole body sprang into action. He talked with his hands, gesticulated with his arms and shoulders, walked up and down before her with violent body contortions. His pulse was rising, his blood was rising, the burning sun sent him into a passion of feverish energy.

The woman listened quietly, never missing a word. From her eyes, he knew she understood. She drank in all he had to say, and still was there, eager and ready to hear more, to understand him, to be the recipient of everything he had to give and could not contain within himself.

He stopped abruptly. He trembled all over with excitement. His eyes and face were red, his limbs quivering. The woman pulled him down beside her.

"Kiss me, Vincent." she said.

He kissed her on the mouth. Her lips were no longer cool. They lay side by side in the rich, crumbly loam. The woman kissed his eyes, his ears, the nostrils of his nose, the declivity of his upper lip, bathed the inside of his mouth with her sweet, soft tongue, ran her fingers down the beard of his neck, down his shoulders and along the sensitive nerve-ends of his arm pit.

Her kisses aroused in him the most excruciating passion he had ever known. Every inch of him ached with the dull ache of the flesh that cannot be satisfied by flesh alone. Never before had a woman given herself to him with the kiss of love. He strained her body to him, feeling, beneath the soft white gown, the heat of her life flow.

"Wait," she said.

She unbuckled the silver clasp at her side and tossed the white gown away from her. Her body was the same burnished gold as her face. It was virgin, every beating pulse of it virgin. He had not known that the body of a woman could be so exquisitely wrought. He had not known that passion could be so pure, so fine, so searing.

"You're trembling, dear," she said. "Hold me to you. Do

356

not tremble, my dear; my sweet, sweet dear. Hold me as you want me."

The sun was slipping down the other side of the heavens. The earth was hot from the beating rays of the day. It smelled of things that had been planted, of things that had grown, been cut away and died again. It smelled of life, rich pungent smells of life ever being created and ever returning to the stuff of its creation.

Vincent's emotion rose higher and higher. Every fibre of him beat inward to some focal core of pain. The woman opened her arms to him, opened her warmth to him, took from him what was the man of him, took into herself all the volcanic turbulence, all the overwhelming passion that hour by hour wracked his nerves and burst his body, led him with gentle caressing undulations to the shattering, creative climax.

Exhausted, he fell asleep in her arms.

When he awoke, he was alone. The sun had gone down. There was a solid cake of mud on one cheek, where he had buried his perspiring face in the loam. The earth was coolish and smelled of buried, crawling things. He put on his coat and rabbit-fur bonnet, strapped the easel to his back, and took the canvas under his arm. He walked the dark road home.

When he reached the yellow house, he threw the easel and blank canvas on the mattress in his bedroom. He went out for a cup of coffee. He leaned his head in his hands on the cold stone-topped table and thought back over the day.

"Maya," he murmured to himself. "Maya. Haven't I heard that name somewhere before? It means ... it means ... I wonder what it means?"

He took a second cup of coffee. After an hour he crossed the Place Lamartine to the yellow house. A cold wind had come up. There was the smell of rain in the air.

He had not bothered to light the kerosene lamp when he had dropped his easel. Now he lit a match and set the lamp on the table. The yellow flame illumined the room. His eye was caught by a patch of colour on the mattress. Startled, he walked over and picked up the canvas that he had taken with him that morning.

There, in a magnificent blaze of light, he saw his autumn garden; the two bottle green, bottle shaped cypresses; the three little chestnut trees with tobacco and orange coloured leaves; the yew with pale lemon foliage and a violet trunk; the two blood-red bushes with scarlet purple leaves; in the foreground some sand and grass, and over all a blue, blue sky with a whorling ball of sulphur-lemon fire.

He stood gazing at the picture for several moments. He tacked it lightly on the wall. He went back to the mattress, sat on it cross-legged, looked at his painting and grinned.

"It is good," he said aloud. "It is well realized."

7

Winter came on. Vincent spent the days in his warm pleasant studio. Theo wrote that Gauguin, who had been in Paris for a day, was in vile frame of mind, and was resisting the Arlesian idea with all his strength. In Vincent's mind the yellow house was not to be simply a home for two men, but a permanent studio for all the artists of the South. He made elaborate plans for enlarging his quarters as soon as he and Gauguin put the place into working order. Any painter who wished to stay there would be welcome; in return for his hospitality he would be obliged to send Theo one canvas a month. As soon as Theo had enough Impressionist pictures on hand, he was to leave Goupils and open an Independent Gallery in Paris.

Vincent made it very clear in his letters that Gauguin was to be the director of the studio, master of all the painters who worked there. Vincent saved every franc he could in order to furnish his bedroom. He painted the walls a pale violet. The floor was of red tile. He bought very light, greenish lemon sheets and pillows, a scarlet covering, and painted the wooden bed and chairs the colour of fresh butter. The toilet table he painted orange, the basin blue, the door lilac. He hung a number of his pictures on the wall, threw away the window shutters, and then transferred the whole scene to canvas for Theo, so that his brother might see how restful his room was. He painted it in free flat washes, like the Japanese prints.

With Gauguin's room it was another matter. He was not willing to buy such cheap furniture for the master of the studio. Madame Roulin assured him that the walnut bed he wanted for Gauguin would come to three hundred and fifty francs, an impossible sum for him to muster. Nevertheless he began buying the smaller articles for the room, keeping himself in a constant state of financial exhaustion.

When he had no money for models, he stood before a mirror and did his own portrait over and over. Rachel came to pose for him; Madame Roulin came one afternoon a week and brought the children; Madame Ginoux, wife of the owner of the café where he took his drinks, sat for him in her Arlesienne costume. He slashed the figure on to the canvas in an hour. The background was pale lemon, the face grey, the clothes black, with raw Prussian blue. He posed her in a borrowed armchair of orange wood, her elbows leaning on a green table.

A Zouave lad with a small face, the neck of a bull, and the eye of a tiger agreed to sit for a small sum. Vincent did a half length of him in his blue uniform, the blue of enamelled saucepans, with a braid of faded reddish orange, and two pale lemon stars on his breast. There was a reddish cap on the bronzed, feline head, set against a green background. The result was a savage combination of incongruous tones, very harsh, common and even loud, but fitting the character of the subject.

He sat at his window for hours with pencil and drawing paper, trying to master the technique which would enable him with a few strokes to put down the figure of a man, a woman, a youngster, a horse, a dog, so that it would have a head, body, and legs all in keeping. He copied a good many of the paintings he had made that summer, for he thought that if he could turn out fifty studies at two hundred francs each within the year, he would not have been so very dishonest in having eaten and drunk as though he had a right to it.

He learned a good many things during the winter; that one must not do flesh in Prussian blue, for then it becomes as wood; that his colour was not as firm as it should have been; that the most important element in southland painting was the contrast of red and green, of orange and blue, of sulphur and lilac; that in pictures he wanted to say something comforting as music is comforting; that he wished to paint men and women with that something of the divine which the halo used to symbolize, and which he sought to give by the actual radiance and vibration of his colouring; and lastly, that for those who have a talent for poverty, poverty is eternal.

One of the Van Gogh uncles died and left Theo a small legacy. Since Vincent was so keen to have Gauguin with him, Theo decided to use half the money to furnish Gauguin's bedroom and send him to Arles. Vincent was delighted. He began planning the decorations for the yellow house. He wanted a dozen panels of glorious Arlesian sunflowers, a symphony of blue and yellow.

Even the news of the free railway fare did not seem to excite Gauguin. For some reason which remained obscure to Vincent, Gauguin preferred to dawdle in Pont-Aven. Vincent was eager to finish the decorations and have the studio ready when the master arrived.

Spring came. The row of oleander bushes in the back yard of the yellow house went raving mad, flowering so riotously that they might well have developed locomotor ataxia. They were loaded with fresh flowers, and heaps of faded flowers as well ; their green was continually renewing itself in strong jets, apparently inexhaustible.

Vincent loaded the easel on his back once again and went into the country-side to find sunflowers for the twelve wall panels. The earth of the ploughed fields was as soft in colour as a pair of sabots, while the forget-me-not blue sky was flecked with white clouds. Some of the sunflowers he did on the stalk, at sunrise, and in a flash. Others he took home with him and painted in a green vase.

He gave the outside of his house a fresh coat of yellow, much to the amusement of the inhabitants of the Place Lamartine.

By the time he finished his work on the house, summer had come. With it came the broiling sun, the driving mistral, the growing excitement in the air, the tortured, tormented, driven aspect of the country-side and the stone city pasted against the hill.

And with it came Paul Gauguin.

He arrived in Arles before dawn and waited for the sun in a little all-night café. The proprietor looked at him and exclaimed, "You are the friend! I recognize you."

"What the devil are you talking about?"

"Monsieur Van Gogh showed me the portrait you sent him.. It looks just like you, Monsieur."

Gauguin went to rouse Vincent. Their meeting was boisterous and hearty. Vincent showed Gauguin the house, helped him unpack his valise, demanded news of Paris. They talked animatedly for several hours.

"Are you planning to work today, Gauguin?"

"Do you think I am a Carolus-Duran, that I can get off the train, pick up my palette, and turn you off a sunlight effect at once?"

"I only asked."

"Then don't ask foolish questions."

360

"I'll take a holiday, too. Come along, I'll show you the town."

He led Gauguin up the hill, through the sun-baked Place de la Mairie, and along the market road at the back of the town. The Zouaves were drilling in the field just outside the barracks; their red fezzes burned in the sun. Vincent led the way through the little park in front of the Roman forum. The Arlesiennes were strolling for their morning air. Vincent had been raving to Gauguin about how beautiful they were.

"What do you think about the Arlesiennes, Gauguin?" he demanded.

"I can't get up a perspiration about them."

"Look at the tone of their flesh, man, not the shape. Look at what the sun has done to their colouring."

"How are the houses here, Vincent?"

"There's nothing but five franc places for the Zouaves."

They returned to the yellow house to work out some sort of living arrangements. They nailed a box to the wall in the kitchen and put half their money into it—so much for tobacco, so much for incidental expenses, including rent. On the top of the box they put a scrap of paper and a pencil with which to write down every franc they took. In another box they put the rest of their money, divided into four parts, to pay for the food each week.

"You're a good cook, aren't you, Gauguin?"

"Excellent. I used to be a sailor."

"Then in the future you shall cook. But tonight I am going to make the soup in your honour."

When he served the soup that night, Gauguin could not eat it.

"How you mixed this mess, Vincent, I can't imagine. As you mix the colours in your pictures, I dare say."

"What is the matter with the colours in my pictures?"

"My dear fellow, you're still floundering in neo-impressionism. You'd better give up your present method. It doesn't correspond to your nature."

Vincent pushed his bowl of soup aside.

"You can tell that at first glance, eh? You're quite a critic."

"Well, look for yourself. You're not blind, are you? Those violent yellows, for example ; they're completely disordered."

Vincent glanced up the sunflower panels on the wall.

"Is that all you find to say about my sunflowers?"

"No, my dear fellow, I can find a good many things to criticize."

"Among them?"

"Among them, your harmonies; they're monotonous and incomplete."

"That's a lie!"

"Oh, sit down, Vincent. Stop looking as though you wanted to murder me. I'm a good deal older than you, and more mature. You're still trying to find yourself. Just listen to me, and I'll give some fruitful lessons."

"I'm sorry, Paul. I do want you to help me."

"Then the first thing you had better do is sweep all the garbage out of your mind. You've been raving all day about Meissonier and Monticelli. They're both worthless. As long as you admire that sort of painting, you'll never turn out a good canvas yourself."

"Monticelli was a great painter. He knew more about colour than any man of his time."

"He was a drunken idiot, that's what he was."

Vincent jumped to his feet and glared at Gauguin across the table. The bowl of soup fell to the red tile floor and smashed.

"Don't you call 'Fada' that! I love him almost as well as I do my own brother! All that talk about his being such a drinker, and off his head, is vicious gossip. No drunkard could have painted Monticelli's pictures. The mental labour of balancing the six essential colours, the sheer strain and calculation, with a hundred things to think of in a single half hour, demands a sane mind. And a sober one. When you repeat that gossip about 'Fada' you're being just as vicious as that beastly woman who started it."

"*Turlututu, mon chapeau pointu!*"

Vincent recoiled, as though a glass of cold water had been thrown in his face. His words and tense emotion strangled within him. He tried to put down his rage, but could not. He walked to his bedroom and slammed the door behind him.

8

The following morning the quarrel was forgotten. They had coffee together and then went their separate ways to find pictures. When Vincent returned that night, exhausted from what he had called the balancing of the six essential colours, he found Gauguin already preparing supper on the tiny gas stove. They talked quietly for a little while ; then the conversation turned to painters and painting, the only subject in which they were passionately interested.

The battle was on.

The painters whom Gauguin admired, Vincent despised. Vincent's idols were anathema to Gauguin. They disagreed on every last approach to their craft. Any other subject they might have been able to discuss in a quiet and friendly manner, but painting was the meat and drink of life to them. They fought for their ideas to the last drop of nervous energy. Gauguin had twice Vincent's brute strength, but Vincent's lashing excitement left them evenly matched.

Even when they discussed things about which they agreed, their arguments were terribly electric. They came out of them with their heads as exhausted as a battery after it has been discharged.

"You'll never be an artist, Vincent," announced Gauguin, "until you can look at nature, come back to your studio and paint it in cold blood."

"I don't want to paint in cold blood, you idiot. I want to paint in hot blood! That's why I'm in Arles."

"All this work you've done is only slavish copying from nature. You must learn to work extempore."

"*Extempore!* Good God!"

"And another thing ; you would have done well to listen to Seurat. Painting is abstract, my boy. It has no room for the stories you tell and the morals you point out."

"I point out morals? You're crazy."

"If you want to preach, Vincent, go back to the ministry. Painting is colour, line, and form ; nothing more. The artist can reproduce the decorative in nature, but that's all."

"Decorative art," snorted Vincent. "If that's all you get out of nature, you ought to go back to the Stock Exchange."

"If I do, I'll come hear you preach on Sunday mornings. What do you get out of nature, Brigadier?"

"I get motion, Gauguin, and the rhythm of life."

"Well, we're off."

"When I paint a sun, I want to make people feel it revolving at a terrific rate of speed. Giving off light and heat waves of tremendous power. When I paint a cornfield I want people to feel the atoms within the corn pushing out to their final growth and bursting. When I paint an apple I want people to

363

feel the juice of that apple pushing out against the skin, the seeds at the core striving outward to their own fruition!"

"Vincent, how many times have I told you that a painter must not have theories."

"Take this vineyard scene, Gauguin. Look out! Those grapes are going to burst and squirt right in your eye. Here, study this ravine. I want to make people feel all the millions of tons of water that have poured down its sides. When I paint the portrait of a man, I want them to feel the entire flow of that man's life, everything he has seen and done and suffered!"

"What the devil are you driving at?"

"At this, Gauguin. The fields that push up the corn, and the water that rushes down the ravine, the juice of the grape, and the life of a man as it flows past him, are all one and the same thing. The sole unity in life is the unity of rhythm. A rhythm to which we all dance; men, apples, ravines, ploughed fields, carts among the corn, houses, horses, and the sun. The stuff that is in you, Gauguin, will pound through a grape tomorrow, because you and a grape are one. When I paint a peasant labouring in the field, I want people to feel the peasant flowing down into the soil, just as the corn does, and the soil flowing up into the peasant. I want them to feel the sun pouring into the peasant, into the field, into corn, the plough, and the horses, just as they all pour back into the sun. When you begin to feel the universal rhythm in which everything on earth moves, you begin to understand life. That alone is God."

"*Brigadier,*" said Gauguin, "*vous avez raison!*"

Vincent was at the height of his emotion, quivering with febrile excitement. Gauguin's words struck him like a slap in the face. He stood there gaping foolishly, his mouth hanging open.

"Now what in the world does that mean, 'Brigadier, you are right?' "

"It means I think it about time we adjourned to the cafe for an absinthe."

At the end of the second week Gauguin said, "Let's try that house of yours tonight. Maybe I can find a nice fat girl."

"Keep away from Rachel. She belongs to me.'"

They walked up the labyrinth of stone alleys and entered the Maison de Tolerance. When Rachel heard Vincent's voice, she skipped down the hallway and threw herself into his arms. Vincent introduced Gauguin to Louis.

"Monsieur Gauguin," said Louis, "you are an artist. Perhaps you would give me your opinion of the two new paintings I bought in Paris last year."

"I'd be glad to. Where did you buy them?"

"At Goupils, in the Place de l'Opéra. They are in this front parlour. Will you step in, Monsieur?"

Rachel led Vincent to the room on the left, pushed him into a chair near one of the tables, and sat on his lap.

"I've been coming here for six months," grumbled Vincent, "and Louis never asked my opinion about his pictures."

"He doesn't think you are an artist, *fou-rou*."

"Maybe he's right."

"You don't love me any more," said Rachel, pouting.

"What makes you think that, Pigeon?"

"You haven't been to see me for weeks."

"That was because I was working hard to fix the house for my friend."

"Then you do love me, even if you stay away?"

"Even if I stay away."

She tweaked his small, circular ears, then kissed each of them in turn.

"Just to prove it, *fou-rou*, will you give me your funny little ears? You promised you would."

"If you can take them off, you can have them."

"Oh, *fou-rou*, as if they were sewed on, like my dolly's ears."

There was a shout from the room across the hall, and the noise of someone screaming, either in laughter or in pain. Vincent dumped Rachel off his lap, ran across the hall and into the parlour.

Gauguin was doubled up on the floor, convulsed, tears streaming down his face. Louis, lamp in hand, was gazing down at him, dumbfounded. Vincent crouched over Gauguin and shook him.

"Paul, Paul, what is it?"

Gauguin tried to speak, but could not. After a moment he gasped, "Vincent ... at last ... we're vindicated ... look ... look ... up on the wall ... the two pictures ... that Louis bought from Goupils ... for the parlour of his brothel. *They are both Bouguereaus!*"

He stumbled to his feet and made for the front door.

"Wait a minute," cried Vincent, running after him. "Where are you going?"

"To the telegraph office. I must wire this to the Club Batignolles at once."

Summer came on in all its terrific, glaring heat. The country-side burst into a riot of colour. The greens and blues and yellows and reds were so stark they were shocking to the eye. Whatever the sun touched, it burnt to the core. The valley of the Rhône vibrated with wave after wave of billowy heat. The sun battered the two painters, bruised them, beat them to a living pulp, sucked out all their resistance. The mistral came up and lashed their bodies, whipped their nerves, shook their heads on their necks until they thought they would burst or break off. Yet every morning they went out with the sun and laboured until the crying blue of night deepened the crying blue of day.

Between Vincent and Gauguin, the one a perfect volcano, the other boiling inwardly, a fierce struggle was preparing itself. At night, when they were too exhausted to sleep, too nervous to sit still, they spent all their energy on each other. Their money ran low. They had no way to amuse themselves. They found an outlet for their pent up passions in mutual exacerbation. Gauguin never tired of whipping Vincent into a rage and, when Vincent was at the height of his paroxysm, throwing into his face, *"Brigadier, vous avez raison!"*

"Vincent, no wonder you can't paint. Look at the disorder of this studio. Look at the mess in this colour box. My God, if your Dutch brain wasn't so fired with Daudet and Monticelli, maybe you could clean it out and get a little order into your life."

"That's nothing to you, Gauguin. This is my studio. You keep your studio any way you like."

"While we're on the subject, I may as well tell you that your mind is just as chaotic as your colour box. You admire every postage stamp painter in Europe, and yet you can't see that Degas ..."

"Degas! What has he ever painted that can be held up alongside of a Millet?"

"Millet! That sentimentalist! That ...!"

Vincent worked himself into a frenzy at this slur at Millet, whom he considered his master and spiritual father. He stormed after Gauguin from room to room. Gauguin fled. The house was small. Vincent shouted at him, harangued him, waved his fists in Gauguin's powerful face. Far into the

366

tropical, oppressive night they kept up their bruising, battering conflict.

They both worked like fiends to catch themselves and nature at the point of fructification. Day after day they battled with their flaming palettes, night after night with each other's strident egos. When they were not quarrelling viciously, their friendly arguments were so explosive that it was impossible to summon sleep. Money came from Theo. They spent it immediately for tobacco and absinthe. It was too hot to eat. They thought absinthe would quiet their nerves. It only excited them the more.

A nasty, lashing mistral came up. It confined the men to the house. Gauguin could not work. He spent his time scourging Vincent into a continuous ebullition. He had never seen anyone grow so violent over mere ideas.

Vincent was the only sport Gauguin had. He made the most of it.

"Better quiet down, Vincent," he said after the fifth day of the mistral. He had baited his friend until the storm within the yellow house had made the howling mistral seem like a mild and gentle breeze.

"What about yourself, Gauguin?"

"It so happens, Vincent, that several men who have been a good deal in my company, and in the habit of discussing things with me, have gone mad."

"Are you threatening me?"

"No, I'm warning you."

"Then keep your warnings to yourself."

"All right, but don't blame me if anything happens."

"Oh, Paul, Paul, let's stop this eternal quarrelling. I know that you're a better painter than I am. I know that you can teach me a great deal. But I won't have you despising me, do you hear. I've slaved nine long years, and by Christ, I have something to say with this beastly paint! Now admit it, haven't I? Speak up, Gauguin."

Brigadier, vous avez raison!

The mistral died down. The Arlesians dared go out in the streets again. The blistering sun came back. An uncontainable fever settled over Arles. The police had to cope with crimes of violence. People walked about with a smouldering excitement in their eyes. No one ever laughed. No one talked. The stone roofs broiled under the sun. There were fights and knife flashes in the Place Lamartine. There was the smell of catastrophe in the air. Arles was too engorged to stand the strain any longer. The valley of the Rhône was about to burst into a million fragments.

Vincent thought of the Parisian journalist.

"Which will it be?" he asked himself. "An earthquake or a revolution."

In spite of it all, he still painted in the fields without a hat. He needed the white, blinding heat to make fluid within him the terrific passions he felt. His brain was a burning crucible, turning out red-hot canvas after canvas.

With each succeeding canvas he felt more keenly that all his nine years of labour were converging in these few surcharged weeks to make him, for one brief instant, the complete and perfect artist. He was by far surpassing his last summer's work. Never again would he produce paintings that so utterly expressed the essence of nature and the essence of himself.

He painted from four in the morning until night stole the scene from him. He created two, and sometimes even three complete pictures a day. He was spilling out a year of his life blood with every convulsive painting that he tore from his vitals. It was not the length of his stay on earth that mattered to him; it was what he did with the days of his life. For him time would have to be measured by the paintings he poured out, not by the fluttering leaves of a calendar.

He sensed that his art had reached a climax; that this was the high spot of his life, the moment toward which he had been striving all these years. He did not know how long it would last. He knew only that he had to paint pictures, and more pictures ... and still more and more pictures. This climax of his life, this tiny point of infinity, had to be held, sustained, pushed out until he had created all those pictures that were gestating in his soul.

Painting all day, fighting all night, sleeping not at all, eating very little, glutting themselves with sun and colour, excitement, tobacco and absinthe, lacerated by the elements and their own drive of creation, lacerating each other with their rages and violence, their gorges mounting higher and higher.

The sun beat them. The mistral whipped them. The colour stabbed their eyes out. The absinthe swelled their empty bowels with turgescent fever. The yellow house rocked and throbbed with the tempest in the tropical, plethoric nights.

Gauguin did a portrait of Vincent while the latter was painting a still life of some ploughs. Vincent stared at the portrait. For the first time he understood clearly just what Gauguin thought of him.

"It is certainly I," he said. "But it is I gone mad!"

That evening they went to the café. Vincent ordered a light absinthe. Suddenly he flung the glass and the contents at Gauguin's head. Gauguin dodged. He picked Vincent up bodily in his arms. He carried him across the Place Lamartine. Vincent found himself in bed. He fell asleep instantly.

"My dear Gauguin," he said very calmly the next morning, "I have a vague memory that I offended you last evening."

"I forgive you gladly and with all my heart," said Gauguin, "but yesterday's scene might occur again. If I were struck I might lose control of myself and give you a choking. So permit me to write to your brother and tell him that I am coming back."

"No! No! Paul, you can't do that. Leave the yellow house? Everything in it I made for you."

During all the hours of the day the storm raged. Vincent fought desperately to keep Gauguin by his side. Gauguin resisted every plea. Vincent begged, cajoled, cursed, threatened, even wept. In this battle he proved to be the stronger. He felt that his whole life depended upon keeping his friend in the yellow house. By nightfall Gauguin was exhausted. He gave in just to get a little rest.

Every room in the yellow house was charged and vibrating with electrical tension. Gauguin could not sleep. Toward dawn he dozed off.

A queer sensation awakened him. He saw Vincent standing over his bed, glaring at him in the dark.

"What's the matter with you, Vincent?" he asked sternly.

Vincent walked out of the room, returned to his bed, and fell into a heavy sleep.

The following night Gauguin was jerked out of his sleep by the same strange sensation. Vincent was standing over his bed, staring at him in the dark.

"Vincent! Go to bed!"

Vincent turned away.

At supper the next day they fell into a fierce quarrel over the soup.

"You poured some paint into it, Vincent, while I wasn't looking!" shouted Gauguin.

Vincent laughed. He walked to the wall and wrote in chalk,

He was very quiet for several days. He looked moody and depressed. He hardly spoke a word to Gauguin. He did not even pick up a paint brush. He did not read. He sat in a chair and gazed ahead of him into space.

On the afternoon of the fourth day, when there was a vicious mistral, he asked Gauguin to take a walk with him.

"Let's go up to the park," he said. "I have something to tell you."

"Can't you tell me here, where we're comfortable?"

"No, I can't talk sitting down. I must walk."

"Very well, if you must."

They took the wagon road which wound up the left side of the town. To make progress they had to plunge through the mistral as though it were a thick, leathery substance. The cypresses in the park were being swayed almost to the ground.

"What is it you want to tell me?" demanded Gauguin.

He had to shout into Vincent's ear. The wind snatched away his words almost before Vincent could catch them.

"Paul, I've been thinking for the past few days. I've hit upon a wonderful idea."

"Forgive me if I'm a little leery of your wonderful ideas."

"We've all failed as painters. Do you know why?"

"What? I can't hear a word. Shout it in my ear."

"DO YOU KNOW WHY WE'VE ALL FAILED AS PAINTERS?"

"No. Why?"

"Because we paint alone!"

"What the devil?"

"Some things we paint well, some things we paint badly. We throw them all together in a single canvas."

"Brigadier, I'm hanging on your words."

"Do you remember the Both brothers? Dutch painters. One was good at landscape. The other was good at figures. They painted a picture together. One put in the landscape. The other put in the figures. They were successful."

"Well, to bring an interminable story to its obscure point?"

"What? I can't hear you. Come closer."

"I SAID, GO ON!"

"Paul. That's what we must do. You and I. Seurat. Cezanne. Lautrec. Rousseau. We must all work together on the same canvas. That would be a true painter's communism. We would

370

each put in what we did best. Seurat the air. You the land-scape. Cezanne the surfaces. Lautrec the figures. I the sun and moon and stars. Together we could be one great artist. What do you say?"

"Turlutut, mon chapeau pointu!"

He burst into raucous, savage laughter. The wind splashed his ridicule into Vincent's face like the spray of the sea.

"Brigadier," he cried, when he could catch his breath, "if that's not the world's greatest idea, I'll eat it. Pardon me while I howl."

He stumbled down the path, holding his stomach, doubled over with delight.

Vincent stood perfectly still.

A rush of blackbirds came out of the sky. Thousands of cawing, beating blackbirds. They swooped down on Vincent, struck him, engulfed him, flew through his hair, into his nose, into his mouth, into his ears, into his eyes, buried him in a thick, black, airless cloud of flapping wings.

Gauguin returned.

"Come on, Vincent, let's go down to Louis's. I feel the need of a celebration after that priceless idea of yours."

Vincent followed him to the Rue des Ricolettes in silence.

Gauguin went upstairs with one of the girls.

Rachel sat on Vincent's lap in the café room.

"Aren't you coming up with me, *fou-rou!*" she asked.

"No."

"Why not?"

"I haven't the five francs."

"Then you will give me your ear instead?"

"Yes."

After a very few moments, Gauguin returned. The two men walked down the hill to the yellow house. Gauguin bolted his supper. He walked out the front door without speaking. He had almost crossed the Place Lamartine when he heard behind him a well known step ; short, quick, irregular.

He whirled about.

Vincent rushed upon him, an open razor in his hand.

Gauguin stood rigid and looked at Vincent.

Vincent stopped just two feet away. He glared at Gauguin in the dark. He lowered his head, turned, ran towards home.

Gauguin went to a hotel. He engaged a room, locked the door and went to bed.

Vincent entered the yellow house. He walked up the red

brick stairs to his bedroom. He picked up the mirror in which he had painted his own portrait so many times. He set it on the toilet table against the wall.

He looked at his red-shot eyes in the mirror.

The end had come. His life was over. He read that in his face.

He had better make the clean break.

He lifted the razor. He felt the keen steel against the gooseflesh of his throat.

Voices were whispering strange tales to him.

The Arlesian sun threw a wall of blinding fire between his eyes and the glass.

He slashed off his right ear.

He left only a tiny portion of the lobe.

He dropped the razor. He bound his head in towels. The blood dripped on to the floor.

He picked up his ear from the basin. He washed it. He wrapped it in several pieces of drawing paper. He tied the bundle in newspaper.

He pulled a Basque beret down over the thick bandage. He walked down the stairs to the front door. He crossed the Place Lamartine, climbed the hill, rang the bell of the Maison de Tolérance, Numero I.

A maid answered the door.

"Send Rachel to me."

Rachel came in a moment.

"Oh, it's you, *fou-rou*. What do you want?"

"I have brought you something."

"For me? A present?"

"Yes."

"How nice you are, *fou-rou*."

"Guard it carefully. It is a souvenir of me."

"What is it?"

"Open, and you will see."

Rachel unwrapped the papers. She stared in horror at the ear. She fell in a dead faint on the flagstones.

Vincent turned away. He walked down the hill. He crossed the Place Lamartine. He closed the door of the yellow house behind him and went to bed.

When Gauguin returned at seven-thirty the following morning he found a crowd gathered in front. Roulin was wringing his hands in despair.

"What have you done to your comrade, Monsieur?" asked a man in a melon shaped hat. His tone was abrupt and severe.

"I don't know."

"Oh, yes . . . you know very well . . . he is dead."

It took Gauguin a long time to gather his wits together. The stares of the crowd seemed to tear his person to pieces, suffocating him.

"Let us go upstairs, Monsieur," he said stammeringly. "We can explain ourselves there."

Wet towels lay on the floor of the two lower rooms. The blood had stained the stairway that led up to Vincent's bedroom. In the bed lay Vincent, rolled in the sheets, humped up like a guncock. He seemed lifelesss. Gently, very gently, Gauguin touched the body. It was warm. For Gauguin, it seemed as if he had suddenly got back all his energy, all his spirit.

"Be kind enough, Monsieur," he said in a low voice to the police superintendent, "to awaken this man with great care. If he asks for me, tell him I have left for Paris. The sight of me might prove fatal to him."

The police superintendent sent for a doctor and a cab. They took Vincent to the hospital. Roulin ran alongside of the carriage, panting.

9

Doctor Felix Rey, young interne of the hospital of Arles, was a short, thickset man with an octagonal head and a weed of black hair shooting up from the top of the octagon. He treated Vincent's wound, then put him to bed in a cell-like room from which everything had been removed. He locked the door behind him when he went out.

At sundown, when he was taking his patient's pulse, Vincent awoke. He stared at the ceiling, then the whitewashed wall, then out of the window at the patch of darkening blue sky. His eyes wandered slowly to Doctor Rey's face.

"Hello," he said, softly.

"Hello," replied Doctor Rey.

"Where am I?"

"You're in the hospital of Arles."

"Oh."

A flash of pain went across his face. He lifted his hand to where his right ear had once been. Doctor Rey stopped him.

"You mustn't touch," he said.

". . . Yes . . . I remember . . . now."

"It's a nice, clean wound, old fellow. I'll have you on your feet within a few days."

"Where is my friend?"

"He has returned to Paris."

". . . I see . . . May I have my pipe?"

"Not just yet, old fellow."

Doctor Rey bathed and bandaged the wound.

"It's an accident of very little importance," he said. "After all, a man doesn't hear with those cabbages he has stuck on the outside of his head. You won't miss it."

"You are very kind, Doctor. Why is the room . . . so bare?"

"I had everything taken out to protect you."

"Against whom?"

"Against yourself."

". . . Yes . . . I see . . ."

"Well, I must go now. I'll send the attendant in with your supper. Try to lie perfectly still. The loss of blood has made you weak."

When Vincent awoke in the morning. Theo was sitting by his bedside. Theo's face was pale and drawn, his eyes bloodshot.

"Theo," said Vincent.

Theo slipped off the chair, went on his knees beside the bed, and took Vincent's hand. He wept without shame or restraint.

"Theo . . . always . . . when I wake up . . . and need you . . . you're by my side."

Theo could not speak.

"It was cruel to make you come all the way down here. How did you know?"

"Gauguin telegraphed yesterday. I caught the night train."

"That was wrong of Gauguin to put you to all that expense. You sat up all night, Theo."

"Yes, Vincent."

They were silent for some time.

"I've spoken to Doctor Rey, Vincent. He says it was a sunstroke. You've been working in the sun without a hat, haven't you?"

"Yes."

"Well, you see, old boy, you mustn't. In the future you must wear your hat. Lots of people here in Arles get sunstroke."

Vincent squeezed his hand gently. Theo tried to swallow the lump in his throat.

"I have some news for you, Vincent, but I think it had better wait a few days."

"Is it nice news, Theo?"

"I think you'll like it."

Doctor Rey walked in.

"Well, how's the patient this morning?"

"Doctor, may my brother tell me some good news?"

"I should say so. Here, wait a minute. Let me look at this. Yes, that's fine, that's fine. It'll be healing fast, now."

When the doctor left the room, Vincent begged for his news.

"Vincent," said Theo, "I've . . . well, I . . . I've met a girl."

"Why, Theo."

"Yes. She's a Dutch girl. Johanna Bunger. She's a lot like mother, I think."

"Do you love her, Theo?"

"Yes. I've been so desperately lonely without you in Paris, Vincent. It wasn't so bad before you came, but after we had lived together for a year . . ."

"I was hard to live with, Theo. I'm afraid I showed you a bad time."

"Oh, Vincent, if you only knew how many times I wished I could walk into the apartment on the Rue Lepic and find your shoes on the sideboard, and your wet canvases all over my bed. But we mustn't talk any more. You must rest. We'll just stay here with each other."

Theo remained in Arles two days. He left only when Doctor Rey assured him that Vincent would make a rapid recovery, and that he would take care of his brother, not only as a patient but as a friend.

Roulin came every evening and brought flowers. During the nights Vincent suffered from hallucinations. Doctor Rey put camphor on Vincent's pillow and mattress to overcome his insomnia.

At the end of the fourth day, when the Doctor saw that Vincent was completely rational, he unlocked the door of the room and had the furniture put back.

"May I get up and dress, Doctor?" asked Vincent.

"If you feel strong enough. Come to my office after you have had a little air."

The hospital of Arles was of two stories, built in a quadrangle, with a patio in the centre, full of riotously coloured flowers, ferns, and gravel walks. Vincent strolled about slowly for a few minutes, then went to Doctor Rey's office on the ground floor.

"How does it feel to be on your feet?" asked the doctor.

"Very good."

"Tell me, Vincent, why did you do it?"

Vincent was silent for a long time.

"I don't know," he said.

"What were you thinking of when you did it?"

". . . I . . . wasn't . . . thinking, Doctor."

Vincent spent the next few days recovering his strength. One morning, while he was chatting with Doctor Rey in the latter's room, he picked up a razor off the washstand and opened it.

"You need a shave, Doctor Rey," he said. "Would you like me to give you one?"

Doctor Rey backed into a corner, the palm of his hand out before his face.

"No! No! Put that down!"

"But I'm really a good barber, Doctor. I could give you a nice shave."

"Vincent! Put that razor down!"

Vincent laughed, closed the razor, and put it back on the washstand. "Don't be afraid, my friend. That's all over now."

At the end of the second week Doctor Rey gave Vincent permission to paint. An attendant was sent down to the yellow house to get the easel and canvas. Doctor Rey posed for Vincent just to humour him. Vincent worked slowly, a tiny bit each day. When the portrait was finished he presented it to the Doctor.

"I want you to keep this as a souvenir of me, Doctor. It is the only way I have of showing my gratitude for your kindness."

"That is very nice of you, Vincent. I am honoured."

The doctor took the portrait home and used it to cover a crack in the wall.

Vincent stayed at the hospital two weeks longer. He painted the patio, baking in the sun. He wore a wide straw hat while he worked. The flower garden took him the full two weeks to paint.

"You must drop in to see me every day," said Doctor Rey, shaking hands with Vincent at the front gate of the hospital. "And remember, no absinthe, no excitement, and no working in the sun without that hat."

"I promise, Doctor. And thank you for everything."

"I shall write your brother that you are completely well."

Vincent found that the landlord had made a contract to turn him out and give the yellow house to a tobacconist. Vincent was deeply attached to the yellow house. It was his sole root in the soil of Provence. He had painted every inch of it, inside and out. He had made it habitable. In spite of the accident, he still considered it his permanent home, and he was determined to fight the landlord to the bitter end.

At first he was afraid to sleep alone in the house because of his insomnia, which not even the camphor could overcome. Doctor Rey had given him bromide of potassium to rout the unbearable hallucinations that had been frightening him. At length the voices that had been whispering queer tales in his ears went away, to come back only in nightmares.

He was still far too weak to go out and work. The serenity returned but slowly to his brain. His blood revived from day to day and his appetite increased. He had a gay dinner with Roulin at the restaurant, quite cheerful and with no dread of renewed suffering. He began working gingerly on a portrait of Roulin's wife, which had been unfinished at the time of the accident. He liked the way he had ranged the reds from rose to orange, rising through the yellows to lemon, with light and sombre greens.

His health and his work picked up slowly. He had known before that one could fracture one's legs and arms, and after that recover, but he was rather astonished that one could fracture the brain in one's head and recover after that, too.

One afternoon he went to ask after Rachel's health.

"Pigeon," he said, "I'm sorry for all the trouble I caused you."

"It's all right, *fou-rou*. You mustn't worry about it. In this town things like that are not out of the way."

His friends came in and assured him that in Provence everyone suffered either from fever, hallucinations, or madness.

"It's nothing unusual, Vincent," said Roulin. "Down here in Tartarin's country we are all a trifle cracked."

"Well, well," said Vincent, "we understand each other like members of the same family."

A few more weeks passed. Vincent was now able to work all day in the studio. Thoughts of madness and death left his mind. He began to feel almost normal.

Finally he ventured out of doors to paint. The sun was burning up the magnificent yellow of the cornfields. But

377

Vincent could not capture it. He had been eating regularly, sleeping regularly, avoiding excitement and intense enthusiasm.

He was feeling so normal he could not paint.

"You are a *grand nerveux*, Vincent," Doctor Rey had told him. "You never have been normal. But then, no artist is normal; if he were, he wouldn't be an artist. Normal men don't create works of art. They eat, sleep, hold down routine jobs, and die. You are hypersensitive to life and nature; that's why you are able to interpret for the rest of us. But if you are not careful, that very hypersensitiveness will lead you to your destruction. The strain of it breaks every artist in time."

Vincent knew that to attain the high yellow note which dominated his Arlesian canvases he had to be on edge, strung up, throbbingly excited, passionately sensitive, his nerves rasped raw. If he allowed himself to get into that state, he could paint again as brilliantly as he had before. But the road led to destruction.

"An artist is a man with his work to do," he murmured to himself. "How stupid for me to remain alive if I can't paint the way I want to paint."

He walked in the fields without his hat, absorbing the power of the sun. He drank in the mad colours of the sky, the yellow ball of fire, the green fields and bursting flowers. He let the mistral lash him, the thick night sky throttle him, the sunflowers whip his imagination to a bursting point. As his excitement rose, he lost his appetite for food. He began to live on coffee, absinthe, and tobacco. He lay awake nights with the deep colours of the countryside rushing past his bloodshot eyes. And at last he loaded his easel on his back and went into the fields.

His powers came back; his sense of the universal rhythm of nature, his ability to smash off a large canvas in a few hours and flood it with glaring, brilliant sunshine. Each day saw a new picture created; each day saw a rise in his emotional gauge. He painted thirty-seven canvases without a pause.

One morning he awoke feeling lethargic. He could not work. He sat on a chair. He stared at a wall. He hardly moved all through the day. The voices came back to his ears and told him queer, queer tales. When night fell he walked to the grey restaurant and sat down at a little table. He ordered soup. The waitress brought it to him. A voice rang sharply in his ear, warning him.

He swept the plate of soup to the floor. The dish smashed in fragments.

"You're trying to poison me!" he screamed. "You put poison in that soup!"

He jumped to his feet and kicked over the table. Some of the customers ran out the door. Others stared at him agape.

"You're all trying to poison me!" he shouted. "You want to murder me! I saw you put poison in that soup!"

Two gendarmes came in and carried him bodily up the hill to the hospital.

After twenty-four hours he became quite calm and discussed the affair with Doctor Rey. He worked a little each day, took walks in the country, returned to the hospital for his supper and sleep. Sometimes he had moods of indescribable mental anguish, sometimes moments when the veil of time and of inevitable circumstance seemed for the twinkling of an eye to be parted.

Doctor Rey allowed him to paint again. Vincent did an orchard of peach trees beside a road, with the Alps in the background; an olive grove with leaves of old silver, silver turning to green against the blue, and with orange-coloured ploughed earth.

After three weeks, Vincent returned to the yellow house. By now the town, and especially the Place Lamartine, was incensed against him. The severed ear and the poisoned soup were more than they could accept with equanimity. The Arlesians were firmly convinced that painting drove men mad. When Vincent passed they stared at him, made remarks out loud, sometimes even crossed the street so as to avoid passing him.

Not a restaurant in the city would allow him to enter the front door.

The children of Arles gathered before the yellow house and made up games to torment him.

"Fou-rou! Fou-rou!" they cried out. "Cut off your other ear."

Vincent locked his windows. The shouts and laughter of the children drifted through.

"Fou-rou! Fou-rou!"

"Crazy man! Crazy man!"

They made up a little song which they sang beneath his window.

379

> *Fou-rou* was a crazy man
> Who cut off his right ear.
> Now no matter how you shout,
> The crazy man can't hear.

Vincent tried going out to escape them. They followed him through the streets, into the fields, a jolly crowd of singing and laughing urchins.

Day after day their number increased as they gathered before the yellow house. Vincent stuffed his ears with cotton. He worked at his easel, making duplicates of his pictures. The words of the children came through the cracks and the walls. They seared into his brain.

The young boys became more bold. They clambered up the drain pipes like little monkeys, sat on the window sills, peered into the room and shouted at Vincent's back.

"*Fou-rou*, cut off your other ear. We want your other ear!"

The tumult in the Place Lamartine increased. The boys put up boarding on which they could climb to the second floor. They broke the windows, poked their heads in, threw things at Vincent. The crowd below encouraged them, echoed their songs and shouts.

"Get us the other ear. We want the other ear!"

"*Fou-rou!* Want some candy? Look out, it's poisoned!"

"*Fou-rou!* Want some soup? Look out, it's poisoned!"

> *Fou-rou* was a crazy man
> Who cut off his right ear.
> Now no matter how you shout,
> The crazy man can't hear.

The boys perched on the window sill led the crowd below in a chant. Together, they sang with an ever rising crescendo.

"*Fou-rou, fou-rou*, throw us your ear, throw us your ear!"

"FOU-ROU, FOU-ROU, THROW US YOUR EAR, THROW US YOUR EAR!"

Vincent lurched up from his easel. There were three urchins sitting on his window sill, chanting. He lashed out at them. They scampered down the boarding. The crowd below roared. Vincent stood at the window, looking down at them.

A rush of blackbirds came out of the sky, thousands of cawing, beating blackbirds. They darkened the Place Lamartine, swooped down on Vincent, struck him, filled the room, engulfed him, flew through his hair, into his nose and mouth and eyes, buried him in a thick, black, airless cloud of flapping wings.

Vincent jumped on to the window sill.

"Go away!" he screamed. "You fiends, go away! For God's sake, leave me in peace!"

"*FOU-ROU, FOU-ROU,* THROW US YOUR EAR, THROW US YOUR EAR!"

"Go away! Let me alone! Do you hear, let me alone!"

He picked up the wash basin from the table and flung it down at them. It smashed on the cobblestones below. He ran about in a rage picking up everything he could lay his hands on and flinging them down into the Place Lamartine to be hopelessly smashed. His chairs, his easel, his mirror, his table, his bedclothing, his sunflower canvases from the walls, all rained down on the urchins of Provence. And with each article there went a flashing panorama of his days in the yellow house, of the sacrifices he had made to buy, one by one, these simple articles with which he was to furnish the house of his life.

When he had laid the room bare, he stood by the window, every nerve quivering. He fell across the sill. His head hung down towards the cobblestone Place.

10

A petition was immediately circulated to the Place Lamartine. Ninety men and women signed it.

To Mayor Tardieu:

We, the undersigned citizens of Arles, are firmly convinced that Vincent Van Gogh, resident at Place Lamartine, 2, is a dangerous lunatic, not fit to be left at large.

We hereby call upon you as our Mayor to have this madman locked up.

It was very close to election time in Arles. Mayor Tardieu did not wish to displease so many voters. He ordered the superintendent of police to arrest Vincent.

The *gendarmes* found him lying on the floor below the window sill. They carried him off to jail. He was put in a cell, under lock and key. A keeper was stationed outside his door.

When Vincent returned to consciousness, he asked to see

381

Doctor Rey. He was refused permission. He asked for pencil and paper to write Theo. It was refused.

At length Doctor Rey gained entrance to the jail.

"Try to restrain your indignation, Vincent," he said, "Otherwise they will convict you of being a dangerous lunatic, and that will be the end of you. Besides, strong emotion can only aggravate your case. I will write to your brother, and between us we will get you out of here."

"I beg you, Doctor, don't let Theo come down here. He's just going to be married. It will spoil everything for him."

"I'll tell him not to come. I think I have a good plan for you."

Two days later Doctor Rey came back. The keeper was still stationed in front of the cell.

"Listen Vincent," he said, "I just watched them move you out of your yellow house. The landlord stored your furniture in the basement of one of the cafés, and he has your paintings under lock and key. He says he won't give them up until you pay the back rent."

Vincent was silent.

"Since you can't go back there, I think you had better try to work out my plan. There is no telling how often these epileptic fits will come back on you. If you have peace and quiet and pleasant surroundings and don't excite yourself, you may have seen the last of them. On the other hand, they may recur every month or two. So to protect yourself, and others about you . . . I think it would be advisable . . . to go into . . ."

". . . *A maison de santé?*"

"Yes."

"Then you think I am . . .?"

"No, my dear Vincent, you are not. You can see for yourself that you are as sane as I. But these epileptic fits are like any other kind of fever. They make a man go out of his head. And when a nervous crisis comes on, you naturally do irrational things. That's why you ought to be in a hospital, where you can be looked after."

"I see."

"There is a good place in St. Remy, just twenty-five kilometres from here. It's called St. Paul de Mausole. They take first, second, and third-class patients. The third class is a hundred francs a month. You could manage that. The place was formerly a monastery, right up against the base of the hills. It is beautiful, Vincent, and quiet, oh, so quiet. You will have a doctor to advise you, and sisters to take care of you. The food will be plain and good. You will be able to recover your health."

"Would I be allowed to paint?"

"Why, of course, old fellow. You'll be allowed to do whatever you wish ... providing it doesn't injure you. It will be just like being in a hospital with enormous grounds. If you live quietly that way for a year, you may be completely cured."

"But how will I get out of this hole?"

"I have spoken to the superintendent of police. He agrees to let you go to St. Paul de Mausole, providing I take you there."

"And you say it is really a nice place?"

"Oh, charming, Vincent. You'll find loads of things to paint."

"How nice. A hundred francs a month isn't so much. Perhaps that's just what I need for a year, to quiet me down."

"Of course it is. I have already written to your brother, telling him about it. I suggested that in your present state of health it would be inadvisable to move you very far; certainly not to Paris. I told him that in my opinion St. Paul would be the very best thing for you."

"Well, if Theo agrees ... Anything, just so long as I don't cause him more trouble ..."

"I expect an answer any hour. I'll come back when I get it."

Theo had no alternative. He acquiesced. He sent money to pay his brother's bills. Doctor Rey took Vincent in a carriage to the station where they boarded the train for Tarascon. At Tarascon they took a little branch line that wound up a green, fertile valley to St. Remy.

It was two kilometres up a steep hill, through the sleeping town, to St. Paul de Mausole. Vincent and Doctor Rey hired a carriage. The road led straight to a ridge of black, barren mountains. From a short way off Vincent saw, nestled at their base, the sod-brown walls of the monastery.

The carriage stopped. Vincent and Doctor Rey got out. On the right of the road there was a cleared, circular space with a Temple of Vesta and a Triumphal Arch.

"How in the world did these get here?" demanded Vincent.

"This used to be an important Roman settlement. The river which you see down there once filled this whole valley. It came right up to where you're standing. As the river receded, the town crawled lower and lower down the hill. Now nothing is left here except these dead monuments, and the monastery."

"Interesting."

"Come, Vincent, Doctor Peyron is expecting us."

They left the road and walked through a patch of pines to the gate of the monastery. Doctor Rey pulled an iron knob which sounded a loud bell. After a few moments the gate opened and Doctor Peyron appeared.

"How do you do, Doctor Peyron?" said Doctor Rey. "I have brought you my friend, Vincent Van Gogh, as we arranged by mail. I know that you will take good care of him."

"Yes, Doctor Rey, we will take care of him."

"You will forgive me if I run, Doctor? I just have time to catch that train back to Tarascon."

"Of course, Doctor Rey. I understand."

"Good-bye, Vincent," said Doctor Rey. "Be happy, and you will get well. I will come to see you as often as I can. By the end of a year I expect to find you a completely well man."

"Thank you, Doctor. You are very kind. Good-bye."

"Good-bye, Vincent."

He turned and walked away through the pines.

"Will you come in, Vincent?" asked Doctor Peyron, stepping aside.

Vincent walked past Doctor Peyron.

The gate of the insane asylum locked behind him.

BOOK SEVEN

ST. REMY

1

The ward in which the inmates slept was like a third-class waiting room in some dead-alive village. The lunatics always wore their hats, spectacles, canes, and travelling cloaks, just as though they were on the point of leaving for somewhere.

Sister Deschanel brought Vincent through the long corridor-like room and indicated an empty bed.

"You will sleep here, Monsieur," she said. "At night you will pull the curtains for privacy. Doctor Peyron wishes to see you in his office when you are settled."

The eleven men sitting about the unlit stove neither noticed nor commented upon Vincent's arrival. Sister Deschanel

384

walked down the long narrow room, her starched white gown, black cape, and black veil standing out stiffly behind her.

Vincent dropped his valise and looked about. Both sides of the ward were lined with beds sloping downward at an angle of five degrees, each surrounded by a framework on which were hung dirty cream-coloured curtains. The roof was of rough beams, the walls were whitewashed, and in the centre was a stove with an angular pipe coming out of its left side. There was a lone lamp in the room, hung just above the stove.

Vincent wondered why the men were so quiet. They did not speak to each other. They did not read or play games. They leaned on their walking sticks and looked at the stove.

There was a box nailed to the wall by the head of his bed, but Vincent preferred to keep his belongings in his valise. He put his pipe, tobacco, and a book in the box, shoved the valise under the bed and walked out into the garden. On the way he passed a row of dark, dank looking rooms, locked tight and abandoned.

The patio cloister was utterly deserted. There were large pines beneath which grew tall and unkempt grass mixed with rampant weeds. The walls enclosed a square of stagnant sunlight. Vincent turned to his left and knocked on the door of the private house in which Doctor Peyron and his family lived.

Doctor Peyron had been a *médecin de marine* at Marseilles, after that an oculist. A severe case of gout had caused him to search for a *maison de santé* in the quiet of the country.

"You see, Vincent," said the Doctor, gripping a corner of the desk with each hand, "formerly I took care of the health of the body. At present I take care of the health of the soul. It is the same *métier*."

"You have had experience with nervous diseases, Doctor. Can you explain why I cut off my ear?"

"That is not at all unusual with epileptics, Vincent. I have had two similar cases. The auditory nerves become extremely sensitive, and the patient thinks he can stop the hallucinations by cutting off the auricle."

"... Oh ... I see. And the treatments I am to have ... ?"

"Treatments? Well ... ah ... you must have at least two hot baths a week. I insist upon that. And you must stay in the baths for two hours. They will calm you."

"And what else am I to do, Doctor?"

"You are to remain perfectly quiet. You must not excite yourself. Do not work, do not read, do not argue or get upset."

"I know . . . I am too weak to work."

"If you do not wish to participate in the religious life of St. Paul, I will tell the sisters not to insist upon it. If there is anything you need, come to me."

"Thank you, Doctor."

"Supper is at five. You will hear the gong. Try to fit into the pattern of the hospital, Vincent, as quickly as you can. It will speed your recovery."

Vincent stumbled through the chaotic garden, passed the crumbling portico at the entrance to the third-class building, and walked by the row of dark, deserted cells. He sat on his bed in the ward. His companions were still sitting about the stove in silence. After a time he heard a noise from another room. The eleven men rose with an air of grim determination and stormed down the ward. Vincent followed them.

The room in which they ate had an earthen floor and no window. There was just one long, rough, wooden table with benches about it. The sisters served the food. It tasted mouldy, as in a shoddy boarding house. First there was soup and black bread; the cockroaches in the soup made Vincent homesick for the restaurants of Paris. Next he was served a dish of chick peas, beans, and lentils. His companions ate with all their might, brushing the crumbs of black bread from the table into their hands, and then licking them off with their tongues.

The meal finished, the men returned to the identical chairs about the stove and digested their food with intense concentration. When the supper had gone down, they rose one by one, undressed, pulled the curtains and went to sleep. Vincent had not as yet heard them utter a sound.

The sun was just setting. Vincent stood at the window and looked over the green valley. There was a superb sky of pale lemon, against which the mournful pines stood out in designs of exquisite black lace. The sight moved Vincent to nothing, not even the faint desire to paint it.

He stood at the window until the heavy Provençal dusk filtered through the lemon sky and absorbed the colour. No one came into the ward to light the lamp There was nothing to do in the darkness but think of one's life.

Vincent undressed and went to bed. He lay there wide-eyed, staring at the rough beams of the ceiling. The angle of the bed pitched him downward toward the base. He had brought Delacroix's book with him. He fumbled in the box, found it and held the leather covering against his heart in the darkness. The feel of it reassured him He did not belong with these lunatics who surrounded him, but with the great master whose words of wisdom and comfort flowed through the stiff binding and into his aching heart.

After a time he fell asleep. He was awakened by a low moaning in the bed next to his. The moans became louder and louder, until they broke into cries and a flood of vehement words.

"Go away! Stop following me! Why do you follow me? I didn't kill him! You can't fool me. I know who you are. You're the secret police! Well, search me if you like! I didn't steal that money! He murdered himself on Wednesday! Go away! For God's sake, leave me alone!"

Vincent jumped up and pushed aside the curtain. He saw a blond haired young boy of twenty-three, tearing at his nightgown with his teeth. When the boy saw Vincent, he sprang to his knees and clasped his hands fervently before him.

"Monsieur Mounet-Sully, don't take me away! I didn't do it, I tell you! I'm not a sodomist! I'm a lawyer. I'll handle all your cases, Monsieur Mounet-Sully, only don't arrest me! I couldn't have killed him last Wednesday! I haven't the money! Look! It isn't here!"

He tore the covers off him and began ripping up the bed in a paroxysm of maniacal frenzy, crying out all the while against the secret police and the false accusations against him. Vincent did not know what to do. All the other inmates seemed to be sleeping soundly.

Vincent ran to the next bed, slipped aside the curtain and shook the man in it. The fellow opened his eyes and stared at Vincent stupidly.

"Get up and help me quiet him," said Vincent. "I'm afraid he will do himself some harm."

The man in bed began to dribble at the right corner of his mouth. He let out a stream of blubbering, inarticulate sounds.

"Quick," cried Vincent. "It will take two of us to hold him down."

He felt a hand on his shoulder. He whirled about. One of the older men was standing behind him.

"No use bothering with this one," said the man. "He's an

387

idiot. Hasn't uttered a word since he's been here. Come, we'll quiet the boy."

The young blond had dug a hole in the mattress with his fingernails and was crouched on his knees above it, pulling out the straw and stuffing. When he saw Vincent again, he began shouting legal quotations. He beat his hands against Vincent's chest.

"Yes, yes, I killed him! I killed him! But it wasn't for pederasty! I didn't do that, Monsieur Mounet-Sully. Not last Wednesday. It was for his money! Look! I have it! I hid the wallet in the mattress! I'll find it for you! Only make the secret police stop following me! I can go free, even if I did kill him! I'll cite you cases to prove ... Here! I'll dig it out of the mattress!"

"Take his other arm," said the old man to Vincent.

They held the boy down on the bed, but his ravings rang out for over an hour. Finally, exhausted, his words sank to a jarred mumbling and he dropped off in a feverish sleep. The older man came around to Vincent's side.

"The boy was studying for the bar," he said. "He overworked his brain. These attacks come on about every ten days. He never hurts anyone. Good night to you, Monsieur."

The older man returned to his bed and promptly fell asleep. Vincent went once again to the window that overlooked the valley. It was still a long time before sunrise and nothing was visible but the morning star. He remembered the painting Daubigny had made of the morning star, expressing all the vast peace and majesty of the universe ... and all the feeling of heartbreak for the puny individual who stood below, gazing at it.

2

The next morning after breakfast the men went out into the garden. Beyond the far wall could be seen the ridge of desolate, barren hills, dead since the Romans first crossed them. Vincent watched the inmates play lackadaisically at bowls. He sat on a stone bench and gazed at the thick trees covered with ivy, then at the ground dotted with periwinkle. The sisters, of the order of St. Joseph d'Aubenas, passed on their way to the old Roman chapel, mouse-like figures in black and white, their eyes drawn deep into their heads, fingering their beads and mumbling the morning prayers.

After an hour at mute bowls, the men returned to the cool of their ward. They sat about the unlit stove. Their utter idleness appalled Vincent. He could not understand why they did not even have an old newspaper to read.

When he could bear it no longer, he went again into the garden and walked about. Even the sun at St. Paul seemed to be moribund.

The buildings of the old monastery had been put up in the conventional quadrangle; on the north was the ward of the third-class patients; on the east Doctor Peyron's house, the chapel, and a tenth century cloister; on the south the buildings of the first and second-class inmates; and on the west, the courtyard of the dangerous lunatics, and a long, dead-clay wall. The locked and barred gate was the only exit. The walls were twelve feet high, smooth and unscaleable.

Vincent returned to a stone bench near a wild rose bush and sat down. He tried to reason with himself and get a clear idea of why he had come to St. Paul. A terrible dismay and horror seized him and prevented him from thinking. In his heart he could find neither hope nor desire.

He stumbled towards his quarters. The moment he entered the portico of the building he heard the queer howling of a dog. Before he reached the door of the ward, the noise had changed from the howl of a dog to the cry of a wolf.

Vincent walked down the length of the ward. In the far corner, his face to the wall, he saw the old man of the night before. The man's face was raised to the ceiling. He was howling with all the strength of his lungs, a bestial look on his face. The cry of the wolf gave way to some strange jungle call. The mournful sound of it flooded the room.

"What sort of a menagerie am I a prisoner in?" Vincent demanded of himself.

The men about the stove paid no attention. The wails of the animal in the corner rose to a pitch of despair.

"I must do something for him," said Vincent, aloud.

The blond boy stopped him.

"It is better to leave him alone," he said. "If you speak to him, he will fly into a rage. It will be over in a few hours."

The walls of the monastery were thick, but all through lunch Vincent could hear the changing cries of the afflicted one straining through the vast silence. He spent the afternoon in a far corner of the garden, trying to escape the frenetic wails.

That night at supper, a young man whose left side was paralyzed, grabbed up a knife, sprang to his feet, and held the knife over his heart with his right hand.

"The time has come!" he shouted. "I shall kill myself!"

The man on his right side rose wearily and gripped the paralytic's arm.

"Not today, Raymond," he said. "Today is Sunday."

"Yes, yes, today! I won't live! I refuse to live! Let go of my arm! I want to kill myself!"

"Tomorrow, Raymond, tomorrow. This isn't the right day."

"Let go of my arm! I shall plunge this knife into my heart! I tell you, I've got to kill myself!"

"I know, I know, but not now. Not now."

He took the knife from Raymond's hand and led him, weeping in a rage of impotence, back to the ward.

Vincent turned to the man next to him, whose red-rimmed eyes were watching his trembling fingers anxiously as he tried to carry the soup to his mouth.

"What is the matter with him?" he asked.

The syphilitic lowered his spoon and said, "Not a day has passed for a whole year that Raymond has not tried to commit suicide."

"Why does he try it here?" asked Vincent. "Why doesn't he steal the knife and kill himself when everyone has gone to sleep?"

"Perhaps he does not wish to die, Monsieur."

While Vincent was watching them play bowls the following morning, one of the men suddenly fell to the ground and went into a convulsive paroxysm.

"Quick. It's his epileptic fit," shouted someone.

"On his arms and legs."

It took four of them to hold his arms and legs. The writhing epileptic seemed to have the strength of a dozen men. The young blond reached into his pocket, pulled out a spoon, and thrust it between the prostrate man's teeth.

"Here, hold his head," he cried to Vincent.

The epileptic went through a rising and falling series of convulsions, their peaks mounting ever higher and higher. His eyes rolled in their sockets and the foam lathered from the corners of his mouth.

"Why do you hold that spoon in his mouth?" grunted Vincent.

"So he won't bite his tongue."

After a half hour the shuddering man sank into unconsciousness. Vincent and two of the others carried him to his bed. That was the end of the affair; no one mentioned it again.

By the end of a fortnight, Vincent had seen every one of his eleven companions go through his own particular form of insanity: the noisy maniac who tore his clothes off his body and smashed everything in sight; the man who howled like an animal; the two syphilitics; the suicide monomaniac; the paralytics who suffered from excess of fury and exaltation; the epileptic; the lymphomaniac with a persecution mania; the young blond who was being pursued by secret police.

Not a day went by without some one of them having a seizure; not a day passed but that Vincent was called to calm some momentary maniac. The third-class patients had to be each other's doctors and nurses. Peyron looked in but once a week, and the guardians bothered only with the first and second-class residents. The men stayed close together, helped each other in the moments of affliction, and had endless patience; each of them knew that his turn was coming again, soon, and that he would need the help and forbearance of his neighbours.

It was a fraternity of *fous*.

Vincent was glad that he had come. By seeing the truth about the life of madmen he slowly lost the vague dread, the fear of insanity. Bit by bit he came to consider madness as a disease like any other. By the third week he found his comates no more frightening than if they had been stricken by consumption or cancer.

He often sat and chatted with the idiot. The idiot could only answer with incoherent sounds, but Vincent felt that the fellow understood him and was pleased to be talking. The sisters never spoke to the men unless it was imperative. Vincent's portion of rational intercourse each week consisted of his five minute conversation with Doctor Peyron.

"Tell me, Doctor," he said, "why do the men never talk to each other? Some of them seem intelligent enough, when they are well."

"They can't talk, Vincent, for the minute they begin to talk, they argue, get excited, and bring a seizure upon themselves. So they've learned that the only way they can live is by remaining utterly quiet."

"They might just as well be dead, mightn't they?"

Peyron shrugged. "That, my dear Vincent, is a matter of opinion."

"But why don't they at least read? I should think that books . . ."

"Reading starts their minds churning, Vincent, and the first thing we know, they have a violent attack. No, my friend, they must inhabit the closed world of their own. There is no need to feel sorry for them. Don't you remember what Dryden said? 'There is pleasure, sure, in being mad, which none but madmen know.' "

A month passed. Not once did Vincent have the least desire to be elsewhere. Nor did he notice in any of the others a definite wish to get away. He knew this came from the feeling that they were all too thoroughly shattered for the life outside.

And over the ward hung the fetid odour of decaying men.

Vincent held the spirit of himself together rigidly, against that day when the desire and strength to paint should return to him. His fellow inmates vegetated in idleness, thinking only of their three meals a day. In order to discipline himself against this surrender, Vincent refused to eat any of the stale and slightly spoiled food. He swallowed only a little black bread and soup. Theo sent him a one-volume edition of Shakespeare; he read "Richard II," "Henry IV," and "Henry V," projecting his mind to other days and other places.

He fought valiantly to keep grief from gathering in his heart like water in a swamp.

Theo was now married. He and his wife Johanna wrote to Vincent often. Theo's health was poor. Vincent worried more about his brother than he did about himself. He begged Johanna to give Theo wholesome Dutch food once more, after ten years of restaurant fare.

Vincent knew that work distracted him infinitely better than anything else, and that if he could only throw himself into it with all his strength, it might possibly be the best remedy. The men in the ward had nothing to save them from a rotting death; he had his painting which would take him out of the asylum a well and happy man.

At the end of the sixth week, Doctor Peyron gave Vincent a little room for a studio. It was done in greenish-grey paper, and had two curtains of sea-green with a design of very pale roses. The curtains, and an old armchair covered with an upholstery splashed like a Monticelli, had been left behind by one of the wealthier inmates who had died. The room looked out on a slanting cornfield, and freedom. There were thick black bars across the window.

Vincent promptly painted the landscape that he saw from the window. In the foreground was a field of corn ruined and dashed to the ground after a storm. A boundary wall ran down a slope, and beyond the grey foliage of a few olive trees were some huts and hills. At the top of the canvas Vincent put a great grey and white cloud drowned in the azure.

He returned to the ward at supper time, exultant. His power had not left him. He had come face to face with nature again. The feeling for work had held him and forced him to create.

The insane asylum could not kill him now. He was on the road to recovery. In a few months he would be out. He would be free to return to Paris and his old friends. Life was beginning for him once more. He wrote Theo a long, tumultuous letter, with demands for pigments, canvas, brushes, and interesting books.

The next morning the sun came out, yellow and hot. The cicadas in the garden began to sing with a harsh cry, ten times stronger than that of the crickets. Vincent took his easel out and painted the pine trees, the bushes and the walks. His ward mates came to look over his shoulder, but remained perfectly silent and respectful.

"They have better manners than the good people of Arles," murmured Vincent to himself.

Late that afternoon he went to see Doctor Peyron. "I am feeling perfectly well, Doctor, and I should like your permission to go outside the grounds to paint."

"Yes, you are certainly looking better, Vincent. The baths and quiet have helped you. But don't you think it a bit dangerous to go out so soon?"

"Dangerous? Why, no. How?"

"Suppose you . . . had an attack . . . in the fields . . . ?"

Vincent laughed. "No more attacks for me. Doctor. I'm through with them. I feel better than I did before they began."

"No, Vincent, I'm afraid . . ."

"Please, Doctor. If I can go wherever I wish, and paint the things I love, don't you see how much happier I will be?"

"Well, if work is what you need . . ."

And so the gate was unlocked for Vincent. He loaded his easel on his back and went in search of pictures. He spent whole days in the hills behind the asylum. The cypress trees about St. Remy began to occupy his thoughts. He wanted to make something of them, like his sunflower canvases. It astonished him that they had not yet been painted as he saw them. He found them as beautiful in line and proportion as an Egyptian obelisk; splashes of black in a sunny landscape.

The old habits of the Arlesian days returned. Each morning at sunrise he trudged out with a blank canvas; each sundown saw it transcribed from nature. If there was any lessening of his power and ability, he could not perceive it. Every day he felt stronger, more sensitive, surer of himself.

Now that he was again master of his own destiny, he no longer feared eating at the asylum board. He devoured his food avidly, even the cockroach soup. He needed food for his working strength. He had nothing to fear now. He was in complete control of himself.

When he had been in the asylum three months, he found a cypress motif that lifted him out of his troubles, beyond all the suffering he had endured. The trees were massive. The foreground was low with brambles and brushwood. Behind were some violet hills, a green and rose sky with a decrescent moon. He painted the clump of brambles in the foreground very thick, with touches of yellow, violet, and green. When he looked at his canvas that night he knew that he had come up out of the pit and was standing once more on solid earth, his face to the sun.

In his overwhelming joy he saw himself once again a free man.

Theo sent some extra money, so Vincent secured permission to go to Arles and recover his pictures. The people in the Place Lamartine were courteous to him, but the sight of the yellow house made him very ill. He thought he was going to faint. Instead of visiting Roulin and Doctor Rey, as he had planned, he went in search of the landlord, who had his pictures.

Vincent did not return to the asylum that night as he had promised. The following day he was found between Tarascon and St. Remy, lying face downward in a ditch.

3

Fever clouded his mind for three weeks. The men in the ward, whom he had pitied because their attacks were recurrent, were very patient with him. When he recovered sufficiently to realize what had happened, he kept repeating to himself.

"It is abominable. It is abominable!"

Toward the end of the third week, when he was beginning to walk about the barren, corridor-like room for a little exercise, the sisters brought in a new patient. He allowed himself to be led to his bed very docilely, but once the sisters were gone, he broke into a violent rage. He ripped all the clothes off his body and tore them to shreds, shouting at the top of his voice all the time. He clawed his bed to pieces, smashed the box nailed to the wall, pulled down the curtains, broke the frame, and kicked his valise into a shapeless mass.

The inmates never touched a newcomer. At length two guardians came and hauled the maniac away. He was locked in a cell down the corridor. He howled like a savage beast for two weeks. Vincent heard him night and day. Then the cries ceased altogether. Vincent watched the guardians bury the man in the little cemetery behind the chapel.

A terrible fit of depression came over Vincent. The more his health returned to normal, the more his brain could reason in cold blood, the more foolish it seemed to him to go on painting when it cost so much and brought in nothing. And yet if he did not work, he could not live.

Doctor Peyron gave him some meat and wine from his own table, but refused to let him go near his studio. Vincent did not mind so long as he was convalescing, but when his strength returned and he found himself condemned to the intolerable idleness of his companions, he revolted.

"Doctor Peyron," he said, "my work is necessary for me to recover. If you make me sit about in idleness, like those madmen, I shall become one of them."

"I know, Vincent, but it was working so hard that brought on your attack. I must keep you from that excitement."

"No, Doctor, it wasn't work. It was going to Arles that did it. I no sooner saw the Place Lamartine and the yellow house, than I became ill. But if I never go back there again, I'll never have another attack. Please let me go to my studio."

"I am unwilling to take the responsibility in this matter. I shall write to your brother. If he gives his consent, then we'll let you work again."

The return letter from Theo, urging Doctor Peyron to allow Vincent to paint, brought a revivifying piece of news. Theo was to become a father. The news made Vincent feel as happy and strong as he had before the last attack. He sat down immediately and wrote Theo a glowing letter.

"Do you know what I hope, Theo? It is that a family will be for you what nature, the clods of earth, the grass, the yellow corn, and the peasants are for me. The baby that Johanna is designing for you will give you a grip on reality that is otherwise impossible in a large city. Now certainly you are yourself deep in nature, since you say that Johanna already feels her child quicken."

Once again he went to his studio and painted the scene from the barred window, the cornfield with a little reaper and a big sun. The canvas was all yellow except for the wall, which ran down the slope at a steep, sharp angle, and the background of violet-tinted hills.

Dr. Peyron acquiesced in Theo's wish, and allowed Vincent to go outside the grounds to work. He painted the cypresses which flowed up out of the ground and poured into the yellow roof of sun. He did a canvas of women gathering olives; the soil violet, and farther off yellow ochre; the trees with bronze trunks and green-grey foliage; the sky and the three figures of the women a deep rose.

On his way to work he would stop and talk to the men labouring in the fields. In his own mind he considered himself below these peasants.

"You see," he told one of them, "I plough on my canvases, just as you plough in your fields."

The late Provençal autumn came to a focal point of beauty. The earth brought forth all its violets; the burnt-up grass flamed about the little rose flowers in the garden; the green skies contrasted with the varying shades of yellow foliage.

And with the late autumn came Vincent's full strength. He saw that his work was getting on. Good ideas began to spring anew in his mind; he was happy in letting them develop. Because of his long stay he began to feel the country keenly. It was very different in character from Arles. Most of the mistral was stopped by the hills which overlooked the valley. The sun was far less blinding. Now that he had come to understand the country about St. Remy, he did not want to leave the asylum. In the early months of his stay he had prayed that the year would pass without breaking his mind. Now that he was wrapped in his work, he did not know whether he was staying in a hospital or a hotel. Although he felt entirely well, he thought it foolish to move to some chance place and spend another six months getting acquainted with strange terrain.

Letters from Paris kept him in high spirits. Theo's wife was cooking at home for him, and his health was recovering rapidly. Johanna was carrying the baby without difficulty. And every week Theo sent tobacco, chocolate, paints, books, and a ten or twenty franc note.

The memory of his attack after the Arlesian trip vanished from Vincent's mind. Again and again he reassured himself that if he had never gone back to that cursed city, he would have had six months of normal health to his credit. When his studies of the cypresses and olive groves dried, he washed them with water and a little wine to take away the oil in the *pâte*, then sent them to Theo. He received Theo's announcement that he was exhibiting a number of his canvases at the Independents with disappointment, for he felt that he had not yet done his best work. He wanted to hold off until he had perfected his technique.

Letters from Theo assured him that his work was going ahead at a remarkable pace. He decided that when his year was up at the asylum, he would take a house in the village of St. Remy and continue his painting of the Southland. He felt once again the exultant joy that had been his in the Arlesian days before Gauguin arrived, when he was painting his sunflower panels.

One afternoon, when he was working calmly in the fields, his mind began to wander. Late that night the guardians of the asylum found him, several kilometres away from his easel. His body was wrapped about the trunk of a cypress.

4

By the end of the fifth day his senses returned to normal. What hurt him most deeply was the way his fellow inmates accepted the seizure as being inevitable.

Winter came on. Vincent could not find the will to get out of bed. The stove in the centre of the ward now glowed brightly. The men sat about it in frozen silence from morning until night. The windows of the ward were small and high, letting in very little light. The stove heated and spread the thick odour of decay. The sisters, withdrawn even farther into their black capes and hoods, went about mumbling prayers and fingering their crosses. The barren hills in the background stood out like death heads.

Vincent lay awake in his slanting bed. What was it that Scheveningen picture of Mauve's had taught him? *"Savoir souffrir sans se plaindre."* Learn to suffer without complaint, to look on pain without repugnance ... yes, but in that he ran the risk of vertigo. If he gave in to that pain, that desolation, it would kill him. There came a time in every man's life when it was necessary to fling off suffering as though it were a filthy cloak.

Days passed, each exactly like the last. His mind was barren of ideas and hope. He heard the sisters discuss his work; they wondered if he painted because he was crazy, or if he was crazy because he painted.

The idiot sat by his bedside and blubbered to him for hours. Vincent felt a warmth in the man's friendliness and did not chase him away. Often he talked to the idiot, for there was no one else who would listen.

"They think my work has driven me crazy," he said to the man one day, as two of the sisters passed. "I know that at the bottom it is fairly true that a painter is a man too much absorbed by what his eyes see, and is not sufficiently master of the rest of his life. But does that make him unfit to live in this world?"

The idiot only drooled.

It was a line from Delacroix's book that finally gave him the strength to get out of bed. "I discovered painting," said Delacroix, "when I no longer had teeth or breath."

For several weeks he did not even have the desire to go into the garden. He sat in the ward near the stove, reading the books that Theo sent from Paris. When one of his neighbours was taken with an attack, he did not look up or get out of his chair. Insanity had become sanity; the abnormal had become the normal. It was so long since he had lived with rational people that he no longer looked upon his fellow inmates as irrational.

"I'm sorry, Vincent," said Doctor Peyron, "but I cannot give you permission to leave the grounds again. In the future you must stay within the walls."

"You will permit me to work in my studio?"

"I advise you against it."

"Would you prefer me to commit suicide, Doctor?"

"Very well, work in your studio. But only for a few hours a day."

Even the sight of his easel and brushes could not destroy Vincent's lethargy. He sat in the Monticelli armchair and stared through the iron bars at the barren cornfields.

A few days later he was summoned to Doctor Peyron's office to sign for a registered letter. When he slit open the envelope, he found a cheque for four hundred francs made out in his name. It was the largest sum of money he had ever possessed at one time. He wondered what on earth Theo had sent it for.

My Dear Vincent:

At last! One of your canvases has been bought for four hundred francs! It was *Red Vineyard*, the one you painted at Arles last spring. It was bought by Anna Bock, sister of the Dutch painter.

Congratulations, old boy! Soon we'll be selling you all over Europe! Use this money to come back to Paris, if Doctor Peyron agrees.

I have recently met a delightful man, Doctor Gachet, who has a home in Auvers-sur-l'Oise, just an hour from Paris. Every important painter since Daubigny has worked in his home. He claims he understands your case thoroughly, and that any time you want to come to Auvers, he will take care of you.

I'll write again tomorrow
Theo

Vincent showed Doctor Peyron and his wife the letter. Peyron read it thoughtfully, then fingered the cheque. He contratulated Vincent on his good fortune. Vincent walked down the path, the soft stuff of his brain springing to firm life again with feverish activity. Half-way across the garden he saw that he had taken the cheque with him but left Theo's letter in the Doctor's office. He turned and walked back quickly.

He was about to knock on the door when he heard his name mentioned inside. He hesitated for a moment, irresolute.

"Then why do you suppose he did it?" demanded Madame Peyron.

"Perhaps he thought it would be good for his brother."

"But if he can't afford the money . . .?"

"I suppose he thought it was worth it, to bring Vincent back to normal."

"Then you don't think there's any chance of it being the truth?"

"My dear Marie, how could there be? This woman is supposed to be the sister of an artist. How in the world could a person with any perception ...?"

Vincent walked away.

At supper he received a wire from Theo.

NAMED THE BOY AFTER YOU. JOHANNA AND VINCENT FEELING FINE.

The sale of his picture and the marvellous news from Theo made Vincent a well man over night. In the morning he went early to his studio, cleaned his brushes, sorted the canvases and studies that were leaning against the wall.

"If Delacroix can discover painting when he no longer has teeth or breath I can discover it when I no longer have teeth or wits."

He threw himself into his work with a dumb fury. He copied *The Good Samaritan* after Delacroix, *The Sower* and *The Digger* after Millet. He was determined to take his recent misfortune with a sort of northern phlegm. The life of art was shattering; he had known that when he began. Then why should he take to complaining at this late date?

Exactly two weeks to the day after receiving the four hundred franc cheque, he found in the mail a copy of the January issue of the *Mercure de France*. He noticed that Theo had checked an article on the title page called "Les Isolées."

That which characterizes all the work of Vincent Van Gogh (he read) is the excess of force, and the violence in expression. In his categorical affirmative of the essential character of things, in his often rash simplification of form, in his insolent desire to look at the sun face to face, in the passion of his drawing and colour, their lies revealed a powerful one, a male, a darer who is sometimes brutal, sometimes ingenuously delicate.

Vincent Van Gogh is of the sublime line of Frans Hals. His realism goes beyond the truth of those great little burghers of Holland, so healthy in body, so well balanced in mind, who were his ancestors. What marks his canvases is his conscientious study of character, his continuous search for the quintessence of each object, his deep and almost childlike love of nature and truth.

400

This robust and true artist with an illumined soul, will he ever know the joys of being rehabilitated by the public? I do not think so. He is too simple, and at the same time too subtle, for our contemporary bourgeois spirit. He will never be altogether understood except by his brother artists.

G. Albert Aurier

Vincent did not show the article to Doctor Peyron.

All his strength and lust for life came back to him. He painted a picture of the ward in which he slept, painted the superintendent of the buildings, and then his wife, made more copies after Millet and Delacroix, filled his nights and days with tumultuous labour.

By going carefully over the history of his illness, he saw clearly that his seizures were cyclical in nature, coming every three months. Very well, if he knew when they were to come, he would be able to take care of himself. When his next attack was due, he would stop work, go to bed, and prepare himself for a brief indisposition. And after a few days he would be up again, just as though he had been suffering from nothing more than a slight cold.

The only thing that now disturbed him at the asylum was the intense religious nature of the place. It seemed to him that with the coming of the dark winter, the sisters had suffered a hysterical seizure. Sometimes, as he watched them mumble their prayers, kiss their crosses, finger their beads, walk with their eyes glued to their Bibles, tiptoe into the chapel for prayer and services five and six times a day, he had difficulty in determining who were the patients in this insane asylum, and who the attendants. Since his days in the Borinage he had had a horror of all religious exaggerations. At moments he found the sisters' aberrations preying upon his mind. He drove himself more passionately into his work, trying to wipe the image of the black-hooded, black-caped creatures from his mind.

He gave himself forty-eight hours leeway before the end of the third month, going to bed in perfect health and spirits. He pulled the curtains of the bed about him so that the sisters, shaken by their ever rising religious exaltation, could not destroy his peace of mind.

The day arrived when his seizure was due. Vincent awaited it eagerly, almost with affection. The hours dragged by. Nothing happened. He was surprised, then disappointed. The

401

second day passed. He still felt completely normal. When the third day drew to an end without mishap, he had to laugh at himself.

"I've been a fool. I've seen the last of those attacks, after all. Doctor Peyron was wrong. From now on I don't have to be afraid. I've been wasting my time, lying in bed this way. Tomorrow morning I'm going to get up and work."

In the dead of the night, when everyone was asleep, he climbed quietly out of bed. He walked down the stone floored ward in his bare feet. He made his way in the dark to the cellar where the coal was stored. He fell to his knees, scooped up a handful of coal-dust, and smeared it over his face.

"You see, Madame Denis? They accept me now. They know I am one of them. They did not trust me before, but now I am a *gueule noire*. The miners will let me bring them the Word of God."

The guardians found him there shortly after dawn. He was whispering chaotic prayers, repeating broken bits of scripture, answering the voices which were pouring queer tales into his ear.

His religious hallucinations continued for several days. When he came back to his senses, he asked one of the sisters to send for Doctor Peyron.

"I think I would have avoided this attack, Doctor," he said, "if it had not been for all the religious hysteria I am exposed to."

Doctor Peyron shrugged, leaned against the bed, and pulled Vincent's curtains behind him.

"What can I do, Vincent? It is just so, every winter. I do not approve but neither can I interfere. The sisters do good work, in spite of all."

"Be that as it may," said Vincent, "it is hard enough to keep sane among all the madmen, without being exposed to religious insanity in the bargain. I had passed the time for my attack . . ."

"Vincent, do not delude yourself. That attack had to come. Your nervous system works itself up to a crisis every three months. If your hallucinations had not been religious, they would have been of some other nature."

"If I have another, Doctor, I shall ask my brother to take me away."

"As you say, Vincent."

He returned to work in his studio on the first real day of

spring. He painted the scene out of his window again, a field of yellow stubble being ploughed. He contrasted the violet-tinted ploughed earth with the strips of yellow stubble against the background of hills. The almond trees began to blossom everywhere, and once again the sky became pale lemon at sunset.

The eternal re-creation of nature brought forth no new life in Vincent. For the first time since he had grown accustomed to his companions, their mad babblings and periodic seizures tore his nerves and ripped into his vitals. Nor was there any escape from the mouse-like, praying creatures in black and white. The very sight of them sent shivers of apprehension through Vincent.

"Theo," he wrote to his brother, "it would make me unhappy to leave St. Remy; there is much good work to be done here yet. But if I have another attack of a religious nature, it will be the fault of the asylum, and not my nerves. It will only take two or three more of them to kill me.

"Be prepared. If I have another religious seizure, I shall leave for Paris the instant I am able to get out of bed. Perhaps it would be best for me to come north again, where one can rely on a certain amount of sanity.

"What about this Doctor Gachet of yours? Will he take a personal interest in my case?"

Theo replied that he had spoken to Doctor Gachet again, and shown him some of Vincent's canvases. Doctor Gachet was eager to have Vincent come to Auvers and paint in his house.

"He is a specialist, Vincent, not only in nervous diseases, but in painters. I am convinced that you could not be in better hands. Any time you wish to come, just wire me and I will catch the first train for St. Remy."

The heat of early spring came on. The cicadas began to sing in the garden. Vincent painted the portico of the third-class ward, the walks and trees in the gardens, his own portrait in the mirror. He worked with one eye on his canvas and the other on the calendar.

His next seizure was due in May.

He heard voices shouting at him in the empty corridors. He answered them, and the echo of his own voice came back like the malignant call of fate. This time they found him in the chapel, unconscious. It was the middle of May before he recovered from the religious hallucinations that went twisting through his brain.

Theo insisted upon coming to St. Remy to get him. Vincent wanted to make the trip alone, with one of the guardians putting him on the train at Tarascon.

Dear Theo:

I am not an invalid, nor yet a dangerous beast. Let me prove to both you and myself that I am a normal being. If I can wrench myself away from this asylum with my own strength, and take up a new life in Auvers, perhaps I shall be able to conquer this malady of mine.

I give myself one more chance. Away from this *maison des fous*, I feel confident that I can become again a rational person. From what you write me, Auvers will be quiet and beautiful. If I live carefully, under the eyes of Doctor Gachet, I am convinced that I will conquer my disease.

I shall wire you when my train leaves Tarascon. Meet me at the Gare de Lyon. I want to leave here Saturday, so that I can spend Sunday at home with you and Johanna and the little one.

BOOK EIGHT

AUVERS

1

Theo could not sleep all that night for anxiety. He left for the Gare de Lyon two hours before Vincent's train could possibly arrive. Johanna had to stay home with the baby. She stood on the terrace of their fourth floor apartment on the Cité Pigalle and peered through the leaves of the great black tree that covered the front of the house. She eagerly watched the entrance of the Cité Pigalle for a carriage would turn in from the Rue Pigalle.

It was a long distance from the Gare de Lyon to Theo's house. To Johanna it seemed an endless time of waiting. She began to fear that something had happened to Vincent on the train. But at length an open *fiacre* turned in from the Rue Pigalle, two merry faces nodded to her, and two hands waved. She strained to catch a glimpse of Vincent.

The Cité Pigalle was a *rue impasse*, blocked off at the end by a garden court and the jutting corner of a stone house. There were only two long buildings on either side of the prosperous and respectable looking street. Theo lived at number 8, the house nearest the impasse; it was set back from a little garden and had a private *trottoir* all its own. It took the *fiacre* but a few seconds to draw up before the big black tree and the entrance.

Vincent bounded up the stairs with Theo at his heels. Johanna had expected to see an invalid, but the man who flung his arms about her had healthy colour, a smile on his face, and an expression of great resoluteness.

"He seems perfectly well. He looks much stronger than Theo," was her first thought.

But she could not bring herself to look at his ear.

"Well, Theo," exclaimed Vincent, holding Johanna's hand and looking at her approvingly, "you certainly picked yourself a fine wife.

"Thanks, Vincent," laughed Theo.

Theo had chosen in the tradition of his mother. Johanna had the same soft brown eyes as Anna Cornelia, the same tender reaching out in full sympathy and compassion. Already, with her child but a few months old, there was the faint touch of the coming matriarch about her. She had plain, good features, an almost stolid oval face, and a mass of light brown hair combed back simply from a high Dutch brow. Her love for Theo included Vincent.

Theo drew Vincent into the bedroom, where the baby was sleeping in his cradle. The two men looked at the child in silence, tears in their eyes. Johanna sensed that they would like to be alone for a moment; she tiptoed to the door. Just as she put her hand on the knob, Vincent turned smilingly to her and said, pointing to the crocheted cover over the cradle,

"Do not cover him too much with lace, little sister."

Johanna closed the door quietly behind her. Vincent, looking down at the child once more, felt the awful pang of barren men whose flesh leaves no flesh behind, whose death is death eternal.

Theo read his thoughts.

"There is still time for you, Vincent. Some day you will find a wife who will love you and share the hardships of your life."

"Ah no, Theo, it's too late."

"I found a woman only the other day who would be perfect for you."

"Not really! Who was she?"

"She was the girl in 'Terre Vierge,' by Turgenev. Remember her?"

"You mean the one who works with the nihilists, and brings the compromising papers across the frontier?"

"Yes. Your wife would have to be somebody like that, Vincent; somebody who had gone through life's misery to the very bottom ..."

"... And what would she want with me? A one-eared man?"

Little Vincent awakened, looked up at them and smiled. Theo lifted the child out of the cradle and placed him in Vincent's arms.

"So soft and warm, like a little puppy," said Vincent, feeling the baby against his heart.

"Here, clumsy, you don't hold a baby like that."

"I'm afraid I'm more at home holding a paint brush."

Theo took the child and held him against his shoulder, his head touching the baby's brown curls. To Vincent they looked as though they had been carved out of the same stone.

"Well, Theo boy," he said resignedly, "each man to his own medium. You create in the living flesh ... and I'll create in paint."

"Just so, Vincent, just so."

A number of Vincent's friends came to Theo's that night to welcome him back. The first arrival was Aurier, a handsome young man with flowing locks and a beard which sprouted out of each side of his chin, but conjured up no hair in the middle. Vincent led him to the bedroom, where Theo had hung a Monticelli bouquet.

"You said in your article, Monsieur Aurier, that I was the sole painter to perceive the chromatism of things with a metallic, gem-like quality. Look at this Monticelli. 'Fada' achieved it years before I even came to Paris."

At the end of an hour Vincent gave up trying to persuade Aurier, and presented him instead with one of the St. Remy cypress canvasses in appreciation for his article.

Toulouse-Lautrec blew in, winded from six flights of stairs, but still as hilarious and ribald as ever.

"Vincent," he exclaimed, while shaking hands, "I passed an undertaker on the stairs. Was he looking for you or me?"

"For you, Lautrec! He couldn't get any business out of me."

"I'll make you a little wager, Vincent. I'll bet your name comes ahead of mine in his little book."

"You're on. What's the stake?"

"Dinner at the Café Athens, and an evening at the Opéra."

"I wish you fellows would make your jokes a trifle less macabre," said Theo, smiling faintly.

A strange man entered the front door, looked at Lautrec, and sank into a chair in a far corner. Everyone waited for Lautrec to present him, but he just went on talking.

"Won't you introduce your friend?" asked Vincent.

"That's not my friend," laughed Lautrec. "That's my keeper."

There was a moment of pained silence.

"Hadn't you heard, Vincent? I was *non compos mentis* for a couple of months. They said it was from too much liquor, so now I'm drinking milk. I'll send you an invitation to my next party. There's a picture on it of me milking a cow from the wrong end!"

Johanna passed out refreshments. Everyone talked at the same time and the air grew thick with tobacco smoke. It reminded Vincent of the old Paris days. "How is Georges Seurat getting along?" Vincent asked Lautrec.

"Georges! Mean to tell me you don't know about him?"

"Theo didn't write anything," said Vincent. "What is it?"

"Georges is dying of consumption. The doctor says he won't last beyond his thirty-first birthday."

"Consumption! Why, Georges was strong and healthy. How in the ...?"

"Overwork, Vincent," said Theo. "It's been two years since you've seen him? Georges drove himself like a demon. Slept two and three hours a day, and worked himself furiously all the rest of the time. Even that good old mother of his couldn't save him."

"So Georges will be going soon," said Vincent, musingly.

Rousseau came in, carrying a bag of home-made cookies for Vincent. Père Tanguy, wearing the same round straw hat, presented Vincent with a Japanese print and a sweet speech about how glad they were to welcome him back to Paris.

At ten o'clock Vincent insisted upon going down and buying a litre of olives. He made everyone eat them, even Lautrec's guardian.

"If you could once see those silver-green olive groves in Provence," he exclaimed, "you would eat olives for the rest of your life."

"Speaking of olive groves, Vincent," said Lautrec, "how did you find the Arlesiennes?"

The following morning Vincent carried the perambulator down to the street for Johanna so that the baby might have his hour of sunshine on the private *trottoir*. Vincent then went back to the apartment and stood about in his shirt sleeves, looking at the walls. They were covered with his pictures. In the dining room over the mantelpiece was the *Potato Eaters*, in the living room the *Landscape from Arles*, and *Night View on the Rhône*, in the bedroom, *Blooming Orchards*. To the despair of Johanna's *femme de ménage*, there were huge piles of unframed canvases under the beds, under the sofa, under the cupboard, and stacked solid in the spare room.

While rummaging for something in Theo's desk, Vincent came across large packages of letters tied with heavy cord. He was amazed to find that they were his own letters. Theo had carefully guarded every line his brother had written to him since that day, twenty years before, when Vincent had left Zundert for Goupils in The Hague. All in all, there were seven hundred letters. Vincent wondered why in the world Theo had saved them.

In another part of the desk he found the drawings that he had been sending to Theo for the past ten years, all ranged neatly in periods; here were the miners and their wives from the Borinage period, leaning over their *terril*; here the diggers and sowers in the fields near Etten; here the old men and women from the Hague, the diggers in the Geest, and the fishermen of Scheveningen; here the potato eaters and weavers of Nuenen; here the restaurants and street scenes of Paris; here the early sunflower and orchard sketches from Arles; and here the garden of the asylum at St. Remy.

"I'm going to have an exhibition all my own!" he exclaimed.

He took all the pictures off the walls, threw down the packages of sketches, and pulled piles of unframed canvases from under every piece of furniture. He sorted them out very carefully into periods. Then he selected the sketches and oils which best caught the spirit of the place in which he had been working. In the foyer, where one entered from the hallway of the house, he pinned up about thirty of his first studies, the

408

Borains coming out of the mines, leaning over their oval stoves, eating supper in their little shacks.

"This is the charcoal room," he announced to himself.

He looked about the rest of the house and decided that the bathroom was the next least important place. He stood on a chair and tacked a row of Etten studies about the four walls in a straight line, studies of the Brabant peasants.

"And this, of course, is the carpenter's pencil room."

His next selection was the kitchen. Here he put up his Hague and Scheveningen sketches, the view from his window over the lumber yard, the sand dunes, the fishing smacks being drawn up on the beach.

"Chamber three," he said; "water-colour room."

In the little spare room he put up his canvas of his friends the De Groots, the *Potato Eaters*; it was the first oil in which he had expressed himself fully. All about it he pinned dozens of studies of the weavers of Nuenen, the peasants in mourning, the graveyard behind his father's church, the slim, tapering steeple.

In his own bedroom he hung the oil paintings from the Paris period, the ones he had put on Theo's walls in the Rue Lepic the night he left for Arles. In the living room he crowded every last blazing Arlesian canvas he could fit on the walls. In Theo's bedroom he put up the pictures he had created while in the asylum at St. Remy.

His job finished, he cleared the floor, put on his hat and coat, walked down the four flights of stairs, and wheeled his namesake in the sunshine of the Cité Pigalle, while Johanna held his arm and chatted with him in Dutch.

Theo swung in from the Rue Pigalle at a little after twelve, waved to them happily, broke into a run, and scooped the baby out of the perambulator with a loving gesture. They left the carriage with the *concierge* and walked up stairs, chatting animatedly. When they came to the front door, Vincent stopped them.

"I'm going to take you to a Van Gogh exhibition, Theo and Jo," he said. "So steel yourself for the ordeal."

"An exhibit, Vincent?" asked Theo. "Where?"

"Just shut your eyes," said Vincent.

He threw the door open and the three Van Goghs stepped into the foyer. Theo and Johanna gazed about, stunned.

"When I was living in Etten," said Vincent, "father once remarked that good could never grow out of bad. I replied that not only it could, but that in art it must. If you will follow me, my dear brother and sister, I will show you the story of a man who began crudely, like an awkward child, and after ten years of constant labour, arrived at ... but you shall decide that for yourselves."

He led them, in the proper chronological sequence, from room to room. They stood like three visitors in an art gallery, looking at this work which was a man's life. They felt the slow, painful growth of the artist, the fumbling toward maturity of expression, the upheaval that had taken place in Paris, the passionate outburst of his powerful voice in Arles, which caught up all the strands of his years of labour ... and then ... the smash ... the St. Remy canvases ... the crucial striving to keep up to the blaze of creation, and the falling slowly away ... falling ... falling ... falling ...

They looked at the exhibit through the eyes of casual strangers. Before them they saw, in a brief half hour, the recapitulation of one man's stay on earth.

Johanna served a typical Brabant lunch. Vincent was happy just to taste Dutch food once again. After she had cleared away, the two men lit their pipes and chatted.

"You must be very careful to do everything Doctor Gachet tells you, Vincent."

"Yes, Theo, I will."

"Because, you see, he's a specialist in nervous diseases. If you carry out his instructions, you are sure to recover."

"I promise."

"Gachet paints, too. He exhibits each year with the Independents under the name of P. Van Ryssel."

"Is his work good, Theo?"

"No, I shouldn't say so. But he's one of those men who have a genius for recognizing genius. He came to Paris at the age of twenty to study medicine, and became friends with Courbet, Murger, Champfleury, and Proudhon. He used to frequent the café La Nouvelle Athens, and soon was intimate with Manet, Renoir, Degas, Durante, and Claude Monet. Daubigny and Daumier painted in his house years before there even was such a thing as Impressionism."

"You don't say!"

"Nearly everything he has was painted either in his garden or his living room. Pissarro, Guillaumin, Sisley, Delacroix, they've all gone out to work with Gachet in Auvers. You'll find canvases of Cezanne, Lautrec, and Seurat on the walls, too. I tell you, Vincent, there hasn't been an important painter since the middle of the century who wasn't Doctor Gachet's friend."

"Whoa! Wait a minute, Theo, you're frightening me. I don't belong in such illustrious company. Has he seen any of my work yet?"

"You idiot, why do you suppose he's so eager to have you come to Auvers?"

"Blessed if I know."

"He thought your Arlesian night scenes in the last Independents the best canvases in the whole show. I swear to you, when I showed him the sunflower panels you painted for Gauguin and the yellow house, the tears came to his eyes. He turned to me and said, 'Monsieur Van Gogh, your brother is a great artist. There has never been anything like the yellow of these sunflowers before in the history of art. These canvases alone, Monsieur, will make your brother immortal.'"

Vincent scratched his head and grinned.

"Well," he said, "if Doctor Gachet feels that way about my sunflowers, he and I shall get along together."

2

Doctor Gachet was down at the station to meet Theo and Vincent. He was a nervous, excited, jumpy little man with an eager melancholy in his eyes. He wrung Vincent's hand warmly.

"Yes, yes, you will find this a real painter's village. You will like it here. I see you have brought your easel. Have you enough paints? You must begin work immediately. You will have dinner with me at my house this afternoon, yes? Have you brought some of your new canvases? You won't find that Arlesian yellow here, I'm afraid, but there are other things, yes, yes, you will find other things. You must come to my house to paint. I will give you vases and tables that have been painted by everyone from Daubigny to Lautrec. How do you feel? You look well. Do you think you will like it here? Yes, yes, we will take care of you. We'll make a healthy man out of you!"

From the station platform Vincent looked over a patch of trees to where the green Oise wound through the fertile valley. He ran a little bit to one side to get a full view. Theo spoke in a low tone to Doctor Gachet.

"I beg of you, watch my brother carefully," he said. "If you see any symptoms of his trouble coming, telegraph to me at once. I must be with him when he . . . he must not be allowed to . . . there are people who say that . . ."

"Tut! Tut!" interrupted Doctor Gachet, dancing from one foot to the other and rubbing his little goatee vigorously with his index finger. "Of course he's crazy. But what would you? All artists are crazy. That's the best thing about them. I love them that way. I sometimes wish I could be crazy myself! 'No excellent soul is exempt from a mixture of madness!' Do you know who said that? Aristotle, that's who."

"I know, Doctor," said Theo, "but he is a young man, only thirty-seven. The best part of life is still before him."

Doctor Gachet snatched off his funny white cap and ran his hand through his hair many times, with no apparent purpose.

"Leave him to me. I know how to handle painters. I will make a well man of him in a month. I'll set him to work. That will cure him. I'll make him paint my portrait. Right away. This afternoon. I'll get his mind off his illness, all right."

Vincent came back, drawing big breaths of pure country air.

"You ought to bring Jo and the little one out here, Theo. It's a crime to raise children in the city."

"Yes, yes, you must come on a Sunday and spend the whole day with us," cried Gachet.

"Thank you. I would like that very much. Here comes my train. Good-bye, Doctor Gachet; thank you for taking care of my brother. Vincent, write to me every day."

Doctor Gachet had a habit of holding people at the elbow and propelling them forward in the direction he wished to go. He pushed Vincent ahead of him, kept up a nervous flow of talk in a high voice, scrambled up his conversation, answered his own questions, and deluged Vincent in a sputtering monologue.

"That's the road to the village," he said, "that long one, straight ahead. But come, I'll take you up this hill and give you a real view. You don't mind walking with the easel on your back? That's the Catholic church on the left. Have you noticed that the Catholics always build their churches on a hill, so that people will look up to them? Dear, dear, I must be getting old; this grade seems steeper every year. Those are lovely cornfields, aren't they? Auvers is surrounded by them. You must come and paint this field some time. Of course it's not as yellow as the Provençal . . . yes, that's the cemetery on the right ... we put it up here on the crest of the hill, overlooking the river and the valley ... do you think it makes much difference to dead people where they lie? ... we gave them the loveliest spot in the whole Oise valley ... shall we go in? ... you get the clearest view of the river from inside ... we'll be able to see almost to Pointoise ... yes, the gate is open, just push it ... that's right ... now isn't this pleasant? ... we built the walls to keep the wind out ... we bury Catholics and Protestants alike here ..."

Vincent slipped the easel off his back and walked a little ahead of Doctor Gachet to escape the flow of words. The cemetery, which had been laid at the very crest of the hill, was a neat square in shape. Part of it ran downward on the slope. Vincent went to the back wall, from where he could see the whole Oise valley flowing beneath him. The cool green river wound its way gracefully between banks of brilliant verdure. To his right he saw the thatched roofs of the village, and just a short distance beyond, another slope on the top of which was a chateau. The cemetery was full of clean May sunshine and early spring flowers. It was roofed by a delicate blue sky. The complete and beautiful quiet was almost the quiet from beyond the grave.

"You know, Doctor Gachet," said Vincent, "it did me good to go south. Now I see the North better. Look how much violet there is on the far river bank, where the sun hasn't struck the green yet."

"Yes, yes, violet, violet, that's just what it is, vio ..."

"And how sane," murmured Vincent. "How calm and restful."

They wound down the hill again, past the cornfields and the church, and took the straight road on their right to the heart of the village.

"I regret I cannot keep you at my house," said Doctor Gachet, "but alas! we have no room. I will take you to a good inn, and every day you will come to my house to paint, and make yourself at home."

The doctor took Vincent by the elbow and propelled him beyond the Mairie, down almost to the river bank, where there was a summer inn. Gachet spoke to the proprietor, who agreed to give Vincent room and board for six francs a day.

"I will give you a chance to get settled now," cried Gachet. "But mind you come to dinner at one o'clock. And bring your

413

easel. You must do my portrait. And let me see some of your new canvases. We will have a grand chat, yes?"

As soon as the doctor was out of sight, Vincent picked up his belongings and stalked out the front door.

"Wait a minute," said the proprietor. "Where are you going?"

"I am a labourer," replied Vincent, "not a capitalist. I cannot pay your six francs a day."

He walked back to the Place and found a little café exactly opposite the Mairie, called Ravoux's, where he could get room and board for three francs fifty a day.

Ravoux's café was the meeting place of the peasants and labourers who worked around Auvers. Vincent found a little bar on the right as he walked in, and all the way down the side of the dark, dispirited room, rough wooden tables and benches. At the rear of the cafe, behind the bar, was a billiard table with a soiled and torn green covering. It was the pride and joy of Ravoux's. A door at the rear led to the back kitchen ; just outside this door was a flight of stairs winding up to three bedrooms. From his window Vincent could see the steeple of the Catholic church, and a small patch of the cemetery wall, a clean, crisp brown in the mild Auvers sunlight.

He took his easel, paints and brushes, a portrait of the Arlesienne, and set out to find Gachet's. The same road which came down from the station, and led past Ravoux's sneaked out of the Place again on the west and climbed another grade. After a short walk, Vincent came to a spot where three roads forked. He saw that the one on his right led up the hill past the chateau, and the one on his left wandered down through fields of peas to the river bank. Gachet had told him to take the centre road, which continued along the contour of the hill. Vincent walked slowly, thinking of the doctor to whose care he had been committed. He noticed how the old thatched houses were being replaced by prosperous villas, and the whole nature of the country-side was changing.

Vincent pulled a brass knob stuck in a high stone wall. Gachet came running to the tinkle of the bell. He led Vincent up three flights of steep stone steps to a terraced flower garden. The house was of three stories, solid and well built. The doctor flexed Vincent's arm, seized the joint of the elbow and pushed him around to the back yard, where he kept ducks, hens, turkeys, peacocks, and a retinue of ill-assorted cats.

"Come into the living room, Vincent," said Gachet, after giving a complete life history of each of the fowls in the yard.

The living room at the front of the house was large and had a high ceiling, but there were only two small windows looking out on the garden. In spite of the size of the room it was so crammed full of furniture, antiques, and bric-a-brac that there was hardly enough space for the two men to move about the table in the centre. The room was dark from lack of window space, and Vincent noticed that every last piece in it was black.

Gachet ran about picking up things, thrusting them into Vincent's hands, taking them away again before Vincent had a chance to look at them.

"See. See that bouquet on the wall? Delacroix used this vase to hold the flowers. Feel it. Doesn't it feel like the one he painted? See that chair? Courbet sat in it by the window when he painted the garden. Aren't these exquisite dishes? Desmoulins brought them back from Japan for me. Claude Monet put this one into a still life. It's upstairs. Come with me. I'll show it to you."

At the dinner table Vincent met Gachet's son, Paul, a vivacious and handsome young lad of fifteen. Gachet, who was a sick man with a poor digestion, served a five course dinner. Vincent was accustomed to the lentils and black bread of St. Remy; he became distressed after the third course and could go no further.

"And now we must go to work," cried the doctor. "You will paint my portrait, Vincent; I will sit for you just as I am, yes?"

"I'm afraid I must come to know you better, Doctor, or it won't be an understanding portrait."

"Perhaps you are right, perhaps you are right. But surely you will paint something? You will let me see how you work? I am eager to watch you."

"I saw a scene in the garden I would like to do."

"Good! Good! I will set up your easel. Paul, carry Monsieur Vincent's easel into the garden. You will show us where you want it, and I will tell you if any other painter has done that exact spot."

While Vincent worked, the doctor ran about him in little circles, gesticulating with rapture, consternation and amazement. He poured a constant stream of advice over Vincent's shoulder, interspersed with hundreds of sharp exclamations.

"Yes, yes, you caught it that time. It's crimson lake. Look out. You'll spoil that tree. Ah, yes, yes, now you've caught it. No. No. No more cobalt. This isn't Provence. Now I see. Yes, yes, its *épatant*. Careful. Careful. Vincent, put a little spot of yellow in that flower. Yes, yes, just so. How you make things live. There's not a still life in your brush. No. No. I beg of you. Be careful. Not too much. Ah, yes, yes, now I catch it. *Merveilleux!*"

Vincent stood the doctor's contortions and monologue as long as he could. Then he turned to the dancing Gachet and said, "My dear friend, don't you think it bad for your health to get yourself so excited and wrought up? As a medical man, you should know how important it is to keep calm."

But Gachet could not be calm when anyone was painting.

When he finished his sketch, Vincent went inside the house with Gachet, and showed him the portrait of the Arlesienne he had brought. The Doctor cocked one eye and looked at it quizzically. After a long and voluble discussion with himself as to its merits and faults, he announced,

"No, I cannot accept it. I cannot fully accept it. I do not see what you have tried to say."

"I haven't tried to say anything," replied Vincent, "She is the synthesis of the Arlesiennes, if you like. I simply tried to interpret her character in terms of colours."

"Alas," said the doctor mournfully, "I cannot accept it."

"Do you mind if I look about the house at your collection?"

"But of course, of course, go look your fill. I will stay here with this lady and see if I cannot come to accept her."

Vincent browsed through the house for an hour, led from room to room by the obliging Paul. Thrown carelessly in one corner he found a Guillaumin, a nude woman lying on a bed. The canvas had obviously been neglected, and was cracking. While Vincent was examining it, Doctor Gachet came running up excitedly and poured out a string of questions about the Arlesienne.

"Do you mean to tell me you have been looking at her all this time?" demanded Vincent.

"Yes, yes, it is coming, it is coming, I am beginning to feel her."

"Forgive my presumption, Doctor Gachet, But this is a

416

magnificent Guillaumin. If you don't have it framed soon, it will be ruined."

Gachet did not even hear him.

"You say you followed Gauguin in the drawing . . . I do not agree . . . that clash of colours . . . it kills her femininity . . . no, not kills, but . . . well, well I will go look again . . . she is coming to me . . . slowly . . . slowly . . . she is jumping out of the canvas to me."

Gachet spent the rest of the long afternoon running about the Arlesienne, pointing at her, waving his arms, talking to himself, asking and answering innumerable questions, falling into a thousand poses. By the time night fell, the woman had completely captured his heart. An exalted quiescence fell upon him.

"How difficult it is to be simple," he remarked, standing in peaceful exhaustion before the portrait.

"Yes."

"She is beautiful, beautiful. I have never felt such depth of character before."

"If you like her, Doctor," said Vincent, "she is yours. And so is the scene I did in the garden this afternoon."

"But why should you give me these pictures, Vincent? They are valuable."

"In the near future you may have to take care of me. I will have no money to pay you. So I pay you in canvases, instead."

"But I would not be taking care of you for money, Vincent. I would be doing it for friendship."

"*Soit!* I give you these pictures for friendship."

3

Vincent settled down once again to be a painter. He went to sleep at nine, after watching the labourers play billiards under a dull lamp in Ravoux's café. He arose at five. The weather was beautiful, with gentle sunshine and the fresh verdancy of the valley. His periods of illness and enforced idleness in St. Paul had taken their toll ; the paint brush slipped in his hand.

He asked Theo to send him Bargue's sixth charcoal studies to copy, for he was afraid that if he did not study proportion and the nude again, he would be badly caught out. He looked about Auvers to see if he could find a little house in which he might settle permanently. He wondered if Theo had been right in thinking that, somewhere in the world, there was a woman who would share his life. He laid out a number of his St. Remy canvases, anxious to retouch and perfect them.

But his sudden activity was only a momentary gesture, the reflex of an organism that was yet too powerful to be destroyed.

Afer his long seclusion in the asylum the days seemed to him like weeks. He was at a loss to know how to fill them, for he did not have the strength to paint all the time. Nor did he have the desire. Before his accident in Arles no day had been long enough to get his work done; now they seemed interminable.

Fewer scenes in nature tempted him, and when he did begin work he felt strangely calm, almost indifferent. The feverish passion to paint in hot blood every minute of the day had left him. He now sketched in what was for him a leisurely fashion. And if he did not finish a canvas by nightfall ... it no longer seemed to matter.

Doctor Gachet remained his only friend in Auvers. Gachet, who spent most of his days at his consulting office in Paris, often came to the Café Ravoux at night to look at pictures. Vincent had often wondered at the look of utter heartbreak in the doctor's eyes.

"Why are you unhappy, Doctor Gachet?" he asked.

"Ah, Vincent, I have laboured so many years ... and I have done so little good. The doctor sees nothing but pain, pain, pain."

"I would gladly exchange my calling for yours," said Vincent.

A rapt eagerness lighted up the melancholy in Gachet's eyes.

"Ah, no, Vincent, it is the most beautiful thing in the world, to be a painter. All my life I wanted to be an artist ... but I could spare only an hour here and there ... there are so many sick people who need me."

Doctor Gachet went on his knees and pulled a pile of canvases from under Vincent's bed. He held a glowing yellow sunflower before him.

"If I had painted just one canvas like this, Vincent, I would consider my life justified. I spent the years curing people's pain ... but they died in the end, anyway ... so what did it matter? These sunflowers of yours ... they will cure the pain in people's hearts ... they will bring people joy ... for centuries and centuries ... that is why your life is successful ... that is why you should be a happy man."

A few days later Vincent painted a portrait of the doctor in his white cap and blue frock coat, against a cobalt blue background. He did the head in a very fair, very light tone, the hands also in a light flesh tint. He posed Gachet leaning on a red table on which were a yellow book and a foxglove plant with purple flowers. He was amused to find, when he finished, that the portrait resembled the one he had done of himself in Arles, before Gauguin arrived.

The doctor went absolutely fanatical about the portrait. Vincent had never heard such a torrent of praise and acclaim. Gachet insisted that Vincent make a copy for him. When Vincent agreed, the doctor's joy knew no bounds.

"You must use my printing machine in the attic, Vincent," he cried. "We'll go to Paris, get all your canvases, and make lithographs of them. It won't cost you a centime, not a centime. Come, I will show you my workshop."

They had to climb a ladder and push open a trap door to get into the attic. Gachet's studio was piled so high with weird and fantastic implements that Vincent thought he had been plunged into an alchemist's workshop of the Middle Ages.

On the way downstairs, Vincent noticed that the Guillaumin nude was still lying about, neglected.

"Doctor Gachet," he said, "I simply must insist that you have this framed. You are ruining a masterpiece."

"Yes, yes, I mean to have it framed. When can we go to Paris and get your paintings? You will print as many lithographs as you like. I will supply the materials."

May slipped quietly into June. Vincent painted the Catholic church on the hill. He wearied in the middle of the afternoon and did not even bother to finish it. By dint of great perseverance he managed to paint a cornfield while lying flat on the ground, his head almost in the corn ; he did a large canvas of Madame Daubigny's house ; another of a white house in the trees, with a night sky, an orange light in the windows, dark greenery and a note of sombre rose colour ; and lastly, an evening effect, two pear trees quite black against a yellowing sky.

But the juice had gone out of painting. He worked from habit, because there was nothing else to do. The terrific momentum of his ten years of colossal labour carried him still a little farther. Where scenes from nature had thrilled and excited him before, they now left him indifferent.

"I've painted that so many times," he would murmur to

himself as he walked along the roads, easel on his back, looking for a motif. "I have nothing new to say about it. Why should I repeat myself? Father Millet was right. *'J'aimerais mieux ne rien dire que de m'exprimer faiblement.'* "

His love for nature had not died; it was simply that he no longer felt the desperate need to fling himself at a scene and re-create it. He was burned out. During the whole month of June he painted only five canvases. He was weary, unspeakably weary. He felt empty, drained, washed out, as though the hundreds upon hundreds of drawings and paintings that had flowed out of him in the past ten years had each taken a tiny spark of his life.

At last he went on working only because he felt he owed it to Theo to capitalize on the years of investment. And yet, when he realized, in the very middle of a painting, that Theo's house was already jammed with more canvases than could be sold in ten lifetimes, a gentle nausea would arise within him, and he would push away his easel with distaste.

He knew that another seizure was due in July, at the end of the three month period. He worried for fear he would do something irrational while the attack was upon him, and ostracize himself in the village. He had not made any definite financial arrangements with Theo when he left Paris, and he worried about how much money he was going to receive. The alternating heartbreak and rapture in Gachet's eyes was driving Vincent's gorge up, day by day.

And to cap the climax, Theo's child became ill.

The anxiety over his namesake almost drove Vincent, frantic. He stood it as long as he could, then took a train to Paris. His sudden arrival at the Cité Pigalle heightened the confusion. Theo was looking pale and ill. Vincent did his best to comfort him.

"It isn't only the little one I'm worrying about, Vincent," he admitted at last.

"What then, Theo?"

"It's Valadon. He has threatened to ask for my resignation."

"Why, Theo, he couldn't! You've been with Goupils for sixteen years!"

"I know. But he says I've been neglecting the regular trade for the Impressionists. I don't sell very many of them, and when I do, the prices are low. Valadon claims my shop has been losing money for the past year."

"But could he really put you out?"

"Why not? The Van Gogh interest has been completely sold."

"What would you do, Theo? Open a shop of your own?"

"How could I? I had a little money saved, but I spent it on my wedding, and the baby."

"If only you hadn't thrown away those thousands of francs on me ..."

"Now, Vincent, please. That had nothing to do with it. You know I ..."

"But what will you do, Theo? There's Jo and the little one."

"Yes. Well ... I don't know ... I'm only worrying about the baby now."

Vincent stayed around Paris a number of days. He kept out of the apartment as much as possible, so as not to disturb the child. Paris and his old friends excited him. He felt a slow, gripping fever arise within him. When little Vincent recovered somewhat, he took the train back to the quiet of Auvers.

But the quiet did him no good. He was tormented by his worries. What would happen to him if Theo lost his job? Would he be thrown out into the streets like some vile beggar? And for that matter, what would happen to Jo and the baby? What if the baby died? He knew that Theo's frail health could never stand the blow. Who was going to support them all while Theo searched for a new job? And where was Theo going to find strength for the search?

He sat for hours in the dark café of Ravoux's. It reminded him of the Café Lamartine, with its odours of stale beer and acrid tobacco smoke. He jabbed around aimlessly with the billiard cue, trying to hit the discoloured balls. He had no money to buy liquor. He had no money to buy paints and canvases. He could not ask Theo for anything at such a crucial moment. And he was deathly afraid that when he had his seizure in July, he would do something insane, something to cause poor Theo even more worry and expense.

He tried working, but it was no good. He had painted everything he wanted to paint. He had said everything he wanted to say. Nature no longer stirred him to a creative passion, and he knew that the best part of him was already dead.

The days passed. The middle of July came, and with it the hot weather. Theo, his head just about to be chopped off by Valadon, frantic with worry over his baby and the doctor bills, managed to squeeze out fifty francs to send to his brother.

Vincent turned them over to Ravoux. That would keep him until almost the end of July. And after that ... what? He could not expect any more money from Theo.

He lay on his back under the hot sun in the cornfields by the little cemetery. He walked along the banks of the Oise, smelling the cool water and the foliage that lined its banks. He went to Gachet's for dinner and stuffed himself with food that he could neither taste nor digest. While the doctor raved on excitedly about Vincent's paintings, Vincent said to himself,

"That's not me he's talking about. Those can't be my pictures. I never painted anything. I don't even recognize my own signature on the canvas. I can't remember putting one single brush stroke on any of them. They must have been done by some other man!"

Lying in the darkness of his room he said to himself, "Suppose Theo doesn't lose his job. Suppose he is still able to send me a hundred and fifty francs a month. What am I going to do with my life? I've kept alive these last miserable years because I had to paint, because I had to say the things that were burning inside of me. But there's nothing burning inside me now. I'm just a shell. Should I go on vegetating like those poor souls at St. Paul, waiting for some accident to wipe me off the earth?"

At other times he worried about Theo, Johanna, and the baby.

"Suppose my strength and spirits return, and I want to paint again. How can I still take money from Theo when he needs it for Jo and the little one? He ought not spend that money on me. He ought to use it to send his family to the country, where they can grow healthy and strong. He's borne me on his back for ten long years. Isn't that enough? Shouldn't I get out and give little Vincent a chance? I've had my say; now the little one ought to have his."

But at the base of everything lay the overwhelming fear of what epilepsy would eventually do to him. Now he was sane and rational; he could do with his life what he wished. But suppose his next attack should convert him into a raving maniac. Suppose his brain should crack under the strain of the seizure. Suppose he became a hopeless, drivelling idiot. What would poor Theo do then? Lock him in an asylum for the lost ones?

He presented Doctor Gachet with two more of his canvases and wormed the truth out of him.

"No. Vincent," said the doctor, "you are all through with your attacks. You'll find yourself in perfect health from now on. But not all epileptics are that fortunate."

"What eventually happens to them, Doctor?"

"Sometimes, when they have had a number of crises, they go out of their minds completely."

"And there is no possible recovery for them?"

"No. They're finished. Oh, they may linger on for some years in an asylum, but they never come back to their right minds."

"How can they tell, Doctor, whether they will recover from the next attack, or whether it will crack their brains?"

"There is no way of telling, Vincent. But come, why should we discuss such morbid questions? Let's go up to the workshop and make some etchings."

Vincent did not leave his room at Ravoux's for the next four days. Madame Ravoux brought him his supper every evening.

"I'm well now, and sane," he kept repeating to himself. "I am master of my own destiny. But when the next seizure catches me . . . if it cracks my skull . . . I won't know enough to kill myself . . . and I'll be lost. Oh, Theo, Theo, what should I do?"

On the afternoon of the fourth day he went to Gachet's. The doctor was in the living room. Vincent walked to the cabinet where he had put the unframed Guillaumin nude some time before. He picked up the canvas.

"I told you to have this framed," he said.

Doctor Gachet looked at him in surprise.

"I know, Vincent. I'll order a stick frame from the joiner in Auvers next week."

"It must be framed now! Today! This minute!"

"Why, Vincent, you're talking nonsense!"

Vincent glared at the doctor for a moment, took a menacing step toward him, then put his hand in his coat pocket. Doctor Gachet thought he saw Vincent grip a revolver and point it at him through the coat.

"Vincent!" he exclaimed.

Vincent trembled. He lowered his eyes, pulled his hand from his pocket, and ran out of the house.

The next day he took his easel and canvas, walked down the long road to the station, climbed the hill past the Catholic church, and sat down in the yellow cornfield, opposite the cemetery.

About noon, when the fiery sun was beating down upon his head, a rush of blackbirds suddenly came out of the sky. They filled the air, darkened the sun, covered Vincent in a thick blanket of night, flew into his hair, his eyes, his nose, his mouth, buried him in a black cloud of tight, airless, flapping wings.

Vincent went on working. He painted the birds above the yellow field of corn. He did not know how long he wielded his brush, but when he saw that he had finished, he wrote *Crows Above a Cornfield* in one corner, carried his easel and canvas back to Ravoux's, threw himself across the bed and went to sleep.

The following afternoon he went out again, but left the Place de la Mairie from the other side. He climbed the hill past the chateau. A peasant saw him sitting in a tree.

"It is impossible!" he heard Vincent say. "It is impossible!"

After a time he climbed down from the tree and walked in the ploughed field behind the chateau. This time it was the end. He had known that in Arles, the very first time, but he had been unable to make the clean break.

He wanted to say good-bye. In spite of all, it had been a good world that he had lived in. As Gauguin said, "besides the poison, there is the antidote." And now, leaving the world, he wanted to say good-bye to it, say good-bye to all those friends who had helped mould his life; to Ursula, whose contempt had wrenched him out of a conventional life and made him an outcast; to Mendes da Costa, who had made him believe that ultimately he would express himself, and that expression would justify his life; to Kay Vos, whose "No, never! never!" had been written in acid on his soul; to Madame Denis, Jacques Verney and Henri Decrucq, who had helped him love the despised ones of the earth; to the Reverend Pietersen, whose kindness had transcended Vincent's ugly clothes and boorish manners; to his mother and father, who had loved him as best they could; to Christine, the only wife with which fate had seen fit to bless him; to Mauve, who had been his master for a few sweet weeks; to Weissenbruch and De Bock, his first painter friends; to his Uncles Vincent, Jan, Cornelius Marius, and Stricker, who had labelled him the black sheep of the Van Gogh family; to Margot, the only woman who had ever loved him, and who had tried to kill herself for that love;

to all his painter friends in Paris; Lautrec, who had been shut up in an asylum again, to die; Georges Seurat, dead at thirty-one from overwork; Paul Gauguin, a mendicant in Brittany; Rousseau, rotting in his hole near the Bastille; Cezanne, a bitter recluse on a hilltop in Aix; to Père Tanguy and Roulin, who had shown him the salt in the simple souls of the earth; to Rachel and Doctor Rey, who had been kind to him with the kindness he needed; to Aurier and Doctor Gachet, the only two men in the world who had thought him a great painter, and last of all, to his good brother Theo, long suffering, long loving, best and dearest of all possible brothers.

But words had never been his medium. He would have to paint good-bye.

One cannot paint good-bye.

He turned his face upward to the sun. He pressed the revolver into his side. He pulled the trigger. He sank down, burying his face in the rich, pungent loam of the field, a more resilient earth returning to the womb of its mother.

4

Four hours later he staggered through the gloom of the café. Madame Ravoux followed him to his room and saw blood on his clothes. She ran at once for Doctor Gachet.

"Oh, Vincent, Vincent, what have you done!" groaned Gachet, when he entered the room.

"I think I have bungled it; what do you say?"

Gachet examined the wound.

"Oh, Vincent, my poor old friend, how unhappy you must have been to do this! Why didn't I know? Why should you want to leave us when we all love you so? Think of the beautiful pictures you have still to paint for the world."

"Will you be so kind as to give me my pipe from my waistcoat pocket?"

"But certainly, my friend."

He loaded the pipe with tobacco, then placed it between Vincent's teeth.

"A light, if you please," said Vincent.

"But certainly, my friend."

Vincent puffed quietly at his pipe.

"Vincent, it is Sunday and your brother is not at the shop. What is his home address?"

"That I will not give you."

"But, Vincent, you must! It is urgent that we reach him!"

"Theo's Sunday must not be disturbed. He is tired and worried. He needs the rest."

No amount of persuasion could get the Cité Pigalle address out of Vincent. Doctor Gachet stayed with him until late that night, tending the wound. Then he went home for a little rest, leaving his son to care for Vincent.

Vincent lay there wide-eyed all night, never uttering a word to Paul. He kept filling his pipe and smoking it constantly.

When Theo arrived at Goupils the following morning, he found Gachet's telegram awaiting him. He caught the first train for Pontoise, then dashed in a carriage to Auvers.

"Well, Theo," said Vincent.

Theo dropped on his knees by the side of the bed and took Vincent in his arms like a little child. He could not speak.

When the doctor arrived, Theo led him outside to the corridor. Gachet shook his head sadly.

"There is no hope, my friend. I cannot operate to remove the bullet, for he is too weak. If he were not made of iron he would have died in the fields."

All through the long day Theo sat by his bed, holding Vincent's hand. When nightfall came, and they were left alone in the room, they began to speak quietly of their childhood in the Brabant.

"Do you remember the mill at Ryswyk, Vincent?"

"It was a nice old mill, wasn't it, Theo?"

"We used to walk by the path along the stream, and plan our lives."

"And when we played in the high corn, in midsummer, you used to hold my hand, just as you're doing now. Remember, Theo?"

"Yes, Vincent."

"When I was in the hospital at Arles, I used to think often about Zundert. We had a nice childhood, Theo, you and I. We used to play in the garden behind the kitchen, in the shade of the acacias, and Mother would make us cheese bakes for lunch."

"That seems so long ago, Vincent."

"... Yes ... well ... life is long. Theo, for my sake, take care of yourself. Guard your health. You must think of Jo and the

426

little one. Take them into the country somewhere so they can grow strong and healthy. And don't stay with Goupils, Theo. They have taken the whole of your life ... and given you nothing in return."

"I'm going to open a tiny gallery of my own, Vincent. And my first exhibition will be a one-man show. The complete works of Vincent Van Gogh ... just as you laid it out in the apartment ... with your own hands."

"Ah, well, my work ... I risked my life for it ... and my reason has almost foundered."

The deep quiet of the Auvers night fell upon the room.

At a little after one in the morning, Vincent turned his head slightly and whispered,

"I wish I could die now, Theo."

In a few minutes he closed his eyes.

Theo felt his brother leave him, forever.

5

Rousseau, Père Tanguy, Aurier, and Emile Bernard came out from Paris for the funeral.

The doors of the Café Ravoux were locked and the blinds pulled down. The little black hearse with the black horses waited out in front.

They laid Vincent's coffin on the billiard table.

Theo, Doctor Gachet, Rousseau, Père Tanguy, Aurier, Bernard, and Ravoux gathered about, speechless. They could not look at each other.

No one thought of calling in a minister.

The driver of the hearse knocked at the front door.

"It is time, gentlemen," he said.

"For God's sake, we can't let him go like this!" cried Gachet.

He brought all the paintings down from Vincent's room, then sent his son Paul running home to get the rest of his canvases.

Six of the men worked putting up the paintings on the walls.

Theo stood alone by the coffin.

Vincent's sunlight canvases transformed the drab, gloomy cafe into a brilliant cathedral.

Once again the men gathered about the billiard table. Gachet alone could speak.

"Let us not despair, we who are Vincent's friends. Vincent is not dead. He will never die. His love, his genius, the great beauty he has created will go on forever, enriching the world. Not an hour passes but that I look at his paintings and find there a new faith, a new meaning of life. He was a colossus . . . a great painter . . . a great philosopher. He fell a martyr to his love of art."

Theo tried to thank him.

". . . I . . . I . . ."

The tears choked him. He could not go on.

The cover was placed on Vincent's coffin.

His six friends lifted it from the billiard table. They carried it out of the little café. They placed it gently in the hearse.

They walked behind the black carriage, down the sunlit road. They passed the thatched cottages and the little country villas.

At the station the hearse turned to the left and began the slow climb up the hill. They passed the Catholic church, then wound through the yellow cornfield.

The black carriage stopped at the gate of the cemetery.

Theo walked behind the coffin while the six men carried it to the grave.

Doctor Gachet had chosen as Vincent's last resting place the spot on which they had stood that very first day, overlooking the lovely verdant valley of the Oise.

Once again Theo tried to speak. He could not.

The attendants lowered the coffin into the ground. Then they shovelled in dirt and stamped it down.

The seven men turned, left the cemetery, and walked down the hill.

Doctor Gachet returned a few days later to plant sunflowers all about the grave.

Theo went home to the Cité Pigalle. His loss pushed out every aching second of the night and day with unassuagable grief.

His mind broke under the strain.

Johanna took him to the *maison de santé* in Utrecht, where Margot had gone before him.

At the end of six months, almost to the day of Vincent's death, Theo passed away. He was buried at Utrecht.

Some time later, when Johanna was reading her Bible for comfort, she came across the line in Samuel:

And in their death they were not divided.

She took Theo's body to Auvers, and had it placed by the side of his brother.

When the hot Auvers sun beats down upon the little cemetery in the cornfields, Theo rests comfortably in the luxuriant umbrage of Vincent's sunflowers.

NOTE

The reader may have asked himself, "How much of this story is true?" The dialogue had to be reimagined; there is an occasional stretch of pure fiction, such as the Maya scene, which the reader will have readily recognized; in one or two instances, I have portrayed a minor incident where I was convinced of its probability even though I could not document it, for example, the brief meeting between Cezanne and Van Gogh in Paris; I have utilized a few devices for the sake of facility, such as the use of the franc as the unit of exchange during Vincent's trek over Europe; and I have omitted several unimportant fragments of the complete story. Aside from these technical liberties, the book is entirely true.

My main source was Vincent Van Gogh's three volumes of letters to his brother Theo (Houghton Mifflin 1927–1930). The greater part of the material I unearthed on the trail of Vincent across Holland, Belgium, and France.

It would be ingratitude indeed if I did not acknowledge my debt to the host of Van Gogh friends and enthusiasts in Europe who gave unsparingly of their time and material: Colin Van Oss and Louis Bron of the Haagshe *Post*; Johan Tersteeg of the Goupil Galleries in The Hague; the family of Anton Mauve in Scheveningen; M. and Mme. Jean Baptiste Denis of Petit Wasmes; the Hofkes family of Nuenen; J. Bart de la Faille of Amsterdam; Dr. Felix Rey of Arles; Dr. Edgar Le Roy of St. Paul de Mausole; Paul Gachet of Auvers-sur L'Oise, who remains Vincent's staunchest friend in Europe.

I am indebted to Lona Mosk, Alice and Ray C. B. Brown, and Jean Factor for editorial assistance. Lastly, I wish to express my profoundest gratitude to Ruth Aley, who first saw the book in the manuscript.

I.S.

June 6, 1934.